Cognitive Reserve

STUDIES ON NEUROPSYCHOLOGY, NEUROLOGY AND COGNITION

Series Editor:

Linas Bieliauskas, Ph.D.
University of Michigan, Ann Arbor, MI, USA

Other titles in this series:

Fundamentals of Functional Brain Imaging: A Guide to the Methods and their Applications to Psychology and Behavioral Neuroscience. A. C. Papanicolaou

Forensic Neuropsychology: Fundamentals and Practice. Edited by J. J. Sweet

Neuropsychological Differential Diagnosis. K. K. Zakzanis, L. Leach, & E. Kaplan

Minority and Cross-Cultural Aspects of Neuropsychological Assessment. Edited by F. R. Ferraro

Ethical Issues in Clinical Neuropsychology. Edited by S. S. Bush & M. L. Drexler

Practice of Child-Clinical Neuropsychology: An Introduction. B. P. Rourke, H. van der Vlugt, & S. B. Rourke

The Practice of Clinical Neuropsychology. A Survey of Practice and Settings. Edited by G. J. Lamberty, J. C. Courtney, & R. L. Heilbronner

Neuropsychological Rehabilitation: Theory and Practice. Edited by B. E. Wilson

Traumatic Brain Injury in Sports. An International Neuropsychological Perspective. Edited by M. R. Lovell, R. J. Echemendia, J. T. Barth, & M. W. Collins

Methodological and Biostatistical Foundations of Clinical Neuropsychology and Medical and Health Disciplines. Edited by D. V. Cicchetti & B. P. Rourke

A Casebook of Ethical Challenges in Neuropsychology. Edited by S. S. Bush

Neurobehavioral Toxicology: Neurological and Neuropsychological Perspectives. Volume I Foundations and Methods. S. Berent & J. W. Albers

Neurobehavioral Toxicology: Neurological and Neuropsychological Perspectives. Volume II Peripheral Nervous System. J. W. Albers & S. Berent

Geriatric Neuropsychology: Practice Essentials. Edited by S. S. Bush & T. A. Martin

Brain Injury Treatment: Theories and Practices. J. Leon-Carrion, K. R. H. Von Wild, & G. Zitnay

The Quantified Process Approach to Neuropsychological Assessment. Edited by A. M. Poreh

Mild Cognitive Impairment: International Perspectives. Edited by H. A. Tuokko & D. F. Hultsch

Forthcoming titles:

Neuropsychology and Substance Misuse: Sate-of-the-Art and Future Directions. A. Kalechstein & W. G. van Gorp

Geriatric Neuropsychology Casebook. J. J. Dunkin

Neuropsychology of Malingering Case Book. J. E. Morgan & J. J. Sweet

For continually updated information about the *Studies on Neuropsychology, Neurology and Cognition* series, please visit: **www.psypress.co.uk/nnc/**

Cognitive Reserve
Theory and Applications

Edited by
Yaakov Stern

Taylor & Francis
Taylor & Francis Group

NEW YORK AND LONDON

Published 2007
by Taylor & Francis, an informa business
270 Madison Avenue
New York, NY 10016
www.taylorandfrancis.com

Published in Great Britain
by Taylor & Francis Group, an informa business
27 Church Road
Hove, East Sussex BN3 2FA
www.tandf.co.uk

Typeset in Times by RefineCatch Limited, Bungay, Suffolk, UK
Printed and bound in the USA by Edwards Brothers, Inc. on acid-free paper
Cover design by Jim Wilkie

10 9 8 7 6 5 4 3 2 1

Library of Congress Cataloging in Publication Data
Cognitive reserve : theory and applications / edited by Yaakov Stern.
    p. ; cm. – (Studies or neuropsychology, neurology, and cognition)
  Includes bibliographical references and index.
  ISBN-13: 978–1–84169–474–0 (hardcover : alk. paper)
  ISBN-10: 1–84169–474–6 (hardcover : alk. paper) 1. Cognition disorders – Diagnosis.
2. Neuropsychology. I. Stern, Yaakov. II. Series.
  [DNLM: 1. Cognition Disorders – diagnosis. 2. Aging – physiology. 3. Alzheimer Disease –
diagnosis. 4. Brain – physiology. 5. Brain Injuries – physiopathology. 6. Cognition –
physiology. 7. Neuropsychological Tests. WM 204 C6768 2006]
  RC553.C64C662 2006
616.8075 – dc22   2006016532

ISBN13: 978-1-84169-474-0 (hbk)

ISBN10: 1-84169-474-6 (hbk)

To Sharon

Contents

List of figures

List of tables

About the editor

Yaakov Stern is Professor of Clinical Neuropsychology in the Departments of Neurology, Psychiatry, and Psychology, and in the G. H. Sergievsky Center and Taub Institute for Research on Alzheimer's Disease and the Aging Brain at Columbia University College of Physicians and Surgeons. Dr. Stern directs the Cognitive Neuroscience Division of the Taub Institute and is Director of Neuropsychology for the Memory Disorders Clinic at the New York State Psychiatric Institute. He also directs the post-doctoral training program Neuropsychology and Cognition in Aging.

List of contributors

Ami Antonucci, Neuropsychology Postdoctoral fellow, University of Michigan Health System, Ann Arbor, MI, USA

Lisa L. Barnes, Ph.D., Clinical Neuropsychologist, Rush Alzheimer's Disease Center, and Assistant Professor, Departments of Neurological Sciences and Psychology, Rush University Medical Center, Chicago, IL, USA

James T. Becker, Ph.D., Professor, Psychiatry and Neurology, School of Medicine, University of Pittsburgh, Pittsburgh, PA, USA

David A. Bennett, M.D., Director, Rush Alzheimer's Disease Center, and Robert C. Borwell, Professor of Neurological Sciences, Rush University Medical Center, Chicago, IL, USA

Linas A. Bieliauskas, Ph.D., Staff Psychologist, Ann Arbor Veterans Administration Healthcare System, and Associate Professor, Neuropsychology Division, University of Michigan Health System, Ann Arbor, MI, USA

Erin D. Bigler, Ph.D., Professor of Psychology and Neuroscience, Brigham Young University, and Adjunct Professor of Psychiatry & Radiology, University of Utah, Salt Lake City, UT, USA

Patricia A. Boyle, Ph.D., Assistant Professor and Neuropsychologist, Department of Psychology, Rush Alzheimer's Disease Center, Rush University Medical Center, Chicago, IL, USA

Bruce A. Cohen, M.D., Professor of Neurology, Feinberg School of Medicine, Northwestern University, Chicago, IL, USA

Ian J. Deary, M.D., Ph.D., Professor of Psychology, School of Philosophy, Psychology and Language Sciences, University of Edinburgh, Edinburgh, Scotland, UK

Dorly J. H. Deeg, Ph.D., Professor of The Epidemiology of Aging, Department of Psychiatry and Institute for Research in Extramural Medicine, VU University Medical Center, Amsterdam, The Netherlands

Maureen Dennis, Ph.D., Senior Scientist, Brain and Behavior Research, The Hospital for Sick Children, Toronto, and Professor of Surgery and Psychology, University of Toronto, Ontario, Canada

Miranda G. Dik, Ph.D., Institute for Research in Extramural Medicine, VU University Medical Center, Amsterdam, The Netherlands

Roger A. Dixon, Ph.D., Canada Research Chair in Cognition and Aging, and Professor of Psychology, University of Alberta, Edmonton, Alberta, Canada

Jack M. Fletcher, Ph.D., ABPP, Distinguished University Professor, Department of Psychology, University of Houston, Houston, TX, USA

David Friedman, Ph.D., Cognitive Electrophysiology Laboratory, New York State Psychiatric Institute, New York, NY, USA

Cheryl L. Grady, Ph.D., Senior Scientist and Assistant Director, Canada Research Chair in Neurocognitive Aging Rotman Research Institute, Baycrest Centre for Geriatric Care, University of Toronto, Ontario, Canada

Elizabeth Gould, Ph.D., Professor of Psychology, Psychology Department, Princeton University, Princeton, NJ, USA

Tiffany F. Hughes, School of Aging Studies, University of South Florida, Tampa, FL, USA

David F. Hultsch, Ph.D., Lansdowne Professor of Psychology, University of Victoria, Victoria, British Columbia, Canada

Cees Jonker, Ph.D., Professor of Diagnosis and Management of Dementia, Department of Psychiatry and Institute for Research in Extramural Medicine, VU University Medical Center, Amsterdam, The Netherlands

Yevgenia Kozorovitskiy, Psychology Department, Princeton University, Princeton, NJ, USA

Joseph H. Lee, Dr.PH, Assistant Professor of Epidemiology, Taub Institute for Research on Alzheimer's Disease and the Aging Brain, Sergievsky Center, College of Physicians and Surgeons, Department of Epidemiology, School of Public Health, Columbia University, New York, NY, USA

Jennifer J. Manly, Ph.D., Assistant Professor of Neuropsychology in Neurology, Cognitive Neuroscience Division, Taub Institute for Research on AD and the Aging Brain, Columbia University College of Physicians and Surgeons, New York, NY, USA

William R. Markesbery, M.D., Director, Sanders-Brown Center on Aging, and Clinical Core Director, Departments of Pathology and Neurology, University of Kentucky, Lexington, KY, USA

Eric N. Miller, Ph.D., Professor, Departments of Psychology, Psychiatry and Behavioral Sciences, UCLA Neuropsychiatric Institute, Los Angeles, CA, USA

James A. Mortimer, Ph.D., Director, Institute on Aging, and Saunders Professor of Gerontology, Epidemiology and Biostatistics, University of South Florida, Tampa, FL, USA

Matthew J. Reinhard, Psy.D., Neuropsychology Fellow, Department of Psychiatry and Biobehavioral Sciences, UCLA Neuropsychiatric Institute, Los Angeles, CA, USA

Marcus Richards, Ph.D., MRC National Survey of Health and Development, Royal Free & University College Medical School, Department of Epidemiology & Public Health, University College London, UK

Susan A. Legendre Ropacki, Ph.D., Department of Psychology, School of Science & Technology, Loma Linda University, Loma Linda, CA, USA

Amanda Sacker, Ph.D., Principal Research Fellow, Life Course Social Research Group, Department of Epidemiology & Public Health, University College London, UK

Ned Sacktor, M.D., Associate Professor of Neurology, Department of Neurology, The Johns Hopkins University School of Medicine, Baltimore, MD, USA

Paul Satz, Ph.D., Chief, The Help Group, UCLA Neuropsychology Program, The David Geffen School of Medicine, University of California, Los Angeles, CA, USA

Nikolaos Scarmeas, M.D., Assistant Professor of Neurology, Department of Neurology, Cognitive Neuroscience Division, G. H. Servievsky Center and Taub Institute, Columbia University Medical Center, New York, NY, USA

Nicole Schupf, Ph.D., DrPH, Associate Professor of Clinical Epidemiology, Department of Neurology, Cognitive Neuroscience Division, Taub Institute for Research on AD and the Aging Brain, Columbia University College of Physicians and Surgeons, New York, NY, USA

Ola A. Selnes, Ph.D., Professor of Neurology and Neuropsychologist, School of Medicine, The Medical Psychology Clinic, The Johns Hopkins University Medical Institutions, Baltimore, MD, USA

Brent J. Small, Ph.D., Associate Professor, School of Aging Studies, University of South Florida, Tampa, FL, USA

David A. Snowdon, Ph.D., Department of Neurology, Graduate Center for Gerontology, University of Kentucky, Lexington, KY, USA

Robert A. Stern, Ph.D., Associate Professor of Neurology, and Associate Director, Alzheimer's Disease Clinical and Research Program, Boston University School of Medicine, Boston, MA, USA

Yaakov Stern, Departments of Neurology and Psychiatry, Cognitive Neuroscience Division, Taub Institute for Research on AD and the Aging Brain, Columbia University College of Physicians and Surgeons, New York, NY, USA

Ming-Xin Tang, Associate Professor and Statistician, Department of Biostatistics, School of Public Health, Columbia University College of Physicians and Surgeons, New York, NY, USA

H. Gerry Taylor, Ph.D., ABPP/CN, Professor of Pediatrics and Psychology, Case Western Reserve University, Rainbow Babies & Children's Hospital, University Hospitals of Cleveland, Cleveland, OH, USA

Marjolein Visser, Ph.D., EMGO Institute, VU University Medical Center and Department of Earth and Life Sciences, Institute of Health Sciences, VU University, Amsterdam, The Netherlands

Christopher C. Weiss, Ph.D., Institute for Social and Economic Research and Policy, Columbia University, New York, NY, USA

Robert S. Wilson, Ph.D., Senior Neuropsychologist, Rush Alzheimer's Disease Center, and Professor, Departments of Neurological Sciences and Behavioral Sciences, Rush University Medical Center, Chicago, IL, USA

Keith Owen Yeates, Ph.D., ABPP/CN, Professor of Pediatrics and Psychology, The Ohio State University, Director, Center for Biobehavioral Health, Columbus Children's Research Institute, and Director, Pediatric Neuropsychology, Columbus Children's Hospital, Columbus, OH, USA

From the series editor

In translating findings in neuropsychological research to appropriate clinical application, it is hard to find a subject worthy of more consideration than that of *Cognitive Reserve*. From the threshold model developed by Paul Satz to the interactive model established by Yaakov Stern, the logical impact of estimates of cognitive reserve on cognitive performance seems obvious. Though study upon study has demonstrated the close relationship between measures of cognitive reserve, and performance on neuropsychological measures, the potential impact of cognitive reserve on test performance remains often neglected. In this worthy volume in our series, Yaakov Stern has gathered a number of prominent authors who address the basis for cognitive reserve, clinical settings in which cognitive reserve has been explored, patterns of the influence of cognitive reserve in clinical conditions, and markers for estimation of cognitive reserve.

There is little doubt that cognitive reserve is the elephant hiding in the closet when estimates are made of the prevalence of cognitive impairment in various disease states. This includes the judgments made about individual cognitive decline in the face of injury or illness, or behaviorally-based disease diagnostic classifications. The need for considering the impact of cognitive reserve on neuropsychological tests and their interpretation is made clear in this volume. Optimistically, Dr. Stern and his colleagues also address the potential for adaptation and compensation in the face of insult, which a cognitive reserve approach may permit us to understand and tap. *Cognitive Reserve: Theory and Applications* provides a contemporary perspective on the appreciation of cognitive performance in many clinical conditions and, as such, presents a valuable resource in further exploring the complexity of brain/behavior relationships. It will prove a fundamental reference for students, clinicians, and researchers for the foreseeable future.

Linas A. Bieliauskas
Ann Arbor
May, 2006

1 The concept of cognitive reserve: A catalyst for research

Yaakov Stern

The idea of reserve against brain damage stems from the repeated observation that there does not appear to be a direct relationship between the degree of brain pathology or brain damage and the clinical manifestation of that damage. Two interrelated concepts have been proposed. Brain reserve is an example of what might be called a passive model of reserve, where reserve derives from brain size or neuronal count. The model is passive because reserve is defined in terms of the amount of brain damage that can be sustained before reaching a threshold for clinical expression. In contrast, the cognitive reserve (CR) model suggests that the brain actively attempts to cope with brain damage by using pre-existing cognitive processing approaches or by enlisting compensatory approaches. Individuals with more CR would therefore be more successful at coping with the same amount of brain damage. As will become clear throughout this volume, these models are by no means mutually exclusive.

The threshold model, critically reviewed by Satz (1993), and suggested by many others, is a well articulated model of how reserve may operate. The threshold model revolves around the construct of "brain reserve capacity" (BRC). This is a hypothetical construct, but concrete examples of brain reserve capacity might include brain size or synapse count. The model recognizes that there are individual differences in BRC. It also presupposes that there is a critical threshold of BRC such that specific clinical or functional deficits emerge once BRC is depleted past this threshold. This formulation begins to account for the disjunction between the extent of pathology and the extent of clinical change. If two patients have different amounts of BRC, a lesion of a particular size may exceed the threshold of brain damage sufficient to produce a clinical deficit in one patient but not the other. Thus more BRC can be considered a protective factor, while less BRC would impart vulnerability.

In contrast, the CR model suggests that the brain actively attempts to compensate for the challenge represented by brain damage (Stern, 2002). The active models of reserve focuses more on the mode in which tasks are processed as opposed to differences in underlying physiologic differences. Thus *neural reserve* could take the form of using brain networks or cognitive paradigms that are more efficient or flexible, and thus less susceptible to disruption. This type of reserve is a normal process used by healthy individuals when coping with task demands, as well as by individuals with brain damage. In contrast, *neural compensation* refers to adopting new, compensatory brain networks or paradigms because pathology has impacted those that are normally used in no affected individuals. Together, these two types of neural mechanisms could underlie CR.

Individual variability in CR can stem from innate or genetic differences or from life experiences, such as education, occupational experience or leisure activities. These factors could also contribute to brain reserve.

The concept of cognitive reserve provides a ready explanation for why many studies have demonstrated that higher levels of educational and occupational attainment, or of intelligence, and are good predictors of which individuals can sustain greater brain damage before demonstrating functional deficit. Rather than positing that these individuals' brains are grossly anatomically different than those with less reserve (e.g. they have more synapses), the cognitive reserve hypothesis posits that they process tasks in a more efficient manner.

The concept of reserve is not just applicable to the emergence of a clinical condition such as Alzheimer's disease. It is equally applicable to the rate of change in clinical function as a result of gradual changes in disease pathology. Similarly, it applies to issues of recovery of function, for example recovery following traumatic brain injury. More generally, reserve is operative whenever there is a balance between some brain change, for example that due to a disease or normal aging, and a person's current level of functioning. A straightforward example of this is in Alzheimer's disease, where both imaging and post-mortem studies have suggested that in individuals with the same amount of brain pathology, those with higher levels of reserve show less severe clinical dementia. Thus an individual's level of function at any point in time is a function of the underlying brain substrate and their ability to make use of this substrate, with the latter influenced by the level of cognitive reserve.

A consistent set of variables have been linked with the concept of cognitive reserve, including IQ, educational and occupational attainment, and enriching activities such as leisure activities. These variables have often been shown to operate independently and additively. This speaks to a conception of CR as a malleable entity, whose level at any point in time is dependent on the summation of life experience and exposures up to that time. This also raises the possibility of enhancing cognitive reserve, and thus improving people's ability to maintain their capacities in the face of insult to brain function.

This volume

This volume assembles a body of work which defines, explores and utilizes the concept of cognitive reserve. I have attempted to gather together a diverse set of research approaches ranging from genetics to neurogenesis, and from neuroepidemiology to neuroimaging.

The volume began as a special issue of the *Journal of Clinical and Experimental Neuropsychology*. For this volume, the authors of those articles were invited to revise and expand their original contributions. This has allowed the majority of the authors to bring the research findings reported previously into a larger theoretical context, and to more thoroughly review and discuss the applicability of the concept of CR to their research domain. In addition, I have invited five additional investigators to contribute chapters to this volume. The intention was to expand to an even greater degree the diversity of domains in which the CR concept is discussed and applied.

Lee (Chapter 2) reviews the genetic basis for cognitive performance and how this might interact with the concept of cognitive reserve. Since a potentially substantial proportion of variability in cognitive abilities can be genetically determined, this is a fitting place to begin the special issue. This is followed by Richards et al. (Chapter 3), who set the stage for a comprehensive consideration of the factors across the lifespan that can contribute to cognitive reserve. They also describe a prospective study that elegantly demonstrates that cognitive reserve is malleable, and that both genetic (childhood IQ) and experiential components contribute to it.

The next four chapters thoughtfully apply the concept of cognitive reserve to conditions and situations that that have received relatively little attention in this context. Dennis et al. (Chapter 4) explore cognitive reserve in the setting of childhood development and brain injury, while Bigler (Chapter 5) explores the implications of CR for recovery from traumatic brain injury. This chapter nicely demonstrates the interplay between supposed brain size, supposedly a passive indicator of reserve, and more active forms of cognitive reserve. Boyle et al. (Chapter 6) consider two situations where the implications of CR can be directly studied: electroconvulsive therapy and coronary artery bypass grafting surgery. Finally, Bieliauskas and Antonucci (Chapter 7) review the implications of CR on the estimation of disease progression, particularly in the context of clinical trials.

The next four chapters evaluate the potential influence on cognitive reserve of lifetime activities, including physical activity, general lifestyle activities, cognitively stimulating activities, and leisure. These activities are explored in relation to outcomes including late life cognition or cognitive decline, as well as the onset of dementia. Dik et al. (Chapter 8) present data from a large cohort of prospectively followed elders regarding the association between early life physical activity and cognition in aging. Wilson et al. (Chapter 9) review their epidemiologic research, focusing on lifetime participation in cognitively stimulating activities. Small et al. (Chapter 10) review the implication of lifestyle activities for cognitive change in aging. Finally, Scarmeas (Chapter 11) reviews my group's and others' studies evaluating the relationship between elders' engagement in leisure activities and two outcomes: cognitive decline in normal aging, and the incidence or severity of Alzheimer's disease.

The following series of chapters incorporate a series of proxies for cognitive reserve, and apply them in three different settings. Reinhard et al. (Chapter 12) followed a cohort of HIV positive individuals, using onset of AIDS, dementia and mortality as outcomes and Shipley IQ as the proxy for cognitive reserve. Manly et al. (Chapter 13) demonstrate that literacy may be an important measure of cognitive reserve in the context of cognitive decline and incident dementia in aging. Finally, Mortimer et al. (Chapter 14) report data from the Nun Study, using the diagnosis of dementia as an outcome. They used education as a proxy measure for reserve, and also looked at head size, which has been associated with reserve against dementia in several studies.

Three chapters review functional imaging studies intended to elucidate the neural substrates of cognitive reserve. In Chapter 15 I attempt to develop a theoretical framework for studying the neural correlates of cognitive reserve, and then describe four studies that incorporate these ideas. Grady (Chapter 16) reviews her ground-breaking work on compensatory brain activity in older adults or AD patients. Then, Friedman (Chapter 17) provides a thoughtful review of event-related potential data that shed light on the concept of compensation.

Finally Kozorovitskiy and Gould (Chapter 18) provide an insightful review on the topic of adult neurogenesis and its potential for being a compensatory mechanism for brain damage. Theoretical treatments of cognitive reserve and compensation have traditionally emphasized mechanisms for coping with brain damage. These approaches typically view the brain as a resource that can be depleted or damaged, and do not incorporate recent information about neurogenesis in the mature brain. This review points to the future, where compensation may not simply be adaptation of alternate brain networks, but regeneration of underlying brain circuitry.

The diversity of the subject matter in this volume highlights the utility and flexibility of the concept of cognitive reserve for understanding how the brain copes with challenge and pathology. Hopefully, the present volume will encourage further exploration of this concept in diverse research domains.

Acknowledgements

This work was supported by NIA grant AG 14671.

References

Satz, P. (1993). Brain reserve capacity on symptom onset after brain injury: A formulation and review of evidence for threshold theory. *Neuropsychology*, 7, 273–295.
Stern, Y. (2002). What is cognitive reserve? Theory and research application of the reserve concept. *Journal of the International Neuropsychological Society*, 8, 448–460.

2 Understanding cognitive reserve through genetics and genetic epidemiology

Joseph H. Lee

The basis for cognitive reserve (CR) arose from the observation that the severity of neuropathological manisfestations of Alzheimer's disease (AD) did not always correlate well with severity of AD (Katzman et al., 1988). This observation led several investigators to propose the concept of CR (Katzman, 1993; Satz, 1993; Stern, Alexander, Prohovnik, & Mayeux, 1992; Stern et al., 1994). They argue that individuals develop cognitive reserve in the presence of favorable environments such as high educational level or by genetic predisposition, or both, and that CR increases the threshold for neuropsychological responses to brain insult. Those with a greater brain reserve capacity have a higher threshold for brain insult before clinical deficit appears. The concept of CR is evolving to include broader phenomena. Others have argued that more efficient circuitry is less likely to be disrupted and more resilient in the event of brain insult (Grady et al., 1996; Grasby et al., 1994). Stern (2002) applies CR to any situation where there is variation in response to brain injury, suggesting that CR can be applied to individuals who are healthy as well as those who are suffering from neurodegeneration.

A multitude of factors may contribute to the variable responses to brain insults observed in individuals. Both genetic and environmental factors are likely to affect the responses to injury. Gene dosage and timing will influence the responses to the insult. Similarly, the strength and timing of environmental factors will bring about variations among individuals. Factors present early in life may influence cognitive reserve and be as important as factors present later. To support the hypothesis of genetic contributions to CR in humans it is necessary to show that: (1) cognitive function(s) are highly heritable, and (2) there is a differential expression of a gene(s) that influences cognitive function.

The majority of the human genetic studies of memory and other cognitive functions are in their infancy, and a few studies have examined the genome systematically. Here I review these studies in the context of the genetics of cognitive reserve. In this review, I first discuss inherent difficulties of complex (non-Mendelian) phenotypes, ranging from the arbitrariness of phenotyic definition multifactorial nature of the trait, and study design issues. I then discuss the outcome from published results to date to consider the magnitude of genetic and environmental factors that contributed to memory and related cognitive functions.

Defining cognitive reserve phenotypes

Cognitive reserve is a complex trait, and many different surrogate phenotypes can be considered as part of CR. Stern (2002) makes a careful delineation of *passive* vs. *active* models of cognitive reserve. Simply, the passive model explores the role of brain capacity, whereas the active model explores the role of efficiency of the neuronal system. The two models are tightly linked. Given the same degree of efficiency, individuals with larger capacity will suffer less impairment. Similarly, given the same level of capacity, individuals with more efficient neuronal circuitry will be able to tolerate a brain insult better. Under either model, the individual's innate ability is likely to influence the capacity or efficiency of the circuitry, and will lead to differential rates of cognitive decline or responses to brain insults. These models can be tested by operationalizing cognitive reserve in a number of different ways. Some researchers have studied physical phenotypes, such as brain capacity, number of neurons, or differential metabolic expression of anatomical subregions in functional magnetic resonance imaging (fMRI). Others have operationalized several domains of neuropsychological traits, including memory, general intelligence, and language. To this end, proper use of biomarkers or inter-mediate risk factors that reflect the biological pathway can provide enormous insight into our understanding of cognitive reserve.

Physical phenotypes

Brain capacity

The simplest phenotype of cognitive reserve is cranial capacity, as measured by head circumference or brain volume. It is employed as a surrogate measure of the number of neurons. The threshold approach to CR supposes that the person with more cranial capacity can afford to lose a greater number of neurons before they begin to show clinical cognitive impairment. However, the relation between brain capacity and memory or other cognitive function is equivocal (Borenstein Graves et al., 2001; Drachman, 2002; Edland et al., 2002; Graves, Mortimer, Larson, Wenzlow, Bowen, & McCormick, 1996; Katzman et al., 1988; MacLullich, Ferguson, Deary, Seckl, Starr, & Wardlaw, 2002; Schofield, Logroscino, Andrews, Albert, & Stern, 1997; Schofield, Mosesson, Stern, & Mayeux, 1995). Some studies have shown that indi-viduals with large cranial capacity are relatively protected from age-related decline in memory when compared with those with smaller cranial capacity, whereas others found no effect. Similarly, investigators have found brain volume to be positively correlated with memory scores and general intelli-gence scores (Andreasen et al., 1993; MacLullich et al., 2002), while another study found no association (Edland et al., 2002). These investigators often use cross-sectional area of the brain, head circumference, or total intracranial volume to approximate premorbid brain size. These surrogate measures, rather than the actual CR phenotype, may contribute to the inconsistent relation between the brain capacity and memory. The use of cranial capacity as a proxy measure for CR is likely to be insensitive, as cognitive functions encompass an array of complex processes that are not likely to be captured in measures such as brain size. In addition, variation in nutritional and cognitive stimuli during in-utero environment, childhood development, as well as educational or vocational environment, are likely to contribute to CR.

Number of neurons or synapses

The number of neurons is directly related to cranial capacity and can be a measure of CR. A positive correlation between the number of neurons and cognitive functions supports the idea that the larger brain can withstand brain insults better. Currently, there is little direct evidence to support a relation between the number of neurons and cognitive functions. Most evidence has come from studies of AD patients. Since AD patients suffer neuronal loss, which in turn leads to brain atrophy, it is plausible that neuronal loss may be associated with cognitive impairment. In addition, Bigio, Hynan, Sontag, Satumtira, and White (2002) reported that the number of synapses measured by an Enzyme-Linked Immuno Sorbent Assay method was lower in early onset AD cases than in late onset ADs.

Imaging

Imaging tools provide accurate measure of neuroanatomy (Edland et al., 2002; MacLullich et al., 2002; Mori et al., 1997) as well as measures of differential metabolism in the sub-regions of the brain (S. A. Small et al., 2000). When used in conjunction with a neuropsychological battery, they can provide a better understanding of memory and related cognitive functions. Positron emission tomography (PET) and single photon emission tomography (SPECT) studies revealed that brain activation in elders differs from that in younger cohorts (Foster, Minoshima, & Kuhl, 1999). These studies can be further exploited to study the neural network by examining how genetic factors are associated with differential ability to encode or retrieve memory. The relation between a gene (or a set of genes) and differential expression in the brain can provide additional information on underlying causes of the variation in functional activities in the brain. However, given the enormous number of brain regions to study and the number of different conditions in which imaging experiments need to be performed, coupled with the number of genes involved in the brain, this approach will require massive efforts. To perform this experiment, it will be necessary to simplify the causal pathway by focusing on simpler models by narrowing down the number of genes involved or number of environmental factors involved (e.g., individuals with PS1 mutation vs. normals).

Cognitive phenotypes

Memory and age-related decline in cognitive function

There are numerous cognitive phenotypes, including memory, language, and processing time. There are large interpersonal variations in these cognitive functions at any age, and the observed variations are likely to increase with age, because there is a greater opportunity for genetic and non-genetic factors to affect the neural network process. Further variations in rate of decline in cognitive functions provide further evidence for a genetic contribution to cognitive reserve. In most people, there is an observed decline in cognitive functions with age, with a 20% decline observed by age 70 (Powell & Whitla, 1994). Yet Benton, Eslinger, and Damasio (1981) reported that about 33% of octogenarians performed as well as a younger group. Others have documented individual variations in age-related decline in memory and other cognitive functions (Christensen et al., 1994; Christensen et al., 1999; Flood & Morley, 2000; Meaney et al., 1995; Mejia, Pineda, Alvarez, & Ardila, 1998; Schaie, 1988). Some attributed the variations to genetic factors (Backman et al., 2000; Markowska & Savonenko, 2002). In these studies, decline in sensory processes appears to be smaller than that in memory and learning.

Processing time

Another approach is to measure the efficiency of the neuronal network system by measuring speed of processing. Both direct measures of processing efficiency as well as rate of age-related decline in processing can be used to evaluate CR. However, processing speed is likely to be controlled by a number of different cognitive functions, including attention, intelligence, and memory. Each of these factors can be under the influence of different genetic factors, with some of these genes interacting with one another.

Cognitive reserve: A complex trait

Complex traits are broadly defined as "any phenotype that does not exhibit Mendelian recessive or dominant inheritance attributable to a single gene locus" (Lander & Schork, 1994, p. 2037). In simple organisms like D. melanogaster and C. elegans, a single genetic mutation or polymorphism can have a substantial effect on learning and memory (Mayford & Kandel, 1999). In humans, twin, adoption and family studies have shown that cognitive functions, such as memory and intelligence, "run in families." However, a single mutation or polymorphism is not likely to explain the familial aggregation of cognitive function. Instead several genes in conjunction with environmental factors are likely to contribute to cognitive functions. To best understand the complex causal network leading to CR, it will require careful study design, analysis, and clear characterization of the CR phenotype.

Study design and methods

Twin, adoption, and family studies provide estimates of heritability or familiality of cognitive functions. These studies test whether the correlation among family members is higher than expected by chance. Because these studies test relatively simple genetic parameters, estimations of genetic contribution are likely to be somewhat inflated (Terwilliger, Göring, Magnusson, & Lee, 2002). Below, I briefly discuss the rationale and limitations of each study design.

In twin studies, the phenotypic correlations among sets of monozygotic (MZ) twins are compared to those among dizygotic (DZ) twins. Because MZ twins are genetically identical while DZ twins share only 50% of their autosomal genetic material, highly heritable traits will show a greater degree of similarity in MZ twins compared with DZ twins. Two important assumptions are that members of MZ and DZ twin pairs have identically distributed environmental risk factors, and that these factors are equally correlated within twin pairs, independent of zygosity. These assumptions are difficult to satisfy as correlations between MZ and DZ twins in many environmental factors (e.g., in-utero environment, lifestyle factors in adulthood) are likely to differ by zygosity. However, the observed differences in concordance between MZs and DZs are attributed to genetic factors. The net effect of the assumptions in twin studies, on average, is likely to lead to some overestimation of the contribution of genetics to the trait.

In adoption studies, many different comparisons of phenotypic correlations can be devised to dissect the role of gene and environment. For example, biological siblings who are adopted to different families can be used to examine the role of environmental factors under the same genetic background. Also non-biological siblings raised in the same family can be studied to examine the role of the genetic factors. When both parent and offspring data are available, parent–offspring correlation between biological parent and adoptee can be compared with the correlation between adoptive parent and adoptee. If the genetic contribution is significant, the parent–offspring correlation with biological parent should be greater than that with adoptive parent. In these studies, the effects of early environment (e.g., in-utero and before adoption environment) cannot be separated from genetics. Certainly, the effects of "being an adoptee" and "having an adoptive sibling" can influence familial environment in the adoptive families. Adoptive parents (representing environment) are a self-selected group who may be healthier than the general population, and a lower correlation with adoptees may be attributed to genetic causes. Given that any of these differences are more likely to be interpreted in the direction of genetic contribution, genetic estimates are likely to be inflated.

In family studies, one examines how traits segregate within the family to see if genetic factors co-segregate. To do so, one often assumes that the environmental contribution to trait has a common distribution for all individuals. In more sophisticated analyses, a household effect may be included, that is assumed to be identically distributed among all members of a given nuclear (or sometimes extended) family. The residual correlation in the phenotype among relatives is assumed to be due solely to genetic factors. These assumptions are difficult to satisfy because sharing of the environmental factors is not uniform among nuclear family members at any one time and tends to change with time. Moreover, transmission of an environmental or cultural factor can mimic transmission of a genetic factor, thereby spuriously favoring a genetic hypothesis.

Genetic analysis

For heritable traits, two different approaches can be taken to identify susceptibility genes: family-based vs. individual-based methods (Ott, 1999; Strachan & Read, 1999). The family-based method assumes that the trait in family members is significantly correlated because the family members share some of the underlying genetic risk factors. When the trait is caused by a single gene, it is possible to localize that trait gene by linkage analysis. Linkage analysis tests whether two closely located loci are inherited more often than by chance. Individuals with the same phenotype are likely to share a genotype at some putative disease locus as well as some genotypes at nearby marker loci. By examining a set of markers evenly distributed across the entire genome, it is possible to localize and identify the gene by searching for the chromosomal regions where genotypes are shared by the affected individuals within a pedigree. This approach has worked successfully for unraveling simple Mendelian traits where phenotypes predict genotypes with high accuracy. Ascertainment of large families increases, in general, the predictive value of phenotype for the underlying genotypes of the loci to be identified. For complex traits with multiple predisposing genes, the phenotypes are less reliable predictors of any one underlying genotype, thereby making the gene mapping difficult.

As an alternative to linkage study, allele association studies have been advocated by some (Chakravarti, 1999; Reich et al., 2001; Risch & Merikangas, 1996; Schork, Fallin, & Lanchbury, 2000). Allelic association studies compare the frequency of risk alleles in affected vs. unaffected individuals. Because they do not require family data, ascertainment of study subjects is somewhat easier. However, allelic association studies require examination of over 500,000 loci for a systematic genome-wide search (in effect test one marker every 3 kb) (Kruglyak, 1999), compared with 350–400 loci required for linkage studies. Some have advocated the use of haplotype blocks to reduce the number of genetic markers. The idea is that it is not necessary to genotype genetic markers within a haplotype block containing comparable genetic information. Therefore, one would genotype only a few markers in a haplotype block, thereby reducing the cost of genotyping as well as statistical testing. However, new studies suggest haplotype blocks may not be as useful as previously believed. Further, while the cost of genotyping is coming down, the cost of multiple statistical testing remains prohibitive, even with the use of haplotype block information. Thus it would be prudent to limit the analysis to a number of candidate genes. However, it is no easy task to select a manageable set of genes from thousands of genes in the genome. Even when there is a candidate gene, it is necessary to test the right allele. For example, there are over 100 different variants of presenilin-1 mutation (PS1) among early onset AD individuals (Rogaeva et al., 2001; http://molgen-www.uia.ac.be/ADMutations) not all of which are associated with increased risk. When there are multiple putative alleles, each allele has little power to predict AD. This example illustrates the difficulty associated with association analysis. Here, we know a priori that the PS1 mutations *cause* AD; thus the case of PS1 should be considered as one of the "best-case scenarios" for the allelic association approach. When we are studying unknown genes, the difficulties will be greater. This will be further complicated when studying cognitive traits since the traits have several different cognitive domains and subdomains (e.g., delayed, immediate memory), where each domain may have different genetic and non-genetic causes.

Many researchers have opted to employ association studies for ease of study subject recruitment. Paradoxically, as the trait becomes more complex, large families still provide greater power to detect genes than a large collection of independent cases. This is because the odds of finding any one putative gene is higher in large families with multiple affected individuals. Traits or diseases *within* families are likely to be caused by the same gene, while traits or diseases *between* families are likely to be caused by a number of different genes. This is illustrated by the fact that all successful mapping studies of complex disease genes to date have involved large families, including PS1, PS2 (Levy-Lahad et al., 1995; Rogaev et al., 1995; Schellenberg et al., 1992; Sherrington et al., 1995; Van Broeckhoven et al., 1992), and APOE (Pericak-Vance et al., 1991) for Alzheimer's disease. It should be noted that in isolated populations with a small number of ancestors (e.g., Finland, Amish population), allelic association methods can work well.

Endophenotype

One of the ways to enhance power to detect genes for complex traits is to study endophenotypes, or intermediate risk factors. Because endophenotype is closer to the action of the gene than the clinical endpoint (e.g., AD), the genotype–phenotype correlation is likely to be stronger. Endophenotypes can range from neuropsychological traits, such as memory decline, to biomarkers, such as amyloid β (Aβ) protein. Consequently, power to identify the susceptibility gene increases. In addition, all individuals in the continuum contribute information toward the genotype–phenotype relation. In contrast, affected individuals contribute much of the genetic information when discrete traits such as AD are studied (Ott, 1999). Although memory encompasses a broader cognitive phenotype than AD, it can be considered an intermediate risk factor for AD because memory impairment precedes AD in all cases. In this light, use of memory as an endophenotype can serve to improve statistical power in AD gene mapping. Identification of genes associated with memory may provide valuable information on genes that contribute to memory impairment in AD.

Genetic contributions to cognitive reserve

Familial aggregation/segregation of cognitive reserve

Many different experimental approaches support genetic contributions to cognitive functions. Genetic contributions to memory and other cognitive functions have been studied both in humans and in animals. In humans, familial correlation studies of cognitive functions based on twin, adoption, and family studies, support genetic contributions.

Twin and family studies consistently support genetic contributions to cognitive functions (Ando, Ono, & Wright, 2001; Devlin, Daniels, & Roeder, 1997; Jensen & Marisi, 1979; McClearn et al., 1997; Plomin, Pedersen, Lichtenstein, & McClearn, 1994; Sahota et al., 1997; Thapar, Petrill, & Thompson, 1994). These studies show how genes contribute to normal variation in human cognition, ranging from memory to general intelligence, and reading ability. Earlier I noted that heritability estimates based on these studies cannot effectively separate shared family environment factors from shared genetic factors, and thus estimates are likely to be skewed toward genetic explanations. Thus weak heritability (e.g., heritability estimate < 0.1) should discourage further genetic studies.

Studies of elderly twins

Most heritability estimates of cognitive function in elderly twins range from 0.4 to 0.6, with some as low as 0.0 and others as high as 0.8 (Table 2.1). McClearn and colleagues (1997) studied heritability of cognitive functions in 110 MZ and 130 DZ healthy elderly Swedish same-sex twins who were 80 years of age or older (median age of 82.3). Overall cognitive function had a significant heritable component, and the magnitude of the heritability estimate varied for different cognitive domains. For example, the estimate for the memory component was 52%. For other components, heritability estimates varied widely, ranging from 62% for general cognitive function and

Table 2.1 Summary of heritability estimates of cognitive functions

Authors (year)	Test (traits)	Heritability estimates#	Mean/median age
Older cohort			
Swan et al. (1990)	Iowa Screening Score	0.30	63
	MMSE	0.60*	
	Digital Symbol Score	0.67*	
Plomin et al. (1994)	*Memory*		64.1
	Digit Span	0.51	
	Name & Faces	0.47	
	Thurston	0.41	
	Processing speed		
	Digit Symbol	0.68	
	Figure Identification	0.51	
	Verbal		
	Information	0.63	
	Synonyms	0.63	
	Analogies	0.53	
	Spatial		
	Blocks	0.55	
	Card Rotation	0.52	
	Figure Logic	0.35	
McClearn et al. (1997)	Memory	0.52	82.3
	General Cognitive Function	0.62	
	WAIS – Short	0.53	
	Verbal Ability	0.55	
	Spatial Ability	0.32	
	Processing Speed	0.62	
Swan and Carmelli (2002)	Executive Control	0.79	71
	Digit Substitution	0.68	
	Trail Making B	0.50	
	Verbal Fluency	0.34	
	Color–Word Interference	0.50	
Younger cohort			
Jensen and Marisi (1979)	Memory Span	0.52	15
Thapar et al. (1994)	Probe Recall Memory	0.38	9.5
	Self-paced Memory	0.55	
	SCA Picture Memory – Immediate	0.33	
	SCA Picture Memory – Delayed	0.59	
	Name & Faces – Immediate	0.32	
	Name & Faces – Delayed	0.38	
	WISC-R Digit Span	0.49	
Petrill et al. (1995)	Learning	0.14–0.28**	9.6
	Self-paced Probe Recall	0.22–0.43	
	Reaction Time	0.00–0.16	
	Stimulus Discrimination	0.23–0.63	

Continued

Table 2.1 (continued)

Authors (year)	Test (traits)	Heritability estimates#	Mean/median age
Petrill et al. (1996)	General cognitive abilities	0.03–0.49**	9.6
	Verbal	0.28–0.48	
	Performance	0.24–0.55	
	Distraction	0.0	
	Speed	0.46–0.50	
Devlin et al. (1997)	IQ	0.33	Meta-analysis
Ando et al. (2001)	Spatial Storage in Working Memory	0.45	19.9
	Spatial Executive	0.49	
	Verbal Storage	0.48	
	Verbal Executive	0.43	
	Spatial Cognitive Ability	0.65	
	Verbal Cognitive Ability	0.65	
Marlow et al. (2001)	Word Recognition	0.63	
	Spelling	0.72*	
	Reading Discrepancy	0.79*	
	Non-verbal Reasoning	0.18	
	Spoonerism	0.33	
	Non-word Naming	0.51*	
	Irregular Word Naming	0.64	
	Pseudohomophone	0.66*	

* $p < .05$
# Adjusted for covariates.
** Range of estimates for multiple tests

speed of processing, to 32% for spatial ability. Interestingly, unlike other cognitive functions (e.g., general intelligence, verbal and spatial abilities), the authors concluded that their models suggest that memory and speed of processing do not have significant contributions from shared environment. However, by design, twin study cannot effectively separate the effects of shared environment factors (including in-utero exposure) from those of shared genetic factors.

Swan and colleagues (1990) found heritability estimates to be high for general cognitive functions but low for memory. Using the NHLBI Twin study that included male twin veterans (mean age of 63) from the World War II and the Korean conflict, they estimated the heritability coefficient for Iowa Screening Battery for Mental Decline to be 0.30, while that for Digit Symbol Substitution test from the Wechsler Adult Intelligence Scale, Revised was 0.67. This study illustrates again that there is likely to be high but variable heritability across different cognitive domains. In a subsequent study, they further dissected cognitive functions by adjusting for the effects of age and education and found 79% of executive function to be explained by genetic contribution (Swan & Carmelli, 2002). Executive functions, such as cooking and other goal-oriented behaviors, have been shown to decline with age. These findings suggest that cognitive efficiency as well as rate of age-related decline of cognitive and other related functions are highly heritable. In this group of healthy elderly twins, greater efficiency and slower decline may explain elevated shared genetic variance. Plomin and colleagues (1994) combined twin and adoption study designs by comparing Swedish MZ and DZ twins who were reared together against those who were reared apart (mean age of 64.1). The authors also found heritability estimates of memory to be in the range of 0.36–0.52. Processing speed measured by the Digit Symbol test was shown to have the highest heritability estimate of 0.68. Spatial and verbal ability had similarly high estimates in the range of 0.33 to 0.57 and 0.46 to 0.65, respectively. It is important to note that these studies require both twin pairs to be willing to participate and to be healthy enough to complete one to two hours of neuropsychological testing.

Studies of twin children

Cognitive function in children should reveal as much information about the genetic contributions to cognitive reserve as that in elder cohorts. Genetic studies of cognitive functions in childhood may provide better assessment of genetic contributions in that they are less influenced by life-long exposures to their environmental factors and, at the same time, minimize the impact of healthy survivor effects. Surprisingly, genetic epidemiologic studies of cognitive functions in children reveal somewhat lower and highly variable heritability estimates. Thapar and colleagues (1994) examined 137 MZ and 127 DZ same-sex twins, aged between 6 and 13, from the Western Reserve Twin Project and reported modest heritability estimates for memory. The highest heritability estimate of 59% was observed for delayed memory (as measured by SCA Picture Memory) and an estimate of 32% was observed for immediate recall (as measured by SCA Names and Faces). Unlike the study of MacClearn and colleagues in elderly twins (McClearn et al., 1997), heritability estimates for Digit Span (0.49) and Picture Memory (0.59) were not statistically significant, even though the sample size was comparable. Other researchers find lower estimates of heritability across different cognitive domains (Petrill, Luo, Thompson, & Detterman, 1996; Petrill, Thompson, & Detterman, 1995).

Thompson and colleagues (2001) conducted a novel study integrating an imaging technique with neuropsychological tests on a small number of twins (10 MZs and 10 DZs). The authors showed that genetic factors contributing to general cognitive function (maximal difference in brain activities between MZs and DZs) were associated with brain regions in Broca's and Wernicke's language areas, as well as the frontal brain region, which is associated with general cognitive functions.

Marlow and colleagues (2001) computed heritability estimates as part of their sibpair genome study. The authors studied 89 nuclear families with at least one pair of siblings who had a reading disability to determine genetic contributions to reading disability. Heritability estimates for different cognitive subdomains were highly variable, ranging from 0.32 to 0.73. To see if there were major factors underlying numerous correlated subdomains, the authors conducted a principal components analysis. The authors found that general reading factor accounted for 54% of the phenotypic variance, a general IQ component 14%, and other factors were negligible. Another twin study by Dale and colleagues (1998) reported that heritability estimates for language ability in developmentally normal children were different from those in developmentally delayed children. When children with the most significant language delay (the lowest 5 percentile) were examined, heritability explained 73% of the variance, and shared environment 18%. In developmentally normal children, however, heritability explained 25% of the variance and shared environment 69%. It is reasonable to conclude that, in a small proportion of children who are most severely affected, putative genes may explain reading disability. In developmentally normal children, genetic contributions are weak, and language delay can be remedied.

These studies suggest that heritability increases (or is at least maintained) with increasing age. Intuitively, the longer an individual lives, the greater the opportunities (and cumulative effects) for environmental exposures to influence the phenotype. Proportionally, the variance due to genetic factors should decrease. Several possible explanations can be given for this paradox. First, the increased heritability estimates may be explained by interactions between shared genetic and environmental factors, and the contribution from the interaction increases exponentially with age (another form of effect). Second, shared environmental factors between twins decrease as they age; therefore, twin studies in the elderly may be able to separate genetic contributions from environmental contributions more effectively. In addition to biological causes, there are numerous methodologic issues that introduce variability in heritability estimates. First, not all neuropsychological instruments measure cognitive functions with equal sensitivity and specificity, and both sensitivity and specificity may be lower in children than in adults. Thus assessment of cognitive performance will depend on test instrument. Second, performances on neuropsychological tests are age-dependent. Even though most tests provide age-specific norms, age-specific norms are difficult to determine and are subject to sampling bias. Third, ascertainment bias has to be considered when interpreting studies of the elderly, since only healthy twin pairs or individuals who survive to a certain age and can complete the neuropsychological tests are included in the study. Fourth, in addition to interindividual variations, there is intraindividual variation of cognitive functions as measured by repeat-testing ranges from 0.6 to 0.9 (Petrill et al., 1995; Plomin et al., 1994; Thapar et al., 1994). Some of these non-differential errors in measurements, such as intraindividual variation, can lower heritability estimates. Lastly, heritability estimates are subject to violation of the assumption of multivariate normality in the distribution of phenotypes, and differential skewness of the underlying distribution of genetic and environmental variance can lead to bias in the estimates (Detterman, Thompson, & Plomin, 1990; Falconer & Mackay, 1996). Despite these methodologic difficulties, the results are remarkably consistent across studies, showing modest to high heritability estimates for memory and related cognitive functions.

Genes that influence cognitive reserve

To date, many animal studies have explored the molecular mechanisms underlying memory. Some studies have been carried out to identify and characterize genes that contribute to those molecular mechanisms involving memory. Yet little work has been done in humans, except for some work in relation of memory impairment in AD. Below I discuss some of the molecular genetics research that illustrates how genes contribute to interindividual variations in cognitive functions, then I discuss the genetics of Alzheimer's disease as a model of memory impairment.

Animal studies of cognitive function

Genoux Haditsch, Knobloch, Michalon, Storm, and Mansuy (2002) reported that in mice, inhibition of the protein phosphatase 1 (PP1) gene reduced time required for learning and slowed down memory loss. Further, the effect was more pronounced in older mice, suggesting that PP1 activity accelerates age-related memory decline. While the precise function of the PP1 gene is unclear, Silva and Josselyn (2002) speculated that it may work by interfering with its target cAMP response element binding protein (CREB), which is required for memory formation, and inhibit formation of new proteins. Earlier work by Yin, Del Vecchio, Zhou, and Tully (1995) and Josselyn, Shi, Carlezon, Neve, Nestler, and Davis (2001) showed that disruption of CREB was associated with a longer period of learning for tasks requiring long-term memory.

Williams, Strom, and Goldowitz (1998) conducted a quantitative trait loci (QTL) study to localize chromosomal regions that explain the variance in the number of neurons in mice. A significant linkage was found for Nnc1 located on chromosome 11. This locus accounts for one third of the genetic variance among the BXH strain and over one half in the BXD strain. The role of Nnc1 appears to be specific in that it increased the number of ganglion cells, but it was not linked to the weight of brain and eye, or to the total number of retinal cells. For this gene to play a role in CR, it will be necessary to show that Nnc1 influences cognitive performance or behavior in association with an increased number of neurons.

Apolipoprotein E (APOE) appears to play a significant role in memory impairment. APOE has three common polymorphisms (ε2, ε3, and ε4). It increases risk of AD significantly, especially in Caucasians (Corder et al., 1993; Farrer et al., 1997; Tang et al., 1998). In numerous studies, patients with the APOE ε4 allele were more likely to have AD and an earlier age of onset, compared with individuals without a copy of the ε4 allele. The role of APOE has been studied in transgenic mice that have been engineered to harbor a human APP717 mutation. This mutation causes an early-onset, autosomal dominant form of AD. APOE-*deficient* mice with the human APP717 mutation deposit fewer Aβ plaques (Bales et al., 1999), and show less memory impairment than wild type mice, compared with mice that express APOE and the mutation, suggesting that APOE plays a role in clearance of Aβ plaques (Dodart, Mathis, Bales, Paul, & Ungerer, 2000). A direct role of APOE on impaired memory has been suggested by others (Dodart et al., 2000; Gordon, Ben-Eliyahu, Rosenne, Sehayek, & Michaelson, 1996). Compared with intact mice, APOE-deficient mice have lower synaptic density in cholinergic, noradrenergic, and serotinergic projections to relevant brain regions (Chapman & Michaelson, 1998) and perform worse in several types of memory tasks (Buttini et al., 1999; Dodart et al., 2000; Raber et al., 1998). Therefore, in animals, the ε4 allele has a direct effect on memory in the absence of AD.

Human studies of cognitive reserve

Several different human studies support a genetic contribution to cognitive reserve. Some studies localized chromosomal locations that influence cognitive function; many have explored the role of APOE as a candidate gene in cognitive function; and others have examined the role of a gene in rare single gene disorders that have cognitive impairment as one of their phenotypes.

Fisher and colleagues (1999) conducted the only systematic survey of the genome to identify three loci on chromosome 4 that could potentially contribute to general cognitive ability. They conducted a two-stage DNA pooling approach to compare allele frequencies in children with high vs. average intelligence (IQ), and identified three markers (D4S2943, MSX, D4S1607). Further studies are needed to narrow down the chromosomal regions, since it is not clear whether these three markers are the putative genes or are located very close to (i.e., are in linkage disequilibrium) the causative gene. No follow-up study of fine mapping is reported from this group.

A number of studies have examined the relation between APOE and cognitive function (see a meta-analysis by Small, Rosnick, Fratiglioni, & Backman, 2004). Some found age-related memory decline to be greater among those with an APOE ε4 allele compared with those without (Bunce, Fratiglioni, Small, Winblad, & Backman, 2004; Deary et al., 2002; Haan, Shemanski, Jagust, Manolio, & Kuller, 1999; Mayeux, Small, Tang, Tycko, & Stern, 2001; Payami et al., 1997; Small et al., 2004; Wilson et al., 2002). The association between the ε4 allele and memory decline was strongest for episodic memory. In contrast, Helkala and colleagues (1995) reported that individuals with at least one copy of the ε2 allele performed better on learning and memory tests. However, they found no significant association with the ε4 allele. Stern and colleague (Stern et al., 1997) raised a different question. Among individuals with AD, do ε4 carriers experience either accelerated rate of memory decline or a higher risk of mortality, compared with non-carriers? Surprisingly, they observed that the ε4 carriers experienced a less aggressive form of AD. For cognitive functions other than memory, the relation was similarly inconsistent. Among non-demented individuals, Mayeux and colleagues (2001) found no significant decline in visuospatial and language functions in individuals with ε4, whereas Wilson and colleagues (2002) found APOE ε4 to be associated with visuospatial ability and a uniformly rapid decline in all cognitive domains. Haan and colleagues (1999) found the ε4 allele to exacerbate the risk of dementia in the presence of comorbid conditions, including peripheral vascular disease, atherosclerosis of the common and internal carotid arteries, and diabetes. In addition, the risk of dementia associated with the apolipoprotein ε4 allele was found to be greatest in individuals between 60 and 70 years of age, and the risk was lower for older and younger age groups. G. W. Small and colleagues (2000) extended the APOE-phenotype relation by evaluating the effect of APOE using cerebral metabolic rate as a marker for cognitive decline in non-demented individuals. Even though neuropsychological test scores for these non-demented individuals did not significantly differ by their ε4 allele status, the authors observed significant decline in cortical metabolic rates among those with at least one copy of the ε4 allele.

Another candidate gene that is attracting the interest of geneticists is the brain-derived neurotrophic factor (BDNF) gene. BDNF contributes to survival, growth and maintenance of neuron development (Barde, 1994). Animal studies have shown that activities that increase BDNF, such as physical exercise, enhance hippocampal-dependent learning (Barde, 1994). When BDNF action was inhibited, the learning and recall abilities of animals were reduced. In a transfection experiment involving a functional polymorphism Val66Met (G196A) of BDNF, the authors observed that the *val* allele was more effective in modulating BDNF-related changes compared with the *met* allele (Egan et al., 2003). Thus it would be of interest to see whether genetic variants in BDNF lead to observable variation in cognitive function *in vivo*. Although the sample size was quite small (*n* = 64 healthy adults), Hariri et al. (2003) observed that individuals with at least one copy of the *met* allele had a lower level of hippocampal activity as measured by fMRI during encoding and retrieval processes, compared with individuals carrying two copies of *val* alleles. Further, individuals with the *met* performed poorly in memory tests compared with those with two *val* alleles. Although this study supports a role of the BDNF gene in some hippocampal activities, this finding does not strongly support the hypothesis of cognitive reserve, since those with the memory deficit (*met* carriers) would require a greater level of cognitive processing than the normals (*val* carriers). In a case-control study of late onset AD, Desai, Nebes, Dekosky, and Kamboh (2005) failed to confirm the association with the Val66Met polymorphism. This discrepancy can be due to the fact, unlike Hariri et al. who examined functional imaging data, Desai and colleagues examined AD and MMSE, which are likely to be less sensitive to preclinical changes. Given the exploratory nature of these studies, further studies are necessary.

To simplify the genetic complexity in cognitive reserve, some researchers have studied single gene disorders as human models to understand the genetics of cognitive functions. These genes can serve as candidate genes for cognitive reserve in the general population. Mutations in three early onset AD genes, namely presenilin-1 (PS1), presenilin-2 (PS2) and amyloid precursor protein (APP), are examples, since they are associated with individual differences in cognitive impairment. In addition, mutations in PS1 were associated with a wide range of phenotypic expressions, including variable age at onset of AD and variable Aβ levels in individuals with AD (Athan et al., 2001; Cruts, 2002; Laws et al., 2002). Thus variable cognitive impairment can be studied using PS1 carriers. Similarly, Olson, Goddard, and Dudek (2001) reported significant linkage between the APP gene and age at onset in families with late onset AD, suggesting that the APP gene has influence even among late onset AD.

Bond and her colleagues (2002) studied genetic contributions to a rare form of microcephaly and reported a homozygous mutation that affects cranial size. The mutation in the ASPM gene causes autosomal recessive primary microcephaly in consanguineous northern Pakistani families. Individuals with the mutation had mild to moderate mental retardation but lacked other clinical problems. In general, this gene is involved in mitotic spindle activity in the central nervous system development. This gene is conserved across species, and there appears to be a positive correlation between protein size and brain size when human, M. musculus, D. melanogaster, and C. elegans were compared.

One study examined cognitive impairment in hereditary spastic paraparesis. Although this disorder is a neurodegenerative movement disorder, affected individuals experience late onset cognitive impairment. Byrne, McMonagle, Webb, Fitzgerald, Parfrey, and Hutchinson (2000) found a putative haplotype at the SPG4 locus on 2p to be associated with cognitive impairment. In five extended families, carriers of the putative haplotype had lower scores on a set of cognitive functions (e.g., memory, orientation, language expression, and comprehension) than non-carrier family members and controls. Even the carriers who had not yet displayed the symptoms of spastic paraparesis showed lower cognitive scores compared with the controls. Gecz and Mulley (2000) reviewed genes that influence cognitive function with emphasis on mental retardation and chromosome X.

Language impairment, in addition to learning and memory, provides insight into the biology underlying cognitive function. Lai, Fisher, Hurst, Vargha-Khadem, and Monaco (2001) confirmed that genetic factors contribute to language impairment when they identified a mutation in FOXP2, located on 7q31, as the cause of severe speech and language impairment in individuals with normal intelligence. They extended this study by comparing sequences of this gene in normal humans with those in primates. Their evolutionary genetics analysis revealed that the human FOXP2 sequence differed from that in primates by one amino acid (Enard et al., 2002). This may provide the first step in understanding how humans develop the ability to speak. However, this mutation was not implicated in autism and other speech impairments (Newbury et al., 2002). These studies illustrate that it is likely that many genes contribute to a wide range of cognitive functions, including memory, intelligence, and language.

Just as genetic factors can influence variations in endophenotypes (that may eventually influence neurodegenerative diseases), it is also possible that genetic factors can lower levels of cognitive reserve by accelerating the rate of aging. One way to examine this possibility is to use telomere length as a surrogate for biological aging (Brenner, 1997). Simply, as cells replicate (or age), the length of telomere shortens until cellular apoptosis occurs. In our earlier report (Honig, Schupf, Lee, Flores, Tang, and Mayeux, 2004), we showed that among 205 randomly selected elderly, those who died during the 10 years of follow-up had significantly shorter telomere length ratios than those were surviving (45.3 vs. 52.3, $p = .01$). Stratifying by AD diagnosis, we found shorter telomere length ratio in AD subjects than in non-demented subjects (45.8 vs. 54.9). Stratifying by both vital status and diagnosis, telomere length was 25% shorter in the deceased AD cases than in the living AD cases (40.1 vs. 53.4, $p < .001$); the difference in telomere length with mortality was much less among non-demented. This suggests leukocyte telomere length may relate to aging, as measured by mortality risk and AD risk, but needs replication in the larger dataset.

Human studies of AD

Most of our understanding of the genetics of memory comes from genetic studies of AD, and those studies have identified four genes. AD genes can be considered a special class that influence memory or memory decline, and can provide insight into the process of memory decline. Recent genetic linkage studies identified some candidate genes and additional genomic regions that support association with late onset familial AD. These genes, if confirmed, are likely to enhance our understanding of how genetic factors contribute to variations in cognitive functions, which may eventually lead to elevated or lowered risk of neurological disorders such as Alzheimer's disease.

Mutations in three genes, the APP gene on chromosome 21, PS1 on chromosome 14, and PS2 on chromosome 1, are usually found in families with an autosomal dominant pattern of disease inheritance beginning as early as the third decade of life (St. George-Hyslop, 2000). Studies of mutant genes from these families indicate that many lead to enhanced generation or aggregation of Aβ that is subsequently deposited in the brain in the form of neuritic plaques, suggesting a pathogenic role. Further, each APOE ε4 allele lowers the age at onset by several years (Corder et al., 1993). This common variant may influence the age at onset in some families with mutations in the amyloid precursor protein gene (Levy-Lahad & Bird, 1996) and in adults with Down syndrome who develop dementia as they age (Schupf et al., 1996).

Three additional candidate loci for AD have been reported. Initially a locus on chromosome 12 conferring susceptibility was reported by Pericak-Vance and colleagues (1997). Subsequent confirmation of this finding has been limited as many studies show strong linkage to 12p (Mayeux et al., 2002; Pericak-Vance et al., 1997; Pericak-Vance et al., 2000; Rogaeva et al., 1998; Wu et al., 1998). However, this candidate region was approximately 40 cM, a region far too broad for gene identification. The observed variation is likely to be due to locus heterogeneity and clinical heterogeneity. As a support, Scott et al. (2000) showed that some AD patients who have Lewy bodies as well as plaques and tangles may represent a distinct subset with different genetic factors contributing to their AD. Similarly, chromosome 10 has been of interest to many groups (Bertram et al., 2000; Blacker et al., 2003; Ertekin-Taner et al., 2000; Lee, Mayeux, et al., 2004; Li et al., 2002; Myers et al., 2000). Initially, three studies reported strong support for a candidate gene on 10q (81 cM) with both Alzheimer's disease (Bertram et al., 2000; Myers et al., 2000) and variation in Aβ level in plasma of family members (Ertekin-Taner et al., 2000). Subsequently, three genes—PLAU gene which encodes urokinase-type plasminogen activator (Ertekin-Taner et al., 2005); VR22 which encodes alpha-T catenin (Ertekin-Taner et al., 2003), and glutathione S-transferase, omega-1 (Li et al., 2003)—have been implicated, but not yet confirmed in independent datasets. Lastly, Pericak-Vance and associates have identified a locus on chromosome 9p with linkage to Alzheimer's disease restricted to a series of families in whom the diagnosis was confirmed by post-mortem examination (Pericak-Vance et al., 2000).

Use of endophenotypes such as Aβ and memory scores will improve the capacity of genetics as a means to understand the pathobiology of AD (Ertekin-Taner et al., 2000; Lee, Mayo, et al., 2004). More importantly, it is also possible to further explore the pathobiology underlying memory decline by examining how a given gene is related to Aβ and memory decline.

In sum, researchers are beginning to localize and identify potential genes that influence memory, memory decline, intelligence and language. Findings from animal studies, human studies, and studies of AD, need to be integrated. Mutations in the AD genes—PS1, PS2, and APP—cause memory decline in early onset AD patients. APOE appears to have significant influence on memory as well as in AD among healthy elders. Other candidate genes—such as genes that cause human single gene disorders that have a memory part of the phenotypes, candidate genes from genome wide searches of familial Alzheimer's disease, as well as those from animal studies that control the number of neurons—need to be explored together to better understand CR.

Environmental and cultural influences on cognitive reserve

The main objective in studies of cognitive reserve is to understand the variability in cognitive function in response to brain insult from environmental risk factor. As in most non-Mendelian traits, environmental factors will influence cognitive functions in conjunction with genetic factors. Therefore, it is necessary to understand how gene together with environment influence cognitive function. Studies have shown that environmental and cultural influences contribute to memory and other cognitive functions (Manly et al., 1998; Stern, Albert, Tang, & Tsai, 1999; Stern et al., 1994; Unverzagt, Hui, Farlow, Hall, & Hendrie, 1998). Educational and occupational attainment have been cited as the most important examples. However, additional risk factors, including severe head injury, estrogen deficiency, diet, AIDS, syphilis, toxic encephalopathy, contribute to memory impairment (Kawas & Katzman, 1999). The phenotypic manifestation of the gene–environment interaction can be differential risk or differential rate of progression. Here I introduce three environmental or host risk factors, namely head injury, estrogen and diet, in the context of gene–environment interaction.

Head injury

Head injury has been known to increase the likelihood of AD (Heyman, Wilkinson, Stafford, Helms, Sigmon, & Weinberg 1984; Mayeux et al., 1995; Mayeux et al., 1993; Mortimer, French, Hutton, & Schuman, 1985; van Duijn et al., 1992), and it may work by increasing deposition of Aβ (Roberts, Gentleman, Lynch, Murray, Landon, & Graham, 1994). The risk of memory impairment following head trauma varied by the individual's ability to clear amyloid or by the propensity for accumulating Aβ. Mayeux and colleagues (1995) observed that the risk of AD following head injury varies with the presence or absence of apolipoprotein ε4 allele. Those with an ε4 allele had a 10-fold increased risk of having AD following head injury compared with those without. The ε4 allele may slow down clearance of Aβ in the brain. However, it is unclear as to whether the head injury has to occur immediately prior to dementia or not, and how severe the injury has to be. It would be more informative to examine rate of memory decline associated with head injury in a longitudinal study. Certainly, genes involved in Aβ production will also interact with these insults.

Estrogen

Estrogen plays an important role in the normal maintenance of brain function in the hippocampus and the basal forebrain. Estrogen may delay cognitive decline through maintenance of cholinergic neurons, stimulation of acetylcholine activity and the formation of synapses and dendritic spines, antioxidant effects, and slowing accumulation of Aβ (McEwen & Alves, 1999).

In ovariectomized rats, estrogen replacement therapy (ERT) increased cholinergic activity and improved performance in memory tasks compared with estrogen-deprived rats (Singh, Meyer, Millard, & Simpkins, 1994). In guinea pigs, ovariectomy led to increased levels of Aβ peptides Aβ1-40 and Aβ1-42 in the brain and the effect was partially reversible with exogenous estrogen treatment (Petanceska, Nagy, Frail, & Gandy, 2000).

In human observation studies, however, the relation between estrogen in postmenopausal women and memory and other cognitive functions appears ambiguous. Several studies showed slower declines in memory and other cognitive functions with the use of estrogen, hormonal replace-ment therapy, or high serum concentrations of non-protein-bound estradiol (Jacobs et al., 1998; Kawas et al., 1997; Tang et al., 1996; Yaffe, Lui, Grady, Cauley, Kramer, & Cummings, 2000), while other studies did not show any significant improvement (Barrett-Connor & Goodman-Gruen, 1999; Barrett-Connor & Kritz-Silverstein, 1993; Yaffe, Sawaya, Lieberburg, & Grady, 1998). Further, randomized controlled clinical trials of ERT in women with moderate to severe AD have failed to show cognitive improve-ment. It may be that the major effect of estrogen is to delay onset rather than reverse cognitive and functional decline (Henderson et al., 2000; Mulnard et al., 2000), and the ERT may require early or longer exposure for it to be effective.

Some of the observed variations in estrogen influence may be due to underlying genetic variations. Yaffe, Haan, Byers, Tangen, and Kuller (2000) found that ERT/HRT was protective for cognitive decline only in women without an APOE ε4 allele. In the brain, two estrogen receptors, ERα and ERβ, have been identified (McEwen & Alves, 1999). Two polymorphisms *Pvu*II (P and p) and *Xba*I (X and x) in ERα, have been reported to influence APOE synthesis and beta amyloid metabolism. Having at least one copy of homozygous PP or XX was associated with earlier onset of menopause (Weel et al., 1999) or increased risk for AD (Brandi et al., 1999; Isoe-Wada et al., 1999; Ji, Urakami, Wada-Isoe, Adachi, & Nakashima, 2000). The increased risk of AD associated with ERα PP and XX genotypes was greater in those with an ε4 allele than in those without (Brandi et al., 1999; Ji et al., 2000; Mattila et al., 2000). Moreover, ERβ was reported to be involved in hippocampal formation, entorhinal cortex, and thalamus. In a small post-mortem study, reduced ERβ mRNA was associated with increased risk of depressive symptoms (Ostlund, Keller, & Hurd, 2003).

Diet

Reduced caloric intake (RCI) has been shown to influence aging for the past 70 years (Koubova & Guarente, 2003; Lee, Klopp, Weindruch, & Prolla, 1999; Mattson, 2003b). The supporting evidence has been coming primarily from animal models. Recent epidemiologic studies are beginning to show that RCI, by the means of reduced oxidative stress, is associated not only with the aging process itself, but also with a number of common neurodegenerative diseases (Luchsinger & Mayeux, 2004; Luchsinger, Tang, Stern, Shea, & Mayeux, 2001; Mattson, 2003b). Some suggested that malnutrition, particularly at an early age, can increase the likelihood of cognitive deficit later in life (Bauer, Boschmann, Green, & Kuehnast, 1998; Bryan, Osendarp, Hughes, Calvaresi, Baghurst, & van Klinken, 2004), and deficiencies in these micronutrients are quite common in developing countries (Sharmanov, 1999). For example, 62.8% of the children age 2–15 surveyed in Kazakhstan had severe folic acid deficiency (Sarbayev, Kudaibergenov, Chuyenbekova, & Imanbayev, 1999). It has been reported that deficiencies in folic acid, vitamin B12, and vitamin B6 can lead to elevated homocysteine levels, and may lead to eventual late-age cognitive impairments (Auer, Lamm, & Eber, 2004; Duthie, Whalley, Collins, Leaper, Berger, & Deary, 2002; Luchsinger & Mayeux, 2004; Mattson, 2003a). Further, life expectancy in these developing countries is increasing rapidly, such that cognitive aging will become a significant public health burden. For this purpose, it would be powerful to compare populations that experience extreme ends of the distribution of nutritional exposure. It would be even more powerful if populations from a single genetic background are utilized. To this end, migrant studies, such as the Korean diaspora study (Terwilliger et al., 2002) and the Ni-Hon-San study of Japanese Americans (Benfante, 1992), can provide an effective means to look into this complex biological process.

Future directions

There is strong evidence that genetic variation accounts for a significant proportion of cognitive variation, supporting the phenomenon of cognitive reserve. Thus the genetic approach can enhance our understanding of cognitive reserve. Fundamentally, this can be achieved by clarifying genotype–phenotype relations. Recent advances in biotechnology have made tremendous improvements in developing cost-effective and accurate methods of identifying genes. Progress has also been made at the phenotypic end, where better characterization of phenotypes is possible via imaging techniques and newly discovered biomarkers. At the same time, it is necessary to design the study that will provide optimal power to test the hypothesis. Only when all three factors are taken into account and methods integrated, will it be possible to understand the complex neuronal networks involved in CR.

Acknowledgments

This work was supported by grants AG20351, AG15473, AG23749, and ES013108 from the National Institutes of Health, Bethesda, MD.

References

Ando, J., Ono, Y., & Wright, M. J. (2001). Genetic structure of spatial and verbal working memory. *Behavioral Genetics, 31*(6), 615–624.

Andreasen, N. C., Flaum, M., Swayze, V., 2nd, O'Leary, D. S., Alliger, R., Cohen, G., et al. (1993). Intelligence and brain structure in normal individuals. *American Journal of Psychiatry, 150*(1), 130–134.

Athan, E. S., Williamson, J., Ciappa, A., Santana, V., Romas, S. N., Lee, J. H., et al. (2001). A founder mutation in presenilin 1 causing early-onset Alzheimer disease in unrelated Caribbean Hispanic families. *Journal of the American Medical Association, 286*(18), 2257–2263.

Auer, J., Lamm, G., & Eber, B. (2004). Homocysteine as a predictive factor for hip fracture in older persons. *New England Journal of Medicine, 351*(10), 1027–1030; author reply 1027–1030.

Backman, L., Ginovart, N., Dixon, R. A., Wahlin, T. B., Wahlin, A., Halldin, C., et al. (2000). Age-related cognitive deficits mediated by changes in the striatal dopamine system. *American Journal of Psychiatry, 157*(4), 635–637.

Bales, K. R., Verina, T., Cummins, D. J., Du, Y., Dodel, R. C., Saura, J., et al. (1999). Apolipoprotein E is essential for amyloid deposition in the APP(V717F) transgenic mouse model of Alzheimer's disease. *Proceedings of the National Academy of Science USA, 96*(26), 15233–15238.

Barde, Y. A. (1994). Neurotrophins: A family of proteins supporting the survival of neurons. *Progress in Clinical and Biological Research, 390*, 45–56.

Barrett-Connor, E., & Goodman-Gruen, D. (1999). Cognitive function and endogenous sex hormones in older women. *Journal of the American Geriatric Society, 47*(11), 1289–1293.

Barrett-Connor, E., & Kritz-Silverstein, D. (1993). Estrogen replacement therapy and cognitive function in older women. *Journal of the American Medical Association, 269*(20), 2637–2641.

Bauer, A., Boschmann, N., Green, D., & Kuehnast, K. (1998). *A generation at risk: Children in the Central Asian Republic of Kazakhstan and Kyrgyzstan.* Manila, Philippines: Asian Development Bank.

Benfante, R. (1992). Studies of cardiovascular disease and cause-specific mortality trends in Japanese-American men living in Hawaii and risk factor comparisons with other Japanese populations in the Pacific region: A review. *Human Biology, 64*(6), 791–805.

Benton, A. L., Eslinger, P. J., & Damasio, A. R. (1981). Normative observations on neuropsychological test performances in old age. *Journal of Clinical Neuropsychology, 3*(1), 33–42.

Bertram, L., Blacker, D., Mullin, K., Keeney, D., Jones, J., Basu, S., et al. (2000). Evidence for genetic linkage of Alzheimer's disease to chromosome 10q. *Science, 290*(5500), 2302–2303.

Bigio, E. H., Hynan, L. S., Sontag, E., Satumtira, S., & White, C. L. (2002). Synapse loss is greater in presenile than senile onset Alzheimer disease: Implications for the cognitive reserve hypothesis. *Neuropathology and Applied Neurobiology, 28*, 218–227.

Blacker, D., Bertram, L., Saunders, A. J., Moscarillo, T. J., Albert, M. S., Wiener, H., et al. (2003). Results of a high-resolution genome screen of 437 Alzheimer's disease families. *Human Molecular Genetics, 12*(1), 23–32.

Bond, J., Roberts, E., Mochida, G. H., Hampshire, D. J., Scott, S., Askham, J. M., et al. (2002). ASPM is a major determinant of cerebral cortical size. *Nature Genetics*, Published online 23 September 2002, doi:10.1038/ng995.

Borenstein Graves, A., Mortimer, J. A., Bowen, J. D., McCormick, W. C., McCurry, S. M., Schellenberg, G. D., et al. (2001). Head circumference and incident Alzheimer's disease: Modification by apolipoprotein E. *Neurology*, *57*(8), 1453–1460.

Brandi, M. L., Becherini, L., Gennari, L., Racchi, M., Bianchetti, A., Nacmias, B., et al. (1999). Association of the estrogen receptor alpha gene polymorphisms with sporadic Alzheimer's disease. *Biochemical and Biophysical Research Communications*, *265*(2), 335–338.

Brenner, S. (1997). *Telomeres and telomerase* (Vol. 211). New York: John Wiley and Sons.

Bryan, J., Osendarp, S., Hughes, D., Calvaresi, E., Baghurst, K., & van Klinken, J. W. (2004). Nutrients for cognitive development in school-aged children. *Nutrition Reviews*, *62*(8), 295–306.

Bunce, D., Fratiglioni, L., Small, B. J., Winblad, B., & Backman, L. (2004). APOE and cognitive decline in preclinical Alzheimer disease and non-demented aging. *Neurology*, *63*(5), 816–821.

Buttini, M., Orth, M., Bellosta, S., Akeefe, H., Pitas, R. E., Wyss-Coray, T., et al. (1999). Expression of human apolipoprotein ε3 or ε4 in the brains of APOE-/- mice: Isoform-specific effects on neurodegeneration. *Journal of Neuroscience*, *19*(12), 4867–4880.

Byrne, P. C., McMonagle, P., Webb, S., Fitzgerald, B., Parfrey, N. A., & Hutchinson, M. (2000). Age-related cognitive decline in hereditary spastic paraparesis linked to chromosome 2p. *Neurology*, *54*(7), 1510–1517.

Chakravarti, A. (1999). Population genetics—making sense out of sequence. *Nature Genetics*, *21*(1 Suppl.), 56–60.

Chapman, S., & Michaelson, D. M. (1998). Specific neurochemical derangements of brain projecting neurons in apolipoprotein E-deficient mice. *Journal of Neurochemistry*, *70*(2), 708–714.

Christensen, H., Mackinnon, A., Jorm, A. F., Henderson, A. S., Scott, L. R., & Korten, A. E. (1994). Age differences and interindividual variation in cognition in community-dwelling elderly. *Psychology and Aging*, *9*(3), 381–390.

Christensen, H., Mackinnon, A. J., Korten, A. E., Jorm, A. F., Henderson, A. S., Jacomb, P., et al. (1999). An analysis of diversity in the cognitive performance of elderly community dwellers: Individual differences in change scores as a function of age. *Psychology and Aging*, *14*(3), 365–379.

Corder, E. H., Saunders, A. M., Strittmatter, W. J., Schmechel, D. E., Gaskell, P. C., Small, G. W., et al. (1993). Gene dose of apolipoprotein E type 4 allele and the risk of Alzheimer's disease in late onset families. *Science*, *261*(5123), 921–923.

Cruts, M. (2002). Alzheimer Disease Mutation Database.

Dale, P. S., Simonoff, E., Bishop, D. V., Eley, T. C., Oliver, B., Price, T. S., et al. (1998). Genetic influence on language delay in two-year-old children. *Nature Neuroscience*, *1*(4), 324–328.

Deary, I. J., Whiteman, M. C., Pattie, A., Starr, J. M., Hayward, C., Wright, A. F., et al. (2002). Cognitive change and the APOE ε4 allele. *Nature*, *418*, 932.

Desai, P., Nebes, R., Dekosky, S. T., & Kamboh, M. I. (2005). Investigation of the effect of brain-derived neurotrophic factor (BDNF) polymorphisms on the risk of late-onset Alzheimer's disease (AD) and quantitative measures of AD progression. *Neuroscience Letters, 379*(3), 229–234.

Detterman, D. K., Thompson, L. A., & Plomin, R. (1990). Differences in heritability across groups differing in ability. *Behavior Genetics, 20*(3), 369–384.

Devlin, B., Daniels, M., & Roeder, K. (1997). The heritability of IQ. *Nature, 388*(6641), 468–471.

Dodart, J. C., Mathis, C., Bales, K. R., Paul, S. M., & Ungerer, A. (2000). Behavioral deficits in APP(V717F) transgenic mice deficient for the apolipoprotein E gene. *Neuroreport, 11*(3), 603–607.

Drachman, D. A. (2002). Hat size, brain size, intelligence, and dementia: What morphometry can tell us about brain function and disease. *Neurology, 59*(2), 156–157.

Duthie, S. J., Whalley, L. J., Collins, A. R., Leaper, S., Berger, K., & Deary, I. J. (2002). Homocysteine, B vitamin status, and cognitive function in the elderly. *American Journal of Clinical Nutrition, 75*(5), 908–913.

Edland, S. D., Xu, Y., Plevak, M., O'Brien, P., Tangalos, E. G., Petersen, R. C., et al. (2002). Total intracranial volume: Normative values and lack of association with Alzheimer's disease. *Neurology, 59*(2), 272–274.

Egan, M. F., Kojima, M., Callicott, J. H., Goldberg, T. E., Kolachana, B. S., Bertolino, A., et al. (2003). The BDNF val66met polymorphism affects activity-dependent secretion of BDNF and human memory and hippocampal function. *Cell, 112*(2), 257–269.

Enard, W., Przeworski, M., Fisher, S. E., Lai, C. S., Wiebe, V., Kitano, T., et al. (2002). Molecular evolution of FOXP2, a gene involved in speech and language. *Nature*, doi:10.1038/nature01025.

Ertekin-Taner, N., Graff-Radford, N., Younkin, L. H., Eckman, C., Baker, M., Adamson, J., et al. (2000). Linkage of plasma Abeta42 to a quantitative locus on chromosome 10 in late-onset Alzheimer's disease pedigrees. *Science, 290*(5500), 2303–2304.

Ertekin-Taner, N., Ronald, J., Asahara, H., Younkin, L., Hella, M., Jain, S., et al. (2003). Fine mapping of the alpha-T catenin gene to a quantitative trait locus on chromosome 10 in late-onset Alzheimer's disease pedigrees. *Human Molecular Genetics, 12*(23), 3133–3143.

Ertekin-Taner, N., Ronald, J., Feuk, L., Prince, J., Tucker, M., Younkin, L., et al. (2005). Elevated amyloid beta protein (Abeta42) and late onset Alzheimer's disease are associated with single nucleotide polymorphisms in the urokinase-type plasminogen activator gene. *Human Molecular Genetics, 14*(3), 447–460.

Falconer, D. S., & Mackay, T. F. C. (1996). *Introduction to quantitative genetics* (4th ed.). Burnt Mill, Harlow, UK: Longman.

Farrer, L. A., Cupples, L. A., Haines, J. L., Hyman, B., Kukull, W. A., Mayeux, R., et al. (1997). Effects of age, sex, and ethnicity on the association between apolipoprotein E genotype and Alzheimer disease. A meta-analysis. APOE and Alzheimer Disease Meta Analysis Consortium. *Journal of the American Medical Association, 278*(16), 1349–1356.

Fisher, P. J., Turic, D., Williams, N. M., McGuffin, P., Asherson, P., Ball, D., et al. (1999). DNA pooling identifies QTLs on chromosome 4 for general cognitive ability in children. *Human Molecular Genetics, 8*(5), 915–922.

Flood, J. F., & Morley, J. E. (2000). Age-related changes in learning, memory, and memory processing. In J. E. Morley, H. J. Armbrecht, R. M. Coe, & B. Vellas (Eds.), *The science of geriatrics* (Vol. 2, pp. 503–514). Paris: Serdi Publisher.

Foster, N. L., Minoshima, S., & Kuhl, D. E. (1999). Brain imaging in Alzheimer disease. In R. D. Terry, R. Katzman, K. L. Bick, & S. S. Sisodia (Eds.), *Alzheimer disease* (2nd ed., pp. 67–93). Philadelphia: Lippincott Williams & Wilkins.

Gecz, J., & Mulley, J. (2000). Genes for cognitive function: Developments on the X. *Genome Research, 10*(2), 157–163.

Genoux, D., Haditsch, U., Knobloch, M., Michalon, A., Storm, D., & Mansuy, M. M. (2002). Protein phosphatase 1 is a molecular constrain on learning and memory. *Nature, 418*, 970–975.

Gordon, I., Ben-Eliyahu, S., Rosenne, E., Sehayek, E., & Michaelson, D. M. (1996). Derangement in stress response of apolipoprotein E-deficient mice. *Neuroscience Letters, 206*(2–3), 212–214.

Grady, C. L., Horwitz, B., Pietrini, P., Mentis, M. J., Ungerleiter, L., Rapoport, S. I., et al. (1996). Effect of task difficulty on cerebral blood flow during perceptual matching of faces. *Human Brain Mapping, 4*, 227–239.

Grasby, P. M., Frith, C. D., Friston, K. J., Simpson, J., Fletcher, P. C., Frackowiak, R. S., et al. (1994). A graded task approach to the functional mapping of brain areas implicated in auditory-verbal memory. *Brain, 117* (Pt 6), 1271–1282.

Graves, A. B., Mortimer, J. A., Larson, E. B., Wenzlow, A., Bowen, J. D., & McCormick, W. C. (1996). Head circumference as a measure of cognitive reserve. Association with severity of impairment in Alzheimer's disease. *British Journal of Psychiatry, 169*(1), 86–92.

Haan, M. N., Shemanski, L., Jagust, W. J., Manolio, T. A., & Kuller, L. (1999). The role of APOE epsilon4 in modulating effects of other risk factors for cognitive decline in elderly persons. *Journal of the American Medical Association, 282*(1), 40–46.

Hariri, A. R., Goldberg, T. E., Mattay, V. S., Kolachana, B. S., Callicott, J. H., Egan, M. F., et al. (2003). Brain-derived neurotrophic factor val66met polymorphism affects human memory-related hippocampal activity and predicts memory performance. *Journal of Neuroscience, 23*(17), 6690–6694.

Helkala, E. L., Koivisto, K., Hanninen, T., Vanhanen, M., Kervinen, K., Kuusisto, J., et al. (1995). The association of apolipoprotein E polymorphism with memory: A population based study. *Neuroscience Letters, 191*(3), 141–144.

Henderson, V. W., Paganini-Hill, A., Miller, B. L., Elble, R. J., Reyes, P. F., Shoupe, D., et al. (2000). Estrogen for Alzheimer's disease in women: Randomized, double-blind, placebo-controlled trial. *Neurology, 54*(2), 295–301.

Heyman, A., Wilkinson, W. E., Stafford, J. A., Helms, M. J., Sigmon, A. H., & Weinberg, T. (1984). Alzheimer's disease: a study of epidemiological aspects. *Annals of Neurology, 15*(4), 335–341.

Honig, L. S., Schupf, N., Lee, J. H., Tang, M. X. & Mayeux, R. (2006). Short telomere length is associated with mortality in those with APOE4 and dementia. *Annals of Neurology, 60*, 181–187.

Isoe-Wada, K., Maeda, M., Yong, J., Adachi, Y., Harada, H., Urakami, K., et al. (1999). Positive association between an estrogen receptor gene polymorphism and Parkinson's disease with dementia. *European Journal of Neurology, 6*(4), 431–435.

Jacobs, D. M., Tang, M. X., Stern, Y., Sano, M., Marder, K., Bell, K. L., et al. (1998). Cognitive function in nondemented older women who took estrogen after menopause. *Neurology, 50*(2), 368–373.

Jensen, A. R., & Marisi, D. Q. (1979). A note on the heritability of memory span. *Behavioral Genetics, 9*(5), 379–387.

Ji, Y., Urakami, K., Wada-Isoe, K., Adachi, Y., & Nakashima, K. (2000). Estrogen receptor gene polymorphisms in patients with Alzheimer's disease, vascular dementia and alcohol-associated dementia. *Dementia & Geriatric Cognitive Disorders*, *11*(3), 119–122.

Josselyn, S. A., Shi, C., Carlezon, W. A., Jr., Neve, R. L., Nestler, E. J., & Davis, M. (2001). Long-term memory is facilitated by cAMP response element-binding protein overexpression in the amygdala. *Journal of Neuroscience*, *21*(7), 2404–2412.

Katzman, R. (1993). Education and the prevalence of dementia and Alzheimer's disease. *Neurology*, *43*(1), 13–20.

Katzman, R., Terry, R., DeTeresa, R., Brown, T., Davies, P., Fuld, P., et al. (1988). Clinical, pathological, and neurochemical changes in dementia: A subgroup with preserved mental status and numerous neocortical plaques. *Annals of Neurology*, *23*(2), 138–144.

Kawas, C., Resnick, S., Morrison, A., Brookmeyer, R., Corrada, M., Zonderman, A., et al. (1997). A prospective study of estrogen replacement therapy and the risk of developing Alzheimer's disease: The Baltimore Longitudinal Study of Aging. *Neurology*, *48*(6), 1517–1521.

Kawas, C. H., & Katzman, R. (1999). Epidemiology of dementia and Alzheimer's disease. In R. D. Terry, K. L. Katzman, & S. S. Sisodia (Eds.), *Alzheimer disease* (2nd ed., pp. 95–116). Philadelphia: Lippincott Williams and Wilkins.

Koubova, J., & Guarente, L. (2003). How does calorie restriction work? *Genes and Development*, *17*(3), 313–321.

Kruglyak, L. (1999). Prospects for whole-genome linkage disequilibrium mapping of common disease genes. *Nature Genetics*, *22*(2), 139–144.

Lai, C. S., Fisher, S. E., Hurst, J. A., Vargha-Khadem, F., & Monaco, A. P. (2001). A forkhead-domain gene is mutated in a severe speech and language disorder. *Nature*, *413*(6855), 519–523.

Lander, E. S., & Schork, N. J. (1994). Genetic dissection of complex traits. *Science*, *265*(5181), 2037–2048.

Laws, S. M., Clarnette, R. M., Taddei, K., Martins, G., Paton, A., Almeida, O. P., et al. (2002). Association between the presenilin-1 mutation Glu318Gly and complaints of memory impairment. *Neurobiology of Aging*, *23*(1), 55–58.

Lee, C. K., Klopp, R. G., Weindruch, R., & Prolla, T. A. (1999). Gene expression profile of aging and its retardation by caloric restriction. *Science*, *285*(5432), 1390–1393.

Lee, J. H., Mayeux, R., Mayo, D., Mo, J., Santana, V., Williamson, J., et al. (2004). Fine mapping of 10q and 18q for familial Alzheimer's disease in Caribbean Hispanics. *Molecular Psychiatry*, *9*(11), 1042–1051.

Lee, J. H., Mayo, D., Mo, J., Santana, V., Williamson, J., Flaquer, A., et al. (2004). Fine mapping of 10 using memory and neuropsychological phenotypes in the Caribbean Hispanics. *Neurobiology of Aging*, *25*(2), S56.

Levy-Lahad, E., & Bird, T. D. (1996). Genetic factors in Alzheimer's disease: A review of recent advances. *Annals of Neurology*, *40*(6), 829–840.

Levy-Lahad, E., Wijsman, E. M., Nemens, E., Anderson, L., Goddard, K. A., Weber, J. L., et al. (1995). A familial Alzheimer's disease locus on chromosome 1. *Science*, *269*(5226), 970–973.

Li, Y. J., Oliveira, S. A., Xu, P., Martin, E. R., Stenger, J. E., Scherzer, C. R., et al. (2003). Glutathione S-transferase omega-1 modifies age-at-onset of Alzheimer disease and Parkinson disease. *Human Molecular Genetics*, *12*(24), 3259–3267.

Li, Y. J., Scott, W. K., Hedges, D. J., Zhang, F., Gaskell, P. C., Nance, M. A., et al. (2002). Age at onset in two common neurodegenerative diseases is genetically controlled. *American Journal of Human Genetics, 70*(4), 985–993.

Luchsinger, J. A., & Mayeux, R. (2004). Dietary factors and Alzheimer's disease. *Lancet Neurology, 3*(10), 579–587.

Luchsinger, J. A., Tang, M. X., Stern, Y., Shea, S., & Mayeux, R. (2001). Diabetes mellitus and risk of Alzheimer's disease and dementia with stroke in a multiethnic cohort. *American Journal of Epidemiology, 154*(7), 635–641.

MacLullich, A. M., Ferguson, K. J., Deary, I. J., Seckl, J. R., Starr, J. M., & Wardlaw, J. M. (2002). Intracranial capacity and brain volumes are associated with cognition in healthy elderly men. *Neurology, 59*(2), 169–174.

Manly, J. J., Jacobs, D. M., Sano, M., Bell, K., Merchant, C. A., Small, S. A., et al. (1998). Cognitive test performance among nondemented elderly African Americans and whites. *Neurology, 50*(5), 1238–1245.

Markowska, A. L., & Savonenko, A. (2002). Retardation of cognitive aging by life-long diet restriction: Implications for genetic variance. *Neurobiology of Aging, 23*(1), 75–86.

Marlow, A. J., Fisher, S. E., Richardson, A. J., Francks, C., Talcott, J. B., Monaco, A. P., et al. (2001). Investigation of quantitative measures related to reading disability in a large sample of sib-pairs from the UK. *Behavior Genetics, 31*(2), 219–230.

Mattila, K. M., Axelman, K., Rinne, J. O., Blomberg, M., Lehtimaki, T., Laippala, P., et al. (2000). Interaction between estrogen receptor 1 and the epsilon4 allele of apolipoprotein E increases the risk of familial Alzheimer's disease in women. *Neuroscience Letters, 282*(1–2), 45–48.

Mattson, M. P. (2003a). Gene–diet interactions in brain aging and neurodegenerative disorders. *Annals of Internal Medicine, 139*(5 Pt 2), 441–444.

Mattson, M. P. (2003b). Will caloric restriction and folate protect against AD and PD? *Neurology, 60*(4), 690–695.

Mayeux, R., Lee, J. H., Romas, S. N., Mayo, D., Santana, V., Williamson, J., et al. (2002). Chromosome-12 mapping of late-onset Alzheimer disease among Caribbean Hispanics. *American Journal of Human Genetics, 70*(1), 237–243.

Mayeux, R., Ottman, R., Maestre, G., Ngai, C., Tang, M. X., Ginsberg, H., et al. (1995). Synergistic effects of traumatic head injury and apolipoprotein-epsilon 4 in patients with Alzheimer's disease. *Neurology, 45*(3 Pt 1), 555–557.

Mayeux, R., Ottman, R., Tang, M. X., Noboa-Bauza, L., Marder, K., Gurland, B., et al. (1993). Genetic susceptibility and head injury as risk factors for Alzheimer's disease among community-dwelling elderly persons and their first-degree relatives. *Annals of Neurology, 33*(5), 494–501.

Mayeux, R., Small, S. A., Tang, M., Tycko, B., & Stern, Y. (2001). Memory performance in healthy elderly without Alzheimer's disease: Effects of time and apolipoprotein-E. *Neurobiology of Aging, 22*(4), 683–689.

Mayford, M., & Kandel, E. R. (1999). Genetic approaches to memory storage. *Trends in Genetics, 15*(11), 463–470.

McClearn, G. E., Johansson, B., Berg, S., Pedersen, N. L., Ahern, F., Petrill, S. A., et al. (1997). Substantial genetic influence on cognitive abilities in twins 80 or more years old. *Science, 276*(5318), 1560–1563.

McEwen, B. S., & Alves, S. E. (1999). Estrogen actions in the central nervous system. *Endocrine Reviews, 20*(3), 279–307.

Meaney, M. J., O'Donnell, D., Rowe, W., Tannenbaum, B., Steverman, A., Walker, M., et al. (1995). Individual differences in hypothalamic-pituitary-adrenal activity in later life and hippocampal aging. *Experimental Gerontology, 30*(3–4), 229–251.

Mejia, S., Pineda, D., Alvarez, L. M., & Ardila, A. (1998). Individual differences in memory and executive function abilities during normal aging. *International Journal of Neuroscience, 95*(3–4), 271–284.

Mori, E., Hirono, N., Yamashita, H., Imamura, T., Ikejiri, Y., Ikeda, M., et al. (1997). Premorbid brain size as a determinant of reserve capacity against intellectual decline in Alzheimer's disease. *American Journal of Psychiatry, 154*(1), 18–24.

Mortimer, J. A., French, L. R., Hutton, J. T., & Schuman, L. M. (1985). Head injury as a risk factor for Alzheimer's disease. *Neurology, 35*(2), 264–267.

Mulnard, R. A., Cotman, C. W., Kawas, C., van Dyck, C. H., Sano, M., Doody, R., et al. (2000). Estrogen replacement therapy for treatment of mild to moderate Alzheimer disease: A randomized controlled trial. Alzheimer's Disease Cooperative Study. *Journal of the American Medical Association, 283*(8), 1007–1015.

Myers, A., Holmans, P., Marshall, H., Kwon, J., Meyer, D., Ramic, D., et al. (2000). Susceptibility locus for Alzheimer's disease on chromosome 10. *Science, 290*(5500), 2304–2305.

Newbury, D. F., Bonora, E., Lamb, J. A., Fisher, S. E., Lai, C. S., Baird, G., et al. (2002). FOXP2 is not a major susceptibility gene for autism or specific language impairment. *American Journal of Human Genetics, 70*(5), 1318–1327.

Olson, J. M., Goddard, K. A., & Dudek, D. M. (2001). The amyloid precursor protein locus and very-late-onset Alzheimer disease. *American Journal of Human Genetics, 69*(4), 895–899.

Ostlund, H., Keller, E., & Hurd, Y. L. (2003). Estrogen receptor gene expression in relation to neuropsychiatric disorders. *Annals of the New York Academy of Science, 1007*, 54–63.

Ott, J. (1999). *Analysis of human genetic linkage* (3rd ed.). Baltimore: Johns Hopkins University Press.

Payami, H., Grimslid, H., Oken, B., Camicioli, R., Sexton, G., Dame, A., et al. (1997). A prospective study of cognitive health in the elderly (Oregon Brain Aging Study): Effects of family history and apolipoprotein E genotype. *American Journal of Human Genetics, 60*(4), 948–956.

Pericak-Vance, M. A., Bass, M. P., Yamaoka, L. H., Gaskell, P. C., Scott, W. K., Terwedow, H. A., et al. (1997). Complete genomic screen in late-onset familial Alzheimer disease. Evidence for a new locus on chromosome 12. *Journal of the American Medical Association, 278*(15), 1237–1241.

Pericak-Vance, M. A., Bebout, J. L., Gaskell, P. C., Jr., Yamaoka, L. H., Hung, W. Y., Alberts, M. J., et al. (1991). Linkage studies in familial Alzheimer disease: Evidence for chromosome 19 linkage. *American Journal of Human Genetics, 48*(6), 1034–1050.

Pericak-Vance, M. A., Grubber, J., Bailey, L. R., Hedges, D., West, S., Santoro, L., et al. (2000). Identification of novel genes in late-onset Alzheimer's disease. *Experimental Gerontology, 35*(9–10), 1343–1352.

Petanceska, S. S., Nagy, V., Frail, D., & Gandy, S. (2000). Ovariectomy and 17beta-estradiol modulate the levels of Alzheimer's amyloid beta peptides in brain. *Neurology, 54*(12), 2212–2217.

Petrill, S. A., Luo, D., Thompson, L. A., & Detterman, D. K. (1996). The independent prediction of general intelligence by elementary cognitive tasks: Genetic and environmental influences. *Behavior Genetics, 26*(2), 135–147.

Petrill, S. A., Thompson, L. A., & Detterman, D. K. (1995). The genetic and environmental variance underlying elementary cognitive tasks. *Behavior Genetics, 25*(3), 199–209.

Plomin, R., Pedersen, N. L., Lichtenstein, P., & McClearn, G. E. (1994). Variability and stability in cognitive abilities are largely genetic later in life. *Behavior Genetics, 24*(3), 207–215.

Powell, D. H., & Whitla, D. K. (1994). *Profiles in cognitive aging.* Cambridge, MA: Harvard University Press.

Raber, J., Wong, D., Buttini, M., Orth, M., Bellosta, S., Pitas, R. E., et al. (1998). Isoform-specific effects of human apolipoprotein E on brain function revealed in APOE knockout mice: Increased susceptibility of females. *Proceedings of the National Academy of Science, USA, 95*(18), 10914–10919.

Reich, D. E., Cargill, M., Bolk, S., Ireland, J., Sabeti, P. C., Richter, D. J., et al. (2001). Linkage disequilibrium in the human genome. *Nature, 411*(6834), 199–204.

Risch, N., & Merikangas, K. (1996). The future of genetic studies of complex human diseases. *Science, 273*(5281), 1516–1517.

Roberts, G. W., Gentleman, S. M., Lynch, A., Murray, L., Landon, M., & Graham, D. I. (1994). Beta amyloid protein deposition in the brain after severe head injury: Implications for the pathogenesis of Alzheimer's disease. *Journal of Neurology, Neurosurgery & Psychiatry, 57*(4), 419–425.

Rogaev, E. I., Sherrington, R., Rogaeva, E. A., Levesque, G., Ikeda, M., Liang, Y., et al. (1995). Familial Alzheimer's disease in kindreds with missense mutations in a gene on chromosome 1 related to the Alzheimer's disease type 3 gene. *Nature, 376*(6543), 775–778.

Rogaeva, E., Premkumar, S., Song, Y., Sorbi, S., Brindle, N., Paterson, A., et al. (1998). Evidence for an Alzheimer disease susceptibility locus on chromosome 12 and for further locus heterogeneity. *Journal of the American Medical Association, 280*(7), 614–618.

Rogaeva, E. A., Fafel, K. C., Song, Y. Q., Medeiros, H., Sato, C., Liang, Y., et al. (2001). Screening for PS1 mutations in a referral-based series of AD cases: 21 novel mutations. *Neurology, 57*(4), 621–625.

Sahota, A., Yang, M., Gao, S., Hui, S. L., Baiyewu, O., Gureje, O., et al. (1997). Apolipoprotein E-associated risk for Alzheimer's disease in the African-American population is genotype dependent. *Annals of Neurology, 42*(4), 659–661.

Sarbayev, B. T., Kudaibergenov, Z., Chuyenbekova, A., & Imanbayev, D. (1999). Nutrition of women and children. In T. S. Sharmanov (Ed.), *Kazakhstan demographic and health survey 1999.* Calverton, MD: Academy of Preventive Medicine & Macro International Inc.

Satz, P. (1993). Brain reserve capacity on symptom onset after brain injury: A formulation and review of evidence for threshold theory. *Neuropsychology, 7*, 273–295.

Schaie, K. W. (1988). Variability in cognitive function in the elderly: Implications for societal participation. *Basic Life Sciences, 43*, 191–211.

Schellenberg, G. D., Bird, T. D., Wijsman, E. M., Orr, H. T., Anderson, L., Nemens, E., et al. (1992). Genetic linkage evidence for a familial Alzheimer's disease locus on chromosome 14. *Science, 258*(5082), 668–671.

Schofield, P. W., Logroscino, G., Andrews, H. F., Albert, S., & Stern, Y. (1997). An association between head circumference and Alzheimer's disease in a population-based study of aging and dementia. *Neurology, 49*(1), 30–37.

Schofield, P. W., Mosesson, R. E., Stern, Y., & Mayeux, R. (1995). The age at onset of Alzheimer's disease and an intracranial area measurement. A relationship. *Archives of Neurology, 52*(1), 95–98.

Schork, N. J., Fallin, D., & Lanchbury, J. S. (2000). Single nucleotide polymorphisms and the future of genetic epidemiology. *Clinical Genetics, 58*(4), 250–264.

Schupf, N., Kapell, D., Lee, J. H., Zigman, W., Canto, B., Tycko, B., et al. (1996). Onset of dementia is associated with apolipoprotein E epsilon4 in Down's syndrome. *Annals of Neurology, 40*(5), 799–801.

Scott, W. K., Grubber, J. M., Conneally, P. M., Small, G. W., Hulette, C. M., Rosenberg, C. K., et al. (2000). Fine mapping of the chromosome 12 late-onset Alzheimer disease locus: Potential genetic and phenotypic heterogeneity. *American Journal of Human Genetics, 66*(3), 922–932.

Sharmanov, T. S. (1999). *Kazakhstan demographic and health survey 1999.* Calverton, MD: Academy of Preventive Medicine & Macro International, Inc.

Sherrington, R., Rogaev, E. I., Liang, Y., Rogaeva, E. A., Levesque, G., Ikeda, M., et al. (1995). Cloning of a gene bearing missense mutations in early-onset familial Alzheimer's disease. *Nature, 375*(6534), 754–760.

Silva, A. J., & Josselyn, S. A. (2002). The molecules of forgetfulness. *Nature, 418*(6901), 929–930.

Singh, M., Meyer, E. M., Millard, W. J., & Simpkins, J. W. (1994). Ovarian steroid deprivation results in a reversible learning impairment and compromised cholinergic function in female Sprague-Dawley rats. *Brain Research, 644*(2), 305–312.

Small, B. J., Rosnick, C. B., Fratiglioni, L., & Backman, L. (2004). Apolipoprotein E and cognitive performance: A meta-analysis. *Psychology and Aging, 19*(4), 592–600.

Small, G. W., Ercoli, L. M., Silverman, D. H., Huang, S. C., Komo, S., Bookheimer, S. Y., et al. (2000). Cerebral metabolic and cognitive decline in persons at genetic risk for Alzheimer's disease. *Proceedings of the National Academy of Science, USA, 97*(11), 6037–6042.

Small, S. A., Wu, E. X., Bartsch, D., Perera, G. M., Lacefield, C. O., DeLaPaz, R., et al. (2000). Imaging physiologic dysfunction of individual hippocampal subregions in humans and genetically modified mice. *Neuron, 28*(3), 653–664.

St. George-Hyslop, P. H. (2000). Molecular genetics of Alzheimer's disease. *Biological Psychiatry, 47*(3), 183–199.

Stern, Y. (2002). What is cognitive reserve? Theory and research application of the reserve concept. *Journal of the International Psychological Society, 8*(3), 448–460.

Stern, Y., Albert, S., Tang, M. X., & Tsai, W. Y. (1999). Rate of memory decline in AD is related to education and occupation: Cognitive reserve? *Neurology, 53*(9), 1942–1947.

Stern, Y., Alexander, G. E., Prohovnik, I., & Mayeux, R. (1992). Inverse relationship between education and parietotemporal perfusion deficit in Alzheimer's disease. *Annals of Neurology, 32*(3), 371–375.

Stern, Y., Brandt, J., Albert, M., Jacobs, D. M., Liu, X., Bell, K., et al. (1997). The absence of an apolipoprotein epsilon4 allele is associated with a more aggressive form of Alzheimer's disease. *Annals of Neurology, 41*(5), 615–620.

Stern, Y., Gurland, B., Tatemichi, T. K., Tang, M. X., Wilder, D., & Mayeux, R. (1994). Influence of education and occupation on the incidence of Alzheimer's disease. *Journal of the American Medical Association, 271*(13), 1004–1010.

Strachan, T., & Read, A. P. (1999). *Human molecular genetics 2* (2nd ed.). New York: Wiley-Liss.

Swan, G. E., & Carmelli, D. (2002). Evidence for genetic mediation of executive control: A study of aging male twins. *Journals of Gerontology Series B: Psychological Sciences and Social Sciences, 57*(2), 133–143.

Swan, G. E., Carmelli, D., Reed, T., Harshfield, G. A., Fabsitz, R. R., & Eslinger, P. J. (1990). Heritability of cognitive performance in aging twins. The National Heart, Lung, and Blood Institute Twin Study. *Archives of Neurology, 47*(3), 259–262.

Tang, M. X., Jacobs, D., Stern, Y., Marder, K., Schofield, P., Gurland, B., et al. (1996). Effect of oestrogen during menopause on risk and age at onset of Alzheimer's disease. *Lancet, 348*(9025), 429–432.

Tang, M. X., Stern, Y., Marder, K., Bell, K., Gurland, B., Lantigua, R., et al. (1998). The APOE-epsilon4 allele and the risk of Alzheimer disease among African Americans, whites, and Hispanics. *Journal of the American Medical Association, 279*(10), 751–755.

Terwilliger, J. D., Göring, H. H. H., Magnusson, P. K. E., & Lee, J. H. (2002). Study design for genetic epidemiology and gene mapping: The Korean diaspora project. *Life Science Research, 6*(2), 95–115.

Thapar, A., Petrill, S. A., & Thompson, L. A. (1994). The heritability of memory in the Western Reserve Twin Project. *Behavior Genetics, 24*(2), 155–160.

Thompson, P. M., Cannon, T. D., Narr, K. L., van Erp, T., Poutanen, V. P., Huttunen, M., et al. (2001). Genetic influences on brain structure. *Nature Neuroscience, 4*(12), 1253–1258.

Unverzagt, F. W., Hui, S. L., Farlow, M. R., Hall, K. S., & Hendrie, H. C. (1998). Cognitive decline and education in mild dementia. *Neurology, 50*(1), 181–185.

Van Broeckhoven, C., Backhovens, H., Cruts, M., De Winter, G., Bruyland, M., Cras, P., et al. (1992). Mapping of a gene predisposing to early-onset Alzheimer's disease to chromosome 14q24.3. *Nature Genetics, 2*(4), 335–339.

van Duijn, C. M., Tanja, T. A., Haaxma, R., Schulte, W., Saan, R. J., Lameris, A. J., et al. (1992). Head trauma and the risk of Alzheimer's disease. *American Journal of Epidemiology, 135*(7), 775–782.

Weel, A. E., Uitterlinden, A. G., Westendorp, I. C., Burger, H., Schuit, S. C., Hofman, A., et al. (1999). Estrogen receptor polymorphism predicts the onset of natural and surgical menopause. *Journal of Clinical Endocrinology & Metabolism, 84*(9), 3146–3150.

Williams, R. W., Strom, R. C., & Goldowitz, D. (1998). Natural variation in neuron number in mice is linked to a major quantitative trait locus on Chr 11. *Journal of Neuroscience, 18*(1), 138–146.

Wilson, R. S., Schneider, J. A., Barnes, L. L., Beckett, L. A., Aggarwal, N. T., Cochran, E. J., et al. (2002). The apolipoprotein E epsilon 4 allele and decline in different cognitive systems during a 6-year period. *Archives of Neurology, 59*(7), 1154–1160.

Wu, W. S., Holmans, P., Wavrant-DeVrieze, F., Shears, S., Kehoe, P., Crook, R., et al. (1998). Genetic studies on chromosome 12 in late-onset Alzheimer disease. *Journal of the American Medical Association, 280*(7), 619–622.

Yaffe, K., Haan, M., Byers, A., Tangen, C., & Kuller, L. (2000). Estrogen use, APOE, and cognitive decline: Evidence of gene–environment interaction. *Neurology*, *54*(10), 1949–1954.

Yaffe, K., Lui, L. Y., Grady, D., Cauley, J., Kramer, J., & Cummings, S. R. (2000). Cognitive decline in women in relation to non-protein-bound oestradiol concentrations. *Lancet*, *356*(9231), 708–712.

Yaffe, K., Sawaya, G., Lieberburg, I., & Grady, D. (1998). Estrogen therapy in postmenopausal women: Effects on cognitive function and dementia. *Journal of the American Medical Association*, *279*(9), 688–695.

Yin, J. C., Del Vecchio, M., Zhou, H., & Tully, T. (1995). CREB as a memory modulator: Induced expression of a dCREB2 activator isoform enhances long-term memory in Drosophila. *Cell*, *81*(1), 107–115.

3 Lifetime antecedents of cognitive reserve

Marcus Richards, Amanda Sacker, and Ian J. Deary

Brain reserve capacity, or cognitive reserve is thought to provide a threshold below which cognitive decline or impairment, during normal aging or through insult to the central nervous system (CNS), begins to impact on daily living. Structural, passive reserve, or "brain reserve capacity," focuses on the protective potential of anatomical features such as brain size, neural density, and synaptic connectivity (Katzman, 1993), whereas functional, active or "cognitive" reserve emphasizes efficiency of neural networks and active compensation by alternative or more extensive neural networks following challenge (Stern, 2002, 2003). Both approaches, however, imply a graded neural substrate that is capable, by degree, of protecting against the functional consequences of neuropathology (Richards & Deary, 2005). An important task in cognitive epidemiology is to understand how this substrate develops across the life course. Before we approach this task, however, it is worth asking what it means to say that reserve protects against the functional consequences of neuropathology. In the context of clinical dementia function is usually equated with activities of daily living (ADL) (American Psychiatric Association, 1994). However, it would be unwise to place too much emphasis on ADL as an index of underlying neuropathological severity since, in practice, the stage at which ADL are likely to be classified as impaired will be at least partly determined by extra-biological factors, such as availability and uptake of clinical services, level of social capital, social and cultural norms, and so forth. Furthermore, education, occupation and lifestyle may interact with this social determination, independently of their effects on the brain.

A more tractable, empirical approach would be to equate function with measured cognitive performance, while acknowledging that it is just one of the effects that determine ADL (Richards & Deary, 2005). In this way, the concept of reserve may become a viable model of cognitive aging, and the task of cognitive epidemiology in this context therefore becomes one of understanding how mature cognitive function develops across the life course (Richards & Deary, 2005).

In this chapter, we highlight two comprehensive models that we hope will advance this task. The first was developed by Richards and Sacker (2003), and is a simple structural model that encompasses paths from parental origins to peak mature cognitive ability in adulthood, via own early cognitive ability and subsequent own socioeconomic attainment. The second model was proposed by Richards and Deary (2005), and suggests how cognitive reserve may develop in a wider life course framework that includes morbid as well as normal function.

A simple path model of mature cognitive ability

First, we turn to the structural model of Richards and Sacker (2003), which encompasses paths from parental origins to peak mature cognitive ability. Peak mature ability may be difficult to capture, however, since cognitive function can be augmented over the adult years (Rabbitt, 1993; Schaie, 1996; Anstey & Christensen, 2000), against a background of age-associated decline (Schaie, 1996). One solution is to use a measure of ability that represents accumulated experience, but is relatively resistant to decline, therefore providing a "high water mark" for cognitive ability at any time in the adult life course. Measures of so-called crystallized intelligence, defined by Carroll (1993) as "a type of broad mental ability that develops through the 'investment' of general intelligence into learning through education and experience" (p. 599), are optimal in this respect. For example, the National Adult Reading Test (NART: Nelson & Willison, 1991) is a pronunciation test, where the words are chosen to violate conventional grapheme–phoneme correspondence rules, and are therefore unlikely to be read correctly unless the reader is familiar with them in written form, rather than relying on intelligent guesswork (Nelson & Willison, 1991). It therefore represents a cognitive skill that depends on the accumulation and use of information. Since this mainly involves recognition, the NART arguably makes minimal demands on processing capacity, and should therefore be relatively insensitive to age-associated decline (Salthouse, 1996), a suggestion for which there is support (Rabbitt, 1993). The NART can be used as a brief measure of general ability, and indeed predicts full-scale IQ (Crawford, Stewart, Parker, Besson, & De Lacey, 1989; Nelson & Willison, 1991).

If the NART provides a working measure of cognitive reserve, what are its major determinants across the life course? Influences on cognitive ability begin with the uterine environment (Barker, 1998; Welberg & Seckl, 2001), and the heritable component of IQ (Plomin, 1999), but many factors that determine early cognition are subsumed under the umbrella of parental social background. The effect of parental occupational social class on cognition is evident by 22 months (Feinstein, 2003), and is detectable at least as far as late middle age (Kaplan, Turrell, Lynch, Everson, Hekala, & Salonen, 2001). However, the paths through which parental background influences cognitive reserve are still unclear.

Historically, cognitive reserve has been strongly linked to education, and there are numerous studies showing the protective effect of this variable on cognitive aging (e.g. Evans et al., 1993; Stern, Gurland, Tatemichi, Tang, Wilder, & Mayeux, 1994; White et al., 1994; Geerlings, Schmand, Jonker, Lindeboom & Boulter, 1999, but see Christensen, Hofer, Mackinnon, Korten, Jorm, & Henderson, 2001). Indeed, a recent study showed that the influence of paternal occupation on midlife cognition was mediated by own educational attainment (Kaplan et al., 2001), although it is worth noting that a portion of the variance attributed to educational attainment may be explained by cognitive ability, which, in turn, has a genetic component (Plomin, 1999). Another crucial mediator is cognitive development itself. Low intellectual ability is a risk factor for cognitive decline (Schmand, Smit, Geelings, & Lindeboom, 1997), a risk that has been traced back through early adulthood (Snowdon, Kemper, Mortimer, Greiner, Wekstein, & Markesbery, 1996) to childhood (Whalley, Starr, Athawes, Hunter, Pattie, & Deary, 2001). In fact an early path analysis failed to show independent effects of paternal education and occupation on adult cognitive ability when own education and childhood cognitive ability were included (see Snow & Yalow, 1982). Furthermore, whatever the direct or indirect role of parental occupation, own adult occupation may also be important, since low occupational attainment is a risk factor for age-associated cognitive decline (Dartigues et al., 1992; Stern et al., 1994; Bonaiuto et al., 1995; Callahan, Hall, Hui, Musick, Unverzagt, & Hendrie, 1996, but see Jorm et al., 1998; Helmer et al., 2001). The paths through which cognitive reserve is shaped by even this small set of fundamental variables are therefore likely to be complex.

A simple model that highlights links between these variables used data from the U.K. Medical Research Council National Survey of Health and Development, also known as the British 1946 birth cohort (Richards & Sacker, 2003). This prospective birth cohort study followed a representative sample of the U.K. general population from their birth in 1946, and repeatedly obtained demographic, medical and psychological information on its members through midlife. Path analysis was used to assess the relative contribution of paternal occupation, childhood cognition, educational attainment, and adult occupation to cognitive ability at 53 years. For simplicity, paths to the NART only are summarized in this chapter, although the interested reader is referred to Richards and Sacker (2003) for details of paths to verbal memory and visual search speed at the same age.

The MRC National Survey of Health and Development (NSHD) is a socially stratified birth cohort of 2548 women and 2814 men, followed up 20 times between their birth during one week of March 1946 and the age of 53 years (Wadsworth, 1991). At 43 years, the population interviewed were representative, in comparison with census data, of the British population of that age in most respects (Wadsworth, Mann, Rodgers, Kuh, Hilder, & Yusuf, 1992). Exceptions were an over-representation among non-responders of the never married, the least literate, those always in manual social class circumstances, and those with psychiatric disturbance. By age 53 years permanent losses comprised 469 (8.7%) deaths, and 640 (11.9%) refusals, and temporary losses were 639 (11.9%) emigrations or residence overseas and 580 (10.8%) failures to contact. Since large-scale Commonwealth immigration to Britain did not begin until the late 1940s, the ethnic composition of this birth cohort is entirely white European.

Paternal occupation was assigned according to the Registrar General system (OPCS, 1970), classified as professional, managerial, intermediate, skilled manual, semi-skilled manual, and unskilled, when the participant was aged 11 years or, if this was unknown, occupation at 4 years or 15 years. At 8 years cohort members took tests of verbal and non-verbal ability devised by the National Foundation for Educational Research (Pigeon, 1964), and administered by teachers or other trained personnel. These tests were: (1) reading comprehension (selecting appropriate words to complete 35 sentences); (2) word reading (ability to pronounce 50 words); (3) vocabulary (ability to explain the meaning of these 50 words); and (4) picture intelligence, consisting of a 60-item non-verbal reasoning test. Scores from these tests were summed to create a total score representing overall cognitive ability at this age. The highest educational or training qualification achieved by 26 years was classified by the Burnham scale (DES, 1972). From this scale they were grouped into no qualification, below ordinary secondary qualifications (vocational), ordinary secondary qualifications ("O" levels and their training equivalents), advanced secondary qualifications ("A" levels and their equivalents), or higher qualifications (degree or equivalent). Own current or last occupation by age 43 years was measured using identical categories to those for paternal occupation.

The path model contained three components: (1) paths from paternal occupation to childhood cognitive function, education and own occupation; (2) simultaneous paths from these variables to the cognitive outcome (NART); and (3) paths within childhood cognition, education and occupation; that is, from childhood cognition to educational attainment and adult occupation, and from educational attainment to adult occupation. A particular hypothesis examined was that the entire effect of father's occupation was entirely mediated through childhood cognitive function, educational attainment, and own occupation.

The analysis was carried out using the latent variable modeling program AMOS 4.01 (Arbuckle, 1999). The estimation method of choice in most latent variable modeling programs is maximum likelihood. The AMOS program also employs maximum likelihood estimation based on incomplete data, i.e., the full information maximum likelihood (FIML) approach. FIML is preferable to estimation based on complete data, i.e., the list-wise deletion (LD) approach, since FIML estimates tend to be less biased and more reliable than LD estimates, even when the data deviate from missing at random and are non-ignorable (Arbuckle, 1996).

Figure 3.1 shows the path model. The numerical values refer to standardized regression weights. All paths are statistically independent.

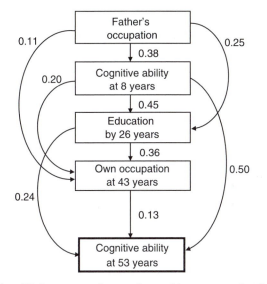

Figure 3.1 Major lifetime antecedents of cognitive reserve in the British 1946 birth cohort (adapted from Richards & Sacker, 2003).

Although a direct path from father's occupation to the NART was significantly different from zero, this path is substantially unimportant ($r = .05$), and is not considered further.

Three independent indirect pathways from paternal occupation were found. Of these, the strongest led to childhood cognition, followed by that to educational attainment, then that to own occupation. Of particular interest are the independent paths from childhood cognitive ability, educational attainment and occupational attainment to the NART. The path from childhood cognitive ability was the strongest, and that from occupational attainment was the weakest. Other notable features of the model are the strong path from cognitive ability to educational attainment, and the relatively weak path from cognitive ability to occupational attainment. As expected, there is a strong internal path from educational attainment to own occupation, since level of occupation is largely dependent on level of educational qualification.

It should be acknowledged that the structure of this model is unlikely to be invariant over time or across cultures. Indeed, it is almost certain to vary across different socioeconomic and sociocultural environments. Instead of constituting a limitation, it is hoped that this fluidity will lead to deeper understanding of cognitive reserve and its determinants through carefully planned comparative research. With this issue in mind, the paths to cognitive reserve via childhood cognition, education and occupation are now considered in detail.

Concerning the path via childhood cognition, previous studies have reported an association between cognition in later life and cognition in childhood (Deary, Whalley, Lemmon, Crawford, & Starr, 2000) and early adulthood (Plassman, Welsh, Helms, Brandt, Page, & Breitner, 1995; Snowdon et al., 1996). The Richards and Sacker (2003) model described above shows that this path receives a substantial initial input from parental social class. A proportion of the variance of this input is almost certainly accounted for by genetic factors, since there is evidence of a strong heritable component to general cognitive ability (Plomin, 1999). In addition, environmental effects of parental background on cognition are demonstrated by evidence that social advantage can benefit cognitive development independently of biological origin (Schiff & Lewontin, 1986; Capron & Duyme, 1989), although evidence from twin and adoption studies suggests that the effect of shared family environments on cognition, while appreciable in early childhood, is overshadowed later in the life course by genetic influence (e.g. Petrill, Pike, Price, & Plomin, 2004; Deater-Deckard, Petrill, Thompson, & DeThorne, 2005; Loehlin, Horn, & Willerman, 1997). Care should be taken, furthermore, in considering the ways in which parental social class exerts an environmental influence on cognitive development. There is a range of possible mediators, including economic conditions (Duncan, Brooks-Gunn, & Klebanov, 1994), school social composition (Sacker, Schoon, & Bartley, 2002), health (Douglas, 1964; McKeown & Record, 1976; Kramer, Allen, & Gergen, 1995), nutrition (Koletzko et al., 1998) and maternal depression (Weinberg & Tronick, 1998). The influence on cognitive development of at least some factors, however, such as material home conditions (Douglas, 1964), parental encouragement (Douglas, 1964), and the home linguistic environment (Tizard, Hughes, Carmichael, & Pinkerton, 1983; Tizard & Hughes, 1984), is not necessarily explained by social class. More complex issues, such as parent–child reciprocity, the variety and meaningfulness of their content, and the active role taken by the child, may need to be taken into account before the influence of parental input on cognition can be fully understood (Rutter, 1985).

The second path to midlife cognition in the Richards and Sacker model, that via educational attainment, is easier to conceptualize, since there is clear evidence that schooling per se can lead to cognitive gains, even in late adolescence (Rutter, 1985). Indeed, earlier data from the 1946 birth cohort show that academic performance of the primary school (i.e., its record in sending pupils to selective secondary schools) was predictive of increased cognitive performance (Douglas, 1964). Furthermore, it has been shown in the British 1958 birth cohort that the academic performance of the school is one of the major contributors to social class differences in childhood cognitive function (Sacker et al., 2002). As with the home, the effect of schooling is not simply a matter of input. In addition to their teaching skills, schools with good scholastic performance tend to promote efficient learning through a variety of factors, including good classroom management, the aiding of high morale, appropriately high teacher expectations, and the fostering of pupils' commitment to educational goals (Rutter, 1985).

The third path to midlife cognition in the Richards and Sacker model, that via adult occupation, is the weakest, and perhaps the least explored. However, several studies show that high occupational attainment can protect cognitive function in adult life (Dartigues et al., 1992; Stern et al., 1994; Bonaiuto et al., 1995; Callahan et al., 1996). An important point in this context is that neuronal plasticity and development are by no means confined to early life. In a striking demonstration, London taxi drivers, who are required to undertake intensive navigational study of the city as part of their training, show significantly larger posterior hippocampi than controls, the size correlating with amount of occupational experience (Maguire et al., 2000). We should note that the classification of occupation in terms of social class (according to the Registrar General system) is relatively crude, and gives few clues as to the specific occupational skills that benefit cognition. This issue warrants further investigation. Again, the model showed paths from paternal occupation to own occupation, independent of childhood cognition and educational attainment, consistent with an earlier analysis (Snow & Yalow, 1982). In addition to the direct effects of occupation on cognition, possible mechanisms underlying this relationship include cultural factors such as the occupational aspirations of parents and children, and greater opportunities for financial aid and social influence among more advantaged families. It should be noted, however, that these paths were weak in the Richards and Sacker model, consistent with some previous studies (Jorm et al., 1998; Helmer et al., 2001).

A life course model of cognitive reserve

A long-term goal is to develop a more comprehensive life course model of cognitive reserve. To this end, Figure 3.2 shows the second model highlighted in this chapter, that proposed by Richards and Deary (2005).

At the center is pre-morbid cognitive ability, which modifies (path a) the clinical expression (path b) of disease that is influenced by CNS lesions. The major proximal input into pre-morbid cognitive ability comes from brain size and function, based on structural neural network complexity (Satz, 1993), and functional processing capacity and efficiency (Stern, 2002, 2003). Influencing brain size and function are a range of more distal factors (path c), beginning with genes (Deary et al., 2002; Hassan et al., 2002; Wilson, Bienia, Berry-Kravis, Evans, & Bennett, 2002; Deary et al., 2004) and pre-natal exposures (Barker, 1998; Seckl, 1998). In regard to the latter, a positive association between birth weight, representing fetal growth, and cognitive development is well established in the normal population (Sorensen, Sabroe, Olsen, Rothman, Gillman, & Fischer, 1997; Matte, Bresnahan, Begg, & Susser, 2001; Richards, Hardy, Kuh, & Wadsworth, 2001; Shenkin, Starr, Pattie, Rush, Whalley, & Deary, 2001; Jefferis, Power, & Hertzman, 2002; Shenkin, Starr, & Deary, 2004), although factors that modify this association are yet to be clarified (Richards, in press). Early post-natal influences include

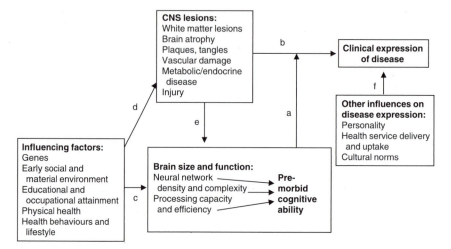

Figure 3.2   A proposed life course model of cognitive reserve (from Richards & Deary, 2005). a. Cognitive reserve is represented by peak pre-morbid cognitive ability. b. Cognitive reserve modifies the clinical expression of CNS lesions. c. Cognitive reserve is influenced by many factors across the life course. d. These same factors influence the accumulation of CNS lesions. e. CNS lesions in turn damage brain size and function. f. There are also factors other than CNS lesions that affect disease (especially dementia) expression.

birth order (Belmont & Marolla, 1973), nutrition (Anderson, Johnstone, & Remley 1999; Koletzko et al., 1998), material home conditions (Douglas, 1964), physical growth (Richards, Hardy, Kuh, & Wadsworth, 2002; Pearce, Deary, Young, & Parker, 2005), physical health (Douglas, 1964; Kramer et al., 1995), and parental encouragement (Douglas, 1964). These influencing factors then extend to the major inputs of education, occupation and the adult socioeconomic environment, to physical health, health behaviors, and degree of engaged lifestyle activity. As already noted, neuronal plasticity permits cognitive reserve to be enhanced or maintained during the adult years. Factors associated with cognitive benefit during maturity include physical activity (Albert et al., 1995; Carmelli, Swan, LaRue, & Eslinger, 1997; Kramer et al., 1999; Richards, Hardy, & Wadsworth, 2003), nutrition (Gale, Martyn, & Cooper, 1996; Jama et al., 1996; La Rue, Koehler, Wayne, Chiulli, Haaland, & Garry, 1997), and social and intellectual engagement (Arbuckle, Gold, Andres, Schwartzman, & Chaikelson, 1992; Bassuk, Glass, & Berkman, 1999; Hultsch, Hertzog, Small, & Dixon, 1999), although the causal direction of these associations is not always clear (Hultsch et al., 1999). These factors are themselves linked to early determinants, so patterns of risk and protection are likely to accumulate across the life course. For example, adult physical health is influenced by childhood health (Kuh & Ben Shlomo, 1997), and propensity towards active lifestyle shows antecedents in childhood (Kuh & Cooper, 1992).

Two further points are important to make. First, although much of the neuropathology highlighted in the CNS lesions box in Figure 3.2 is associated with later life, the model is capable of application to earlier phases of the life course. For example, it might apply to protection against the cognitive effects of head injury at any age. Second, it is important to emphasize that influencing factors not only determine cognitive ability at any given age, but also are capable of augmenting ability (or protecting it from decline) over time. That is, taking prior ability into account, the signature of the accrual of reserve is the identification of something that adds variance to later cognitive function. For example, education and occupation are positively associated with mature ability, even after taking childhood ability into account, as shown in Figure 3.1 (Richards & Sacker, 2003); physical exercise is associated with slower cognitive decline in midlife after taking adolescent ability into account, as well as educational and occupational attainment, and cardio-respiratory function (Richards et al., 2003). Occupation contributes significant variance in fluid reasoning in old age after childhood ability and white matter lesions are taken into account (Staff, Murray, Deary, & Whalley, 2004). As these latter authors suggest, "reserve should account for significant variance in the cognitive outcomes in old age after adjusting for variance contributed by childhood mental ability and burden. In other words, possessing some reserve means that one's cognitive score is greater than would be predicted from the person's childhood ability and the amount of overt, accumulated burden" (p. 1192).

Note that there are paths connecting the Influencing factors to Brain structures (path c) *and* to CNS lesions (path d). For example, poor education may not only inhibit optimal brain development, but may also lead to increased risk of cerebrovascular damage, via cardiovascular disease and diabetes (Roman, Erkinjuntti, Wallin, Pantoni, & Chui, 2002), exacerbated by negative health behaviors such as sedentary lifestyle, poor diet and smoking (Meyer et al., 1999; Starr et al., 2004; Taylor et al., 2003). As already noted, from the perspective of dementia, brain reserve and neuropathology are regarded as fully independent entities; there is no suggestion that education protects against the *acquisition* of AD neuropathology, only against its clinical expression. If, however, the model is broadened to address a range of CNS pathologies, particularly cerebrovascular disease, but also injury and toxic or metabolic disruption, it is clear that this independence is not sustainable.

This, however, raises a difficulty for the concept of cognitive reserve. Note that CNS lesions by definition damage brain size and function, as represented by path e in Figure 3.2. If brain size and function are the major proximal determinants of peak pre-morbid cognitive ability, then the model is capable of working in a negative circular manner. That is, negative influences on brain size and function, such as low educational and occupational attainment, are also risk factors for the development of CNS lesions, which in turn can deplete cognitive reserve and lower protection against their clinical expression. However, only certain cognitive domains, particularly "fluid" skills requiring effortful information processing, are likely to be vulnerable to the effects of CNS damage. Crystallized ability, on the other hand, is not only resistant to age-associated decline but is also capable of being augmented across the adult life course (Rabbitt, 1993; Richards & Sacker, 2003), and is to some extent robust to the effects of frank neuropathology (McGurn et al., 2004), although it does eventually decline with increasing severity of dementia (Taylor, 1999; Cockburn, Keene, Hope, & Smith, 2000). This recapitulates the issue raised in the presentation of the path model of Richards and Sacker (2003) above, that measures of crystallized intelligence provide the optimum opportunity to capture peak mature cognitive ability, in terms of cognitive reserve. The question of whether preserved crystallized ability in the face of impaired fluid ability is sufficient to protect against the clinical expression of neuropathology is a matter for further debate.

Conclusions

The concept of reserve has proved to be heuristic in neuroscience, as a potential mechanism to explain why diseases of the CNS that affect cognition are less likely to be detected, and less likely to impair daily function, in some individuals than in others. However, since disease detection and perceived functional capacity are partly determined by factors that are independent of the individual, the most important focus for reserve theory should arguably be cognitive function itself. This is not a new idea. Indeed, Stern (2003) has argued that an active approach to reserve is equally viable for normal cognitive function as it is for explaining the clinical manifestations of disease. Our suggestion is to extend this further by allowing the reserve model to apply across the life course, to cognitive development in childhood, as well as to adulthood and later life, recognizing that cognitive ability is modifiable at all stages of the life course. We suggest that cognitive reserve reflects the combined influence of factors that promote physical and mental health across the life course, that in turn enhance and maintain neural integrity. Rather than an entity that is fixed during development, cognitive reserve represents a dynamic process in development and aging, with crucial implications for cognitive function in later life. We close with one further thought; our life course approach highlights an important distinction—that between reserve factors, i.e., the class of processes and events that affect reserve and its indicators, and reserve per se. The latter is the biological instantiation of the construct, by far the most interesting and enigmatic aspect of the entire approach that is cognitive reserve theory.

Acknowledgments

Funding for Dr. Richards was provided by the Medical Research Council. Professor Deary is the recipient of a Royal Society-Wolfson Research Merit Award.

References

Albert, M. S., Jones, K., Savage, C. R., Berkman, L., Seeman, T., Blazer, D., et al. (1995). Predictors of cognitive change in older persons: MacArthur Studies of Successful Aging. *Psychology and Aging, 10*, 578–589.

American Psychiatric Association (1994). *Diagnostic and statistical manual of mental disorders (DSM–IV)* (4th ed.). Washington, DC: APA.

Anderson, J. A., Johnstone, B. M., & Remley, D. T. (1999). Breast-feeding and cognitive development: A meta-analysis. *American Journal of Clinical Nutrition, 70*, 525–535.

Anstey, K., & Christensen, H. (2000). Education, activity, health, blood pressure and apolipoprotein E as predictors of cognitive change in old age: A review. *Gerontology, 46*, 163–177.

Arbuckle, J. C. (1996). Full information estimation in the presence of incomplete data. In G. A. Marcoulides & R. E. Schumacker (Eds.), *Advanced structural equation modeling techniques* (pp. 243–277). Mahwah, NJ: Lawrence Erlbaum Associates, Inc.

Arbuckle, J. C. (1999). *Amos for Windows. Analysis of moment structures. Version 4.01.* Chicago: SmallWaters Corp.

Arbuckle, T. Y., Gold, D. P., Andres, D., Schwartzman, A. E., & Chaikelson, J. (1992). The role of psychosocial context, age, and intelligence in memory performance of older men. *Psychology and Aging, 7*, 25–36.

Barker, D. J. P. (1998). *Mothers, babies and health in later life* (2nd ed.). Edinburgh, UK: Churchill Livingstone.

Bassuk, S. S., Glass, T. A., & Berkman, L. F. (1999). Social disengagement and incident cognitive decline in community-dwelling elderly persons. *Annals of Internal Medicine, 131*, 165–173.

Belmont, L., & Marolla, F. A. (1973). Birth order, family size, and intelligence. *Science, 182*, 1096–1101.

Bonaiuto, S., Rocca, W. A., Lippi, A., Giannandrea, E., Mele, M., Cavarzeran, F., et al. (1995). Education and occupation as risk factors for dementia: A population-based case-control study. *Neuroepidemiology, 14*, 101–109.

Callahan, C. M., Hall, K. S., Hui, S. L., Musick, B. S., Unverzagt, F. W., & Hendrie, H. C. (1996). Relationship of age, education, and occupation with dementia among a community-based sample of African Americans. *Archives of Neurology, 53*, 134–140.

Capron, C., & Duyme, M. (1989). Assessment of effects of socio-economic status on IQ in a full cross-fostering study. *Nature, 340*, 552–554.

Carmelli, D., Swan, G. E., LaRue, A. & Eslinger, P. J. (1997). Correlates of change in cognitive function in survivors from the Western Collaborative Group Study. *Neuroepidemiology, 16*, 285–295.

Carroll, J. B. (1993). *Human cognitive abilities: A survey of factor analytic studies.* Cambridge, UK: Cambridge University Press.

Christensen, H., Hofer, S. M., Mackinnon, A. J., Korten, A. E., Jorm, A. F., & Henderson, A. S. (2001). Age is no kinder to the better educated: Absence of an association investigated using latent growth techniques in a community sample. *Psychological Medicine, 31*, 15–28.

Cockburn, J., Keene, J., Hope, T., & Smith, P. (2000). Progressive decline in NART score with increasing dementia severity. *Journal of Clinical and Experimental Neuropsychology, 22*, 508–517.

Crawford, J. R., Stewart, L. E., Parker, D. M., Besson, J. A. O., & De Lacey, G. (1989). Prediction of WAIS IQ with the National Adult Reading Test: Cross-validation and extension. *British Journal of Clinical Psychology, 28*, 267–273.

Dartigues, J. F., Gagnon, M., Letenneur, L., Barberger-Gateau, P., Commenges, D., Evaldre, M., et al. (1992). Principal lifetime occupation and cognitive impairment in a French elderly cohort (Paquid). *American Journal of Epidemiology, 135*, 981–988.

Deary, I., Whalley, L., Lemmon, H., Crawford, J., & Starr, J. (2000). The stability of individual differences in mental ability from childhood to old age: Follow-up of the 1932 Scottish Mental Survey. *Intelligence, 28*, 49–55.

Deary, I. J., Whiteman, M. C., Pattie, A., Starr, J. M., Hayward, C., Wright, A. F., et al. (2002). Cognitive change and the APOE ε4 allele. *Nature, 418*, 932.

Deary, I. J., Whiteman, M. C., Pattie, A., Starr, J. M., Hayward, C., Wright, A. F., et al. (2004). Apolipoprotein E gene variability and cognitive functions at age 79: Follow up of the Scottish Mental Survey. *Psychology and Aging, 19*, 361–371.

Deater-Deckard, K., Petrill, S. A., Thompson, L. A., & DeThorne, L. S. (2005). A cross-sectional behavioural genetic analysis of task persistence in the transition to middle childhood. *Developmental Science, 8*, F21–F26.

Department of Education and Science (DES) (1972). *Burnham further education committee grading courses.* London: HMSO.

Douglas, J. W. B. (1964). *The home and the school.* London: MacGibbon & Kee.

Duncan, G. J., Brooks-Gunn, J., & Klebanov, P. K. (1994). Economic deprivation and early childhood development. *Child Development, 65*, 296–318.

Evans, D. A., Beckett, L. A., Albert, M. S., Hebert, L. E., Scherr, P. A., Funkenstein, H. H., et al. (1993). Level of education and change in cognitive function in a community population of older persons. *Annals of Epidemiology, 3*, 71–77.

Feinstein, L. (2003). Inequality in the early cognitive development of British children in the 1970 cohort. *Economica, 277*, 73–98.

Gale, C. R., Martyn, C. N., & Cooper, C. (1996). Cognitive impairment and mortality in a cohort of elderly people. *British Medical Journal, 312*, 608–611.

Geerlings, M. I., Schmand, B., Jonker, C., Lindeboom, J., & Bouter, L. M. (1999). Education and incident Alzheimer's disease: A biased association due to selective attrition and use of a two-step diagnostic procedure? *International Journal of Epidemiology, 28*, 492–497.

Hassan, A., Lansbury, A., Catto, A. J., Guthrie, A., Spencer, J., Craven, C., et al. (2002). Angiotensin converting enzyme insertion/deletion genotype is associated with leukoaraiosis in lacunar syndromes. *Journal of Neurology, Neurosurgery and Psychiatry, 72*, 343–346.

Helmer, C., Letenneur, L., Rouch, I., Richard-Harston, S., Barberger-Gateau, P., Fabrigoule, C., et al. (2001). Occupation during life and risk of dementia in French elderly community residents. *Journal of Neurology, Neurosurgery and Psychiatry, 71*, 303–309.

Hultsch, D. F., Hertzog, C., Small, B. J., & Dixon, R. A. (1999). Use it or lose it: Engaged lifestyle as a buffer of cognitive decline in aging. *Psychology and Aging, 14,* 245–263.

Jama, J. W., Launer, L. J., Witteman, J. C., den Breeijen, J. H., Breteler, M. M., Grobbee, D. E., et al. (1996). Dietary antioxidants and cognitive function in a population-based sample of older persons. The Rotterdam Study. *American Journal of Epidemiology, 144,* 275–280.

Jefferis, B. J. M. H., Power, C., & Herztman, C. (2001). Birth weight, childhood socioeconomic environment, and cognitive development in the 1958 British birth cohort study. *British Medical Journal, 325,* 305–308.

Jorm, A. F., Rodgers, B., Henderson, A. S., Korten, A. E., Jacomb, P. A., Christensen, H., et al. (1998). Occupation type as a predictor of cognitive decline and dementia in old age. *Age and Aging, 27,* 477–483.

Kaplan, G. A., Turrell, G., Lynch, J. W., Everson, S. A., Helkala, E. L., & Salonen, J. T. (2001). Childhood socioeconomic position and cognitive function in adulthood. *International Journal of Epidemiology, 30,* 256–263.

Katzman, R. (1993). Education and the prevalence of Alzheimer's disease. *Neurology, 43,* 13–20.

Koletzko, B., Aggett, P. J., Bindrels, J. G., Bung, P., Ferre, P., Gil, A., et al. (1998). Growth, development and differentiation: A functional food science approach. *British Journal of Nutrition, 80* (Suppl. 1), S5–45.

Kramer, A. F., Hahn, S., Cohen, N. J., Banich, M. T., McAuley, E., Harrison, C. R., et al. (1999). Ageing, fitness and neurocognitive function. *Nature, 400,* 418–419.

Kramer, R. A., Allen, L., & Gergen, P. J. (1995). Health and social characteristics and children's cognitive functioning: Results from a national cohort. *American Journal of Public Health, 85,* 312–318.

Kuh, D., & Ben-Shlomo, Y. (Eds.) (1997). *A life course approach to chronic disease epidemiology.* Oxford, UK: Oxford University Press.

Kuh, D., & Cooper, C. (1992). Physical activity at 36 years: Patterns and childhood predictors in a longitudinal study. *Journal of Epidemiology and Community Health, 46,* 114–119.

La Rue, A., Koehler, K. M., Wayne, S. J., Chiulli, S. J., Haaland, K. Y., & Garry, P. J. (1997). Nutritional status and cognitive functioning in a normally aging sample: A 6-y reassessment. *American Journal of Clinical Nutrition, 65,* 20–29.

Loehlin, J. C., Horn, J. M., & Willerman, L. (1997). Heredity, environment, and IQ in the Texas Adoption Project. In R. J. Sternberg & E. L. Grigorenko (Eds.), *Intelligence, heredity, and environment* (pp. 105–125). Cambridge, UK: Cambridge University Press.

Maguire, E. A., Gadian, D. G., Johnsrude, I. S., Good, C. D., Ashburner, J., Frackowiak, R. S., et al. (2000). Navigation-related structural change in the hippocampi of taxi drivers. *Proceedings of the National Academy of Science, USA, 97,* 4398–4403.

Matte, T. D., Bresnahan, M., Begg, M. D., & Susser, E. (2001). Influence of variation in birth weight within normal range and within sibships on IQ at age 7 years: Cohort study. *British Medical Journal, 323,* 310–314.

McGurn, B., Starr, J. M., Topfer, J. A., Pattie, A., Whiteman, M. C., Lemmon, H. A., et al. (2004). Pronunciation of irregular words is preserved in dementia, validating premorbid IQ estimation. *Neurology, 62,* 1184–1186.

McKeown, T., & Record, R. C. (1976). Relationship between childhood infections and measured intelligence *British Journal of Preventative and Social Medicine, 30*, 101–106.

Meyer, J. S., Rauch, G. M., Crawford, K., Rauch, R. A., Konno, S., Akiyama, H., et al. (1999). Risk factors accelerating cerebral degenerative changes, cognitive decline and dementia. *International Journal of Geriatric Psychiatry, 14*, 1050–1061.

Nelson, H. E., & Willison, J. R. (1991). *National Adult Reading Test (NART)* (2nd ed.). Windsor, UK: NFER-Nelson.

Office of Population Censuses and Surveys (OPCS) (1970). *Classification of occupations*. London: HMSO.

Pearce, M. S., Deary, I. J., Young, A. H., & Parker, L. (2005). Growth in early life and childhood IQ at age 11 years: The Newcastle Thousand Families Study. *International Journal of Epidemiology, 34*, 673–677.

Petrill, S. A., Pike, A., Price, T., & Plomin, R. (2004). Chaos in the home and socioeconomic status are associated with cognitive development in early childhood: Environmental mediators identified in a genetic design. *Intelligence, 32*, 445–460.

Pigeon, D. A. (1964). Tests used in the 1954 and 1957 surveys. In J. B. W. Douglas (Ed.), *The home and the school* (Appendix 1). London: Macgibbon & Key.

Plassman, B., Welsh, K., Helms, M., Brandt, J., Page, W., & Breitner, J. (1995). Intelligence and education as predictors of cognitive state in late life: A 50-year follow-up. *Neurology, 45*, 1446–1450.

Plomin, R. (1999). Genetics and general cognitive ability. *Nature, 402* (6761 Suppl.), C25–29.

Rabbitt, P. (1993). Does it all go together when it goes? The nineteenth Bartlett Memorial Lecture. *Quarterly Journal of Experimental Psychology, 46A*, 385–434.

Richards, M. (in press). Do heavier babies make brighter children? In R. Murray, J. MacCabe, P. McGuffin, O. O'Daly, & P. Wright (Eds.), *Beyond nature and nurture: Genes, environment and their interplay in psychiatry*. London: Martin Dunitz.

Richards, M., & Deary, I. J. (2005). A life course approach to cognitive reserve: A model for cognitive aging and development? *Annals of Neurology, 58*, 617–622.

Richards, M., & Sacker, A. (2003). Lifetime antecedents of cognitive reserve. *Journal of Clinical and Experimental Neuropsychology, 25*, 614–624.

Richards, M., Hardy, R., Kuh, D., & Wadsworth, M. (2001). Birthweight and cognitive function in the British 1946 birth cohort. *British Medical Journal, 322*, 199–202.

Richards, M., Hardy, R., Kuh, D., & Wadsworth, M. E. J. (2002). Birth weight, postnatal growth and cognitive function in a national birth cohort. *International Journal of Epidemiology, 31*, 342–348.

Richards, M., Hardy, R., & Wadsworth, M. (2003). Does active leisure protect cognition? Evidence from a national birth cohort. *Social Science & Medicine, 56*, 785–792.

Roman, G. C., Erkinjuntti, T., Wallin, A., Pantoni, L., & Chui, H. C. (2002). Subcortical ischaemic vascular dementia. *Lancet Neurology, 1*, 426–436.

Rutter, M. (1985). Family and school influences on cognitive development. *Journal of Child Psychology & Psychiatry, 26*, 683–704.

Sacker, A., Schoon, I., & Bartley, M. (2002). Social inequality in educational achievement and psychosocial adjustment throughout childhood: Magnitude and mechanisms. *Social Science and Medicine, 55*, 863–880.

Salthouse, T. A. (1996). The processing speed theory of adult age differences in cognition. *Psychological Review*, *103*, 403–428.

Satz, P. (1993). Brain reserve capacity on symptom onset after brain injury: A formulation and review of evidence for threshold theory. *Neuropsychology*, *7*, 273–295.

Schaie, K. W. (1996). *Intellectual development in adulthood*. Cambridge, UK: Cambridge University Press.

Schiff, M., & Lewontin, R. (1986). *Education and class: The irrelevance of IQ genetic studies*. Oxford, UK: Clarendon.

Schmand, B., Smit, J. H., Geerlings, M. I., & Lindeboom, J. (1997). The effect of intelligence and education on the development of dementia. A test of the brain reserve hypothesis. *Psychological Medicine*, *27*, 1337–1344.

Seckl, J. (1998). Physiologic programming of the fetus. *Emerging Concepts in Perinatal Endocrinology*, *25*, 939–962.

Shenkin, S. D., Starr, J. M., Pattie, A., Rush, M. A., Whalley, L. J., & Deary, I. J. (2001). Birth weight and cognitive function at age 11 years: The Scottish Mental Survey 1932. *Archives of Diseases in Childhood*, *85*, 189–197.

Shenkin, S. D., Starr, J. M., & Deary, I. J. (2004). Birth weight and cognitive ability in childhood: A systematic review. *Psychological Bulletin*, *130*, 989–1013.

Snow, R. E., & Yalow, E. (1982). Education and intelligence. In R. J. Sternberg (Ed.), *Handbook of human intelligence*. Cambridge, UK: Cambridge University Press.

Snowdon, D. A., Kemper, S. J., Mortimer, J. A., Greiner, L. H., Wekstein, D. R., & Markesbery, W. R. (1996). Linguistic ability in early life and cognitive function and Alzheimer's disease in late life. Findings from the Nun Study. *Journal of the American Medical Association*, *275*, 528–532.

Sorensen, H. T., Sabroe, S., Olsen, J., Rothman, K. J., Gillman, M. W., & Fischer, P. (1997). Birth weight and cognitive function in young adult life: Historical cohort study. *British Medical Journal*, *315*, 401–403.

Staff, R. T., Murray, A. D., Deary, I. J., & Whalley, L. J. (2004). What provides cerebral reserve? *Brain*, *127*, 1191–1199.

Starr, J. M., Taylor, M. D., Hart, C. L., Davey Smith, G., Whalley, L. J., Hole, D. J., et al. (2004). Childhood mental ability and blood pressure at midlife: Linking the Scottish Mental Survey 1932 and the Midspan studies. *Journal of Hypertension*, *22*, 893–897.

Stern, Y. (2002). What is cognitive reserve? Theory and research application of the reserve concept. *Journal of the International Neuropsychological Society*, *8*, 448–460.

Stern, Y. (2003). The concept of cognitive reserve: A catalyst for research. *Journal of Clinical and Experimental Neuropsychology*, *25*, 589–593.

Stern, Y., Gurland, B., Tatemichi, T. K., Tang, M. X., Wilder, D. & Mayeux, R., (1994). Influence of education and occupation on the incidence of Alzheimer's disease. *Journal of the American Medical Association*, *271*, 1004–1010.

Taylor, M. D., Hart, C. L., Davey Smith, G., Starr, J. M., Hole, D. J., Whalley, L. J., et al. (2003). Childhood mental ability and smoking cessation in adulthood: Prospective observational study linking the Scottish Mental Survey 1932 and the Midspan studies. *Journal of Epidemiology and Community Health*, *57*, 464–465.

Taylor, R. (1999). National Adult Reading Test performance in established dementia. *Archives of Gerontology and Geriatrics*, *29*, 291–296.

Tizard, B., & Hughes, M. (1984). *Young children learning: Talking and thinking at home and school*. London: Fontana.

Tizard, B., Hughes, M., Carmichael, H., & Pinkerton, G. (1983). Language deprivation and social class: Is verbal deprivation a myth? *Journal of Child Psychology & Psychiatry, 24*, 533–542.

Wadsworth, M. E. J. (1991). *The imprint of time: Childhood, history and adult life.* Oxford, UK: Martin Robertson.

Wadsworth, M. E. J., Mann, S. L., Rodgers, B., Kuh, D. L., Hilder, W. S., & Yusuf, E. J. (1992). Loss and representativeness in a 43 year follow-up of a national birth cohort. *Journal of Epidemiology and Public Health, 46*, 300–304.

Weinberg, M. K., & Tronick, E. Z. (1998). Emotional characteristics of infants associated with maternal depression and anxiety. *Pediatrics, 102* (5 Suppl. E), 1298–1304.

Welberg, L. A. A., & Seckl, J. R. (2001). Prenatal stress, glucocorticoids and the programming of the brain. *Journal of Neuroendocrinology*, 13, 113–128.

Whalley, L., Starr, J., Athawes, R., Hunter, D., Pattie, A., & Deary, I. (2001). Childhood mental ability and dementia. *Neurology, 55*, 1455–1459.

White, L., Katzman, R., Losonczy, K., Salive, M., Wallace, R., Berkman, L., et al. (1994). Association of education with incidence of cognitive impairment in three established populations for epidemiologic studies of the elderly. *Journal of Clinical Epidemiology, 47*, 363–374.

Wilson, R. S., Bienia, J. L., Berry-Kravis, E., Evans, D. A., & Bennett, D. A. (2002). The apolipoprotein E ε2 allele and decline in episodic memory. *Journal of Neurology, Neurosurgery and Psychiatry, 73*, 672–677.

4 Brain reserve capacity, cognitive reserve capacity, and age-based functional plasticity after congenital and acquired brain injury in children

Maureen Dennis, Keith Owen Yeates, H. Gerry Taylor, and Jack M. Fletcher

An intrinsic property of any brain, mature or immature, intact or injured, is to learn and to change. In a perfectly malleable brain, any brain lesion would be followed by structural and functional changes sufficient to restore or maintain function. Such is not the case, and the response to brain lesions is often incomplete or maladaptive. More important, the functional outcome of brain insult in both children and adults is usually predictable for groups but variable for individuals. In adults, individual differences in functional outcome have been explained by the construct of reserve capacity (Katzman, 1993; Satz, 1993; Stern, 2002), which encompasses both the passive capacity of the brain (brain reserve capacity, BRC) and the active capacity in the individual (cognitive reserve capacity, CRC) that maintain function after brain insult.

BRC is not directly observed, but is rather a hypothetical construct referring to a critical or threshold level of brain size, synapse count, or the like, with functional deficits occurring when the pathology burden is such that the brain substance is reduced below a critical level. In some formulations of BRC (e.g., Satz, 1993), the idea is that deficits emerge when a BRC threshold is reached and, compared to those with less BRC, individuals with more BRC will be deficit-free for longer after similar-sized lesions or require larger lesions to generate symptoms. Variables like head circumference, brain volume, and less direct indices such as education and occupation have been used as proxies for BRC (e.g., Kesler, Adams, Blasey, & Bigler, 2003; Mortimer, Snowdon, & Markesbery, 2003).

CRC is the ability to optimize or maximize performance through differential recruitments of brain networks that reflect the use of alternate cognitive strategies (Stern, 2002). Cognitive reserve is present in healthy individuals: an individual who uses a brain network more efficiently or generates cognitive strategies in response to increased demand is deemed to have more CRC. In the standard formulation, cognitive reserve refers to individual differences in recruiting either the same or alternative networks (Stern, 2002).

The concept of functional plasticity links outcomes to brain-related changes in behavior and cognition, and encourages the search for a biological account of the effects of age and risk and resilience factors on children's response to brain insult. In the most general sense, plasticity is an intrinsic property of the human brain to adapt to environmental pressures, physiologic changes, and experiences by dynamic shifts in the strength of pre-existing neural connections, or by modifications of neural circuits in response to changes in afferent input or efferent demand (Pascual-Leone, Amedi, Fregni, & Merabet, 2005). In this chapter, we define the term more narrowly to refer to brain-based changes in behavior and cognition, and we focus specifically on those changes potentially explained by BRC and CRC. Because we are interested in accounting for outcomes following childhood brain insult, we emphasize those forms of functional plasticity in children that appear to vary with age and that may distinguish how reserve operates in cases of child versus adult neuropathology.

Outcome after childhood brain insult involves multiple domains of function. *Physical* outcome refers to whether the child's height, weight, fatigue tolerance, endurance, and motor performance are normal for age. *Cognitive-academic* outcome is usually measured by a standard intelligence test and by assessment of academic skill attainments. *Neuropsychological* outcome refers to capacities such as motor speed, attention, perception, memory, language, and executive function. *Psychosocial* outcome refers to an individual's ability to function in the social world of family, school, and community.

This chapter examines evidence for childhood reserve and considers factors that contribute to variations in BRC and CRC as moderators of functional plasticity in this age group. We propose that childhood brain insult constitutes a pathological load, but that functional outcome is mediated by reserve, as evidenced by accelerated aging in adulthood, greater vulnerability to subsequent brain insult, or diminished capacity to make age-appropriate developmental progress. Our views about these constructs are developed in the individual difference model in Figure 4.1, which assumes:

1. There is a quantum of brain reserve capacity or BRC, a form of passive reserve (Stern, 2003) that varies in degree among children due to both single or multiple challenges to brain status.
2. The amount of BRC can be measured directly by variables such as residual brain volume on voxel-based morphometry or structural connectivity on diffuse tensor imaging (DTI). Alternatively, BRC can be measured by the extent or likelihood of brain abnormality in persons subsequently exposed to unrelated brain insults or the effects of aging. In the latter instance, proxies for reduced BRC include genetic anomalies (polymorphisms, microdeletions, repeats, or mutations) that affect brain development and prior brain lesions stemming, for example, from past concussions or from treatment-related insults such as radiotherapy and chemotherapy.

3. BRC may additionally be indexed by multiple brain insults. Some individuals suffer an initial brain insult that is followed either by a second injury of the same type, such as a repetitive concussion, or by treatment required by the initial insult, such as radiation and chemotherapy. Childhood brain tumors represent a well-studied childhood model of multiple brain insults in that a primary insult, the tumor, is treated either by a relatively benign procedure, surgery that does not seem to add to tumor morbidity, or by treatments such as radiotherapy and chemotherapy that by themselves constitute an additional brain insult that diminishes BRC.

4. There is a quantum of CRC after developmental brain insult, a form of active reserve that varies in degree among individuals, again reflecting both single and multiple challenges.

5. The amount of CRC is not measured directly, but rather by proxies such as pre-injury cognitive function, socioeconomic status, and family function.

6. BRC and CRC mutually influence each other.

7. Moderators are variables that specify the condition under which a given effect occurs, as well as the conditions under which the direction or strength of the effect will vary, and so interact with a predictor variable to affect outcome (Holmbeck, 1997). Outcomes of brain disorders in childhood are moderated by two sets of variables that contribute to variations in BRC and CRC as mediators of functional plasticity and thus of functional outcome.

8. The first moderators are age and time variables: the age of the child at the time of injury, the amount of time that has passed since the injury, and the child's age at the time of outcome evaluation. Age- and time-related issues are relevant to the outcomes of brain insult at any point in the lifespan, but they are especially important in understanding the outcomes of childhood brain insult (Dennis, 2000; Taylor & Alden, 1997). Almost all neurocognitive skills show age-related improvements, and a number of outcomes vary with age at onset of brain insult. Time is important because outcome may be different when evaluated at different time points after brain insult, from acute, subacute, and long-term to very long-term (Dennis, Spiegler, Riva, & MacGregor, 2004).

9. The second moderators are gradients of lesion location, whether up–down, left–right, or front–back. Recent studies of childhood brain lesions have allowed BRC in children to be conceptualized in terms of spatial gradients with varying degrees of age-based functional plasticity and outcomes. Spatial gradients are considered to be moderators because they interact with BRC to influence outcome.

10. Functional plasticity is the reorganization within an individual that emerges from the action of the two mediators BRC and CR, measured in physical, cognitive, academic, neuropsychological, and psychosocial domains.

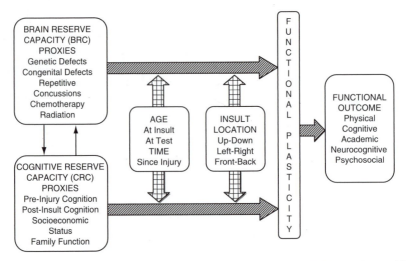

Figure 4.1 Developmental model of brain reserve capacity (BRC) and cognitive reserve capacity (CRC) showing mediated (striped) and moderated (cross-hatched) relations.

11. The moderating influences of age variables and lesion characteristics predict individual differences in functional plasticity and thus help to explain group and individual variability in functional outcome.

Proxies for brain reserve capacity

BRC may be measured directly. Diffusion tensor imaging (DTI) measures diffusion of water throughout the brain. Water diffusing equally in all directions (e.g., in cerebrospinal fluid) is isotropic, whereas restricted diffusion of water (e.g., within axons) is anisotropic. Areas of dense white matter have more directional diffusion (fractional anisotropy) than areas of lower density, and DTI images outlining cortical and subcortical white matter tracts can be used to examine models of connectivity between cortical areas with respect to the number and strength of fiber paths. Childhood brain trauma reduces functional brain connectivity, as evidenced by changes in the directionality and integrity of white matter tracts (Lee, Byun, Jang, Ahn, Moon, & Chang, 2003). Residual brain connectivity constitutes a direct measure of BRC.

More commonly, BRC can be measured indirectly in terms of brain integrity prior to a neurological insult. Proxies such as head size have generally not been studied in children: for one reason, head and brain size in children change over development; for another, some of these size changes are not linear increases (e.g., frontal cortical development involves thinning of the frontal polar cortex, O'Donnell, Noseworthy, Levine, Brandt, & Dennis, 2005).

Genetic heterogeneity

Investigation of children with genetic disorders provides a method of examining the effects of reduced BRC. Genetic defects in children (repeats, microdeletions, mutations, or polymorphisms) are associated with deficits in the functions specific to brain regions that depend on neurotransmitters controlled by the deficient genes. Evidence suggests that these children have a reduced normal brain substrate compared with children without genetic disorders, so that study of the effects of genetic defects on recovery from childhood brain insults and on later age-related loss of skills can illuminate the consequences of diminished BRC.

Phenylketonuria is a genetic disorder associated with atypically high levels of phenylalanine and low dopamine. The catechol gene affects the duration of dopamine activity in the prefrontal cortex, and the methionine polymorphism results in a slower breakdown of prefrontal dopamine. Children with phenylketonuria and high phenylalanine levels have impairments, not only in the dorsolateral prefrontal cortex functions of inhibitory control and working memory, but also in visual contrast sensitivity, which varies with retinal dopamine levels (Diamond, 1996). Children homozygous for the methionine polymorphism perform poorly on tasks sensitive to the level of dopamine (Diamond, Briand, Fossella, & Gehlback, 2004).

Genetic disorders may progressively slow the trajectory of development. Males with the fragile X mutation show loss of cognitive abilities as they mature, with increasing inability to master more complex cognitive skills as they progress into adolescence (Hodapp et al., 1990). In this instance, reduced BRC is evidenced by slowing in the rate of development.

Just as genetic heterogeneity in the apolipoprotein E (ApoE) genotype is a factor in diminished reserve in adults with Alzheimer disease (e.g., Massart, Reginster, & Brandi, 2001), so is genetic heterogeneity in childhood genetic disorders associated with accelerated aging. Williams-Beuren syndrome is a rare genetic disorder related to a sporadic heterozygous contiguous gene deletion on chromosome 7 (Osborne, 1999). Individuals with this condition have physical signs of premature aging (reduced longevity, graying of hair in early adult life, and premature aging of skin, as well as chronic anxiety and hypertension; Mervis, Morris, Bertrand, & Robinson, 1999). Adults with Williams-Beuren syndrome show a chronologically early and precipitous age-associated decrease in long-term episodic memory, a decrease not observed in age peers with unspecified mental retardation (Devenny, Krinsky-McHale, Kittler, Flory, Jenkins, & Brown, 2004).

Another form of genetically based mental retardation, Down syndrome, produces premature aging and Alzheimer disease. Because of the triplication of chromosome 21, individuals with this condition have an increased gene dosage for amyloid precursor protein (cleavage of which is involved in generating the main constituents of neuritic plaques), and they develop amyloid plaques and neurofibrillary tangles during the fourth and fifth decades of life (Janicki & Dalton, 1998; Karlinsky, 1986). Risk factors for development of Alzheimer disease in individuals with Down syndrome include age, apolipoprotein E (ApoE) genotype, brain size, ability level, and head trauma (Ward, 2004).

Individuals with spina bifida meningomyelocele (SBM) have genetic anomalies that are associated with specific brain dysmorphologies and specific cognitive deficits. It has been hypothesized that those with a genetic mutation in the folate metabolic pathway have more compromised brain tissue in the cerebellum and midbrain, and corpus callosum dysgenesis, especially in the splenium, which results in more severe neurocognitive deficits than occur in children with the condition without the genetic mutation (Fletcher et al., 2005). As adults, individuals with spina bifida meningomyelocele have clinical memory problems (Dennis et al., 2000), and the hypothesis that their aging is accelerated is supported by proposals such as those arguing for faulty folate metabolism and B-group vitamin deficiency as risk factors for Alzheimer disease in Down syndrome (Ward, 2004), and for declines in the corpus callosum splenium as part of the neuropathology of Alzheimer disease (Rose et al., 2000). Evaluation of these hypotheses awaits modeling of variability at genetic, neural, and cognitive levels.

Multiple insults

Repetitive concussions

Repetitive brain injuries in adults, such as those from sports injuries, diminish BRC and accelerate dementia, likely because of cumulative damage to hippocampal cells (Slemmer, Matser, DeZeeuw, & Weber, 2002). For many children, brain insult involves a single event, although repetitive insults, such as a series of concussions, may additionally impair cognitive function. Compared to those with no prior concussion, amateur athletes with a history of three or more concussions show more preseason cognitive problems and are nearly eight times more likely to show a major drop in memory function after an additional concussion (Iverson, Gaetz, Lovell, & Collins, 2004).

Treatment-related insults

RADIOTHERAPY

In children, compromised intelligence is associated with conventional cranial radiation treatment (Ellenberg, McComb, Siegel, & Stowe, 1987; Jannoun & Bloom, 1990; LeBaron, Zeltzer, Zeltzer, Scott, & Martin, 1988). The mechanism is thought to involve a progressive vascular and demyelinating neuropathology, beginning after the end of treatment, reaching a peak over the next few years, and then maintaining a persisting but less steep decline (Cohen & Duffner, 1994). The concomitant cognitive impairment is inversely related to age of treatment (Eiser, 1978; Packer et al., 1989) and directly related to the dose and field of cerebral radiation (Mulhern, Horowitz, Kovnar, Langston, Sanford, & Kun, 1989). Attempts to adjust radiation dose on the basis of age or tumor site have not fully eliminated the cognitive deficits (Cohen & Duffner, 1994), and hyperfractionation of the radiation dose reduces but does not eliminate cognitive deficits (Riva, 1995).

Brain scans of children treated with cranial radiation for primary brain- or skull-based tumors show generalized brain atrophy, calcifications in brain matter distant from the site of the primary tumor, and white matter abnormalities (Davis, Hoffman, Pearl, & Braun, 1986). Serial neuroimaging has demonstrated an increasing number and size of lacunae within the white matter in a proportion of children whose brain tumors were treated with radiation (Fouladi et al., 2000). Progressive white matter damage has also been documented after cranial radiation for medulloblastoma (Mulhern et al., 1999, 2001; Reddick et al., 2000), and the volume of normal-appearing white matter declines over time in children radiated for medulloblastoma, a decline that is faster in children with higher radiation dose (Mulhern et al., 1999, 2001). Children with higher radiation doses may have less BRC to maintain age-appropriate rates of skill acquisition.

CHEMOTHERAPY

Intrathecal chemotherapy, particularly methotrexate, produces significant cognitive morbidity (Maria, Dennis, & Obonsawin, 1993), and the risk is greater when intrathecal methotrexate is used in association with radiotherapy (Bleyer & Poplack, 1985). Intravenous chemotherapy alone may have a good outcome in young children (Copeland, deMoor, Moore, & Ater, 1999; Moore, Ater, & Copeland, 1992). In children treated for medulloblastoma, radiotherapy in association with intrathecal methotrexate impairs cognitive development (Riva et al., 2002). Intraventricular methotrexate combined with radiotherapy produces poor outcome (Ottensmeier & Kuhl, 2000).

Proxies for CRC

CRC involves risk and resilience factors that hamper or promote various outcomes (Guralnick, 1989; Masten, Hubbard, Gest, Tellegen, Garmezy, & Ramirez, 1999). Some CRC factors are intrinsic to the child (e.g., pre-injury cognitive ability), while others reflect environmental influences (e.g., socio-economic status, parenting skills).

Pre-injury cognitive ability

Several recent studies have investigated proxies for CRC, including pre-morbid cognitive and behavioral status, to predict outcome after childhood traumatic brain injury (TBI). Cass, Yeates, Taylor, and Minich (2005) hypothesized that CRC moderates neuropsychological outcome attributable to TBI, such that outcome would be poorer among children with lower rather than higher CRC as measured by pre-injury cognitive status. Growth curve analyses revealed that CRC predicted individual differences in neuro-psychological functioning. An additional finding was that children with higher reserve showed more rapid cognitive growth than children with lower reserve on some measures, although these effects did not differ by group. An effect of CRC on subsequent cognitive development is consistent with the hypothesis that additional CRC was conferred by higher cognitive abilities prior to injury, but CRC was not confirmed as a moderator of the effects of TBI.

One of the challenges of studying attention problems in children with TBI is that they have more attention problems and higher rates of attention-deficit hyperactivity disorder (ADHD) prior to injury compared with non-injured controls or normative expectations (Bloom et al., 2001; Gerring et al., 1998; Max et al., 1997; Max, Lansing, Koele, Castillo, Bokura, & Schachar 2004; but see Schachar, Levin, Max, Purvis, & Chen, 2004). Unfortunately, studies of outcomes of TBI frequently fail to obtain information about pre-morbid attention problems, or do so long after the TBI, increasing the likelihood of retrospective bias (Anderson, Fenwick, Manly, & Robertson, 1998; Fenwick & Anderson, 1999; Konrad, Gauggel, Manz, & Scholl, 2000; Max et al., 1997, 1998; Schachar et al., 2004; Vriezen & Piggott, 2000; Wassenberg, Max, Lindgren, & Schatz, 2004). Yeates et al. (2005) examined predictors of post-injury attention problems in children with severe TBI, moderate TBI, or orthopedic injuries, comparing pre-injury ratings to ratings obtained an average of 4 years post-injury. At the long-term follow-up, the severe TBI group displayed significantly more attention problems than the orthopedic injury group at 4 years post-injury, both behaviorally and cognitively.

Evidence for CRC is that group differences in behavioral symptoms were significantly larger for children with more pre-morbid symptoms than for children with fewer pre-morbid problems. Interestingly, pre-injury attention problems did not moderate group differences on long-term cognitive outcomes assessed by neuropsychological tests, but only on long-term behavioral symptoms assessed with rating scales, the latter more like methods used to assess CRC. In previous research with this same sample, behavioral and adaptive outcomes were more likely than cognitive outcomes to be affected by moderators extrinsic to the child, such as family functioning or parental perceived burden (Taylor, Yeates, Wade, Drotar, Stancin, & Minich, 2002; Yeates et al., 2002). The current findings suggest that the same may be true for moderators intrinsic to the child, such as pre-injury attention function. The dissociation may reflect a greater susceptibility of behavioral outcomes to environmental influences, as well as the weak relationship between cognitive and behavioral outcomes following childhood TBI (Fletcher, Ewing-Cobbs, Miner, Levin, & Eisenberg, 1990).

Socioeconomic status and family function

Childhood TBI increases the likelihood of deficits in social information processing, and hence of atypical social interaction and poor social adjustment (Janusz, Kirkwood, Yeates, & Taylor, 2002; Warschausky, Cohen, Parker, Levendosky, & Okun, 1997). Broader aspects of the family environment, including poverty and parental unemployment, parental conflict, and parent mental health, also may influence children's social outcomes (Cochran & Niego, 2002; Zahn-Waxler, Duggal, & Gurber, 2002). To the extent that the latter factors serve as proxies for CRC, they may also play a role in mediating functional plasticity.

In a study that illustrates the influences of environmental factors on child outcomes following childhood brain insult, Yeates and colleagues (2004) conducted growth curve analyses of social outcomes from TBI baseline to the 4-year follow-up. Examining predictors of long-term post injury social outcomes using contemporaneous measures of executive functions, language pragmatics, and social problem solving, the results indicated that childhood TBI was associated with adverse social outcomes, effects that were exacerbated by fewer family resources and poorer family function. Although the better outcomes observed in children with TBI from more advantaged circumstances may be explained in terms of higher level of environmental supports for behavioral change, they are also consistent with the hypothesis that privileged environments impart greater CRC.

Moderators of the relation between BRC, CRC and outcome

Study of age-related factors on outcomes of childhood brain insult suggests that BRC and CRC are not constant across development, but vary with age at insult, age at testing, and time since insult.

Age at insult

Further evidence for both BRC and CRC in children is provided by data suggesting that brain insults early in life are more detrimental to longer-term development than are later-occurring lesions. To illustrate, lower intelligence is related to an earlier age at diagnosis and treatment in children with brain tumors (Duffner, Cohen, & Parker, 1988; Packer et al., 1989; Hoppe-Hirsch, Renier, Lellouch-Tubiana, Sainte-Rose, Pierre-Kahn, & Hirsch, 1990; Jannoun & Bloom, 1990), and a younger age at brain tumor onset is associated with more deficits in expressive language 8 months post-onset (Doxey, Bruce, Sklar, Swift, & Shapiro, 1999). Additionally, younger children with TBI demonstrate a slower rate of change over time and more significant residual deficits after their recovery plateaus than do older children with injuries of equivalent severity (Anderson & Moore, 1995; Anderson et al., 1997; Ewing-Cobbs, Fletcher, Levin, Francis, Davidson, & Miner, 1997). A prospective longitudinal study that tracked a large cohort of children with mild head injury found that, after accounting for several demographic, family features, and pre-injury characteristics, psychosocial deficits (but not cognitive or academic deficits) were more prevalent in the group injured before 5 years of age (McKinlay, Dalrymple-Alford, Horwood, & Fergusson, 2002). Similarly, Dennis, Wilkinson, Koski, & Humphreys (1995) found that selective attention was inversely correlated with age at injury and time since injury. Recent studies of preschool children suggest that acquired brain injuries sustained during infancy or early childhood are associated with more persistent deficits in a range of outcome domains, including social cognition, than are injuries occurring during later childhood and adolescence (Anderson & Moore, 1995; Anderson et al., 1997; Dennis, Barnes, Wilkinson, & Humphreys, 1998; Ewing-Cobbs et al., 1997). It is not surprising that younger children are more adversely affected by a number of brain insults than are older children, because younger children have brains that are in more rapid phases of development and that have had less opportunity to develop cognitive skills. Compared to later insult, early brain insult diminishes BRC and CRC over a larger portion of the development period, making the child's neural substrate unable to support subsequent developmental change.

Time since insult

Children generally display a gradual recovery over the first few years after an acquired brain injury, with the most rapid improvement occurring soon after the injury. The initial rate of recovery is often more rapid among children with severe injuries than among those with milder injuries, although severe injuries also are associated with persistent deficits after the rate of recovery slows down (Taylor et al. 2002; Yeates et al., 2002). It is difficult to disentangle age and time dimensions, even in longitudinal research (Taylor & Alden, 1997). In the case of brain insult at birth, these two factors are indistinguishable. Nevertheless, studies that have followed children after brain insults and examined the influences of both factors, including recent investigations of meningitis and of TBI in children, have found that time since injury predicts outcomes independent of the effects of age at injury (Taylor, Schatschneider, & Minich, 2000; Yeates et al., 2004), consistent with the hypothesis that childhood brain insult depletes CRC, yielding less capacity to support post-injury skill acquisition.

Age at evaluation

Of the three age-related dimensions potentially related to the outcomes of childhood brain disorder, the influence of age at evaluation has been the focus of the least research. The effects of age at testing would be reflected in demonstrations of latent or delayed sequelae resulting from children's failure to meet new developmental demands as a result of a brain disorder. Levin et al. (1988) found greater memory impairment in adolescents than in children following severe TBI, and suggested that adolescents need to use more advanced memory strategies to perform according to normative expectations, and that such strategies might be especially vulnerable to TBI. Although Yeates, Enrile, Loss, Blumenstein, and Delis (1995) did not observe a similar age-related deficit, Taylor and colleagues have examined the consequences of several forms of early brain insult across the school-age years (Taylor et al., 2000; Taylor et al., 2002; Taylor, Minich, Klein, & Hack, 2004). Findings from these studies show that some skills decline relative to age expectations with advancing age, while other deficits remain stable over time. Declines relative to age standards have also been observed in children treated for cancer (Dennis, Spiegler, Hetherington, & Greenberg, 1996). The inability of children to maintain age-appropriate rates of skill acquisition implies loss of reserve, although it is unclear from these results, however, if age-related declines in functioning reflect loss of BRC, CRC, or both.

Spatial gradients of brain insult

Up–down: Outcomes after subtentorial, brainstem and subcortical lesions in children

An earlier era of research into the effects of brain injury in children concluded that cortical lesions in children had fewer consequences for outcome than did cortical lesions in adults (e.g., Basser, 1962), although comparisons were often made between different pathologies or without appropriate benchmarks of typical development (Dennis, 2003). A revision in the view of privileged cortical plasticity in children was prompted by outcome studies involving children with subtentorial and brainstem lesions, which has suggested an up–down BRC gradient in the immature brain, with limited plasticity and thus reduced reserve, following subtentorial, midbrain, and subcortical lesions.

SUBTENTORIAL LESIONS

Timing information generates predictions about the durations of different perceptual events and the sensory consequences of movement (Franz, Zelaznik, & Smith, 1992; Ivry & Richardson, 2002; Keele, Pokorny, Corcos, & Ivry, 1985; Rao, Mayer, & Harrington, 2001). The cerebellum is important for short-duration timing, deficits in which are apparent over the lifespan in individuals with cerebellar lesions, including adults with acquired cerebellar lesions (Ivry & Keele, 1989); adult survivors of childhood cerebellar lesions (Hetherington, Dennis, & Spiegler, 2000); children with genetic cerebellar disease, such as ataxia-telangiectasia (Mostofsky, Kunze, Cutting, Lederman, & Denckla, 2000); children with cerebellar pathologies (Mostofsky, Bunoski, Morton, Goldberg, & Bastian, 2004), and children with embryogenetic cerebellar defects, such as SBM, who have deficits in short-duration timing on both perceptual and motor timing tasks (Dennis, Edelstein et al., 2004). Further, children with SBM have reduced cerebellar volumes on quantitative MRI studies (Fletcher et al., 2005), with timing deficits being related to reduced cerebellar volume (Dennis, Edelstein et al., 2004).

MIDBRAIN LESIONS

The posterior attention system (Posner, Cohen, & Rafal, 1982) concerns stimulus-driven processes such as orienting to salient or unexpected events, and its operation is measured by functions such as cued covert orienting and inhibition of return. The brain bases of stimulus-driven orienting involve a distributed noradrenergically modulated system that includes the midbrain, superior colliculus, pulvinar, and posterior parietal lobe. Inhibition of return depends on midbrain structures such as the superior colliculus (Rafal & Henik, 1994). School-aged children with SBM have a deficit in covert attention orienting. They orient more slowly to, and take longer to disengage from, what has captured their attention (Dennis et al., 2005a). The deficit is selective because they have difficulty disengaging from salient stimuli but not when orienting to cognitively interesting stimuli, which are under goal-directed, top-down control (Dennis et al., 2005a).

Adaptive visual search requires that attention not be returned to a recently explored location. A mechanism for this is inhibition of return (IOR), which is operationalized as the increase in time to react to a target in a previously attended location (Posner & Cohen, 1984; Posner, Rafal, Choate, & Vaughan, 1985). As an adaptive function, IOR increases the chance that exploration will occur with new objects and in new locations, and thereby provides a strategy for effective visual search and foraging in a complex visual environment (Klein, 1988, 2000). Compared to controls, children with SBM show attenuated IOR in the vertical plane (Dennis et al., 2005b). The midbrain, including the superior colliculus, is part of a circuit that controls orienting to salience. Children with SBM who are born with abnormality of the midbrain and tectum (tectal beaking, the characteristic midbrain malformation of SBM) are particularly compromised in attention orienting, both overtly with eye movement, and covertly, in shifting attention, showing more difficulties with orienting to salience and a more attenuated inhibition of return response in the vertical plane than children with SBM who do not have tectal beaking (Dennis et al., 2005b).

PERIVENTRICULAR LESIONS

Deficits following early periventricular brain insults are also highly persistent. Evidence for limited plasticity of functions mediated by this brain region is provided by a recent study (Taylor, Minich, Bangert, Filipek, & Hack, 2004) that examined long-term outcomes at age 16 of below 750 g birth-weight children. Compared to term-born controls, the low birth-weight group had memory and executive function deficits, suggesting a limited capacity for recovery after subcortical, frontostriatal, and medial temporal insults. A related study found slower age-related increases in tests of executive function in the low birth-weight group compared with the term-born controls (Taylor et al., 2004), offering further evidence for limitations in plasticity following perinatal subcortical lesions.

Left–right: Syntax after left-sided or right-sided lesions in children

Components of the language production system are important for producing free-standing function words and inflectional morphemes in sentences, including the inflectional (I) system subcategories, tense, subject agreement, and object agreement. Compared to those with right hemispherectomy, children with left hemispherectomy have difficulty producing inflectional morphology (Dennis & Whitaker, 1976), use a restricted range and number of I-system morphemes, and have particular problem with auxiliaries, despite intact syntactic and morphological structures of other types (Curtiss & Schaeffer, 2005). As with the effects of lower brain lesions on timing, attention orienting, and executive functions, left-hemisphere insult may allow for only a limited form of plasticity, implying a relatively constrained capacity of reserve in this hemisphere to support certain language skills.

Syntactic structures are representations that assign important aspects of sentence meaning (Caplan & Hildebrandt, 1988), especially of functional roles (who is acting, who is being acted on). The adult left hemisphere has a strong association with syntax; functionally, it constructs syntactically licensed dependencies in real time (Swinney, Zurif, Prather, & Love, 1996) and assigns syntactic structure during language comprehension (Caplan, 1992; Caplan & Hildebrandt, 1988; Stromswold, Caplan, Alpert, & Rausch, 1996). The immature left hemisphere also has a strong association with syntax. Compared to those with early right-hemisphere damage and hemispherectomy, individuals with congenital damage to, and removal of, the left hemisphere are slower and less accurate in understanding sentences with non-canonical word orders (e.g., reversible passive sentences such as *the dog is chased by the cat*) in which meaning is provided by syntactic structure but not semantic plausibility, whether comparisons are made between hemidecorticate groups with early lateralized hemispheric damage from varying pathologies (Dennis & Kohn, 1975) or from a single pathology (Dennis & Whitaker, 1976). The syntactic comprehension deficit after left-hemisphere damage is evident whether comparisons are made to chronological age (Aram, Ekelman, Rose, & Whitaker, 1985; Dennis, 1980; Dennis & Kohn, 1975; Dennis & Whitaker, 1976; Paquier & Van Dongen, 1993), mental age (Stark, Bleile, Brandt, Freeman, & Vining, 1995), or brain-intact co-twins (Feldman, Holland, & Keefe, 1989; Hetherington & Dennis, 2004).

Syntactic comprehension disorders in adults arise from at least two separable impairments (Caplan & Hildebrandt, 1988): a specific disturbance with parsing processes and/or linguistic representations, including problems with functional argument structure and difficulties with non-canonical orders of sentence constituents (Berndt, Mitchum, & Wayland, 1997), and a reduction in the computational resources available for syntactic comprehension (Crain, Ni, & Shankweiler, 2001). Individuals with hemispherectomy for early left-hemisphere injury appear to have a combined impairment. They are insensitive to the role of function words that cue syntactic structure, even on metacognitive tasks with no time constraints (Dennis, 1980), which suggests that they have trouble constructing functional argument structures. In addition, they make fewer errors on non-canonical sentences when they respond slowly (Dennis & Kohn, 1975), which suggests a limitation in processing resources whereby performance deficits become attenuated when more resources are allocated to comprehension.

Measurement of language recovery is a precondition for investigation of brain reserve. To do so demands that the researcher both assesses language skills compared with a reference group of the same age, and projects the level of language development that would have been attained had the neurological insult not occurred. Age-referenced language skills measure recovery rather than individual development; that is, they indicate whether a particular language skill is below, at, or above age expectations, but do not reveal how language would have developed without the stroke. Individual developmental trajectories for language after childhood stroke have been difficult to establish, because language development varies with many of the factors (perinatal history, socioeconomic status, education; Aylward, Verhulst, & Bell, 1989; Selzer, Lindgren, & Blackman, 1992) that also affect language recovery (Yeates, 2000).

Later in childhood, more restricted left-sided lesions to the perisylvian region as a result of left middle cerebral artery ischemic stroke produce language deficits, the syntactic component of which shows some recovery but limited development. In a co-twin control study, Hetherington and Dennis (2004) studied language in 13-year-old same-sex twins raised together but discordant for left hemisphere stroke that one twin sustained at age 7, which caused him to change handedness. Five years post-stroke, syntactic deficits were apparent in the form of deficits in rules for negation and polarity and understanding sentences with non-canonical word orders, which suggests that one part of the disorder is a specific difficulty with parsing and syntactic representations. The affected twin also required additional time to perform syntactic operations in sentences with either canonical or non-canonical word order, suggesting some limitation in the computational resources required for successful syntactic comprehension. Importantly, he showed recovery but not development of syntax: syntax skills improved to their level at the time of the injury, but were developmentally arrested thereafter. Follow-up of the affected twin provides a case illustration of the effect of depleted BRC, and the arrest of syntactic development is presumptive evidence of limited BRC.

Front–back: Frontal lobe functions after anterior lesions in children

Traumatic brain injury, a common form of acquired brain disorder, is often associated with damage to anterior brain regions, and provides a model of anterior damage to compare to more posterior lesions. The prefrontal damage following childhood TBI is of three types. The first is contusional injury to the frontal cortex, which, like the temporal lobe, is especially vulnerable to contusional injuries (Levin et al., 1996). The second is diffuse axonal injury, which is seen on late MRI in the form of gliosis, hemosiderin deposits, and volume loss, occurs throughout the corpus callosum and frontal lobe white matter, and becomes more evident in the 3 years following severe childhood TBI (Levin et al., 2000). The third is a reduction in brain connectivity, as shown by changes in the directionality and integrity of white matter tracts (Lee et al., 2003). Examination of regionally specific effects of TBI suggest that some cognitive-behavioral outcomes are highly vulnerable to frontal lesions, implying that frontal reserve may be limited in support of these functions.

The prefrontal lobes have two processing resources, inhibitory control (the ability to stop or modulate ongoing actions or to hold competing representations) and working memory (the process by which information is temporarily activated in memory for rapid manipulation and retrieval). Children with TBI have difficulty maintaining selective attention (Dennis et al., 1995); withholding an action in response to a signal (Konrad et al., 2000; Levin et al., 1993; Schachar et al., 2004); maintaining a counterfactual rule (Manly, Robertson, Anderson, & Nimmo-Smith, 1999), and switching between salient and non-salient responses (Roncadin, Rich, Pascual-Leone, & Dennis, 2003). Moderate or severe childhood TBI is associated with working memory deficits (Levin, Hanten et al., 2004; Roncadin, Guger, Archibald, Barnes, & Dennis, 2004), which, in turn, are associated with impairments in sentence comprehension (Dennis & Barnes, 1990; Hanten, Levin, & Song, 1999; Montgomery, 1995), inferencing (Barnes & Dennis, 2001), and discourse (Chapman et al., 1992; Dennis & Barnes, 1990, 2000). Outcomes of pediatric TBI on behavioral inhibition also reveal effects of diminished BRC in the anterior brain system on post-injury cognitive development. Levin et al. (1993), for example, found that GO/NOGO performance on a response inhibition task was impaired in children 2 years post-injury, with performance related to volume of left prefrontal lesions (Levin et al., 1993).

The ability to link the past and the future, termed *time travel* (Fuster, 2000) or *chronesthesia* (Tulving, 2002), is an important prefrontal function, possibly a distinctly humanly one (Roberts, 2002). Time travel enables autobiographical memory, prospective memory, and planning. School-age children who have sustained a TBI at least 2 years prior to testing are impaired on event-based and activity-based prospective memory tasks (McCauley & Levin, 2000, 2001). For adolescents with TBI, event-based prospective memory worsens with increased cognitive demands (Shum, 2005). Compared with children with mild TBI, children with severe TBI do not benefit from prospective memory reminders (McCauley & Levin, 2004). Planning deficits are also evident in children with TBI (Levin, Song, Ewing-Cobbs, & Robertson, 2001), and performance is correlated with lesion volume, including orbitofrontal, dorsolateral, and frontal white matter lesions (Levin et al., 1994, 2001). Adolescents with early damage to the pre-frontal cortex are inaccurate planners, like younger, typically developing children (Ratterman, Spector, Grafman, Levin, & Harwood, 2001).

Flexible access to one's own mind (through metacognition) and to the minds of others (through theory of mind) is important for the development of socially appropriate behavior. Children with TBI exhibit problems with metacognitive monitoring, being unable to judge the adequacy of ambiguous directions, or to detect anomalies in sentences (Dennis, Barnes, Donnelly, Wilkinson, & Humphreys, 1996), especially sentences presented under con-ditions of high memory load (Hanten et al., 1999) and with metacognitive knowledge, being unable to predict the ease with which they will learn specific items or to estimate their memory span accurately (Hanten, Dennis, Zhang, Barnes, & Robertson, 2004). Problems in metacognition are especially apparent when TBI occurs early in development and/or includes CT evidence of contusional damage to the frontal lobes (Dennis, Barnes et al., 1996).

Theory of mind involves the ability to think about mental states (thoughts, beliefs, intentions, and desires) and to use them to understand and predict what other people need to know and how they will act (Bibby & McDonald, 2005). Childhood TBI in the school-age years is associated with deficits in making pragmatic inferences about the presuppositions, entailments, and implications of mental state verbs (Dennis & Barnes, 2000), a class of words that includes *know, remember, forget, think, believe,* and *pretend* (Hall & Nagy, 1986; Kiparsky & Kiparsky, 1970; Karttunen, 1971), and in producing speech acts (Dennis & Barnes, 2000), prototypical forms of pragmatic com-munication that express the mutual intentions of a speaker and a listener. Children with severe TBI, although not those with mild TBI, have difficulty understanding literal statements concerned with first- and second-order beliefs and intentions (Dennis, Purvis, Barnes, Wilkinson, & Winner, 2001).

Children with TBI have deficits in social information processing that predict their social and academic function (Warschausky et al., 1997). They prefer solutions to social dilemmas and evaluate the outcome of dilemmas in a less developmentally advanced fashion than their peers, although they can define the problem and generate alternative solutions (Janusz et al., 2002). Adolescents with TBI have poorer social information processing than age peers (Turkstra, McDonald, & DePompei, 2001).

The ability to link affect and cognition fosters hedonic encoding and decision making that combines affect and thought, allows expression of emotions to be regulated according to the cognitive understanding of the situation, and allows social-affective messages to be communicated with a softening of the negative affect (e.g., in ironic criticism) or a heightening of the positive affect (e.g., in empathic lies). Children with TBI understand emotional facial expressions, but do not regulate the social display of emotive facial expressions (Dennis et al., 1998). Emotive identification is particularly impaired in children with early-onset injuries or injuries that involve the frontal lobes (Dennis et al., 1998). Irony and empathy engage complex theory of mind processes concerned with affective evaluations of one individual that manipulate the mental states and feelings of another. Children with TBI have difficulty understanding the affective valence of first- and second-order intentions in irony and empathy, even when they understand the intentions of literal statements (Dennis et al., 2001).

Neuroimaging studies of childhood TBI have shown that focal lesions are larger and more numerous in the anterior cortex (Wilde et al., 2005), and that these lesions are related to social-cognitive and social-behavioral outcomes (Levin et al., 1989; Mendelsohn et al., 1992). The link has been made between focal frontal lesions and psychosocial outcomes. In a recent study of childhood TBI (Levin, Zhang, et al., 2004), children with frontal lesions (but not those with non-frontal lesions) displayed poor socialization and maladaptive behaviors compared to children with non-frontal lesions, and frontal lobe lesion volume (but not posterior lesion volume) predicted poor socialization (Levin, Zhang, et al., 2004). A related study found that personality change, including changes in social behavior, is associated with lesions of the dorsal prefrontal cortex (Max et al., 2005). Persistent personality change occurred in 18% of children with TBI in this sample. The most common changes involved affective lability, aggressive behavior, and poor social judgment (e.g., tactless comments about the listener, inappropriate sharing of personal information). Personality change was more common with more severe injuries, and was associated with lesions to several distinct regions as seen on MRI. However, only lesions in the superior frontal gyrus accounted for unique variance in this outcome.

Children with preserved anterior brain regions provide a useful contrast to those with lesions in this area, and allow assessment of variations in BRC along an anterior-to-posterior gradient. Children with preserved anterior brain appear to have more preserved anterior brain functions. For example, children with SBM have normal frontal volumes (on voxel-based morphometry), despite volume loss and loss of connectivity in the posterior cortex (Fletcher et al., 2005). These children have deficits in the posterior attention functions of attention orienting and inhibition of return, but retain normal top-down attention control on endogenous orienting tasks (Dennis et al., 2005a). The implication of these data for BRC is that there are distinct ways in which anterior and posterior brain insults constrain subsequent development.

Discussion

That children sustain brain insults does not speak to the issue of reserve. Both children and adults have a pathological burden as a direct effect of brain insult. What does speak to reserve is that the functional outcome of childhood brain insult is mediated by BRC and CRC, as evidenced by accelerated aging in adulthood, greater vulnerability to subsequent brain insult, or diminished capacity to make age-appropriate developmental progress. Whereas in general terms the data reviewed in this chapter validate the utility of the constructs of BRC and CRC in interpreting the outcome of brain insults in children, they also highlight some important differences between reserve in adults and children.

Normal cognitive development may require more neural resources (more BRC and CRC) than the maintenance of cognitive structures already developed (Hebb, 1942). After brain insult, the task of the mature brain is to support the restitution and reorganization of functions that have been lost or disrupted. The child with a central nervous system (CNS) insult faces the normal task of cognitive development involving the acquisition of new functions, skills, and knowledge and the abnormal task of formulating a strategic, adaptive response to the insult to recover functions existing at the time of the injury. Thus children with brain injury exhibit two kinds of changes, one an adaptive or maladaptive response to the injury, the other a normal or abnormal trajectory of skills not yet acquired at the time of injury (Dennis, 1988).

The cognitive deficits of children with genetic deficits reflect deficient genetic control of the neurotransmitter systems and other neural processes underlying cognition. Genetic syndromes and genetically based congenital malformations of the brain are more common in children than in adults. Genetic heterogeneity is a proxy for diminished brain reserve in a number of childhood conditions. As these individuals age, the consequences of diminished BRC become increasingly evident in the form of accelerated normal or abnormal aging. For many years, genetic anomalies such as those in Down syndrome have been known to reduce BRC brain reserve and accelerate aging. What is emerging as a new research area is normal and abnormal aging in childhood brain disorders such as SBM. Recent advances in the genetics of complex neurobehavioral conditions, including dyslexia, ADHD, and autism, also raise the possibility of investigations of BRC and CRC in these populations. Finally, it may be that forms of genetic anomalies in adults other than the apolipoprotein allele diminish brain reserve and accelerate aging.

Children with congenital forms of brain insult have predictable patterns of brain dysmorphology. Whereas selective midbrain lesions in the adult superior colliculus are rare single cases (e.g., Sapir, Soroker, Berger, & Henik, 1999), congenital malformations of the midbrain are relatively common in childhood conditions such as SBM. Follow-up of children with such conditions enables study of age-based variations in functional plasticity over the lifespan after damage to midbrain structures and encourages comparison of the relative capacity for functional plasticity in midbrain as opposed to cortical lesions. The higher frequency of subtentorial and midbrain lesions in children enables a number of useful comparisons over the lifespan and in relation to the spatial gradients in the brain. Aging in conditions such as SBM, with genetic mutations that affect brain development in highly specific ways but that are congruent with normal intelligence, may provide an impetus for future research. For example, comparison of rate of cognitive aging in individuals with SBM with and without callosal dysgenesis of the splenium is theoretically relevant to recent hypotheses about the role of the splenium in adult-onset Alzheimer disease (reviewed in Reuter-Lorenz & Mikels, 2005).

In recent years, medical advances have created cohorts of survivors of formerly lethal or cognitively devastating childhood brain disorders who are moving from childhood to adulthood and gradually into old age. Older individuals who face aging with diminished reserve because of early brain insults have diminished BRC and CRC and so are at high risk for poor outcome (Dennis, Spiegler, & Hetherington, 2000); for example, children with lower IQ scores are more likely than those with higher IQ to develop cognitive decline in mid-life and beyond (Richards, Shipley, Fuhrer, & Wadsworth, 2004). As new treatments improve survival rates and reduce cognitive morbidity for children with genetic-metabolic disorders, strokes, severe brain trauma, and malignant brain tumors, these new populations provide the opportunity to study questions about reserve in adults using measures of childhood BRC and CRC. These measures supplement the traditional reserve proxies such as head size, IQ or education used in some previous child-to-adult longitudinal studies of reserve and dementia.

Advances in pediatric neuroimaging now allow direct measures of BRC. Measures of fractional anisotropy from DTI measure residual connectivity in the brain, and studies of DTI in relation to various forms of functional plasticity after childhood TBI should provide important new perspectives on BRC in pediatric populations, and add to the information base for studying reserve as these individuals reach adulthood.

Most studies of reserve have emerged from cortical function in adults. New studies of adult aging have suggested that white matter hyperintensities on MRI correlate with cognitive burden in old age (Leaper et al., 2001). White matter lesions are more common in children than in adults, and important evidence about age-based functional plasticity will come from comparisons of similar outcomes following white matter lesions in children and adults.

Studies of how the outcome of childhood brain lesions is moderated according to different spatial gradients provide a new perspective on functional plasticity and, by implication, BRC. An up–down gradient is supported by evidence of some cortically mediated functional plasticity.

However, the timing functions of the cerebellum, the attention orienting functions of the midbrain, and executive and memory functions mediated by the periventricular region exhibit little age-based functional plasticity, and deficits appear similar over the child-to-adult age span. In the case of the midbrain, there is little functional tissue to afford reserve, so attention-orienting deficits follow midbrain lesions over the lifespan. A left–right BRC gradient appears to allow for some functional plasticity following early brain disease, but is insufficient to support normal syntactic development after left-hemisphere cortical lesions, whether focal in the perisylvian area or involving the entire hemisphere, and whether sustained congenitally or in mid-childhood. Compared to similar lesions of the right hemisphere, large, hemisphere-wide congenital pathology of the left hemisphere is associated with syntactic deficits: use of the inflectional morphology system; a specific disturbance with parsing processes and/or linguistic representations; and a reduction in the computational resources available for syntactic comprehension. Depletion of BRC is implicated to the extent that children with early left-hemisphere lesions fail to acquire skills at a normal rate and children with later left-hemisphere lesions have syntactic skills arrested at the time of the insult. With respect to an anterior-to-posterior gradient, anterior cortical lesions in children produce deficits in a number of functions associated with the prefrontal lobes, and, further, these impairments are correlated with the presence of frontal lobe injury (Scheibel & Levin, 1997). Similar lesion–function relations are not observed with posterior lesions, evidencing a front-to-back gradient for a number of functional outcomes.

Studies of childhood brain insult can also address issues of compensation (Stern, 2002), whether reserve involves undamaged brain tissue in a typical substrate or new functionality in an atypical substrate. For children with hemispherectomy, the limitation is clearly related to an atypical substrate because all the cortical mass of one hemisphere has been removed. Syntactic comprehension deficits for non-canonical word orders are evident when only part of the left hemisphere is removed but speech control has shifted to the right hemisphere (Kohn, 1980), showing that residual left-hemisphere tissue does not support normal syntax when language has shifted to the right hemisphere. Despite the presence of undamaged tissue in the right hemisphere, the right hemisphere is not specified as a substrate for syntactic function, as is the left hemisphere in right dominant individuals. Supporting the idea of atypical cognitive strategies, individuals with either congenital or acquired lesions require additional time to make accurate syntactic discriminations, and those with left hemispherectomy use a simpler, canonical functional argument structure (Dennis, 1980), both of which suggest recruitment of distinct, top-down networks.

Further studies are needed to advance knowledge of the vulnerabilities of children with congenital or acquired brain disorders to further brain insult or to difficulties in making developmental transitions. Little research has been conducted in this area, and children with pre-existing conditions are often excluded from studies of long-term outcomes of brain insult. Additional research is also required to examine brain regions that have greater reserve capacities and the neural basis of reserve, perhaps using cortical activation and functional imaging methods. The notion of a gradient of reserve, rather than all-or-none thresholds, deserves further study as well. Although there may be thresholds of damage that, when exceeded, preclude plasticity of function, the concept that reserve varies in degree finds considerable support in the literature reviewed in this chapter. Interpretative and methodological issues are also important, as Stern (2002) emphasizes. For example, investigators must consider the possibility that impaired developmental progress after brain insult reflects lack of environmental supports or motivational changes, as well as the brain-based mechanisms implied by brain reserve; and measures of reserve must be distinguished from the outcomes they are purported to explain.

At the most general level, it is clear even now that issues of reserve—both BRC and CRC—concern the brain's capacity to mediate adaptive changes, optimal or suboptimal, at any point in development. While reserve questions about BRC, CRC and compensation have not generally been addressed with children, new research suggests that comparative studies of reserve in adults and in children might be mutually informative.

Acknowledgments

This chapter describes research supported by project grants from the National Institute of Child Health and Human Development Grant P01 HD-35946 "Spina Bifida: Cognitive and Neurobiological Variability," and HD-44099, "Outcomes of Traumatic Brain Injury in Children," and by grants from the National Institute of Neurological Diseases and Stroke Grant NS-21889, "Neurobehavioral Outcome of Head Injury in Children," and NS-36335, "Recovery from Traumatic Brain Injury in Children-Phase 2." Support was also provided by grant MCJ-390611 from the Maternal and Child Health Bureau (Title V, Social Security Act, Health Resources and Services Administration, Department of Health and Human Services).

References

Anderson, V., & Moore, C. (1995). Age at injury as a predictor of outcome following pediatric head injury: A longitudinal perspective. *Child Neuropsychology, 1,* 187–202.

Anderson, V., Fenwick, T., Manly, T., & Robertson, I. (1998). Attentional skills following traumatic brain injury in childhood: A componential analysis. *Brain Injury, 12,* 937–949.

Anderson, V. A., Morse, S. A., Klug, G., Catroppa, C., Haritou, F., Rosenfeld, J., et al. (1997). Predicting recovery from head injury in young children: A prospective analysis. *Journal of the International Neuropsychological Society, 3,* 568–580.

Aram, D. M., Ekelman, B. L., Rose, D. F., & Whitaker, H. A. (1985). Verbal and cognitive sequelae following unilateral lesions acquired in early childhood. *Journal of Clinical and Experimental Neuropsychology*, *7*, 55–78.

Aylward, G. P., Verhulst, S. J., & Bell, S. (1989). Correlation of asphyxia and other risk factors with outcome: A contemporary view. *Developmental Medicine and Child Neurology*, *31*, 329–340.

Barnes, M. A., & Dennis, M. (2001). Knowledge-based inferencing after childhood head injury. *Brain & Language*, *76*, 253–265.

Basser, L. S. (1962). Hemiplegia of early onset and the faculty of speech with reference to the effects of hemispherectomy. *Brain*, *85*, 427–460.

Berndt, R. S., Mitchum, C. C., & Wayland, S. (1997). Patterns of sentence comprehension in aphasia: A consideration of three hypotheses. *Brain and Language*, *60*, 197–221.

Bibby, H., & McDonald, S. (2005). Theory of mind after traumatic brain injury. *Neuropsychologia*, *43*, 99–114.

Bleyer, W. A., & Poplack, D. G. (1985). Prophylaxis and treatment of leukemia in the central nervous system and other sanctuaries. *Seminars in Oncology*, *12*, 131–148.

Bloom, D. R., Levin, H. S., Ewing-Cobbs, L., Saunders, A. E., Song, J., Fletcher, J. M., et al. (2001). Lifetime and novel psychiatric disorders after pediatric traumatic brain injury. *Journal of the American Academy of Child and Adolescent Psychiatry*, *40*, 572–579.

Caplan, D. (1992). *Language, structure, processing, and disorders*. Cambridge, MA: Bradford/MIT Press.

Caplan, D., & Hildebrandt, N. (1988). *Disorders of syntactic comprehension*. Cambridge, MA: Bradford/MIT Press.

Cass, J. E., Yeates, K. O., Taylor, M. G., & Minich, N. M. (2005). Cognitive reserve capacity and neuropsychological outcome following pediatric traumatic brain injury [Abstract]. *Journal of the International Neuropsychological Society*, *11* (Suppl. 51), available online at http://journals.cambridge.org/action/displayIssue?jid=INS&volumeId=11&issueId=S1 accessed February 2005.

Chapman, S. B., Culhane, K. A., Levin, H. S., Harward, H., Mendelsohn, D., Ewing-Cobbs, L., et al. (1992). Narrative discourse after closed head injury in children and adolescents. *Brain and Language*, *43*, 42–65.

Cochran, M., & Niego, S. (2002). Parenting social networks. In M. Bornstein (Ed.), *The handbook of parenting: Social conditions and applied parenting* (2nd ed., Vol. 4, pp. 123–149). Mahwah, NJ: Lawrence Erlbaum Associates, Inc.

Cohen, M. E., & Duffner, P. K. (1994). *Brain tumors in children* (2nd ed., pp. 455–481). New York: Raven Press.

Copeland, D. R., deMoor, C., Moore, B. D. I., & Ater, J. L. (1999). Neurocognitive development of children after cerebellar tumor in infancy: A longitudinal study. *Journal of Clinical Oncology*, *17*, 3476–3486.

Crain, S., Ni, W., & Shankweiler, D. (2001). Grammatism. *Brain and Language*, *77*, 294–304.

Curtiss, S., & Schaeffer, J. (2005). Syntactic development in children with hemispherectomy: The I-, D-, and C-systems. *Brain and Language*, *94*, 147–166.

Davis, P. C., Hoffman, J. C., Pearl, G. S., & Braun, I. F. (1986). CT evaluation of effects of cranial radiation therapy in children. *American Journal of Neuroradiology*, *7*, 639–644.

Dennis, M. (1980). Capacity and strategy for syntactic comprehension after left or right hemidecortication. *Brain and Language, 10*, 287–317.

Dennis, M. (1988). Language and the young damaged brain. In T. Boll & B. K. Bryant (Eds.), *Clinical neuropsychology and brain function: Research, measurement, and practice*. Master Lecture Series (Vol. 7, pp. 85–123). Washington, DC: American Psychological Association.

Dennis, M. (2000). Childhood medical disorders and cognitive impairment: Biological risk, time, development, and reserve. In K. O. Yeates, M. D. Ris, & H. G. Taylor (Eds.), *Pediatric neuropsychology: Research, theory, and practice* (pp. 3–22). New York: Guilford Press.

Dennis, M. (2003). Acquired disorders of language in children. In T. E. Feinberg & M. J. Farah (Eds.), *Behavioural neurology and neuropsychology* (pp. 783–799). New York: McGraw-Hill, Inc.

Dennis, M., & Barnes, M. A. (1990). Knowing the meaning, getting the point, bridging the gap, and carrying the message: Aspects of discourse following closed head injury in childhood and adolescence. *Brain and Language, 39*, 428–446.

Dennis, M., & Barnes, M. A. (2000). Speech acts after mild or severe childhood head injury. *Aphasiology, 14*, 391–405.

Dennis, M., & Kohn, B. (1975). Comprehension of syntax in infantile hemiplegics after cerebral hemidecortication: Left hemisphere superiority. *Brain and Language, 2*, 472–482.

Dennis, M., & Whitaker, H.A. (1976). Language acquisition following hemidecortication: Linguistic superiority of the left over the right hemisphere. *Brain and Language, 3*, 404–433.

Dennis, M., Barnes, M. A., Donnelly, R. E., Wilkinson, M., & Humphreys, R. (1996). Appraising and managing knowledge: Metacognitive skills after childhood head injury. *Developmental Neuropsychology, 12*, 17–34.

Dennis, M., Barnes, M. A., Hetherington, P., Robitaille, J., Hopyan, T., Spiegler, B. J., et al. (2000). Retrospective and prospective memory in adult survivors of spina bifida. International Neuropsychological Society, Annual Meeting, Denver, Colorado. *Journal of the International Neuropsychological Society, 6*, 160.

Dennis, M., Barnes, M. A., Wilkinson, M., & Humphreys, R. P. (1998). How children with head injury represent real and deceptive emotion in short narratives. *Brain and Language, 61*, 450–483.

Dennis, M., Edelstein, K., Copeland, K., Francis, D., Hetherington, R., Frederick, J., et al. (2005a). Covert orienting to exogenous and endogenous cues in children with spina bifida. *Neuropsychologia, 42*, 976–987.

Dennis, M., Edelstein, K., Copeland, K., Frederick, J., Francis, D. J., Hetherington, R., et al. (2005b). Space-based inhibition of return in children with spina bifida. *Neuropsychology, 19*, 456–465.

Dennis, M., Edelstein, K., Hetherington, R., Copeland, K., Frederick, J., Blaser, S. E., et al. (2004). Neurobiology of perceptual and motor timing in children with spina bifida in relation to cerebellar volume. *Brain, 127*, 1–10.

Dennis, M., Purvis, K., Barnes, M. A., Wilkinson, M., & Winner, E. (2001). Understanding of literal truth, ironic criticism, and deceptive praise after childhood head injury. *Brain and Language, 78*, 1–16.

Dennis, M., Spiegler, B. J., & Hetherington, R. (2000). New survivors for the new millennium: Cognition in adults with childhood brain insults. *Brain and Cognition, 42*, 102–105.

Dennis, M., Spiegler, B. J., Hetherington, C. R., & Greenberg, M. L. (1996). Neuro-psychological sequelae of the treatment of children with medulloblastoma. *Journal of Neuro-Oncology, 29*, 91–101.

Dennis, M., Spiegler, B., Riva, D., & MacGregor, D. (2004). Neuropsychological outcome. In D. Walker, G. Perilongo, J. Punt, & R. Taylor (Eds.), *Brain and spinal tumors of childhood* (pp. 213–227). New York: Oxford University Press.

Dennis, M., Wilkinson, M., Koski, L., & Humphreys, R. P. (1995). Attention deficits in the long term after childhood head injury. In S. Broman & M.E. Michel (Eds.), *Traumatic head injury in children* (pp. 165–187). New York: Oxford University Press.

Devenny, D. A., Krinsky-McHale, S. J., Kittler, P. M., Flory, M., Jenkins, E., & Brown, W. T. (2004). Age-associated memory changes in adults with Williams syndrome. *Developmental Neuropsychology, 26*, 691–706.

Diamond, A. (1996). Evidence for the importance of dopamine for prefrontal cortex functions early in life. *Philosophical Transactions of the Royal Society of London B, 351*, 1483–1494.

Diamond, A., Briand, L., Fossella, J., & Gehlback, L. (2004). Genetic and neuro-chemical modulation of prefrontal cognitive functions in children. *The American Journal of Psychiatry, 161*, 125–132.

Doxey, D., Bruce, D., Sklar, F., Swift, D., & Shapiro, K. (1999). Posterior fossa syndrome: Identifiable risk factors and irreversible complications. *Pediatric Neurosurgery, 31*, 131–136.

Duffner, P. K., Cohen, M. E., & Parker, M. S. (1988). Prospective intellectual testing in children with brain tumors. *Annals of Neurology, 23*, 575–579.

Eiser, C. (1978). Intellectual abilities among survivors of childhood leukaemia as a function of CNS irradiation. *Archives of Diseases of Childhood, 53*, 391–395.

Ellenberg, L., McComb, J. G., Siegel, S. E., & Stowe, S. (1987). Factors affecting intellectual outcome in pediatric brain tumor patients. *Neurosurgery, 21*, 638–644.

Ewing-Cobbs, L., Fletcher, J. M., Levin, H. S., Francis, D. J., Davidson, K., & Miner, M. E. (1997). Longitudinal neuropsychological outcome in infants and pre-schoolers with traumatic brain injury. *Journal of the International Neuro-psychological Society, 3*, 581–591.

Feldman, H., Holland, A., & Keefe, K. (1989). Language abilities after left hemisphere brain injury: A case study of twins. *Topics in Early Childhood Special Education, 9*, 32–47.

Fenwick, T., & Anderson, V. (1999). Impairments of attention following childhood traumatic brain injury. *Child Neuropsychology, 5*, 213–223.

Fletcher, J. M., Copeland, K., Frederick, J., Blaser, S. E., Kramer, L. A., Hannay, H. J., et al. (2005). Spinal lesion level in spina bifida meningomyelocele: A source of neural and cognitive heterogeneity. *Journal of Neurosurgery: Pediatrics, 102*, 268–279.

Fletcher, J. M., Ewing-Cobbs, L., Miner, M., Levin, H., & Eisenberg, H. (1990). Behavioral changes after closed head injury in children. *Journal of Consulting and Clinical Psychology, 58*, 93–98.

Fouladi, M., Langston, J., Mulhern, R., Jones, D., Xiong, X., Yang, J., et al. (2000). Silent lacunar lesions detected by magnetic resonance imaging of children with brain tumors: A late sequelae of therapy. *Journal of Clinical Oncology, 18*, 824–831.

Franz, E. A., Zelaznik, H. N., & Smith, A. (1992). Evidence of common timing processes in the control of manual, orofacial, and speech movement. *Journal of Motor Behavior, 24*, 281–287.

Fuster, J. (2000). The prefrontal cortex of the primate. A synopsis. *Psychobiology, 28,* 125–131.

Gerring, J. P., Brady, K. D., Chen, A., Vasa, R., Grados, M., Bandeen-Roche, K. J., et al. (1998). Premorbid prevalence of ADHD and development of secondary ADHD after closed head injury. *Journal of the American Academy of Child and Adolescent Psychiatry, 37,* 647–654.

Guralnick, M. J. (1989). Social competence as a future direction for early intervention programs. *Journal of Mental Deficiency Research, 33,* 275–281.

Hall, W. S., & Nagy, W. E. (1986). Theoretical issues in the investigation of the words of internal report. In A. Gopnik & M. Gopnik (Eds.), *From models to modules: Studies in cognitive science from the McGill workshops* (pp. 26–65). Norwood, NJ: Ablex.

Hanten, G., Dennis, M., Zhang, L., Barnes, M., & Robertson, G. (2004). Childhood head injury and metacognitive processes in language and memory. *Developmental Neuropsychology, 25,* 85–106.

Hanten, G., Levin, H. S., & Song, J. X. (1999). Working memory and metacognition in sentence comprehension by severely head-injured children: A preliminary study. *Developmental Neuropsychology, 16,* 393–414.

Hebb, D. O. (1942). The effect of early and late brain injury upon test scores, and the nature of normal adult intelligence. *Proceedings of the American Philosophical Society, 85,* 275–292.

Hetherington, R., & Dennis, M. (2004). Plasticity for recovery, plasticity for development: Cognitive function in twins discordant for childhood left hemisphere stroke. *Child Neuropsychology, 10,* 117–128.

Hetherington, R., Dennis, M., & Spiegler, B. (2000). Perception and estimation of time in long-term survivors of childhood posterior fossa tumors. *Journal of the International Neuropsychological Society, 6,* 682–692.

Hodapp, R. M., Dykens, E. M., Hagerman, R. J., Schreiner, R., et al. (1990). Developmental implications of changing trajectories of IQ in males with fragile X syndrome. *Journal of the American Academy of Child and Adolescent Psychiatry, 29,* 214–219.

Holmbeck, G. N. (1997). Toward terminological, conceptual, and statistical clarity in the study of mediators and moderators: Examples from the child-clinical and pediatric psychology literature. *Journal of Consulting and Clinical Psychology, 65,* 599–610.

Hoppe-Hirsch, E., Renier, D., Lellouch-Tubiana, A., Sainte-Rose, C., Pierre-Kahn, A., & Hirsch, J. F. (1990). Medulloblastoma in childhood: Progressive intellectual deterioration. *Child's Nervous System, 6,* 60–65.

Iverson, G. L., Gaetz, M., Lovell, M. R., & Collins, M. W. (2004). Cumulative effects of concussion in amateur atheletes. *Brain Injury, 18,* 433–443.

Ivry, R., & Keele, S. (1989). Timing functions of the cerebellum. *Journal of Cognitive Neuroscience, 1,* 136–152.

Ivry, R. B., & Richardson, T. C. (2002). Temporal control and coordination: The multiple timer model. *Brain and Cognition, 48,* 117–132.

Janicki, M. P., & Dalton, A. J. (Eds.). (1998). *Dementia, aging and intellectual disabilities.* Castleton, NY: Hamilton Printing.

Jannoun, L., & Bloom, H. J. G. (1990). Long-term psychological effects in children treated for intracranial tumors. *International Journal of Radiation Oncology, Biology, Physics, 18,* 747–753.

Janusz, J. A., Kirkwood, M. W., Yeates, K. O., & Taylor, H. G. (2002). Social problem-solving skills in children with traumatic brain injury: Long-term outcomes and prediction of social competence. *Child Neuropsychology, 8*, 179–194.

Karlinsky, M. (1986). Alzheimer's disease in Down's syndrome: A review. *Journal of the American Geriatric Society, 34*, 728–734.

Karttunen, L. (1971). Implicative verbs. *Language, 47*, 340–358.

Katzman, R. (1993). Education and the prevalence of dementia and Alzheimer's disease. *Neurology, 43*, 13–20.

Keele, S. W., Pokorny, R. A., Corcos, D. M., & Ivry, R. B. (1985). Do perception and motor production share common timing mechanisms: A correctional analysis. *Acta Psychologica (Amst) 60*, 173–191.

Kesler, S., Adams, H., Blasey, C., & Bigler, E. (2003). Premorbid intellectual functioning, education, and brain size in traumatic brain injury: An investigation of the cognitive reserve hypothesis. *Applied Neuropsychology, 10*, 153–162.

Kiparsky, P., & Kiparsky, C. (1970). Fact. In M. Bierwisch & K. Heidolph (Eds.), *Progress in linguistics* (pp. 143–173). The Hague, Netherlands: Mouton.

Klein, R. M. (1988). Inhibitory tagging system facilitates visual search. *Nature, 334*, 430–431.

Klein, R. M. (2000). Inhibition of return. *Trends in Cognitive Sciences, 4*, 138–147.

Kohn, B. (1980). Right-hemisphere speech representation and comprehension of syntax after left cerebral injury. *Brain and Language, 9*, 350–361.

Konrad, K., Gauggel, S., Manz, A., & Scholl, M. (2000). Lack of inhibition: A motivational deficit in children with attention deficit/hyperactivity disorder and children with traumatic brain injury. *Child Neuropsychology, 6*, 286–296.

Leaper, S. A., Murray, A. D., Lemmon, H. A., Staff, R. T., Deary, I. J., Crawford, J. R., et al. (2001). Neuropsychological correlates of brain white matter lesions depicted on MR images: 1921 Aberdeen Birth Cohort. *Radiology, 221*, 51–55.

LeBaron, S., Zeltzer, P. M., Zeltzer, L. K., Scott, S. E., & Martin, A. E. (1988). Assessment of quality of survival in children with medulloblastoma and cerebellar astrocytoma. *Cancer, 62*, 1215–1222.

Lee, Z. I., Byun, W. M., Jang, S. H., Ahn, S. H., Moon, H. K., & Chang, Y. (2003). Diffusion tensor magnetic resonance imaging of microstructural abnormalities in children with brain injury. *American Journal of Physical Medicine and Rehabilitation, 82*, 556–559.

Levin, H., Amparo, E., Eisenberg, H., Miner, M., High, W. Jr., Ewing-Cobbs, L., et al. (1989). MRI after closed head injury in children. *Neurosurgery, 24*, 223–227.

Levin, H. S., Benavidez, D., Verger-Maestre, K., Perachio, N., Song, J., Mendelsohn, D. B., et al. (2000). Reduction of corpus callosum growth after severe traumatic brain injury in children. *Neurology, 54*, 647–653.

Levin, H. S., Culhane, K. A., Mendelsohn, D., Lilly, M. A., Bruce, D., Fletcher, J. M., et al. (1993). Cognition in relation to MRI in head injured children and adolescents. *Archives of Neurology, 50*, 897–905.

Levin, H. S., Fletcher, J. M., Kusnerik, L., Kufera, J., Lilly, M. A., Duffy, F. F., et al. (1996). Semantic memory following pediatric head injury: Relationship to age, severity of injury, and MRI. *Cortex, 32*, 461–478.

Levin, H. S., Hanten, G., Zhang, L., Swank, P.R., Ewing-Cobbs, L., Dennis, M., et al. (2004). Changes in working memory after traumatic brain injury in children. *Neuropsychology, 18*, 240–247.

Levin, H. S., High, W. M., Ewing-Cobbs, L., Fletcher, J. M., Eisenberg, H. M., Miner, M. E., et al. (1988). Memory functioning during the first year after closed head injury in children and adolescents. *Neurosurgery*, *22*, 1043–1052.

Levin, H. S., Mendelsohn, D., Lilly, M., Fletcher, J., Culhane, K., Chapman, S., et al. (1994). Tower of London performance in relation to magnetic resonance imaging following closed head injury in children. *Neuropsychology*, *8*, 171–179.

Levin, H. S., Song, J., Ewing-Cobbs, L., & Robertson, G. (2001). Porteus maze performance following traumatic brain injury in children. *Neuropsychology*, *15*, 557–567.

Levin, H. S., Zhang, L., Dennis, M., Ewing-Cobbs, L., Schachar, R., Max, J., et al. (2004). Psychosocial outcome of TBI in children with unilateral frontal lesions. *Journal of the International Neuropsychological Society*, *10*, 305–316.

Manly, T., Robertson, I. H., Anderson, V., & Nimmo-Smith, I. (1999). *Test of every-day attention for children*. Bury St. Edmunds, UK: Thames Valley.

Maria, B. L., Dennis, M., & Obonsawin, M. (1993). Severe permanent encephalopathy in acute lymphoblastic leukemia. *Canadian Journal of Neurological Science*, *20*, 199–205.

Massart, F., Reginster, J. Y., & Brandi, M. L. (2001). Genetics of menopause-associated diseases. *Maturitas*, *40*, 103–116.

Masten, A. S., Hubbard, J. J., Gest, S. D., Tellegen, A., Garmezy, N., & Ramirez, M. (1999). Competence in the context of adversity: Pathways to resilience and maladaptation from childhood to late adolescence. *Development and Psychopathology*, *11*, 143–169.

Max, J. E., Arndt, S., Castillo, C. S., Bokura, H., Robin, D. A., Lindgren, S. D., et al. (1998). Attention-deficit hyperactivity symptomatology after traumatic brain injury: A prospective study. *Journal of the American Academy of Child and Adolescent Psychiatry*, *37*, 841–847.

Max, J. E., Lansing, A. E., Koele, S. L., Castillo, C. S., Bokura, H., & Schachar, R. (2004). Attention deficit hyperactivity disorder in children and adolescents following traumatic brain injury. *Developmental Neuropsychology*, *25*, 159–177.

Max, J. E., Levin, H. S., Landis, J., Schachar, R., Saunders, A. E., Ewing-Cobbs, L., et al. (2005). Predictors of personality change due to traumatic brain injury in children and adolescents in the first six months after injury. *Journal of the American Academy of Child and Adolescent Psychiatry*, *44*, 435–442.

Max, J. E., Lindgren, S. D., Knutson, C., Pearson, C. S., Ihrig, D., & Welborn, A. (1997). Child and adolescent traumatic brain injury: Psychiatric findings from a paediatric outpatient specialty clinic. *Brain Injury*, *11*, 699–711.

McCauley, S. R., & Levin, H. S. (2000). *Prospective memory deficits in children and adolescents sustaining severe closed-head injury*. Presentation at the annual meeting of the Cognitive Neuroscience Society, San Francisco, CA.

McCauley, S. R., & Levin, H. S. (2001). *Prospective memory and executive function in children with severe traumatic brain injury*. Presentation at the 3rd International Conference on Memory (ICOM-3), Valencia, Spain.

McCauley, S. R., & Levin, H. S. (2004). Prospective memory in pediatric traumatic brain injury: A preliminary study. *Developmental Neuropsychology*, *25*, 5–20.

McKinlay, A., Dalrymple-Alford, J. C., Horwood, L. J., & Fergusson, D. M. (2002). Long term psychosocial outcomes after mild head injury in early childhood. *Journal of Neurology, Neurosurgery & Psychiatry*, *73*, 281–288.

Mendelsohn, D., Levin, H. S., Bruce, D., Lilly, M., Harward, H., Culhane, K. A., et al. (1992). Late MRI after head injury in children: Relationship to clinical features and outcome. *Child Nervous System, 8*, 445–452.

Mervis, C. B., Morris, C. A., Bertrand, J., & Robinson, B. F. (1999). Williams syndrome: Findings from an integrated program of research. In H. Tager-Flusberg (Ed.), *Neurodevelopmental disorders* (pp. 65–110). Cambridge, MA: The MIT Press.

Montgomery, J. W. (1995). Sentence comprehension in children with specific language impairment: The role of phonological working memory. *Journal of Speech and Hearing Research, 33*, 187–199.

Moore, B. D., Ater, J. L., & Copeland, D. R. (1992). Improved neuropsychological outcome in children with brain tumors diagnosed during infancy and treated without cranial radiation. *Journal of Child Neurology, 7*, 281–290.

Mortimer, J. A., Snowdon, D. A., & Markesbery, W. R. (2003). Head circumference, education and risk of dementia: Findings from the Nun Study. *Journal of Clinical and Experimental Neuropsychology, 25*, 671–679.

Mostofsky, S. H., Bunoski, R., Morton, M., Goldberg, M. C., & Bastian, A. J. (2004). Children with autism adapt normally during a catching task requiring the cerebellum. *Neurocase, 10*, 60–64.

Mostofsky, S. H., Kunze, J. C., Cutting, L. E., Lederman, H. M., & Denckla, M. B. (2000). Judgment of duration in individuals with ataxia-telangiectasia. *Developmental Neuropsychology, 17*, 63–74.

Mulhern, R. K., Horowitz, M. E., Kovnar, E. H., Langston, J., Sanford, R. A., & Kun, L. E. (1989). Neurodevelopmental status of infants and young children treated for brain tumors with preirradiation chemotherapy. *Journal of Clinical Oncology, 7*, 1660–1666.

Mulhern, R. K., Palmer, S. L., Reddick, W. E., Glass, J. O., Kun, L. E., Taylor, J., et al. (2001). Risks of young age for selected neurocognitive deficits in medulloblastoma are associated with white matter loss. *Journal of Clinical Oncology, 19*, 472–479.

Mulhern, R. K., Reddick, W. E., Palmer, S. L., Glass, J. O., Elkin, T. D., Kun, L. E., et al. (1999). Neurocognitive deficits in medulloblastoma survivors and white matter loss. *Annals of Neurology, 46*, 834–841.

O'Donnell, S., Noseworthy, M., Levine, B., Brandt, M., & Dennis, M. (2005). Cortical thickness of the frontopolar area in typically developing children and adolescents. *Neuroimage, 24*, 948–954.

Osborne, L. R. (1999). Williams-Beuren syndrome: Unraveling the mysteries of a microdeletion disorder. *Molecular Genetics and Metabolism, 67*, 1–10.

Ottensmeier, H., & Kuhl, J. (2000). A retrospective neuropsychological study in children less than 3 years of age with medulloblastoma. In *Proceedings of the IX International Symposium of Pediatric Neuro-Oncology*, San Francisco, CA.

Packer, J. R., Sutton, L. N., Atkins, T. E., Radcliffe, J., Bunin, G. R., D'Angio, G., et al. (1989). A prospective study of cognitive function in children receiving whole-brain radiotherapy and chemotherapy: 2-year results. *Journal of Neurosurgery, 70*, 707–713.

Paquier, P., & Van Dongen, H. R. (1993). Current trends in acquired childhood aphasia: An introduction. *Aphasiology, 7*, 421–440.

Pascual-Leone, A., Amedi, A., Fregni, F., & Merabet, L. B. (2005). The plastic human brain cortex. *Annual Review of Neuroscience, 28*, 377–401.

Posner, M. I., & Cohen, Y. (1984). Components of visual orienting. In H. Bouma &

D. G. Bouwhuis (Eds.), *Attention and performance* (pp. 531–556). Hillsdale, NJ: Lawrence Erlbaum Associates, Inc.

Posner, M. I., Cohen, Y., & Rafal, R. D. (1982). Neural systems control of spatial orienting. *Philosophical Transactions of the Royal Society of London, 298*, 187–198.

Posner, M. I., Rafal, R. D., Choate, L., & Vaughan, J. (1985). Inhibition of return: Neural basis and function. *Cognitive Neuropsychology, 2*, 211–228.

Rao, S. M., Mayer, A. R., & Harrington, D. L. (2001). The evolution of brain activation during temporal processing. *Nature Neuroscience, 4*, 317–323.

Rafal, R. D., & Henik, A. (1994). The neurology of inhibition. In D. Dagenbach & T. H. Carr (Eds.), *Inhibitory processes in attention, memory, and language* (pp. 1–51). San Diego, CA: Academic Press.

Ratterman, M., Spector, L., Grafman, J., Levin, H., & Harwood, H. (2001). Partial and total-order planning: Evidence from normal and prefrontally damaged populations. *Cognitive Science, 25*, 941–975.

Reddick, W. E., Russell, J. M., Glass, J. O., Xiong, X., Mulhern, R. K., Langston, J. W., et al. (2000). Subtle white matter volume differences in children treated for medulloblastoma with conventional or reduced dose craniospinal irradiation. *Magnetic Resonance Imaging, 18*, 787–793.

Reuter-Lorenz, P. A., & Mikels, J. A. (2005). A split-brain model of Alzheimer's disease? Behavioral evidence for comparable intra and interhemispheric decline. *Neuropsychologia, 43*, 1307–1317.

Richards, M., Shipley, B., Fuhrer, R., & Wadsworth, M. (2004). Cognitive ability in childhood and cognitive decline in mid-life: Longitudinal birth cohort study. *British Medical Journal, 328*, 552–556.

Riva, D. (1995). Criteri prognostici neuropsicologici per la scelta del trattamento dei tumori cerebrali infantili [Prognostic neuropsychological criteria for the choice of treatment of infantile cerebral tumors]. *Technical report of the Italian Ministry of Health*. Milan: Italian Ministry of Health.

Riva, D., Giorgi, C., Nichelli, F., Bulgheroni, S., Massimino, M., Cefalo, G., et al. (2002). Intrathecal methotrexate affects higher functions in children with medulloblastoma. *Neurology, 59*, 48–53.

Roberts, W. A. (2002). Are animals stuck in time? *Psychological Review, 128*, 473–489.

Roncadin, C., Guger, S., Archibald, J., Barnes, M., & Dennis, M. (2004). Working memory after mild, moderate, or severe childhood head injury. *Developmental Neuropsychology, 25*, 21–36.

Roncadin, C., Rich, J. B., Pascual-Leone, J., & Dennis, M. (2003). Working memory and inhibitory control after early childhood closed head injury [Abstract]. *Journal of the International Neuropsychological Society, 9*, 141.

Rose, S. E., Chen, F., Chalk, J. B., Zelaya, F. O., Strugnell, W. E., Benson, M., et al. (2000). Loss of connectivity in Alzheimer's disease: An evaluation of white matter tract integrity with colour coded MR diffusion tensor imaging. *Journal of Neurology, Neurosurgery & Psychiatry, 69*, 528–530.

Sapir, A., Soroker, N., Berger, A., & Henik, A. (1999). Inhibition of return in spatial attention: Direct evidence for collicular generation. *Nature Neuroscience, 2*, 1053–1054.

Satz, P. (1993). Brain reserve capacity on symptom onset after brain injury: A formulation and review of evidence for threshold theory. *Neuropsychology, 7*, 273–295.

Schachar, R., Levin, H. S., Max, J. E., Purvis, K., & Chen, S. (2004). Attention deficit hyperactivity disorder symptoms and response inhibition after closed head injury in children: Do preinjury behavior and injury severity predict outcome? *Developmental Neuropsychology, 25,* 179–198.

Scheibel, R. S., & Levin, H. S. (1997). Frontal lobe dysfunction following closed head injury in children: Findings from neuropsychology and brain imaging. In N. A. Krasnegor, G. R. Lyon, & P. S. Goldman-Rakic (Eds.), *Development of the prefrontal cortex: Evolution, neurobiology, and behavior* (pp. 241–260). Baltimore, MD: Paul H. Brookes.

Selzer, S. C., Lindgren, S. D., & Blackman, J. A. (1992). Long-term neuropsychological outcome of high risk infants with intracranial hemorrhage. *Journal of Pediatric Psychology, 17,* 407–422.

Shum, D. (2005). *Prospective memory following traumatic brain injury in children and adolescents.* Presentation at the Joint Mid-Year Meeting of the International Neuropsychology Society, Dublin, Ireland.

Slemmer, J. E., Matser, E. J. T., De Zeeuw, C. I., & Weber, J. T. (2002). Repeated mild injury causes cumulative damage to hippocampal cells. *Brain, 125,* 2699–2709.

Stark, R. E., Bleile, K., Brandt, J., Freeman, J., & Vining, E. P. (1995). Speech-language outcomes of hemispherectomy in children and young adults. *Brain and Language, 51,* 406–421.

Stern, Y. (2002). What is cognitive reserve? Theory and research application of the reserve concept. *Journal of the International Neuropsychological Society, 8,* 448–460.

Stern, Y. (2003). The concept of cognitive reserve: A catalyst for research. *Journal of Clinical and Experimental Neuropsychology, 25,* 589–593.

Stromswold, K., Caplan, D., Alpert, N., & Rausch, S. (1996). Localization of syntactic comprehension by positron emission tomography. *Brain and Language, 52,* 452–473.

Swinney, D., Zurif, E., Prather, P., & Love, T. (1996). Neurological distribution of processing resources underlying language comprehension. *Journal of Cognitive Neuroscience, 8,* 174–184.

Taylor, H. G., & Alden, J. (1997). Age-related differences in outcome following childhood brain injury: An introduction and overview. *Journal of the International Neuropsychological Society, 3,* 555–567.

Taylor, H. G., Minich, N., Bangert, B., Filipek, P. A., & Hack, M. (2004). Long-term neuropsychological outcomes of very low birth weight: Associations with early risks and periventricular insults. *Journal of the International Neuropsychological Society, 10,* 987–1004.

Taylor, H. G., Minich, N. M., Klein, N., & Hack, M. (2004). Longitudinal outcomes of very low birth weight. *Journal of the International Neuropsychological Society, 10,* 1–15.

Taylor, H. G., Schatschneider, C., & Minich, N. M. (2000). Longitudinal outcomes of Haemophilus influenzae meningitis in school-age children. *Neuropsychology, 14,* 509–518.

Taylor, H. G., Yeates, K. O., Wade, S. L., Drotar, D., Stancin, T., & Minich, N. (2002). A prospective study of short- and long-term outcomes after traumatic brain injury in children: Behavior and achievement. *Neuropsychology, 16,* 15–27.

Tulving, E. (2002). Chronesthesia: Conscious awareness of subjective time. In D. T. Stuss & R. T. Knight (Eds.), *Principles of frontal lobe function* (pp. 311–325). New York: Oxford University Press.

Turkstra, L., McDonald, S., & DePompei, R. (2001). Social information processing in adolescents: Data from normally developing adolescents and preliminary data from their peers with traumatic brain injury. *Journal of Head Trauma Rehabilitation, 16,* 469–483.

Vriezen, E. R., & Piggott, S. (2000). Sensitivity of measures of attention to pediatric brain injury. *Brain and Cognition, 44,* 67–82.

Ward, L. (2004). Risk factors for Alzheimer's disease in Down syndrome. In L. M. Glidden (Ed.), *International review of research in mental retardation* (Vol. 29, pp. 63–117). San Diego, CA: Academic Press.

Warschausky, S., Cohen, E. H., Parker, J. G., Levendosky, A. A., & Okun, A. (1997). Social problem-solving skills of children with traumatic brain injury. *Pediatric Rehabilitation, 1,* 77–81.

Wassenberg, R., Max, J. E., Lindgren, S. D., & Schatz, A. (2004). Sustained attention in children and adolescents after traumatic brain injury: Relation to severity of injury, adaptive functioning, ADHD and social background. *Brain Injury, 18,* 751–764.

Wilde, E. A., Hunter, J. V., Newsome, M. R., Scheibel, R. S., Bigler, E. D., Johnson, J., et al. (2005). Frontal and temporal morphometric findings on MRI in children after moderate to severe traumatic brain injury. *Journal of Neurotrauma, 22,* 333–344.

Yeates, K. O. (2000). Closed-head injury. In K. O. Yeates, M. D. Ris, & H. G. Taylor (Eds.), *Pediatric neuropsychology: Research, theory, and practice* (pp. 92–116). New York: Guilford.

Yeates, K. O., Armstrong, K., Janusz, J., Taylor, H. G., Wade, S., Stancin, T., et al. (2005). Long-term attention problems in children with traumatic brain injury. *Journal of the American Academy of Child & Adolescent Psychiatry, 44,* 574–584.

Yeates, K. W., Enrile, B. G., Loss, N., Blumenstein, E., & Delis, D. E. (1995). Verbal learning and memory in children with myelomeningocele. *Journal of Pediatric Psychology, 20,* 801–815.

Yeates, K. O., Swift, E., Taylor, H. G., Wade, S. L., Drotar, D., Stancin, T., et al. (2004). Short- and long-term social outcomes following pediatric traumatic brain injury. *Journal of the International Neuropsychological Society, 10,* 412–426.

Yeates, K. O., Taylor, H. G., Wade, S. L., Drotar, D., Stancin, T., & Minich, N. (2002). A prospective study of short- and long-term neuropsychological outcomes after pediatric traumatic brain injury. *Neuropsychology, 16,* 514–523.

Zahn-Waxler, C., Duggal, S., & Gurber, R. (2002). Parental psychopathology. In M. Bornstein (Ed.), *The handbook of parenting: Social conditions and applied parenting* (2nd ed., Vol. 4, pp. 295–327). Mahwah, NJ: Lawrence Erlbaum Associates, Inc.

5 Traumatic brain injury and cognitive reserve

Erin D. Bigler

At the time of a traumatic brain injury (TBI) a complex array of factors converge to contribute to recovery or the lasting cognitive and neuro-behavioral effects of the injury (Tucker, 2005). Since TBI is an acquired injury, a brain's "health" and overall functional integrity at the time of injury should be key factors in the ultimate effects of the injury. In this context, two obvious factors that relate to outcome are a brain's ability to withstand the initial injury (i.e., protective factors) and its capacity for repair and recovery (i.e., recuperative or promoting factors of healing and adaptation). Such factors relate to a given brain's reserve capacity first to withstand the injury and then to repair itself and potentially recover. Within each general factor are hosts of potential contributing factors that, at any given time, may influence outcome. "Protective" factors were first observed early in the course of animal brain-behavior research, three-quarters of a century ago (see Schulkin, 1989). It was noted that prior to surgical ablation of a given brain structure, pre-surgical experience made a difference in outcome (Schulkin, 1989). Evidently, the amount and type of functional neural networks in place at the time of injury have a bearing on outcome. From a developmental perspective, complex interactions between experience and neural development lead to overall brain development. Therefore, the interaction of neural growth, experience, and the timing and mastery of cognitive abilities relates to opti-mal brain function at any given point in life. If these factors are important in brain development for a given brain to reach optimal levels of function, they are likely also to be important for how a brain responds and recovers when injured. In fact, although not coined in terms of contemporary theories of "cognitive reserve," this was notably part of Karl Lashley's (1950) quest more than 70 years ago in his search for the "engram," the neural locus of memory. At the conclusion of this chapter, the concepts introduced by Lashley are revisited in light of contemporary methods of neuroimaging analysis, cognitive reserve theory, and acquired brain injury.

Reserve theory of brain function also applies to cases of TBI with regard to the remote sequela of the injury, not observed during the recovery and stabilization phase but expressed later in life, sometimes decades after injury. For example, in individuals who have ostensibly recovered from TBI there is an increased risk of developing neuropsychiatric and neurodegenerative disorders later in life (Fann, Burington, Leonetti, Jaffe, Katon, & Thompson, 2004; Jorge, Robinson, Moser, Tateno, Crespo-Facorro, & Arndt, 2004; Murrey, Starzinski, & LeBlanc, 2004; Plassman et al., 2000; Streeter, Van Reekum, Shorr, & Bachman, 1995; Timonen et al., 2002; Tucker, 2005). As such, the brain injury becomes a vulnerability factor for the expression of disorders later in life. These three main topics—protective, promoting and vulnerability factors—provide the theme for discussion of cognitive reserve theory and the effects of TBI. Cognitive reserve has, at times, been used interchangeably with brain reserve and one metric of brain reserve has been overall brain volume. For the purposes of this chapter, the size of the brain and its component structures serve as a marker for reserve capacity, as explained below.

Total brain volume (TBV) and total intracranial volume (TICV) as markers of cognitive reserve

Hominid evolution shows a progression in brain size related to various operational definitions of cognitive complexity (Bruner, 2004; Lefebvre, Reader, & Sol, 2004). The intellectual quotient (IQ) has been a psychometric tool for approximately a century and is widely recognized as one index of cognitive ability, including tasks that assess complex cognitive abilities (Frey & Detterman, 2004; Vernon, Wickett, Bazana, & Stelmack, 2000). In fact, IQ is the best predictor of neuropsychological test performance across a broad band of neuropsychological tests (Diaz-Asper, Schretlen, & Pearlson, 2004). Therefore, from an evolutionary perspective there should be some positive relationship between the size of the organ that gives rise to complex mental functions and complex mental functions however measured. Thus IQ and brain size should be positively related. Interestingly, this concept had to first overcome the pseudoscientific history of phrenology, the critique of which discounted the potential association between the size of an organ like the brain and intellectual ability (Gould, 1996). Thus the relationship between IQ and brain size was not systematically investigated until the late 1980s when Willerman and colleagues first examined the association between total brain volume (TBV) and IQ (Willerman, Schultz, Rutledge, & Bigler, 1991). They observed a positive correlation of approximately .4. Similar findings have now been replicated in numerous studies (Haier, Jung, Yeo, Head, & Alkire, 2004; Ivanovic et al., 2004; Toga & Thompson, 2005; Vernon et al., 2000) and likewise the control of TBV is well established statistical parameter essential to any study examining cognitive ability, brain structure and function (Bigler et al., 2004).

Total intracranial volume (TICV) is a proxy for TBV, a fact that can be readily appreciated by viewing Figure 5.1 from Courchesne et al. (2000). There is a dynamic relationship between brain growth and development and expansion of the cranium. Expanding brain parenchyma stimulates cranial

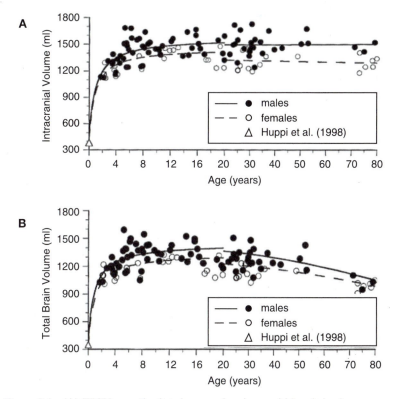

Figure 5.1 (A) TICV growth plots by age, showing rapid head size increase over the first few years of life, but stable TICV after about age 8. (B) TBV growth plots that mirror TICV until after age 20 when subtle volume decreases occur. Used with permission from Courchesne et al. (2000).

vault expansion, reflected in increased head size. The correlation between TBV and TICV in control subjects exceeds .85 (Courchesne et al., 2000; Lainhart, Lazar, Alexander, & Bigler, 2005) and therefore, TICV can be used as a proxy for TBV. Furthermore, since head circumference (HC), typically measured in the occipito-frontal plane or OFC, represents the outer circumference of the skull, it is another proxy for TBV. Because HC measurements are external, and therefore influenced by such things as skull thickness, size of the frontal sinus, hair, and so on, the relationship between HC and TBV is less robust than the TBV–TICV relationship, but is nonetheless positive, where correlations in the .5 range have been reported (Lainhart et al., 2005). In fact, the first demonstration of smaller head size as a risk factor for dementia was the Schofield, Mosesson, Stern, & Mayeux (1995) study that used HC as a proxy for TBV. TICV becomes invariant over the life span (see Figure 5.1), but since its peak value is determined by maximum brain expansion, TICV represents a proxy for original brain volume before the effects of volume loss from aging, disease or disorder reduce peak TBV earlier in life (Lainhart et al., 2005).

The reason that these measures give some index of brain health and reserve can also be appreciated from Figure 5.1. As shown in this figure, at birth TBV is approximately 25% of its adult size, but by age 5, it is 90 to 95% of its adult size. So TBV, TICV and OFC are early markers of brain growth and all three are inexorably interrelated. In other words, a change in one measure affects the other two during the first years of life, and each represents a measure of brain integrity. Accordingly, any adverse events during developmental stages, such as injury, infection, poor nutrition, and so on, would likely be expressed in smaller values (Peterson, 2003; Peterson et al., 2000). Indeed, it is well established that prematurity, early stroke, brain infection or TBI result in not only reduced brain volume (Cooke, 2005) but lower IQ levels (Grunau, Whitfield, & Fay, 2004), where the children never get back to levels seen in age-matched controls (Cooke, 2005; Cooke & Foulder-Hughes, 2003). Smaller brain volume later in childhood in those receiving whole brain radiation as part of their treatment for cerebral neoplasm is associated with greater cognitive deficits (Mulhern, Merchant, Gajjar, Reddick, & Kun, 2004). Relatedly, TICV and TBV have been found to be significantly smaller in childhood neuropsychiatric disorders including schizophrenia and attention deficit hyperactivity disorder (ADHD), the interpretation of such findings being related to some adverse effects early in brain development (Gogtay et al., 2004; Thompson et al., 2004). Of particular interest in these associations is that IQ in these neuropsychiatric groups is found to be lower than in matched cohorts without neuropsychiatric disorder (Badcock, Dragovic, Waters, & Jablensky, 2005; Hervey, Epstein, & Curry, 2004; Toulopoulou et al., 2004). Also, there are genetic disorders, manifested in part by deficits in brain growth and head size, that relate to deficits in intellectual level (i.e., microcephaly) (Lainhart et al., 2005). From a cognitive reserve perspective optimal brain growth is also influenced by experience, including the complexity of the environment and adequacy of the diet (Ivanovic et al., 2004). For example, in animal models, optimal brain growth, when all other factors are controlled but the enrichment of the environment, occurs in those exposed to enriched environments (Levitt, 2003). Thus the relationship between experience, neural function and brain growth sets the stage for TBV as an index of cognitive reserve. So a "healthy" brain exposed to the most favorable cognitive and behavioral experiences while simultaneously tolerating typical adverse consequences of childhood (i.e., routine illnesses, infections, etc.), represents a brain that may be optimized from a cognitive reserve standpoint and, therefore, the most resilient when injury occurs. Since peak TBV and TICV occur prior to puberty and OFC is set prior to adulthood, these markers, when used to study cognitive reserve, reflect the cumulative effects of diverse factors potentially affecting the function of the brain.

TBV and the intellectual quotient (IQ)

As already mentioned, in 1991 Willerman et al. published the first study using magnetic resonance imaging (MRI) to assess the relationship between TBV and IQ, where TBV was positively related to IQ. This has now been replicated by numerous studies (Vernon et al., 2000). Recently, Haier et al. (2004, 2005) demonstrated the importance of frontal and temporal regions in their contribution to TBV–IQ relationships, which had been demonstrated earlier by Flashman, Andreasen, Flaum, and Swayze (1998). If diverse cognitive functions that underlie what is psychometrically assessed by IQ tests relate positively to TBV, this merely underscores the importance of optimal brain development in understanding the neural basis of cognition (Deary & Caryl, 1997; Isaacs, Edmonds, Chong, Lucas, Morley, & Gadian, 2004).

TBI and TBV

Moderate-to-severe TBI has been consistently shown to result in reduced overall brain volume (Bigler, 2001b; Bigler, 2005). In fact, it has been estimated that the average volume loss associated with severe TBI is a 50 cm^3 reduction in brain parenchyma, which is an astonishing figure when one considers the complexity of brain function and that billions of synapses reside in one cubic millimeter (Bigler, 2001a). MacKenzie et al. (2002), in a within-subjects prospective study of brain volume, found subtle volume loss even in cases of mild TBI. Figures 5.2 and 5.3, taken from a patient who sustained a severe TBI, graphically show the reduction in brain volume and the global atrophic processes that occur over time following a brain injury. Brain imaging studies prior to injury were available so the patient acts as his own control in demonstrating the principle that acquired cerebral atrophy in TBI is reflected as overall brain volume loss. Figure 5.2 also demonstrates the calculation of a common metric to measure brain atrophy—the ventricle-to-brain ratio or VBR (Bigler et al., 2004), which has also been used in studies of cognitive reserve in cases of TBI. As a ratio, the VBR automatically adjusts for head size differences. Because of the considerable heterogeneity in head size, and since head size is also related to sex and overall physical size, significant confounds occur when TBV is not corrected for head size differences. Figure 5.4 shows the age-dependent increase in VBR from age 16 to over 90 in control subjects without neuropsychiatric disorder. As distinctly reflected in Figure 5.4 a "normal" brain volume loss occurs in healthy individuals as they age. Returning to Figure 5.2 and comparing this patient's VBR of 3.43 to those subjects in his decade of life (35–45), where the normal VBR value should be under 2.0 (standard deviation of 0.5), the VBR in this TBI patient is indicative of massive tissue loss as a consequence of the brain injury. This is also easily appreciated in Figure 5.3 where the three-dimensional depiction of the ventricle is presented and compared to that of an age-matched control.

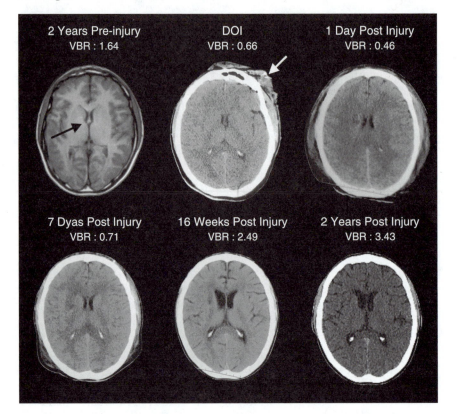

Figure 5.2 Neuroimaging depiction of cerebral atrophy is unmistakably identified in this sequential series of scans. The image in the upper left was obtained 2 years prior to sustaining a TBI, when the patient underwent routine head MRI (inverted T2 image) as part of an evaluation for headaches. The arrow points to the normal size of the ventricle, pre-injury. Pre-injury VBR was well within normal limits for age (see Figure 5.4). Computerized tomography clearly shows diffuse edema on the day of injury (DOI) scan where the VBR is reduced to 0.66 because of massive brain swelling. Note that most cortical sulci are indistinct, also a reflection of generalized cerebral edema. The arrow points to focal extracerebral edema in the frontal region where the patient sustained a blow to the head, resulting in extensive swelling as well. Note by 1 day post-injury, the patient's VBR has been reduced to 0.46, but begins to recover by 1 week post-injury. However, by 16 weeks post-injury VBR has markedly increased with clear dilation of the ventricular system. By 2 years post-injury, even greater cerebral atrophy has taken place, where the VBR is approaching six standard deviations above what is normal for age.

As a general principle the more severe the injury the greater the likelihood of the presence of diffuse damage and generalized parenchymal volume loss as reflected in increased VBR. Similarly, VBR as an expression of global damage also relates to cognitive outcome, where increased VBR is typically

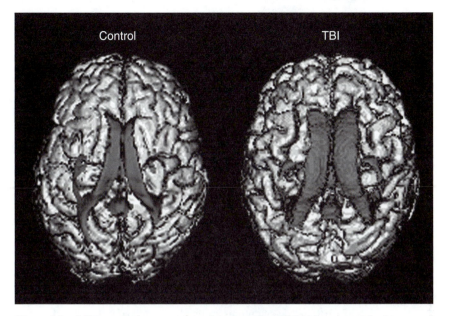

Figure 5.3 3-D ventricular reconstruction depicting TBI-induced ventricular expansion is presented in this dorsal view of the brain on the right, from the patient described in Figure 5.2, compared to the age-matched control subject on the left. Note that all aspects of the ventricular system are dilated.

associated with worse cognitive and neurobehavioral functioning (Bigler, 2005). Because of these features, brain volume and/or VBR are excellent metrics to test cognitive reserve theories as they relate to TBI.

TBV as an indicator of cognitive reserve

As introduced above, many diverse, complicated and intertwined factors influence optimal brain growth. However, it is safe to assume that some factors that promote optimal brain growth and cognitive development also likely optimize the brain against injury. For example, from conception to just prior to birth, neurogenesis and neuropil development occur at astonishing rates (Levitt, 2003), with remarkable neural organization occurring within a short time span. For that organization to be optimized there has to be an orchestration between neurogenesis and apoptosis and the establishment and functionality of almost an infinite number of synapses. When this process occurs optimally it could be theorized that it also confers some ability for that brain to either better withstand an injury or, once injured, have a greater capacity for recovery and/or reorganization. The intrauterine environment is a challenge for the fetus and if that is successfully mastered, the next challenge occurs—birth. In fact, the theory of redundancy and adaptability

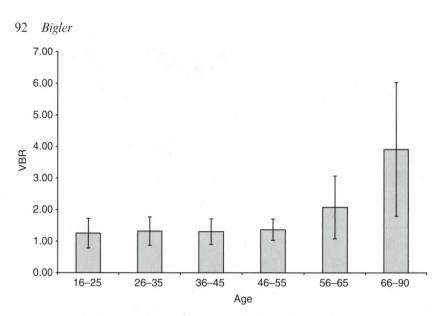

Figure 5.4   Plotting VBR by age shows a relatively stable ventricular volume to brain volume ratio until middle age in normal controls who have no neurologic or psychiatric symptoms and had volunteered to be part of a comparison group for studies involving aging and dementia (see Bigler et al., 2000; Blatter et al., 1995). However, starting in the mid-50s, VBR starts to change significantly, reflecting age-related brain volume loss, basically associated simply with aging. Accordingly, injury from cerebral trauma that occurs in the older individual is happening in a brain that has already lost volume. If volume is a proxy for brain reserve then the diminished volume would result in greater vulnerability of the brain to injury.

of the infant brain at the time of birth has long been assumed to represent a protective factor related to survivability and the inevitability of brain damage occurring during *any* birth (Towbin, 1978; Villablanca, Carlson-Kuhta, Schmanke, & Hovda, 1998). Natural birth is considered a traumatic event and the mechanical distortion of the skull as it passes through the birth canal likely exposes the infant brain to its first chance for a traumatic injury (Towbin, 1978). So how the brain meets the first challenge of birth becomes an important factor in a brain's reserve capacity (Adelson, Dixon, & Kochanek, 2000). In fact from an evolutionary perspective, there probably has been some selection between manageable head size for exiting the birth canal that produces the least injury, since large fetal head size is associated with greater injury (Nassar, Usta, Khalil, Melhem, Nakad, & Abu Musa, 2003; Raio et al., 2003) but head size must be large enough to result in optimal brain growth after birth, particularly in the first year. For those with perinatal complications such as hypoxic brain injury, traumatic birth, prematurity and low-birth weight are all known risk factors associated with smaller brain volume and greater risks for cognitive sequela (Cooke, 2005; Grunau et al., 2004; Marlow, Wolke, Bracewell, & Samara, 2005; Peterson,

2003; Peterson et al., 2000). In fact, Abernethy, Palaniappan, and Cooke (2002) demonstrated that the presence of any lesion was associated with lower IQ, and that caudate volume positively correlated with IQ. From the reserve standpoint, optimal size occurs because during the pre- and perinatal periods of early brain development multiple potentially adverse biological and environmental factors were successfully navigated, resulting in maximum brain development.

Once life begins independent of the womb, a host of environmental influences are at play including illness, diet and stress-mediated factors. Illness is important because it is well known that high fevers increase the risk of febrile seizures, and history of febrile seizures is associated with various neurological sequelae (MacDonald, Johnson, Sander, & Shorvon, 1999; Sulzbacher, Farwell, Temkin, Lu, & Hirtz, 1999). Experimental models of febrile epilepsy show subtle changes in neural function at a pathological cellular level in otherwise healthy appearing brains, particularly at the temporal lobe level (Dube, da Silva Fernandes, & Nehlig, 2001). This implies that subtle environmental effects like fever can have a deleterious effect on brain function and development, which could detract from any reserve potential (see MacDonald et al., 1999). Several studies have also demonstrated that adverse psychosocial stressors may also impact brain development, including brain volume (King, Ferris, & Lederhendler, 2003). Ivanovic et al. (2004) have shown the relationship between poor diet, lower brain volume and reduced IQ. Thus, just as with the intrauterine environment, post-birth is fraught with many challenges to be overcome for optimal postnatal brain growth. However, as shown in Figure 5.1, peak TBV and TICV occur early in childhood, so from a cognitive reserve standpoint, when TICV is used, it is a reflection of the cumulative influences of brain development before puberty.

Cognitive reserve, brain size, pre-experience as a protective factor and TBI

The edited text by Schulkin (1989) reviewed numerous studies on pre-injury factors that influence outcome after brain injury. However, of the 14 chapters, only one dealt with any aspect of pre-injury factors related to outcome in humans after TBI (Grafman, Lalonde, Litvan, & Fedio, 1989). The only major previous human study that attempted to systematically address pre-morbid factors in post-injury outcome was Weinstein and Teuber (1957), where using army data on education and ability testing prior to injury they evaluated the relationship of pre-injury education and intelligence; however, these factors were not very predictive of outcome in their study (see also Teuber, 1972). Of course, Teuber's work was done prior to any contemporary imaging and, likewise, prior to current concepts in cognitive neuroscience and recovery of function. Grafman et al. (1989) explored pre-morbid factors more systematically, including various quantitative methods of brain image analysis examining the effects of the size and location of the lesion on recovery of function. Grafman et al. found that after controlling for size and location of acquired injuries to the brain: "Premorbid level of cognitive ability remains the most powerful factor in predicting postinjury level of recovery" (p. 299). This has also been demonstrated in more recent research (Salazar, Schwab, & Grafman, 1995). Grafman et al. (1989) speculated that the reason for the positive influence of pre-morbid ability on post-morbid recovery following TBI was the potential for neural redundancy in information processing systems, so that if one system is injured others could assume a compensatory role.

Seshadri et al. (2004), as part of a long-term longitudinal study of aging, examined "participants who where free of clinical stroke and dementia" (p. 1591), measuring TBV and assessing their cognitive status on a variety of neuropsychological measures. They observed that smaller TBV was associated with poorer cognitive function in general. From a brain reserve perspective, this could be interpreted as smaller brain volume being associated with less cognitive reserve.

Assuming a relationship between pre-injury ability level, TBV and cognitive function, Bigler, Johnson, and Blatter (1999) performed a retrospective analysis of 33 cases of moderate-to-severe TBI. All subjects received standard IQ testing and underwent a uniform MR imaging protocol that included quantitative MRI measures. Not surprisingly, those with more severe intellectual deficits had greater overall atrophy (i.e. smaller TBV) and specifically had more prominent temporal lobe atrophy. However, what was particularly interesting from a cognitive reserve standpoint and the earlier work by Grafman et al. (1989), was that those with post-injury IQ scores at or below 90 (i.e. low average) as a group had the smallest TICV. This group with the lowest IQ scores after moderate-to-severe TBI also had the smallest TBV, consistent with what the brain reserve hypothesis would predict: smaller TICV and TBV would be most likely associated with greater lowering of IQ following brain injury.

While the Bigler et al. (1999) study inferred a role of cognitive reserve in TBI, it was not designed to control for actual pre-injury cognitive status. As a follow-up, a larger group of TBI patients ($N = 59$), some of whom were in the original Bigler et al. (1999) study, were contacted post-injury by Kesler and Colleagues (Kesler, Adams, Blasey, & Bigler, 2003). They attempted to get standardized academic testing, most typically the American College Testing Program or ACT scores that were performed in high school, and use the overall achievement score as an index of pre-injury cognitive ability. Since these types of standardized tests have a significant positive relationship with IQ (Frey & Detterman, 2004), they represent an excellent index of pre-injury IQ. Knowing the pre-injury IQ estimate it was possible to calculate a standardized change score of pre-injury IQ to post-injury level. For those post-TBI who had IQ scores 90 or above, their change in IQ scores, based on pre-injury estimates from standardized achievement testing, was less than those with IQ scores less than 90, but what was most interesting about this group with IQ scores below 90 was that their TICV was significantly smaller. These findings would be fitting with the cognitive reserve hypothesis that having a larger brain resulted in less difference between pre-morbid and post-morbid IQ following TBI, and overall higher TICV was associated with having post-injury IQ scores above 90. Thus, from a brain reserve perspective, the Kesler et al. (2003) study supports the notion that smaller pre-morbid brain size and lowered achievement ability result in greater vulnerability in terms of neuropsychological outcome from TBI.

Pre-injury factors that increase the vulnerability of TBI

Fann, Leonetti, Jaffe, Katon, Cummings, and Thompson (2002) used a case control method to study the potential influence of prior psychiatric illness and subsequent brain injury, where they found the relative risk significantly elevated, concluding that "psychiatric illness appears to be associated with an increased risk for TBI" (p. 615). Obviously, complex factors are at play, but one may be diminished cognitive reserve in those with psychiatric disorder resulting in greater likelihood for TBI being expressed when injury occurs. Farmer, Kanne, Haut, Williams, Johnstone, & Kirk (2002) tested this in a more direct manner by examining the outcome of TBI in children who had been previously diagnosed with a learning deficit (LD). Those with well-defined learning deficits, from well-documented assessments done prior to brain injury, had worse outcome following TBI than injury-matched controls who did not have an LD when injured. These types of outcomes would be predicted from the cognitive reserve theory as it relates to TBI. This type of vulnerability would also suggest that following TBI, there would be a greater likelihood of expression of neuropsychiatric disorder, which is also the case (see Levin et al., 2004; Bombardier, Machamer, Fann, & Temkin Dikmen, 2004).

Latent or delayed effects of TBI on neurobehavioral and neuropsychiatric status

To understand the long-term latent effects of TBI, it is important to briefly review its typical underlying neuropathology. As already mentioned, there is a diffuse component to TBI particularly at the level of moderate-to-severe injury. This observation is supported by post-mortem (Graham, Gennarelli, & McIntosh, 2002) as well as numerous imaging studies (see Bigler, 2005). A major component of this diffuse damage is white matter pathology (Wu et al., 2004), which can be generalized and nonspecific. However, what is also clear is that there is greater vulnerability for damage to frontal, temporal and limbic regions of the brain (Bigler, Anderson, & Blatter, 2002; Hurley, Hayman, Puryear, & Goldstein, 1995). The selectivity of frontotemporo-limbic damage is critical in understanding the initial as well as long-term effects of brain injury. The most common sequelae associated with TBI have been summarized as reduced processing speed (Mathias, Beall, & Bigler, 2004; Mathias, Bigler et al., 2004), impaired short-term memory (Vakil, 2005), and reduced executive functioning (Scheibel et al., 2003; Suchy, Leahy, Sweet, & Lam, 2003) along with changes in personality and temperament (Salazar et al., 1995; Swanson, Rao, Grafman, Salazar, & Kraft, 1995). Of particular interest is that the sequelae just listed have, independent of TBI studies, been shown to be at least partly dependent on frontotemporolimbic regions. The associations become even more important when one examines the type of neuropsychiatric disorders that increase in frequency after TBI, such as major depression, anxiety and stress-mediated disorders, obsessive-compulsive disorder and schizophrenia to list the most prominent (Fann et al., 2004; Fann et al., 2002; Holsinger et al., 2002; Jaskiw & Kenny, 2002; Jorge et al., 2004; Tucker, 2005). What is particularly interesting about these studies is that they have examined the long-term sequelae wherein TBI patients have ostensibly "recovered" or at least reached some level of post-injury stability, but subsequently develop neuropsychiatric disorders or dementia. One interpretation of such findings is that the brain injury creates "vulnerability" for later expression of a disorder given the right interface of environmental and genetic effects. Accordingly, having a brain injury increases the risk for later in life neuropsychiatric disorder.

One particularly interesting factor associated with TBI and dementia later in life (Bachman, Green, Benke, Cupples, & Farrer, 2003; Plassman et al., 2000), is that at a molecular level, brain injury results in increased deposition of beta-amyloid (Blasko et al., 2004; Bramlett, Kraydieh, Green, & Dietrich, 1997; Chen et al., 2004; Olsson et al., 2004; Verhoeff et al., 2004). This same pathology is found in Alzheimer's disease, where the senile plaques diagnostic of Alzheimer's disease are largely composed of aggregated beta-amyloid (Verhoeff et al., 2004). Futhermore, Ikonomovic et al. (2004) undertook histological analysis of actual excised temporal cortex following TBI and further documented a variety of Alzheimer's-like neuropathology. Thus the connection between brain injury and subsequent dementing disorders may be related to how a particular brain handles the biochemical and neuro-pathological cascade of damage and repair, which undoubtedly relates in some fashion to that brain's "reserve" ability.

Normal aging and prior TBI

The brain changes with age, both in structure and function (Richter & Richter, 2003). As discussed elsewhere in this text, those who age optimally have successfully navigated various challenges to the integrity of the brain throughout their life span. Living longer and intactly implies better brain reserve capabilities. This also probably applies to factors that relate to TBI. Any factor that adversely impacts the health of the brain, such as a brain injury, would have a deleterious effect on successful aging (Colantonio, Ratcliff, Chase, & Vernich, 2004). In fact, prior TBI is associated with shorter life span and there is also an association between lower levels of cognitive ability and mortality later in life (Kuh, Richards, Hardy, Butterworth, & Wadsworth, 2004). At one level this means that those with better reserve and longevity probably withstood any minor central nervous system insults or threats. At another level though, there would be a "cost" to using any reserve to combat injury or illness. In that sense, prior brain injury would be more likely to result in adverse influences on aging, particularly late in the aging process when it would be hypothesized that the greatest reserves would be necessary to promote the most successful aging.

There are numerous metrics that can be applied to successful aging, but since decline in memory is one of the most common occurrences associated with "normal" aging (Salthouse, 2004) and is also the most common sequela of TBI (Vakil, 2005), it would be hypothesized that prior TBI would be associated with an accelerated expression of memory disorders in aging. As impressively demonstrated by Salthouse (2004) "normal" aging is associated with reduced memory performance as distinctly illustrated in Figure 5.5. From a neurological perspective, however, what is also impressive is that "normal" age-mediated reduction in TBV as well as mesial temporal lobe structures also matches this rate of decline (Bigler et al., 2002; Bigler & Snyder, 1995; Raz, Rodrigue, Head, Kennedy, & Acker, 2004). So what Salthouse demonstrates in Figure 5.5 is most likely the actual neurocognitive reflection of underlying so-called "normal" loss of brain parenchyma in

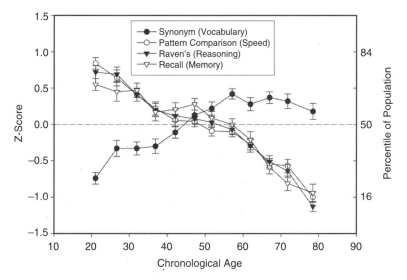

Figure 5.5   The inexorable decline in some cognitive functions is plotted over the lifespan, depicting decrease in memory function with age in normal aging individuals. From Salthouse (2004). If certain cognitive functions steadily decrease with age, then it is likely that brain injury to critical structures of memory later in life will have a greater effect because ability level is diminished to begin with.

structures critical for memory processes. It would also stand to reason that anything that accelerated pathology or damage to such brain regions would adversely disrupt this slow, subtle but inexorable change in brain structure and cognition. By age 65 the beginnings of a more rapid volume loss begins to occur in some structures. For example Raz et al. (2004) have shown approximately 0.33% per annum reduction in the hippocampus. At one level, that may not seem like much, but when one considers that a single hippocampal neuron has been estimated (see Levitan & Kaczmarek, 2001) to have in excess of 10,000 synaptic connections (and of course, an almost limitless manner in which a single neuron could interact with other neurons via these synaptic connections) any loss has the potential to impact function.

The susceptibility of temporal lobe damage from TBI may explain the long-term effects of TBI and the natural aging of the temporal lobe (Tucker, 2005). In a large study that examined risk of epilepsy over a 30-year time span post-injury, Annegers, Hauser, Coan, and Rocca (1998) clearly demonstrated prior moderate to severe head injury increased the lifetime probability of developing epilepsy (see Figure 1 in Annegers et al., 1998). Studies also clearly show that over the life span, history of seizures has an adverse impact of cognitive and neurobehavioral function (Oyegbile et al., 2004). From a cognitive reserve perspective, because the interaction effect of having epilepsy or even sub-clinical seizure-like effects would adversely impact aging, the longer the duration of epilepsy, the greater the likelihood of impaired cognitive functioning. The longer duration of active epilepsy would also mean increased likelihood for the total number of seizures, and the total number of seizures has an adverse effect on cognitive abilities (Dodrill & Matthews, 1992; Fastenau Shen, Dunn, Perkins, Hermann, & Austin, 2004). In a nicely done study by Oyegbile et al. (2004), 96 patients with temporal lobe epilepsy were compared to rigorously matched control subjects that did not differ on various standard demographic factors. As would be predicted by the cognitive reserve theory, duration of epilepsy was positively related to the proportion of abnormal neuropsychological test scores (see Figure 5.6a) and less education, as a marker for less cognitive reserve, was associated with increased cognitive morbidity (see Figure 5.6b). Since the disruptive effects of temporal lobe epilepsy on cognition occur in large part through their effects on the hippocampus and amygdala (Weniger, Boucsein, & Irle, 2004), from the perspective of the reserve hypothesis it takes little speculation to see the connection to prior head injury, the vulnerability of hippocampus and amygdala in head injury, increased risk of seizures, and the potential for adverse long-terms effects of the brain injury.

Lastly, if cognitive reserve is diminished over the aging process, then it would be predicted that brain injury later in life would likely result in greater deficits, once severity of injury was controlled. In fact, this is generally the case, where greater cognitive sequelae are associated with older age (Dunning et al., 2004; Goldstein, Levin, Goldman, Clark, & Altonen, 2001; Sandhir, Puri, Klein, & Berman, 2004). Along these lines, diminished brain reserve

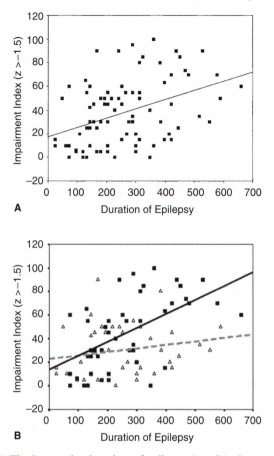

Figure 5.6 (A) The longer the duration of epilepsy (*x* axis), the greater the level of cognitive impairment (*y* axis); however, (B) the effect is lessened in those with greater education (open triangles, dashed line have > 12 years formal education) when compared to those with less education (dark squares, solid line have ≤ 12 years formal education). Cognitive impairment is based on a *z*-score deviation derived from the proportion of tests scores performed in the impaired range. Used with permission from Oyegbile et al. (2004).

from TBI and its associated risks with such medical problems as seizures would be predicted to shorten mortality, which in fact has been shown (Harrison-Felix, Whiteneck, DeVivo, Hammond, & Jha, 2004). More interestingly, however, is the study by Brown, Leibson, Malec, Perkins, Diehl, and Larson (2004) that also demonstrated increased mortality in TBI victims, that was dose-dependent on severity of injury, including a small, but nonetheless significant, reduction in long-term survival of those with mild TBI (see also Brown, Leibson, & Malec, 2005).

Cognitive reserve models as heuristics for the study of prior TBI and aging

Testable hypotheses represent the hallmark of scientific progress. Cognitive reserve theory offers many testable hypotheses in the study of the effects of TBI.

As an example what follows is a cognitive reserve heuristic that speculates on the impact of hippocampal damage early in life and for function later in life. The essence of this hypothesis is that brain injury damages the hippocampus, resulting in smaller hippocampal volumes (Bigler et al., 2002). Because the hippocampus is one of the temporal lobe structures that shows a significant age-mediated decrease even in healthy aging (Raz et al., 2004), cognitive reserve theory would predict that those with TBI-induced hippocampal atrophy early in life would exhibit a different course over the aging process. This could explain, in part, why there is a relationship between TBI and Alzheimer's. From a cognitive reserve perspective the *interaction* between aging and TBI would be predicted to produce greater deficits than just aging alone. Since the peak years of TBI occurrence are between the ages of 15 and 35 (Kraus & Chu, 2005), cognitive reserve theory would speculate that these individuals would, in fact, do worse as they age. Since organized and systematic acute, sub-acute and chronic care for TBI victims is a relatively new phenomena (circa the 1970s), life span data are simply not available at this time to fully test such hypotheses in prospective studies. For example, Corkin, Rosen, Sullivan, and Clegg (1989) found that those veterans with brain injury deteriorated faster by their 50s and 60s than their age-matched cohorts in a study involving military related penetrating brain injuries incurred during combat in World War II. More recently, in a prospective study, some support for more rapid deterioration with aging also was found by Millar, Nicoll, Thornhill, Murray, and Teasdale (2003). They followed TBI patients for up to 25 years post-injury, most of whom were injured in childhood and adolescence and the mean age at follow-up was 42.1 years. Thus the mean age was considerably lower than the subjects in the Corkin et al. study, and much younger than the typical age range associated with age-mediated memory decline (i.e., above 65 years of age); nonetheless, the follow-up by Millar et al. (2003) did find some support for age-mediated decline associated with prior brain injury. Guided by these findings and returning to the use of cognitive reserve as a heuristic, the discussion that follows provides a testable neuroimaging hypothesis that may explain the more rapid deterioration in memory and related cognitive function when a brain injury has occurred earlier in life.

If TBI selectively damages the hippocampus (Bigler et al., 1997; Tomaiuolo et al., 2004), yet the hippocampus is also one of those structures sensitive to age-related changes (Bigler et al., 2002), particularly late in life (Driscoll et al., 2003; Raz et al., 2004), it would be hypothesized that having earlier TBI and hippocampal volume loss would, in fact, predispose an individual to more rapid volume loss than would have occurred had the injury not happened. Similarly, if reduced hippocampal volume relates to memory performance (Cohen-Gadol, Westerveld, Alvarez-Carilles, & Spencer, 2004; Serra-Grabulosa, Junque, Verger, Salgado-Pineda, Maneru, & Mercader, 2005) and the expression of neuropsychiatric disorders (Gilbertson et al., 2002), the more rapidly the hippocampus declines in volume the greater the impact on memory function. Figure 5.7 takes a large cohort of young TBI victims, 35 years of age and under, from the Bigler et al. (2002) study and plots, as a group, their actual hippocampal volume and then their *expected* reduction in hippocampal volume from aging. Using other studies of aging and the hippocampus (Bigler et al., 2000; Bigler & Tate, 2001; Bigler et al., 2003) the typical trajectory of subtle hippocampal volume loss is also plotted over time in a cohort of non-TBI, normal controls. For average hippocampal volume in Alzheimer's disease (AD) patients, for those 65 and older another cohort of dementia subjects is used, since hippocampal

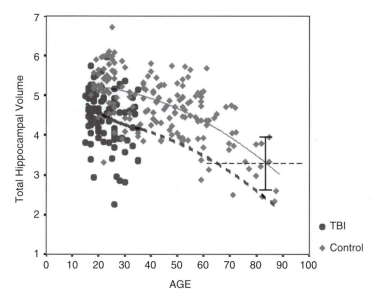

Figure 5.7 Diamonds represent hippocampal volume from age 16 to 88 years of age, taken from Bigler et al. (2002, 1997, 2000). Note that hippocampal volume does decline with age. Solid dots represent hippocampal volume in patients with TBI. Note that volume is reduced. Only TBI subjects 35 years of age and younger were included, because the least amount of age-related change in hippocampal volume occurs in those age ranges. Using the same slope projected by "normal" aging, merely lowered because in TBI subjects hippocampal volume is less, due to atrophy, the volume of the hippocampus in the projected "aging" TBI cohort crosses the mean volume of patients with AD somewhere around age 65. The vertical bar represents the mean hippocampal volume in AD subjects with a mean age of 82 from the Cache County Memory and Aging Project (Bigler et al., 2000).

atrophy is one of the defining features of the disorder (Kramer et al., 2004). In the "normal" aging process, those in the original control group would not be projected to "cross-over" to a range where the hippocampal atrophy of "normal" aging matched the hippocampal volume of those with AD until somewhere around age 83 (vertical solid line, s. d. reflected by the whiskers). In contrast, as a group, assuming the same rate of decline over time, the TBI patients would "cross-over" about 15 to 20 years earlier. Such a scenario may in fact be one of the reasons why prior TBI is a risk factor for dementia, as shown by Plassman et al. (2000), where there is a dose–response association with prior brain injury and risk of later in life dementia, where more severe injury further increases the risk.

Another interesting factor, genetics, complicates this issue to an even greater degree. One of the most thoroughly examined genetic risk factors for AD is the Apolipoprotein E (APOE) gene. Presence of the ε4 allele has been associated with development of AD (Breitner et al., 1999; Huang, Qiu, von Strauss, Winblad, & Fratiglioni, 2004), although the relationship between prior head injury, APOE genotype and risk for dementia is complex (Chamelian, Reis, & Feinstein, 2004; Jellinger, 2004; Koponen et al., 2004; Mayeux, 2004; Millar et al., 2003). Nonetheless some studies have shown presence of the APOE ε4 allele may be associated with lower memory function (Bondi et al., 1995; Deary & Caryl, 1997). From a cognitive reserve perspective, Mayeux and colleagues (Mayeux, 2004; Mayeux et al., 1995) demonstrated an interaction effect between presence of the APOE ε4 allele, TBI and the risk of AD. Plassman et al. (1997), in a study of identical twins with and without the ε4 allele who were also asymptomatic for dementia, demonstrated that those with the ε4 allele had smaller hippocampi. Smaller hippocampi have been associated with less memory ability (Serra-Grabulosa et al., 2005) and as Raz et al. (2004) have shown, late in life smaller hippocampi may predispose one to memory impairment. It is also interesting to note that small hippocampi may be a critical factor in the evolution of neuropsychiatric symptomology after stress (Gilbertson et al., 2002), which may also be a risk factor for development of dementia. So from a heuristic standpoint, the cognitive reserve hypothesis would predict that the interaction of genetic risk *and* brain injury would put those with less cognitive reserve at risk, ultimately leading to worse outcome.

In another recent demonstration of the potential role of genetics and cognitive outcome in TBI, McAllister, Rhodes, Flashman, McDonald, Belloni, and Saykin (2005) examined the dopamine D2 receptor T allele on response latency after mild TBI. Possessing the T allele was found to be associated with worse neuropsychological outcome. This is an excellent example, showing genetic vulnerability as part of the explanation between two groups, one with better and the other with worse outcome, but both with ostensibly the same level of initial brain injury.

Animal studies show that older animals have increased vulnerability to injury (Hoane, Lasley, & Akstulewicz, 2004). Accordingly, returning to

Figure 5.7. It would be predicted that if "normal" aging results in hippo-campal atrophy *and* decline in episodic memory, *and* TBI selectively injures the hippocampus, TBI that occurs later in life should result in a different recovery curve and outcome in older individuals compared to when injury occurs earlier in life. This has been reported in several studies. In particular, simply being older than 65 significantly increases the risk of adverse sequelae associated with even mild TBI (Dunning et al., 2004; Mosenthal et al., 2004; Shavelle, Strauss, Whyte, Day, & Yu, 2001). From a mortality standpoint there is greater risk for loss of life following a TBI (Shavelle et al., 2001).

Lastly, even in severe TBI, some patients recover. Research, using cognitive reserve models, should focus on what variables relate to outcome. For example, Nybo, Sainio, and Muller (2004) followed children who sustained moderate-to-severe TBI as preschoolers, but were followed-up in adulthood. Two thirds of the brain injured individuals remained impaired, but one third had been able to achieve and maintain employment. It could be argued that maintenance of employment is another potential important factor in cogni-tive reserve and outcome. Another childhood study, by Tasker et al. (2005), has shown that early brain injury results in smaller brain and hippocampal growth at approximately 5 years post-injury. If TBI results in smaller ultimate hippocampal volume, this would implicate greater vulnerability of this struc-ture with the aging process, which also results in volume reduction. Rempel-Clower, Zola, Squire, and Amaral (1996) have shown that dense amnesia occurs once hippocampal volume is reduced below 40% of its original volume. Thus anything that leads to reducing hippocampal volume likely increases the adverse consequences of the aging process.

Mild TBI (mTBI) and cognitive reserve

If all concussions were totally benign, then a prior concussion from which an individual purportedly has "recovered" should not increase the likelihood of recurrent concussion (see also McAllister, 2005). However, the independent studies by Guskiewicz et al. (2003) and Schulz et al. (2004) clearly found that prior concussion significantly increased the likelihood of a subsequent concussion in North American collegiate football players (also see Creeley, Wozniak, Bayly, Olney, & Lewis, 2004; Munirathinam & Bahr, 2004). This should not be surprising since mTBI has been shown to result in subtle neuropathology, particularly at the level of white matter (Bigler, 2004; Goetz, Blamire, Rajagopalan, Cadoux-Hudson, Young, & Styles, 2004). Also, animal models have demonstrated the cumulative effects of repetitive brain injury (Raghupathi, 2004; Slemmer, Matser, De Zeeuw, & Weber, 2002). Thus, if injury occurs from concussion, reserve theory would predict that a subsequent injury would be superimposed on existing pathology, where recovery took place via alternate systems that were adaptive, but not as resilient as the primary, non-injured brain. This circumstance would also predict that in performing cognitive functions, during attentional and working memory tasks, mTBI patients would have to recruit more neural resources to maintain a similar level of performance when compared to non-injured controls. This, in fact, has been demonstrated by McAllister et al. (1999) and Chen, Kareken, Fastenau, Trexler, and Hutchins (2003) using functional neuroimaging. This also has been observed in human immuno-deficiency virus (HIV) infected individuals with minor attention/concentration problems (Chang et al., 2004), where the brain injury comes via infection rather than trauma, but results in a similar effect.

Substance abuse prior to and at the time of injury

Returning to the animal literature, pre-treatment with drugs that promote excitoxicity at the time of injury results in worse long-term outcome (Kleim, Jones, & Schallert, 2003). The analog in humans may be drug or alcohol use at the time of injury. Using this hypothesis, Wilde and colleagues (2005) examined morphological and neuropsychological outcome comparing those with history of alcohol abuse at the time of injury with those without such history. This study focused on TBI victims under 45 years of age, so that the long-term adverse effects of alcoholism could be avoided. This is a very important area to investigate because there is a high frequency of substance abuse in those who sustain a brain injury (i.e., intoxicated at the time of injury) (see Jorge, Starkstein, Arndt, Moser, Crespo-Facorro, & Robinson, 2005) and, likewise, there is considerable risk for development of substance abuse or relapse after brain injury (Corrigan, Bogner, Lamb-Hart, Heinemann, & Moore, 2005; Horner, Ferguson, Selassie, Labbate, Kniele, & Corrigan, 2005). The reserve hypothesis would speculate that history of alcohol abuse would be adverse to the health of the brain at the time of injury and, therefore, would likely promote the effects of brain injury. Wilde et al. (2004) used the VBR as a dependent variable as the index of cerebral atrophy. Presence of elevated blood alcohol level at the time of injury and/or history of moderate to heavy alcohol use prior to injury were associated with greater cerebral atrophy when controlling for injury severity, education and age. Pre-injury polysubstance abuse has also been shown to be associated with greater reduction in hippocampal size post-injury after controlling for age, injury severity and education (Barker et al., 1999).

Lashley, mass action and equipotentiality

Early in the last century, Karl Lashley began his systematic search for the "memory trace," or what he labeled the engram (1950). More than 70 years ago he published a study examining the percent of cortex damaged and its influence on error rate in maze learning in a rat model of brain injury and recovery of function (Lashley & Wiley, 1933). Results of that study are reproduced in Figure 5.8 and show that the amount of cerebral tissue damaged is exponentially related to the error rate. This became, in part, the

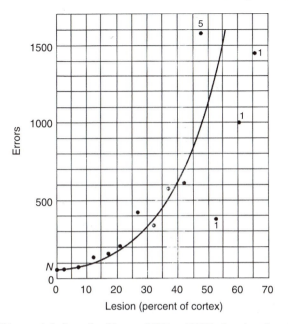

Figure 5.8 This graph is from Lashley and Wiley (1933) showing the relationship of errors in maze learning to the extent of cerebral damage in the rat. Brain damage is expressed as the percentage of the surface area of the isocortex destroyed as histologically verified at post-mortem, based on 60 normal animals and 127 brain-operated animals averaged by class intervals of 5% destruction. The curve is the best fitting one of logarithmic form. For lesions above 45% the number of cases (indicated by the numerals on the graph) was too small for reliability. While this study was performed more than 70 years ago, this principle holds true not only for non-humans but for humans as well, where greater lesion volume predicts greater cognitive impairment. Accordingly, anything that relates to lessening total lesion volume will likely lessen overall cognitive impact when a brain injury occurs.

basis for his "law of mass action," essentially meaning that disrupted learning following brain injury was not so much related to the location of brain damage, but rather to the total quantity of damage. While initial studies that attempted to examine this in humans proved unsuccessful (Teuber, 1972), recent studies using quantitative neuroimaging measures support this principle in humans as well. From a cognitive reserve standpoint, this has implications for how reserve capacity can be linked to factors that relate to lessening the total amount of damage. Also, from the viewpoint of cognitive reserve it would be predicted that the total amount of tissue loss from acquired brain damage would be more important than the etiology of how the brain was injured. In other words, if a certain amount of brain tissue is injured, the total amount of injured tissue becomes important rather than whether the parenchymal damage occurs from injury, infection, disease or stroke. This has recently been shown to be the case by Hopkins, Tate, and Bigler (2005), where they compared patients with TBI with those who had sustained brain damage as a result of anoxic brain injury. The amount of cortical volume loss was the major predictor of cognitive deficit, not the etiology of injury. This is very important because in examining risk factors for dementia, late in life diverse potential brain insults, such as those from diabetes, obesity, stroke, and so on, increase the risk of late in life dementia, as would be predicted by cognitive reserve theory (Gustafson, Lissner, Bengtsson, Bjorkelund, & Skoog, 2004; Rasquin, Verhey, van Oostenbrugge, Lousberg, & Lodder, 2004; Skoog, 2004).

Summary and conclusions

The cognitive reserve hypothesis provides a very reasonable framework to study the effects of TBI in terms of not only initial recovery, but recovery over the lifespan. The cognitive reserve hypothesis helps explain the relationship between prior brain injury and the increased likelihood of dementia and neuropsychiatric disorder later in life. This research also clearly shows how important early factors are in optimizing brain development, where even more research should be directed.

References

Abernethy, L. J., Palaniappan, M., & Cooke, R. W. (2002). Quantitative magnetic resonance imaging of the brain in survivors of very low birth weight. *Archives of Diseases in Childhood, 87*(4), 279–283.

Adelson, P. D., Dixon, C. E., & Kochanek, P. M. (2000). Long-term dysfunction following diffuse traumatic brain injury in the immature rat. *Journal of Neurotrauma, 17*(4), 273–282.

Annegers, J. F., Hauser, W. A., Coan, S. P., & Rocca, W. A. (1998). A population-based study of seizures after traumatic brain injuries. *New England Journal of Medicine, 338*(1), 20–24.

Bachman, D. L., Green, R. C., Benke, K. S., Cupples, L. A., & Farrer, L. A. (2003). Comparison of Alzheimer's disease risk factors in white and African American families. *Neurology, 60*(8), 1372–1374.

Badcock, J. C., Dragovic, M., Waters, F. A., & Jablensky, A. (2005). Dimensions of intelligence in schizophrenia: Evidence from patients with preserved, deteriorated and compromised intellect. *Journal of Psychiatric Research, 39*(1), 11–19.

Barker, L. H., Bigler, E. D., Johnson, S. C., Anderson, C. V., Russo, A. A., Boineau, B., et al. (1999). Polysubstance abuse and traumatic brain injury: Quantitative magnetic resonance imaging and neuropsychological outcome in older adolescents and young adults. *Journal of the International Neuropsychological Society, 5*(7), 593–608.

Bigler, E. D. (2001a). The lesion(s) in traumatic brain injury: implications for clinical neuropsychology. *Archives of Clinical Neuropsychology, 16*(2), 95–131.

Bigler, E. D. (2001b). Quantitative magnetic resonance imaging in traumatic brain injury. *Journal of Head Trauma Rehabilitation, 16*(2), 1–21.

Bigler, E. D. (2004). Neuropsychological results and neuropathological findings at autopsy in a case of mild traumatic brain injury. *Journal of the International Neuropsychological Society, 10*(5), 794–806.

Bigler, E. D. (2005). Structural Imaging. In J. M. Silver, T. W. McAllister, & S. C. Yudofsky (Eds.), *Textbook of traumatic brain injury* (2nd ed.). Washington, DC: American Psychiatric Publishing, Inc.

Bigler, E. D., & Snyder, J. L. (1995). Neuropsychological outcome and quantitative neuroimaging in mild head injury. *Archives of Clinical Neuropsychology, 10*(2), 159–174.

Bigler, E. D., & Tate, D. F. (2001). Brain volume, intracranial volume and dementia. *Investigative Radiology, 36*, 539–546.

Bigler, E. D., Anderson, C. V., & Blatter, D. D. (2002). Temporal lobe morphology in normal aging and traumatic brain injury. *American Journal of Neuroradiology, 23*(2), 255–266.

Bigler, E. D., Blatter, D. D., Anderson, C. V., Johnson, S. C., Gale, S. D., Hopkins, R. O., et al. (1997). Hippocampal volume in normal aging and traumatic brain injury. *American Journal of Neuroradiology, 18*(1), 11–23.

Bigler, E. D., Johnson, S. C., & Blatter, D. D. (1999). Head trauma and intellectual status: Relation to quantitative magnetic resonance imaging findings. *Applied Neuropsychology, 6*(4), 217–225.

Bigler, E. D., Lowry, C. M., Anderson, C. V., Johnson, S. C., Terry, J., & Steed, M. (2000). Dementia, quantitative neuroimaging, and apolipoprotein E genotype. *American Journal of Neuroradiology, 21*(10), 1857–1868.

Bigler, E. D., Neeley, E. S., Miller, M. J., Tate, D. F., Rice, S. A., Cleavinger, H., et al. (2004). Cerebral volume loss, cognitive deficit and neuropsychological performance: Comparative measures of brain atrophy: I. Dementia. *Journal of the International Neuropsychological Society, 10*(3), 442–452.

Bigler, E. D., Tate, D. F., Neeley, E. S., Wolfson, L. J., Miller, M. J., Rice, S. A., et al. (2003). Temporal lobe, autism, and macrocephaly. *American Journal of Neuroradiology, 24*(10), 2066–2076.

Blasko, I., Beer, R., Bigl, M., Apelt, J., Franz, G., Rudzki, D., et al. (2004). Experimental traumatic brain injury in rats stimulates the expression, production and activity of Alzheimer's disease beta-secretase (BACE-1). *Journal of Neural Transmission, 111*(4), 523–536.

Blatter, D. D., Bigler, E. D., Gale, S. D., Johnson, S. C., Anderson, C. V., Burnett, B. M., et al. (1995). Quantitative volumetric analysis of brain MR: Normative database spanning 5 decades of life. *American Journal of Neuroradiology, 16*(2), 241–251.

Bondi, M. W., Salmon, D. P., Monsch, A. U., Galasko, D., Butters, N., Klauber, M. R., et al. (1995). Episodic memory changes are associated with the APOE-epsilon 4 allele in nondemented older adults. *Neurology, 45*(12), 2203–2206.

Bramlett, H. M., Kraydieh, S., Green, E. J., & Dietrich, W. D. (1997). Temporal and regional patterns of axonal damage following traumatic brain injury: A beta-amyloid precursor protein immunocytochemical study in rats. *Journal of Neuropathology and Experimental Neurology, 56*(10), 1132–1141.

Breitner, J. C., Wyse, B. W., Anthony, J. C., Welsh-Bohmer, K. A., Steffens, D. C., Norton, M. C., et al. (1999). APOE-epsilon4 count predicts age when prevalence of AD increases, then declines: The Cache County Study. *Neurology, 53*(2), 321–331.

Brown, A. W., Leibson, C. L., Malec, J. F., Perkins, P. K., Drehl, N. N., & Larson, D. R. (2004). Long-term survival after traumatic brain injury: A population-based analysis. *NeuroRehabilitation, 19*(1), 37–43.

Brown, A. W., Leibson, C. L., & Malec, J. F. (2005). Letters to the editors. *Neuro-Rehabilitation, 20*(1), 67.

Bruner, E. (2004). Geometric morphometrics and paleoneurology: Brain shape evolution in the genus Homo. *Journal of Human Evolution, 47*(5), 279–303.

Chamelian, L., Reis, M., & Feinstein, A. (2004). Six-month recovery from mild to moderate traumatic brain injury: The role of APOE-epsilon4 allele. *Brain, 127*(Pt 12), 2621–2628.

Chang, L., Tomasi, D., Yakupov, R., Lozar, C., Arnold, S., Caparelli, E., et al. (2004). Adaptation of the attention network in human immunodeficiency virus brain injury. *Annals of Neurology, 56*(2), 259–272.

Chen, S. F., Richards, H. K., Smielewski, P., Johnstrom, P., Salvador, R., Pickard, J. D., et al. (2004). Relationship between flow-metabolism uncoupling and evolving axonal injury after experimental traumatic brain injury. *Journal of Cerebral Blood Flow and Metabolism, 24*(9), 1025–1036.

Chen, S. H., Kareken, D. A., Fastenau, P. S., Trexler, L. E., & Hutchins, G. D. (2003). A study of persistent post-concussion symptoms in mild head trauma using positron emission tomography. *Journal of Neurology, Neurosurgery and Psychiatry, 74*(3), 326–332.

Cohen-Gadol, A. A., Westerveld, M., Alvarez-Carilles, J., & Spencer, D. D. (2004). Intracarotid Amytal memory test and hippocampal magnetic resonance imaging volumetry: Validity of the Wada test as an indicator of hippocampal integrity among candidates for epilepsy surgery. *Journal of Neurosurgery, 101*(6), 926–931.

Colantonio, A., Ratcliff, G., Chase, S., & Vernich, L. (2004). Aging with traumatic brain injury: Long-term health conditions. *International Journal of Rehabilitation Research, 27*(3), 209–214.

Cooke, R. W. (2005). Perinatal and postnatal factors in very preterm infants and subsequent cognitive and motor abilities. *Archives of Disease in Childhood Fetal and Neonatal Edition, 90*(1), F60–63.

Cooke, R. W., & Foulder-Hughes, L. (2003). Growth impairment in the very preterm and cognitive and motor performance at 7 years. *Archives of Diseases in Childhood, 88*(6), 482–487.

Corkin, S., Rosen, T. J., Sullivan, E. V., & Clegg, R. A. (1989). Penetrating head injury in young adulthood exacerbates cognitive decline in later years. *Journal of Neuroscience, 9*(11), 3876–3883.

Corrigan, J. D., Bogner, J., Lamb-Hart, G., Heinemann, A. W., & Moore, D. (2005). Increasing substance abuse treatment compliance for persons with traumatic brain injury. *Psychology of Addictive Behaviors, 19*(2), 131–139.

Courchesne, E., Chisum, H. J., Townsend, J., Cowles, A., Covington, J., Egaas, B., et al. (2000). Normal brain development and aging: Quantitative analysis at in vivo MR imaging in healthy volunteers. *Radiology, 216*(3), 672–682.

Creeley, C. E., Wozniak, D. F., Bayly, P. V., Olney, J. W., & Lewis, L. M. (2004). Multiple episodes of mild traumatic brain injury result in impaired cognitive performance in mice. *Academic Emergency Medicine, 11*(8), 809–819.

Deary, I. J., & Caryl, P. G. (1997). Neuroscience and human intelligence differences. *Trends in Neuroscience, 20*(8), 365–371.

Diaz-Asper, C. M., Schretlen, D. J., & Pearlson, G. D. (2004). How well does IQ predict neuropsychological test performance in normal adults? *Journal of the International Neuropsychological Society*, *10*(1), 82–90.

Dikmen, S. S., Bombardier, C. H., Machamer, J. E., Fann, J. R., & Temkin, N. R. (2004). Natural history of depression in traumatic brain injury. *Archives of Physical Medicine and Rehabilitation*, *85*, 1457–1464.

Dodrill, C. B., & Matthews, C. G. (1992). The role of neuropsychology in the assessment and treatment of persons with epilepsy. *American Psychologist*, *47*(9), 1139–1142.

Driscoll, I., Hamilton, D. A., Petropoulos, H., Yeo, R. A., Brooks, W. M., Baumgartner, R. N., et al. (2003). The aging hippocampus: Cognitive, biochemical and structural findings. *Cerebral Cortex*, *13*(12), 1344–1351.

Dube, C., da Silva Fernandes, M. J., & Nehlig, A. (2001). Age-dependent consequences of seizures and the development of temporal lobe epilepsy in the rat. *Developmental Neuroscience*, *23*(3), 219–223.

Dunning, J., Stratford-Smith, P., Lecky, F., Batchelor, J., Hogg, K., Browne, J., et al. (2004). A meta-analysis of clinical correlates that predict significant intracranial injury in adults with minor head trauma. *Journal of Neurotrauma*, *21*(7), 877–885.

Fann, J. R., Burington, B., Leonetti, A., Jaffe, K., Katon, W. J., & Thompson, R. S. (2004). Psychiatric illness following traumatic brain injury in an adult health maintenance organization population. *Archives of General Psychiatry*, *61*(1), 53–61.

Fann, J. R., Leonetti, A., Jaffe, K., Katon, W. J., Cummings, P., & Thompson, R. S. (2002). Psychiatric illness and subsequent traumatic brain injury: A case control study. *Journal of Neurology, Neurosurgery & Psychiatry*, *72*(5), 615–620.

Farmer, J. E., Kanne, S. M., Haut, J. S., Williams, J., Johnstone, B., & Kirk, K. (2002). Memory functioning following traumatic brain injury in children with premorbid learning problems. *Developmental Neuropsychology*, *22*(2), 455–469.

Fastenau, P. S., Shen, J., Dunn, D. W., Perkins, S. M., Hermann, B. P., & Austin, J. K. (2004). Neuropsychological predictors of academic underachievement in pediatric epilepsy: Moderating roles of demographic, seizure, and psychosocial variables. *Epilepsia*, *45*(10), 1261–1272.

Flashman, L. A., Andreasen, N. C., Flaum, M., & Swayze, V. W. (1998). Intelligence and regional brain volumes in normal controls. *Intelligence*, *25*, 149–160.

Frey, M. C., & Detterman, D. K. (2004). Scholastic assessment or g? The relationship between the Scholastic Assessment Test and general cognitive ability. *Psychological Science*, *15*(6), 373–378.

Gilbertson, M. W., Shenton, M. E., Ciszewski, A., Kasai, K., Lasko, N. B., Orr, S. P., et al. (2002). Smaller hippocampal volume predicts pathologic vulnerability to psychological trauma. *Nature Neuroscience*, *5*(11), 1242–1247.

Goetz, P., Blamire, A., Rajagopalan, B., Cadoux-Hudson, T., Young, D., & Styles, P. (2004). Increase in apparent diffusion coefficient in normal appearing white matter following human traumatic brain injury correlates with injury severity. *Journal of Neurotrauma*, *21*(6), 645–654.

Gogtay, N., Giedd, J. N., Lusk, L., Hayashi, K. M., Greenstein, D., Vaituzis, A. C., et al. (2004). Dynamic mapping of human cortical development during childhood through early adulthood. *Proceedings of the National Academy of Science, USA*, *101*(21), 8174–8179.

Goldstein, F. C., Levin, H. S., Goldman, W. P., Clark, A. N., & Altonen, T. K. (2001). Cognitive and neurobehavioral functioning after mild versus moderate traumatic brain injury in older adults. *Journal of the International Neuropsychological Society,* *7*(3), 373–383.

Gould, S. J. (1996). *The mismeasure of man.* New York: W. W. Norton & Company.

Grafman, J., Lalonde, F., Litvan, I., & Fedio, P. (1989). Premorbid effects on recovery from brain injury in humans: Cognitive and interpersonal indexes. In J. Schulkin (Ed.), *Preoperative events: Their effects on behavior following brain damage* (pp. 277–303). Hillsdale, NJ: Lawrence Erlbaum Associates, Inc.

Graham, D. I., Gennarelli, T. A., & McIntosh, T. K. (2002). Trauma. In D. I. Graham & P. L. Lantos (Eds.), *Greenfield's neuropathology* (7th ed., pp. 823–898). New York: Arnold.

Grunau, R. E., Whitfield, M. F., & Fay, T. B. (2004). Psychosocial and academic characteristics of extremely low birth weight (< or = 800 g) adolescents who are free of major impairment compared with term-born control subjects. *Pediatrics, 114*(6), e725–732.

Guskiewicz, K. M., McCrea, M., Marshall, S. W., Cantu, R. C., Randolph, C., Barr, W., et al. (2003). Cumulative effects associated with recurrent concussion in collegiate football players: The NCAA Concussion Study. *Journal of the American Medical Association, 290*(19), 2549–2555.

Gustafson, D., Lissner, L., Bengtsson, C., Bjorkelund, C., & Skoog, I. (2004). A 24-year follow-up of body mass index and cerebral atrophy. *Neurology, 63*(10), 1876–1881.

Haier, R. J., Jung, R. E., Yeo, R. A., Head, K., & Alkire, M. T. (2004). Structural brain variation and general intelligence. *Neuroimage, 23*(1), 425–433.

Haier, R. J., Jung, R. E., Yeo, R. A., Head, K., & Alkire, M. T. (2005). The neuro-anatomy of general intelligence: Sex matters. *Neuroimage, 25*(1), 320–327.

Harrison-Felix, C., Whiteneck, G., DeVivo, M., Hammond, F. M., & Jha, A. (2004). Mortality following rehabilitation in the Traumatic Brain Injury Model Systems of Care. *NeuroRehabilitation, 19*(1), 45–54.

Hervey, A. S., Epstein, J. N., & Curry, J. F. (2004). Neuropsychology of adults with attention-deficit/hyperactivity disorder: A meta-analytic review. *Neuropsychology, 18*(3), 485–503.

Hoane, M. R., Lasley, L. A., & Akstulewicz, S. L. (2004). Middle age increases tissue vulnerability and impairs sensorimotor and cognitive recovery following traumatic brain injury in the rat. *Behavioral Brain Research, 153*(1), 189–197.

Holsinger, T., Steffens, D. C., Phillips, C., Helms, M. J., Havlik, R. J., Breitner, J. C., et al. (2002). Head injury in early adulthood and the lifetime risk of depression. *Archives of General Psychiatry, 59*(1), 17–22.

Hopkins, R. O., Tate, D. F., & Bigler, E. D. (2005). Anoxia versus traumatic brain injury: The amount of tissue loss not etiology. *Neuropsychology, 19*(2), 233–242.

Horner, M. D., Ferguson, P. L., Selassie, A. W., Labbate, L. A., Kniele, K., & Corrigan, J. D. (2005). Patterns of alcohol use 1 year after traumatic brain injury: A population-based, epidemiological study. *Journal of the International Neuro-psychological Society, 11*(3), 322–330.

Huang, W., Qiu, C., von Strauss, E., Winblad, B., & Fratiglioni, L. (2004). APOE genotype, family history of dementia, and Alzheimer disease risk: A 6-year follow-up study. *Archives of Neurology, 61*(12), 1930–1934.

Hurley, R. A., Hayman, L. A., Puryear, L. J., & Goldstein, J. R. (1995). Pathways for declarative memory and emotion. II. Clinical brain imaging. *International Journal of Neuroradiology, 1*, 90–101.

Ikonomovic, M. D., Uryu, K., Abrahamson, E. E., Ciallella, J. R., Trojanowski, J. Q., Lee, V. M., et al. (2004). Alzheimer's pathology in human temporal cortex surgically excised after severe brain injury. *Experimental Neurology, 190*(1), 192–203.

Isaacs, E. B., Edmonds, C. J., Chong, W. K., Lucas, A., Morley, R., & Gadian, D. G. (2004). Brain morphometry and IQ measurements in preterm children. *Brain, 127*, 2595–2607.

Ivanovic, D. M., Leiva, B. P., Perez, H. T., Olivares, M. G., Diaz, N. S., Urrutia, M. S., et al. (2004). Head size and intelligence, learning, nutritional status and brain development. Head, IQ, learning, nutrition and brain. *Neuropsychologia, 42*(8), 1118–1131.

Jaskiw, G. E., & Kenny, J. F. (2002). Limbic cortical injury sustained during adulthood leads to schizophrenia-like syndrome. *Schizophrenia Research, 58*(2–3), 205–212.

Jellinger, K. A. (2004). Traumatic brain injury as a risk factor for Alzheimer's disease. *Journal of Neurology, Neurosurgery & Psychiatry, 75*(3), 511–512.

Jorge, R. E., Robinson, R. G., Moser, D., Tateno, A., Crespo-Facorro, B., & Arndt, S. (2004). Major depression following traumatic brain injury. *Archives of General Psychiatry, 61*(1), 42–50.

Jorge, R. E., Starkstein, S. E., Arndt, S., Moser, D., Crespo-Facorro, B., & Robinson, R. G. (2005). Alcohol misuse and mood disorders following traumatic brain injury. *Archives of General Psychiatry, 62*(7), 742–749.

Kesler, S. R., Adams, H. F., Blasey, C. M., & Bigler, E. D. (2003). Premorbid intellectual functioning, education, and brain size in traumatic brain injury: An investigation of the cognitive reserve hypothesis. *Applied Neuropsychology, 10*(3), 153–162.

King, J. A., Ferris, C. F., & Lederhendler, I. I. (Eds.). (2003). *Roots of mental illness in children* (Vol. 1008). New York: The New York Academy of Sciences.

Kleim, J. A., Jones, T. A., & Schallert, T. (2003). Motor enrichment and the induction of plasticity before or after brain injury. *Neurochemical Research, 28*(11), 1757–1769.

Koponen, S., Taiminen, T., Kairisto, V., Portin, R., Isoniemi, H., Hinkka, S., et al. (2004). APOE-epsilon4 predicts dementia but not other psychiatric disorders after traumatic brain injury. *Neurology, 63*(4), 749–750.

Kramer, J. H., Schuff, N., Reed, B. R., Mungas, D., Du, A. T., Rosen, H. J., et al. (2004). Hippocampal volume and retention in Alzheimer's disease. *Journal of the International Neuropsychological Society, 10*(4), 639–643.

Kraus, J. F., & Chu, L. D. (2005). Epidemiology. In J. M. Silver, T. W. McAllister, & S. C. Yudofsky (Eds.), *Textbook of traumatic brain injury* (2nd ed.). Washington, DC: American Psychiatric Publishing, Inc.

Kuh, D., Richards, M., Hardy, R., Butterworth, S., & Wadsworth, M. E. (2004). Childhood cognitive ability and deaths up until middle age: A post-war birth cohort study. *International Journal of Epidemiology, 33*(2), 408–413.

Lainhart, J. E., Lazar, M., Alexander, A., & Bigler, E. D. (2005). The brain during life in autism: Advances in neuroimaging research. In M. Casanova (Ed.), *Advances in autism research* (pp. 55–105). Hauppauge, NY: Nova Science Publishers.

Lashley, K. S. (1950). In search of the engram. *Symposia of the Society for Experimental Biology, 4*, 454–482.

Lashley, K. S., & Wiley, L. E. (1933). Studies of cerebral function in learning: IX. Mass action in relation to the number of elements in the problem to be learned. *Journal of Comparative Neurology, 57*, 3–55.

Lefebvre, L., Reader, S. M., & Sol, D. (2004). Brains, innovations and evolution in birds and primates. *Brain Behavior, 63*(4), 233–246.

Levin, H. S., McCauley, S. R., Josie, C. P., Boake, C., Brown, S. A., Goodman, H. S., et al. (2004). Predicting depression following mild traumatic brain injury. *Archives of General Psychiatry, 62*, 523–528.

Levitan, I. B., & Kaczmarek, L. K. (2001). *The neuron: Cell and molecular biology.* New York: Oxford University Press.

Levitt, P. (2003). Structural and functional maturation of the developing primate brain. *Journal of Pediatrics, 143*(4 Suppl), S35–45.

MacDonald, B. K., Johnson, A. L., Sander, J. W., & Shorvon, S. D. (1999). Febrile convulsions in 220 children—neurological sequelae at 12 years follow-up. *European Neurology, 41*(4), 179–186.

MacKenzie, J. D., Siddiqi, F., Babb, J. S., Bagley, L. J., Mannon, L. J., Sinson, G. P., et al. (2002). Brain atrophy in mild or moderate traumatic brain injury: A longitudinal quantitative analysis. *American Journal of Neuroradiology, 23*(9), 1509–1515.

Marlow, N., Wolke, D., Bracewell, M. A., & Samara, M. (2005). Neurologic and developmental disability at six years of age after extremely preterm birth. *New England Journal of Medicine, 352*(1), 9–19.

Mathias, J. L., Beall, J. A., & Bigler, E. D. (2004). Neuropsychological and information processing deficits following mild traumatic brain injury. *Journal of the International Neuropsychological Society, 10*(2), 286–297.

Mathias, J. L., Bigler, E. D., Jones, N. R., Bowden, S. C., Barrett-Woodbridge, M., Brown, G. C., et al. (2004). Neuropsychological and information processing performance and its relationship to white matter changes following moderate and severe traumatic brain injury. *Applied Neuropsychology, 11*(3), 134–152.

Mayeux, R. (2004). Dissecting the relative influences of genes and the environment in Alzheimer's disease. *Annals of Neurology, 55*(2), 156–158.

Mayeux, R., Ottman, R., Maestre, G., Ngai, C., Tang, M. X., Ginsberg, H., et al. (1995). Synergistic effects of traumatic head injury and apolipoprotein-epsilon 4 in patients with Alzheimer's disease. *Neurology, 45*(3 Pt 1), 555–557.

McAllister, T. W. (2005). Mild brain injury and the postconcussion syndrome. In J. M. Silver, T. W. McAllister, & S. C. Yudofsky (Eds.), *Textbook of traumatic brain injury.* Washington, DC: American Psychiatric Publishing.

McAllister, T. W., Rhodes, C. H., Flashman, L. A., McDonald, B. C., Belloni, D., & Saykin, A. J. (2005). Effects of the dopamine D2 receptor T allele on response latency after mild traumatic brain injury. *American Journal of Psychiatry, 162*, 1749–1751.

McAllister, T. W., Saykin, A. J., Flashman, L. A., Sparling, M. B., Johnson, S. C., Guerin, S. J., et al. (1999). Brain activation during working memory 1 month after mild traumatic brain injury: A functional MRI study. *Neurology, 53*(6), 1300–1308.

Millar, K., Nicoll, J. A., Thornhill, S., Murray, G. D., & Teasdale, G. M. (2003). Long term neuropsychological outcome after head injury: Relation to APOE genotype. *Journal of Neurology, Neurosurgery & Psychiatry, 74*(8), 1047–1052.

Mosenthal, A. C., Livingston, D. H., Lavery, R. F., Knudson, M. M., Lee, S., Morabito, D., et al. (2004). The effect of age on functional outcome in mild traumatic brain injury: 6-month report of a prospective multicenter trial. *Journal of Trauma, 56*(5), 1042–1048.

Mulhern, R. K., Merchant, T. E., Gajjar, A., Reddick, W. E., & Kun, L. E. (2004). Late neurocognitive sequelae in survivors of brain tumours in childhood. *Lancet Oncology*, *5*(7), 399–408.

Munirathinam, S., & Bahr, B. A. (2004). Repeated contact with subtoxic soman leads to synaptic vulnerability in hippocampus. *Journal of Neuroscience Research*, *77*(5), 739–746.

Murrey, G. J., Starzinski, D. T., & LeBlanc, A. J. (2004). Base rates of traumatic brain injury history in adults admitted to state psychiatric hospitals: A 3-year study. *Rehabilitation Psychology*, *49*, 259–261.

Nassar, A. H., Usta, I. M., Khalil, A. M., Melhem, Z. I., Nakad, T. I., & Abu Musa, A. A. (2003). Fetal macrosomia (> or = 4500 g): Perinatal outcome of 231 cases according to the mode of delivery. *Journal of Perinatology*, *23*(2), 136–141.

Nybo, T., Sainio, M., & Muller, K. (2004). Stability of vocational outcome in adulthood after moderate to severe preschool brain injury. *Journal of the International Neuropsychological Society*, *10*(5), 719–723.

Olsson, A., Csajbok, L., Ost, M., Hoglund, K., Nylen, K., Rosengren, L., et al. (2004). Marked increase of beta-amyloid(1-42) and amyloid precursor protein in ventricular cerebrospinal fluid after severe traumatic brain injury. *Journal of Neurology*, *251*(7), 870–876.

Oyegbile, T. O., Dow, C., Jones, J., Bell, B., Rutecki, P., Sheth, R., et al. (2004). The nature and course of neuropsychological morbidity in chronic temporal lobe epilepsy. *Neurology*, *62*(10), 1736–1742.

Peterson, B. S. (2003). Brain imaging studies of the anatomical and functional consequences of preterm birth for human brain development. *Annals of the New York Academy of Science*, *1008*, 219–237.

Peterson, B. S., Vohr, B., Staib, L. H., Cannistraci, C. J., Dolberg, A., Schneider, K. C., et al. (2000). Regional brain volume abnormalities and long-term cognitive outcome in preterm infants. *Journal of the American Medical Association*, *284*(15), 1939–1947.

Plassman, B. L., Havlik, R. J., Steffens, D. C., Helms, M. J., Newman, T. N., Drosdick, D., et al. (2000). Documented head injury in early adulthood and risk of Alzheimer's disease and other dementias. *Neurology*, *55*(8), 1158–1166.

Plassman, B. L., Welsh-Bohmer, K. A., Bigler, E. D., Johnson, S. C., Anderson, C. V., Helms, M. J., et al. (1997). Apolipoprotein E epsilon 4 allele and hippocampal volume in twins with normal cognition. *Neurology*, *48*(4), 985–989.

Raghupathi, R. (2004). Cell death mechanisms following traumatic brain injury. *Brain Pathology*, *14*(2), 215–222.

Raio, L., Ghezzi, F., Di Naro, E., Buttarelli, M., Franchi, M., Durig, P., et al. (2003). Perinatal outcome of fetuses with a birth weight greater than 4500 g: An analysis of 3356 cases. *European Journal of Obstetrics, Gynecology, and Reproductive Biology*, *109*(2), 160–165.

Rasquin, S. M., Verhey, F. R., van Oostenbrugge, R. J., Lousberg, R., & Lodder, J. (2004). Demographic and CT scan features related to cognitive impairment in the first year after stroke. *Journal of Neurology, Neurosurgery & Psychiatry*, *75*(11), 1562–1567.

Raz, N., Rodrigue, K. M., Head, D., Kennedy, K. M., & Acker, J. D. (2004). Differential aging of the medial temporal lobe: A study of a five-year change. *Neurology*, *62*(3), 433–438.

Rempel-Clower, N. L., Zola, S. M., Squire, L. R., & Amaral, D. G. (1996). Three cases of enduring memory impairment after bilateral damage limited to the hippocampal formation. *Journal of Neuroscience, 16*(16), 5233–5255.

Richter, W., & Richter, M. (2003). The shape of the fMRI BOLD response in children and adults changes systematically with age. *Neuroimage, 20*(2), 1122–1131.

Salazar, A. M., Schwab, K., & Grafman, J. H. (1995). Penetrating injuries in the Vietnam war. Traumatic unconsciousness, epilepsy, and psychosocial outcome. *Neurosurgery Clinics of North America, 6*(4), 715–726.

Salthouse, T. A. (2004). What and when of cognitive aging. *Current Directions in Psychological Science, 13*, 140–144.

Sandhir, R., Puri, V., Klein, R. M., & Berman, N. E. (2004). Differential expression of cytokines and chemokines during secondary neuron death following brain injury in old and young mice. *Neuroscience Letters, 369*(1), 28–32.

Scheibel, R. S., Pearson, D. A., Faria, L. P., Kotrla, K. J., Aylward, E., Bachevalier, J., et al. (2003). An fMRI study of executive functioning after severe diffuse TBI. *Brain Injury, 17*(11), 919–930.

Schofield, P. W., Mosesson, R. E., Stern, Y., & Mayeux, R. (1995). The age at onset of Alzheimer's disease and an intracranial area measurement. A relationship. *Archives of Neurology, 52*(1), 95–98.

Schulkin, J. (Ed.). (1989). *Preoperative events: Their effects on behavior following brain damage.* Hillsdale, NJ: Lawrence Erlbaum Associates, Inc.

Schulz, M. R., Marshall, S. W., Mueller, F. O., Yang, J., Weaver, N. L., Kalsbeek, W. D., et al. (2004). Incidence and risk factors for concussion in high school athletes, North Carolina, 1996–1999. *American Journal of Epidemiology, 160*(10), 937–944.

Serra-Grabulosa, J. M., Junque, C., Verger, K., Salgado-Pineda, P., Maneru, C., & Mercader, J. M. (2005). Cerebral correlates of declarative memory dysfunctions in early traumatic brain injury. *Journal of Neurology, Neurosurgery & Psychiatry, 76*(1), 129–131.

Seshadri, S., Wolf, P. A., Beiser, A., Elias, M. F., Au, R., Kase, C. S., et al. (2004). Stroke risk profile, brain volume, and cognitive function: the Framingham Offspring Study. *Neurology, 63*(9), 1591–1599.

Shavelle, R. M., Strauss, D., Whyte, J., Day, S. M., & Yu, Y. L. (2001). Long-term causes of death after traumatic brain injury. *American Journal of Physical Medicine & Rehabilitation, 80*(7), 510–516; quiz 517–519.

Skoog, I. (2004). Subcortical vascular dementia. *Clinical Neuropsychology, 18*(1), 4–5.

Slemmer, J. E., Matser, E. J., De Zeeuw, C. I., & Weber, J. T. (2002). Repeated mild injury causes cumulative damage to hippocampal cells. *Brain, 125*(Pt 12), 2699–2709.

Streeter, C. C., Van Reekum, R., Shorr, R. I., & Bachman, D. L. (1995). Prior head injury in male veterans with borderline personality disorder. *Journal of Nervous and Mental Disease, 183*(9), 577–581.

Suchy, Y., Leahy, B., Sweet, J. J., & Lam, C. S. (2003). Behavioral Dyscontrol Scale deficits among traumatic brain injury patients, part II: Comparison to other measures of executive functioning. *Clinical Neuropsychology, 17*(4), 492–506.

Sulzbacher, S., Farwell, J. R., Temkin, N., Lu, A. S., & Hirtz, D. G. (1999). Late cognitive effects of early treatment with phenobarbital. *Clinical Pediatrics (Phila), 38*(7), 387–394.

Swanson, S. J., Rao, S. M., Grafman, J., Salazar, A. M., & Kraft, J. (1995). The relationship between seizure subtype and interictal personality. Results from the Vietnam Head Injury Study. *Brain, 118* (Pt 1), 91–103.

Tasker, R. C., Salmond, C. H., Westland, A. G., Pena, A., Gillard, J. H., Sahakian, B. J., et al. (2005). Head circumference and brain and hippocampal volume after severe traumatic brain injury in childhood. *Pediatric Research, 58*(2), 302–308.

Teuber, H. L. (1972). Unity and diversity of frontal lobe functions. *Acta Neurobiologiae Experimentalis (Wars), 32*(2), 615–656.

Thompson, P. M., Hayashi, K. M., Sowell, E. R., Gogtay, N., Giedd, J. N., Rapoport, J. L., et al. (2004). Mapping cortical change in Alzheimer's disease, brain development, and schizophrenia. *Neuroimage, 23*, (Suppl 1), S2–18.

Timonen, M., Miettunen, J., Hakko, H., Zitting, P., Veijola, J., von Wendt, L., et al. (2002). The association of preceding traumatic brain injury with mental disorders, alcoholism and criminality: The Northern Finland 1966 Birth Cohort Study. *Psychiatry Research, 113*(3), 217–226.

Toga, A. W., & Thompson, P. M. (2005). Genetics of brain structure and intelligence. *Annual Review of Neuroscience, 28*, 1–23.

Tomaiuolo, F., Carlesimo, G. A., Di Paola, M., Petrides, M., Fera, F., Bonanni, R., et al. (2004). Gross morphology and morphometric sequelae in the hippocampus, fornix, and corpus callosum of patients with severe non-missile traumatic brain injury without macroscopically detectable lesions: A T1 weighted MRI study. *Journal of Neurology, Neurosurgery & Psychiatry, 75*(9), 1314–1322.

Toulopoulou, T., Grech, A., Morris, R. G., Schulze, K., McDonald, C., Chapple, B., et al. (2004). The relationship between volumetric brain changes and cognitive function: A family study on schizophrenia. *Biological Psychiatry, 56*(6), 447–453.

Towbin, A. (1978). Cerebral dysfunction related to perinatal organic damage: clinical–neuropathologic correlations. *Journal of Abnormal Psychology, 87*(6), 617–635.

Tucker, G. J. (2005). Siezures. In J. M. Silver, T. W. McAllister, & S. C. Yudofsky (Eds.), *Textbook of traumatic brain injury* (2nd ed., pp. 309–318). Washington, DC: American Psychiatric Publishing, Inc.

Vakil, E. (2005). The effect of moderate to severe traumatic brain injury (TBI) on different aspects of memory: A selective review. *Journal of Clinical and Experimental Neuropsychology, 27*, 977–1021.

Verhoeff, N. P., Wilson, A. A., Takeshita, S., Trop, L., Hussey, D., Singh, K., et al. (2004). In-vivo imaging of Alzheimer disease beta-amyloid with [11C]SB-13 PET. *American Journal of Geriatric Psychiatry, 12*(6), 584–595.

Vernon, P. A., Wickett, J. C., Bazana, G., & Stelmack, R. M. (2000). The neuropsychology and psychophysiology of human intelligence. In R. J. Sternberg (Ed.), *Handbook of intelligence*. New York: Cambridge University Press.

Villablanca, J. R., Carlson-Kuhta, P., Schmanke, T. D., & Hovda, D. A. (1998). A critical maturational period of reduced brain vulnerability to developmental injury. I. Behavioral studies in cats. *Brain Research. Developmental Brain Research, 105*(2), 309–324.

Weinstein, S., & Teuber, H. L. (1957). Effects of penetrating brain injury on intelligence test scores. *Science, 125*(3256), 1036–1037.

Weniger, G., Boucsein, K., & Irle, E. (2004). Impaired associative memory in temporal lobe epilepsy subjects after lesions of hippocampus, parahippocampal gyrus, and amygdala. *Hippocampus, 14*(6), 785–796.

Wilde, E. A., Bigler, E. D., Gandhi, P. V., Lowry, C. M., Blatter, D. D., Brooks, J., et al. (2004). Alcohol abuse and traumatic brain injury: Quantitative magnetic resonance imaging and neuropsychological outcome. *Journal of Neurotrauma*, *21*(2), 137–147.

Wilde, E. A., Hunter, J. V., Newsome, M. R., Scheibel, R. S., Bigler, E. D., Johnson, J. L., et al. (2005). Frontal and temporal morphometric findings on MRI in children after moderate to severe traumatic brain injury. *Journal of Neurotrauma*, *22*(3), 333–344.

Willerman, L., Schultz, R., Rutledge, J. N., & Bigler, E. D. (1991). In vivo brain size and intelligence. *Intelligence*, *15*, 223–228.

Wu, H. M., Huang, S. C., Hattori, N., Glenn, T. C., Vespa, P. M., Hovda, D. A., et al. (2004). Subcortical white matter metabolic changes remote from focal hemorrhagic lesions suggest diffuse injury after human traumatic brain injury. *Neurosurgery*, *55*(6), 1306–1317.

6 Electroconvulsive therapy and coronary artery bypass grafting surgery: Pseudoexperimental paradigms for studying cognitive reserve

Patricia A. Boyle, Susan A. Legendre Ropacki, and Robert A. Stern

It is widely recognized that individuals show varying degrees of susceptibility to cognitive and functional impairment associated with neurodegenerative disease or acquired brain injury. Although two individuals may suffer a similar neurological insult, underlying neuropathologies may produce profound clinical impairment in one individual but minimal or no impairment in the other. The theory of cognitive reserve (CR) was proposed to explain variations in symptom presentation among individuals with similar types and degrees of brain damage (Stern, 2002; 2003). The CR hypothesis posits that certain genetic and experiential variables protect against the expression of cognitive and functional impairment subsequent to brain injury or degenerative process, and an individual's *reserve* determines his or her threshold for the clinical manifestation of symptoms. CR therefore partially mediates the association between brain injury and its expression, such that individuals with high CR are able to tolerate a greater degree of neuropathology than are those with low CR prior to the onset of symptoms (Stern, 2002).

In this chapter, we discuss methodological issues related to the study of CR and propose strategies for developing more sophisticated tests of the CR hypothesis. First, we review several commonly studied markers of CR and present evidence of their inter-relatedness. Next, we provide a brief summary of studies that have examined the CR hypothesis and discuss methodological limitations and challenges related to the study of CR. Finally, we propose that medical procedures such as electroconvulsive therapy (ECT) and coronary artery bypass grafting (CABG) provide alternative and potentially advantageous pseudoexperimental paradigms for studying CR. Recent findings from studies examining CR in the context of ECT and CABG are presented.

How is cognitive reserve quantified?

Several markers of CR have been proposed, including premorbid intelligence, head circumference, neuronal density, neuronal processing efficiency, educational achievement, occupational attainment, and lifestyle factors such as participation in cognitively stimulating activities (e.g., Glatt et al., 1996, Snowdon, Kemper, Mortimer, Greiner, Wekstein, & Markesbery, 1996; Stern, Albert, Tang, & Tsai, 1999; Stern, 2002; Wilson, Bennett, Bienias, Mendes de Leon, Morris, & Evans, 2003). Educational achievement and occupational attainment arguably are the most easily measured indices of CR and are commonly used to estimate reserve, although lifestyle factors are gaining increasing attention in the literature as potentially important determinants of CR.

Perhaps the most critical aspect of the study of CR involves the selection and measurement of indicators of reserve. Markers of reserve can be studied alone or in combination, and studies use varying approaches to estimate CR. Importantly, CR is multifactorial in nature and indicators of CR are inter-related (i.e., not independent). Individual markers of CR may act additively and/or synergistically with other markers, and some purportedly experiential markers actually reflect genetic influences (Scarmeas & Stern, 2004). For example, education typically is considered an experiential or environmental marker of CR; however, highly educated individuals generally have higher premorbid intelligence, heavier brains, more dendrites, and more synaptic connections than less educated people (Dartigues et al., 1992; Jacobs, Schall, & Scheibel, 1993; Mortimer, 1997), suggesting that an individual's educational achievement may reflect his or her genetic predisposition for learning. It has also been proposed that education increases synaptic density (Katzman, Terry, & DeTeresa, 1998) and neurochemical transmission in the neocortical association cortex (Stern, 2002), and education may influence CR via its effect on brain processing efficiency. Educational achievement there-fore is related to other neurological and genetic markers of reserve and should be considered an indirect measure of CR.

Occupational attainment also may be considered an indirect measure of CR. Although occupational attainment is influenced less by socioeconomic and cultural factors than by education, occupational attainment is highly correlated with educational achievement (Scarmeas & Stern, 2004). More-over, occupational attainment in and of itself may represent a form of education; that is, an individual's occupation may provide opportunities for cognitive stimulation and new learning, which could promote the develop-ment of cognitive skills that minimize or delay the expression of clinical symptoms following neurological insult.

Evidence supporting the CR hypothesis

Most investigations of the CR hypothesis have focused on elderly individuals at risk for dementia or individuals with clinically diagnosed dementia, and many of the available studies provide support for the theory of CR. Epidemiologic evidence suggests that several of the proposed markers of CR are associated with differential susceptibility to age-related cognitive impairment and dementia; those factors most consistently found to be associated with the risk of cognitive decline include educational achievement (Evans et al., 1993; Letenneur, Commenges, Dartigues, & Barberger-Gateau, 1994), occupational attainment (Karp, Kareholt, Qui, Bellander, Winblad, & Fratiglioni, 2004; Stern et al., 1994), and lifestyle factors such as engagement in cognitively stimulating activities (Fabrigoule, Letenneur, Dartigues, Zarrouk, Commenges, & Barberger-Gateau, 1995; Riley, Snowdon, Desrosiers, & Markesbery, 2005; Wilson et al., 2003). That is, individuals with high educational and occupational attainment and frequent engagement in positive lifestyle activities (e.g., reading, participation in cognitively stimulating activities) have a reduced risk of cognitive impairment and dementia as compared to those with low educational and occupational attainment and/or who participate less frequently in positive lifestyle activities. Y. Stern and colleagues (1994) reported a significantly reduced rate of dementia among individuals with high educational or occupational attainment as compared to those with low educational or occupational attainment, and the risk was even lower for individuals with high educational *and* occupational attainment. Stern et al. (1999) also reported a significant association between educational and occupational attainment and the rate of memory decline in Alzheimer's disease (AD), suggesting that markers of CR influence both the expression and the course of dementia.

Evidence from functional and structural neuroimaging studies also supports the theory of CR. Individuals with high educational and occupational achievement and/or who frequently participate in cognitively stimulating activities can sustain a greater degree of neuropathology prior to the onset of clinical dementia than those who participate less frequently in such activities (Stern, 2002; Stern et al., 1995; Scarmeas et al., 2003; Scarmeas et al., 2004). In addition, one study showed that Alzheimer's patients with high CR outperformed individuals with low CR on a battery of neuropsychological tests, even though both groups showed a similar degree of neuropathology on neuroimaging (Scarmeas et al., 2003). Taken together, the available epidemiologic and neuroimaging findings suggest that individuals with high CR can tolerate a greater degree of neuropathology than individuals with low CR prior to symptom onset, and that individuals with high CR may function better than individuals with low CR even after symptoms manifest, despite relatively similar degrees of neuropathology (see Figure 6.1).

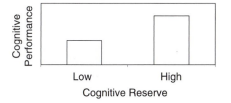

Figure 6.1 Cognitive reserve in degenerative disease: The traditional approach to the study of cognitive reserve without pre-disease cognitive testing.

Limits of traditional approaches to the study of CR

It is clear that there is extensive support for the CR hypothesis, and the notion that some form of reserve may serve to protect against the clinical expression of disease is very encouraging. However, many studies investigating the CR hypothesis have been retrospective and/or cross-sectional and have method-ological limitations that prevent a clear interpretation and synthesis of study findings. Among the most important of these limitations are: (1) the lack of reliable data regarding indices of CR, (2) limited data regarding individuals' cognitive functioning *prior* to the onset of disease, and (3) the absence of longitudinal data.

The use of retrospective accounts to document indices of CR (e.g., reports of educational and occupational achievement and participation in cognitively challenging activities) and other historic variables (e.g., premorbid cognitive functioning) is problematic for various reasons, not the least of which is the high potential for inaccuracy. Individuals with AD and their family members commonly fail to provide accurate information regarding historical variables such as educational status or lifestyle habits; this inaccuracy may be the result of a lack of knowledge, recall bias (e.g., reporters may over- or underestimate factors they think are involved in the development of dementia) or both. Additionally, the use of retrospective accounts of cognitive status (rather than pre–post cognitive testing) is often used in studies examining CR in order to document cognitive decline for the diagnosis of dementia; however, an individual's cognitive status prior to the onset of illness or brain injury is related to his or her performance in the early stages of the illness, and the use of retrospective accounts therefore calls into question the accuracy of the dementia diagnosis. Moreover, individuals with high education typically perform better than those with low education on the cognitive tests used to diagnose dementia. Finally, the use of cross-sectional data raises concerns regarding causal directionality (Scarmeas & Stern, 2004). In fact, data from some cross-sectional studies that reported associations between measures of CR and age-related cognitive impairment (e.g., occupational attainment and dementia) have been refuted following the re-analysis of data longitudinally (Dartigues et al., 1992; Helmer et al., 2001; Richards & Sacker, 2003).

How can we improve our methods for testing the cognitive reserve hypothesis?

Investigations into the theory of CR have significant potential for increasing awareness of strategies to prevent, minimize, or delay the clinical manifest-ation of symptoms following the onset of dementia and other neurological disorders. However, the extent to which CR mediates the association between brain pathology and the clinical expression of disease remains to be elucidated via carefully designed, prospective, longitudinal investigations. We propose that studies of the effects of CR in humans using *pseudoexperimental* paradigms may provide an alternative, feasible, and informative approach to the study of CR. Studies of individuals who undergo major medical procedures such as ECT and CABG allow for the prospective, longitudinal evaluation of cognition following procedures with known or suspected neurological effects. Moreover, such treatments are readily amenable to pre–post assessments of cognitive function. Examinations of individuals undergoing ECT and CABG may provide rare opportunities for the careful investigation of the effect of CR on cognitive and functional impairment secondary to acquired central nervous system (CNS) dysfunction. The use of such paradigms will undoubtedly enhance our understanding of the extent to which CR mediates the association between brain insult and its clinical expression.

A new paradigm for testing the CR hypothesis: ECT

Although ECT is generally considered a safe and highly effective treatment for chronic and severe major depression (Pagnin, Queiroz, Pini, & Cassano, 2004), ECT can often have deleterious effects on cognition. Individuals who undergo ECT exhibit varying degrees of post-treatment cognitive impairment, typically characterized by anterograde and retrograde amnesia (Sobin, Sackeim, Prudic, Devanand, Moody, & McElhiney, 1995; Weiner, 2000). Whereas some patients experience little or no cognitive impairment, others experience moderate to severe impairment that can last from a few days to 2 or 3 months post-treatment. At present, however, there remains a lack of consensus regarding methods to predict which patients will suffer post-treatment cognitive deficits. CR may mediate the effects of ECT on cognitive function, and studies examining the extent to which CR is associated with cognitive outcomes will serve several important purposes. First, they may facilitate the identification of individuals likely to suffer the greatest post-treatment cognitive deficits and, therefore, lead to decisions about selection of ECT treatment parameters that may minimize cognitive impairment in the most susceptible patients. Moreover, an examination of the influence of CR on post-ECT cognitive impairment provides the unique opportunity to prospectively test the CR hypothesis. In this patient population, there is no expected degenerative brain pathology *prior* to the ECT procedure. Therefore, one can directly examine the amount of variance in post-ECT cognitive impairment accounted for by markers of CR.

Legendre, Stern, Solomon, Furman, and Smith (2003) recently conducted the first investigation of the effect of CR on memory impairment among individuals undergoing ECT. Participants included 50 depressed patients treated with bilateral ECT three times per week. All participants were between the ages of 18 and 75, had at least 6 years of education, and scored >16 on the Hamilton Rating Scale for Depression (Hamilton, 1960). Participants were rated as having high or low CR on the basis of a combined index of education and occupational attainment. Educational level was measured using years of education completed, and occupational attainment was measured using the Hollingshead Occupation Rating Scale (Hollingshead, 1975). Using an approach employed by Stern and colleagues (Stern, Silva, Chaisson, & Evans, 1996), years of education and occupational attainment were transformed into *z*-scores using standard procedures and the rank value of each *z*-score was used to calculate a CR score for each participant; a median split of the CR scores was then used to classify individuals as having high or low CR. Memory was assessed pre- and post-ECT via the Randt Memory Test (Randt & Brown, 1983), which assesses aspects of memory most commonly affected by ECT, including immediate and delayed recall of verbal information and rate of forgetting. Depression severity was also assessed in order to control for the potential confounding effect of depressive symptoms on memory performance. The authors hypothesized that individuals with high CR would exhibit significantly less memory impairment than individuals with low CR following three ECT treatments.

At baseline (pre-ECT), there were no significant differences between CR groups in terms of immediate recall, delayed recall, rate of forgetting, or level of depression. At follow-up (after three ECT treatments), the high CR group forgot significantly less information after a delay (30.0%) than the low CR group (54.0%; $p < .01$). The group differences were not accounted for by age or depression severity (see Figure 6.2).

Findings from this first study of the effects of CR on memory impairment following ECT provide support for the CR hypothesis. Specifically, these findings suggest that CR may account for some of the individual differences in cognitive functioning following treatment with ECT. That post-treatment memory performance was considerably better in patients with high CR indicates that individuals with high CR were better able to tolerate the deleterious effects of this treatment and were less vulnerable to negative cognitive outcomes; that is, the high CR patients appear to have a higher threshold for

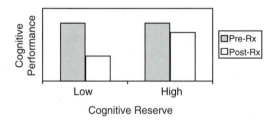

Figure 6.2 Electroconvulsive therapy: A pseudoexperimental approach to the study of cognitive reserve with pre-treatment cognitive testing in a condition without pre-treatment CNS disease burden. In this case, there are no pre-treatment CR-related group differences in cognitive performance, but the low CR group is more susceptible to the cognitive side effects of the treatment.

the deleterious effects of ECT. These findings have important clinical implications. If replicated, findings showing that CR mediates the association between ECT-related brain dysfunction and cognition may influence both the choice of treatment regimens and follow-up care provisions for individuals at risk for post-treatment cognitive impairment. For example, unilateral ECT and/or less intensive weekly treatment schedules are associated with a reduced risk of cognitive impairment (American Psychiatric Association Task Force on Electroconvulsive Therapy, 2000), and individuals with low CR, therefore, may benefit maximally from interventions designed to minimize the risk of cognitive dysfunction.

A second pseudoexperimental paradigm for studying CR: Coronary artery bypass grafting (CABG)

As is the case with ECT, CABG is another major medical procedure with a high incidence of post-treatment cognitive impairment. Despite important advances in surgical techniques and the clinical management of CABG patients, cognitive decline remains a problematic side effect for as many as three quarters of patients at the time of discharge from the hospital and a third of patients after 6 months (Newman et al., 2001; Raja, Blumenthall, & Doraiswamy, 2004; Roach et al., 1996). Typically, deficits are observed in the areas of attention, verbal fluency, verbal learning and recall, spatial skills, and psychomotor speed (e.g., Bruggemans, Van Dijk, & Huysmans, 1995; Hall et al., 1999; Newman et al., 2001; Walzer, Herrmann, & Wallesch, 1997; Weinstein, Woodard, & DeSilva, 1998; Wimmer-Greinecker et al., 1998).

The cause of cognitive dysfunction following CABG remains unclear. Historically, cerebral injury after CABG was attributed to the use of cardiopulmonary bypass (CPB; Roach et al., 1996); however, studies examining the extent to which CPB is associated with brain injury have reported mixed results. Kilo et al. (2001) reported that the use of CPB predicted post-operative cognitive dysfunction, and results of a study by Van Dijk and colleagues (2002) revealed that patients who underwent CABG without CPB had improved cognitive outcomes 3 months after surgery as compared to those who had CABG with CPB. However, other investigators have reported no association between CPB and cognitive impairment following CABG (Selnes, Grega, Borowicz, Royall, McKhann, & Baumgartner, 2003; Taggart, Browne, Halligan, & Wade, 1999).

The impact of CPB duration on cognitive outcome also has been examined, and some findings suggest that CPB duration is predictive of cognitive impairment (Murkin, Martzke, Buchan, Bentley, & Wong 1995). However, others have reported no association (e.g., Selnes, Goldsborough, Borowicz, & McKhann, 1999; Vingerhoets, Van Nooten, Vermassen, De Soete, & Jannes, 1997). Inadequate or fluctuating cerebral perfusion during CPB may also influence post-operative cognitive functioning (Mills, 1993;

Nussmeier, 1994; Pugsley, Treasure, Klinger, Newman, Pascalis, & Harrison, 1990), but again results are contradictory.

Although the cause of cognitive impairment following CABG requires further investigation, CABG provides a unique setting in which to examine the association between CR and post-operative cognitive outcomes. In an early study of the association between educational attainment and cognitive functioning post-CABG, Newman et al. (1994) found that high educational attainment was associated with less post-treatment cognitive impairment on a series of cognitive measures. Interestingly, although education was significantly associated with cognitive outcomes, education was not significantly associated with pre-surgical cognitive performance. Newman's findings therefore suggest that high educational attainment conferred some degree of protection from cognitive *decline* following surgery.

In a more recent study, Newman and colleagues (2001) investigated the potential effect of educational achievement and post-CABG cognitive functioning on long-term cognitive outcomes. Findings indicated that low educational attainment, presence of cognitive impairment at discharge, and older age were predictive of poor outcomes 5 years post-surgery. In a similar study, Hall and others (1999) examined whether certain patient variables, including education, were related to perfusion level and thus to post-surgical cognitive functioning. Patients with high educational achievement exhibited less deterioration on tests of psychomotor speed, verbal fluency, and attention than patients with low educational achievement. The authors suggested that individuals with low education may be among those patients most vulnerable to the deleterious effects of CABG.

Although there have been several studies suggesting that low education, per se, is a risk factor for post-CABG cognitive impairment, Legendre, Stern, Bert, and Rogers (2003) reported on the first study examining the impact of more broadly and appropriately defined CR on CABG-related cognitive decline. Participants included 42 men and women who underwent elective CABG. All were between the ages of 18 and 90 and had at least 6 years of education. Participants underwent pre–post cognitive testing using a neuropsychological battery designed to assess a broad range of cognitive abilities. Results were analyzed using raw factor scores for four identified cognitive domains: (1) psychomotor speed, (2) working memory/executive functions, (3) visual learning and memory, and (4) verbal learning and memory.

For the purpose of this study, CR was estimated via a combination of estimated full-scale IQ and occupational attainment. IQ estimate was made using the Oklahoma Premorbid Intelligence Estimate (OPIE-3V; Schoenberg, Scott, Duff, & Adams, 2002), a method of estimation that incorporates several indirect markers of cognitive reserve into one regression formula. The variables included in the regression equation include the WAIS-III Vocabulary subtest raw score, years of education, ethnicity, region of the country, and gender. Occupational attainment was classified based on seven United States census occupation categories as described by Stern and colleagues (1994): student; housewife; unskilled/semi-skilled; skilled trade or craft; clerical/office worker; manager of business/government; professional/ technical. This combination of estimated premorbid intelligence and occupa- tion was utilized in order to reduce the difficulties associated with using education alone, including the inherent socioeconomic and cultural biases. To calculate CR scores, OPIE-3V and occupational attainment scores were transformed into z-scores and the rank value of each z-score was summed and used to calculate a CR score for each participant; a median split of the CR scores was then used to classify individuals as having high or low CR.

Results indicated that participants with low CR demonstrated significantly poorer performance on measures of psychomotor speed and working memory/executive functions at baseline as compared to those with high CR. However, contrary to the authors' expectations, the low CR group did not demonstrate greater post-CABG cognitive decline on these measures or on tests of verbal or visual memory. In fact, although both groups exhibited post-operative declines on measures of psychomotor speed, working memory/executive functions, and verbal memory, the *high* CR group demon- strated significantly *greater* decline in the area of working memory/executive functions than the low CR group.

These findings did not provide support for Legendre et al.'s (2003) initial hypothesis that individuals with high CR would suffer less post-surgical cognitive impairment than individuals with low CR. However, the authors argued that their findings may provide support for the role of CR in the broader context of vascular disease. According to the threshold model of CR, persons with high CR are able to sustain a greater degree of pathology before clinical expression of a disease, while persons with low CR are more likely to exhibit the negative cognitive consequences of a disease earlier in its course. Thus, given that the low CR group performed significantly below the high CR group on several cognitive measures at the baseline (pre-surgical) evaluation, it is possible that individuals in the low CR group may have already begun to manifest the clinical symptoms of vascular disease (de Groot et al., 2000), while the high CR group had not. Alternatively, the authors reasoned that the threshold hypothesis also posits that symptoms that remain subthreshold in individuals with high CR may become evident following the presence of a new injury or disease sufficient to produce func- tional impairment (Satz et al., 1993; Stern et al., 1999). Therefore, in light of the pre-surgery differences in cognitive function, the decline observed in the high CR group may have reflected the clinical expression of symptoms that were previously subthreshold but that became evident secondary to CABG (see Figure 6.3). Legendre et al. (2003) suggest that future research should include markers of pre-CABG cerebrovascular disease burden (e.g., MRI, SPECT) to address this issue.

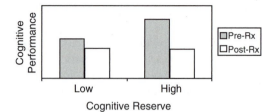

Figure 6.3   Coronary artery bypass grafting: A pseudoexperimental approach to the study of cognitive reserve with pre-treatment cognitive testing in a condition with possible pre-treatment CNS disease burden. In this case, there are significant pre-treatment CR-related group differences in cognitive performance due to a decreased threshold, similar to that seen in the traditional approach to CR (Figure 6.1). However, the high CR group exhibits greater post-treatment decline because the treatment creates an additional challenge, putting them over the threshold for the clinical presentation of cognitive impairment.

Conclusion

A growing body of evidence suggests that CR may mediate the association between brain pathology and the clinical expression of symptoms. Much of the available support for the theory of reserve comes from epidemiologic or cross-sectional clinical studies; however, methodological limitations inherent in such research paradigms must be considered. The concept of CR is complex, and well-designed, prospective, longitudinal investigations are greatly needed to further our understanding of the extent to which CR is associated with a reduced risk of cognitive and functional impairment following brain injury. ECT and CABG may provide alternative and informative pseudo-experimental paradigms for examining CR. In the context of ECT and CABG, investigators can reliably measure CR and conduct prospective, longitudinal investigations of the CR hypothesis without the time requirements inherent in the study of degenerative disease processes. In the case of ECT, this line of research provides a unique pseudoexperimental design in which there are no expected pre-treatment CR-related group differences in cognition; that is, there is no underlying degenerative disease process that would put some patients at a greater risk (i.e., decreased threshold) for treatment-related cognitive impairment (Figure 6.2). CABG similarly provides a pseudoexperimental design, but the possibility of pre-treatment cerebrovascular disease results in the ability to test *both* the association between CR and the clinical manifestation of the underlying disease prior to treatment *and* the impact of CR on post-treatment cognitive decline (Figure 6.3). Additional research using such alternative approaches to the study of CR may facilitate our understanding of the impact of CR on the clinical manifestation of a variety of neurological disorders as well as on the cognitive side effects of various medical treatments.

References

American Psychiatric Association Task Force on Electroconvulsive Therapy (2000). *Practice of electroconvulsive therapy: Recommendations for treatment, training, and privileging* (2nd ed.). Washington, DC: American Psychiatric Publishing, Inc.

Bruggemans, E. F., Van Dijk, J. G., & Huysmans, H. A. (1995). Residual cognitive dysfunctioning at 6 months following coronary artery bypass graft surgery. *European Journal of Cardiothoracic Surgery, 9*, 636–643.

Dartigues, J. F., Gagnon, M., Letenneur, L., Barberger-Gateau, P., Commenges, D., Evaldre, M., et al. (1992). Principal lifetime occupation and cognitive impairment in a French elderly cohort (Paquid). *American Journal of Epidemiology, 135*, 981–988.

de Groot, J. C., de Leeuw, F.-E., Oudkerk, M., Gijn, J. v., Hofman, A., Jolles, J., et al. (2000). Cerebral white matter lesions and cognitive function: The Rotterdam scan study. *Annals of Neurology, 47*, 145–151.

Evans, D. A., Beckett, L. A., Albert, M. S., Hebert, L. E., Scherr, P. A., Funkenstein, H. H., et al. (1993). Level of education and change in cognitive function in a community population of older persons. *Annals of Epidemiology, 3*, 71–77.

Fabrigoule, C., Letenneur, L., Dartigues, J. F., Zarrouk, M., Commenges, D., & Barberger-Gateau, P. (1995). Social and leisure activities and risk of dementia: A prospective longitudinal study. *Journal of the American Geriatric Society, 43*, 485–490.

Glatt, S. L., Hubble, J. P., Lyons, K., Paolo, A., Troster, A. I., Hassanein, R. E., et al. (1996). Risk factors for dementia in Parkinson's disease: Effect of education. *Neuroepidemiology, 15*, 20–25.

Hall, R. A., Fordyce, D. J., Lee, M. E., Eisenberg, B., Lee, R. F., Holmes, J. H. T., et al. (1999). Brain SPECT imaging and neuropsychological testing in coronary artery bypass patients: Single photon emission computed tomography. *The Annals of Thoracic Surgery, 68*, 2082–2088.

Hamilton, M. (1960). A rating scale for depression. *Journal of Neurology, Neurosurgery and Psychiatry, 23*, 56–62.

Helmer, C., Letenneur, L., Rouch, I., Richard-Harston, S., Barberger-Gateau, P., Fabrigoule, C., et al. (2001). Occupation during life and risk of dementia in French elderly community residents. *Journal of Neurology, Neurosurgery and Psychiatry, 71*, 303–309.

Hollingshead, A. B. (1975). *Four factor index of social status*. Unpublished manuscript, Yale University, New Haven, CT.

Jacobs, B., Schall, M., & Scheibel, A. B. (1993). A quantitative dendritic analysis of Wernicke's area in humans. II. Gender, hemispheric, and environmental factors. *Journal of Comparative Neurology, 327*, 97–111.

Karp, A., Kareholt, I. Qui, C., Bellander, T., Winblad, B., & Fratiglioni, L. (2004). Relation of education and occupation-based socioeconomic status to incident Alzheimer's disease. *American Journal of Epidemiology, 159*, 175–183.

Katzman, R., Terry, R., & DeTeresa, R., et al. (1998). Clinical, pathological, and neurochemical changes in dementia: A subgroup with preserved mental status and numerous neocortical plaques. *Annals of Neurology, 23*, 138–144.

Kilo, J., Czerny, M., Gorlitzer, M., Zimpfer, D., Baumer, H., Wolner, E., et al. (2001). Cardiopulmonary bypass affects cognitive brain function after coronary artery bypass grafting. *The Annals of Thoracic Surgery, 72*, 1926–1932.

Legendre, S. A., Stern, R. A., Bert, A. A., & Rogers, B. L. (2003). The influence of cognitive reserve on after CABG [Abstract]. *Archives of Clinical Neuropsychology, 18*, 726.

Legendre, S. A., Stern, R. A., Solomon, D. A., Furman, M. J., & Smith, K. E. (2003). The influence of cognitive reserve on memory following electroconvulsive therapy. *Journal of Neuropsychiatry and Clinical Neurosciences, 15*, 333–339.

Letenneur, L., Commenges, D., Dartigues, J. F., & Barberger-Gateau, P. (1994). Incidence of dementia and Alzheimer's disease in elderly community residents of south-western France. *International Journal of Epidemiology, 23*, 1256–1261.

Mills, S. (1993). Cerebral injury and cardiac operations. *The Annals of Thoracic Surgery, 56* (Suppl. 1), 89–91.

Mortimer, J. A. (1997). Brain reserve and the clinical expression of Alzheimer's disease. *Geriatrics, 52* (Suppl. 2), 50–53.

Murkin, J. M., Martzke, J. S., Buchan, A. M., Bentley, C., Wong, C. J. (1995). A randomized study of the influence of perfusion technique and pH management strategy in 316 patients undergoing coronary artery bypass surgery. II. Neurologic and cognitive outcomes. *Journal of Thoracic Cardiovascular Surgery, 110*, 349–362.

Newman, M. F., Croughwell, N. D., Blumenthal, J. A., White, W. D., Lewis, J. B., Smith, L. R., et al. (1994). Effect of aging on cerebral autoregulation during cardiopulmonary bypass. Association with postoperative cognitive dysfunction. *Circulation, 90*, 243–249.

Newman, M. F., Kirchner, J. L., Phillips-Bute, B., Gaver, V., Grocott, H., Jones, R. H., et al. (2001). Longitudinal assessment of neurocognitive function after coronary-artery bypass surgery. *New England Journal of Medicine, 344*, 395–402.

Nussmeier, N. A. (1994). Neuropsychiatric complications of cardiac surgery. *Journal of Cardiothoracic and Vascular Anesthesiology, 8*, 13–18.

Pagnin, D., de Queiroz, V., Pini, S., & Cassano, G. B. (2004). Efficacy of ECT in depression: A meta-analytic review. *Journal of ECT, 20*, 13–20.

Pugsley, W., Treasure, T., Klinger, L., Newman, S., Pascalis, C., & Harrison, M. (1990). Microemboli and cerebral impairment during cardiac surgery. *Vascular Surgery, 24*, 34–43.

Raja, P. V., Blumenthal, J. A., & Doraiswamy, P. M. (2004). Cognitive deficits following coronary artery bypass grafting: Prevalence, prognosis, and therapeutic strategies. *CNS Spectrums, 9*, 763–772.

Randt, C. T., & Brown, E. R. (1983). *Randt memory test*. New York: Life Sciences.

Richards, M., & Sacker, A. (2003). Lifetime antecedents of cognitive reserve. *Journal of Clinical and Experimental Neuropsychology, 25*, 614–624.

Riley, K. P., Snowdon, D. A., Desrosiers, M. F., & Markesbery, W. R. (2005). Early life linguistic ability, late life cognitive function, and neuropathology: Findings from the Nun Study. *Neurobiology of Aging, 26*, 341–347.

Roach, G. W., Kanchuger, M., Mangano, C. M., Newman, M., Nussmeier, N., Wolman, R., et al. (1996). Adverse cerebral outcomes after coronary bypass surgery. Multicenter Study of Perioperative Ischemia Research Group and the Ischemia Research and Education Foundation Investigators. *New England Journal of Medicine, 335*, 1857–1863.

Satz, P., Morgenstern, H., Miller, E. N., Selnes, O. A., McArthur, J. C., Cohen, B. A., et al. (1993). Low education as a possible risk factor for cognitive abnormalities in HIV-1: Findings from the multicenter AIDS Cohort Study (MACS). *Journal of Acquired Immune Deficiency Syndromes, 6*, 503–511.

Scarmeas, N., & Stern, Y. (2004). Cognitive reserve: Implications for diagnosis and prevention of Alzheimer's disease. *Current Neurology and Neuroscience Reports, 4*, 374–380.

Scarmeas, N., Zarahn, E., Anderson, K. E., Habeck, C. G., Hilton, J., Flynn, J., et al. (2003). Association of life activities with cerebral blood flow in Alzheimer disease: Implications for the cognitive reserve hypothesis. *Archives of Neurology, 60*, 359–65.

Scarmeas, N., Zarahn, E., Anderson, K. E., Honig, L. S., Park, A., Hilton, J., et al. (2004). Cognitive reserve-mediated modulation of PET activations during memory tasks in AD. *Archives of Neurology, 61*, 73–78.

Schoenberg, M. R., Scott, J. G., Duff, K., & Adams, R. L. (2002). Estimation of WAIS-III intelligence from combined performance and demographic variables: Development of the OPIE-3. *Clinical Neuropsychology, 16*, 426–437.

Selnes, O. A., Goldsborough, M. A., Borowicz, L. M., & McKhann, G. M. (1999). Neurobehavioural sequelae of cardiopulmonary bypass. *Lancet, 353*, 1601–1606.

Selnes, O. A., Grega, M. A., Borowicz, L. M. Jr., Royall, R. M., McKhann, G. M., & Baumgartner, W. A. (2003). Cognitive changes with coronary artery disease: A prospective study of coronary artery bypass graft patients and nonsurgical controls. *Annals of Thoracic Surgery, 75*, 1377–1384.

Snowdon, D. A., Kemper, S. J., Mortimer, J. A., Greiner, L. H., Wekstein, D. R., & Markesbery, W. R. (1996). Linguistic ability in early life and cognitive function and Alzheimer's disease in late life. Findings from the Nun Study. *Journal of the American Medical Association, 275*, 528–532.

Sobin, C., Sackeim, H. A., Prudic, J., Devanand, D., Moody, B., & McElhiney, M. C. (1995). Predictors of retrograde amnesia following ECT. *American Journal of Psychiatry, 152*, 995–1001.

Stern, R. A., Silva, S. G., Chaisson, N., & Evans, D. L. (1996). Influence of cognitive reserve on neuropsychological functioning in asymptomatic Human Immuno-deficiency Virus-1 infection. *Archives of Neurology, 53*, 148–153.

Stern, Y. (2003). The concept of cognitive reserve: A catalyst for research. *Journal of Clinical and Experimental Neuropsychology, 25*, 589–593.

Stern, Y. (2002). What is cognitive reserve? Theory and research applications of the reserve concept. *Journal of the International Neuropsychological Society, 8*, 448–460.

Stern, Y., Albert, S., Tang, M. X., & Tsai, W. Y. (1999). Rate of memory decline in AD is related to education and occupation: Cognitive reserve? *Neurology, 53*, 1942–1947.

Stern, Y., Alexander, G. E., Prohovnik, I., Stricks, L., Link, B., Lennon, M. C., et al. (1995). Relationship between lifetime occupation and parietal flow: Implications for a reserve against Alzheimer's disease pathology. *Neurology, 45*, 55–60.

Stern, Y., Gurland, B., Tatemichi, T. K., Tang, M. X., Wilder, D., & Mayeux, R. (1994). Influence of education and occupation on the incidence of Alzheimer's disease. *Journal of the American Medical Association, 271*, 1004–1010.

Stern, Y., Zarahn, E., Hilton, H. J., Flynn, J., DeLaPaz, R., & Rakitin, B. (2003). Exploring the neural basis of cognitive reserve. *Journal of Clinical and Experimental Neuropsychology, 25*, 691–701.

Taggart, D. P., Browne, S. M., Halligan, P. W., & Wade, D. T. (1999). Is cardiopulmonary bypass still the cause of cognitive dysfunction after cardiac operations? *Journal of Thoracic Cardiovascular Surgery, 118*, 414–420.

Van Dijk, D., Jansen, E. W., Hijman, R., Nierich, A. P., Diephuis, J. C., Moons, K. G., et al. (2002). Cognitive outcome after off-pump and on-pump coronary artery bypass graft surgery: A randomized trial. *Journal of the American Medical Association*, *287*, 1405–1412.

Vingerhoets, G., Van Nooten, G., Vermassen, F., De Soete, G., Jannes, C. (1997). Short-term and long-term neuropsychological consequences of cardiac surgery with extracorporeal circulation. *European Journal of Cardiothoracic Surgery*, *11*, 424–431.

Walzer, T., Herrmann, M., & Wallesch, C. W. (1997). Neuropsychological disorders after coronary bypass surgery. *Journal of Neurology, Neurosurgery and Psychiatry*, *62*, 644–648.

Weiner, R. D. (2000). Retrograde amnesia with electroconvulsive therapy: Characteristics and implications. *Archives of General Psychiatry*, *57*, 591–592.

Weinstein, C. S., Woodard, W. J., & DeSilva, R. A. (1998). Late neurocognitive changes from neurological damage following coronary bypass surgery. *Archives of General Psychiatry*, *24*, 131–137.

Wilson, R. S., Bennett, D. A., Bienias, J. L., Mendes de Leon, C. F., Morris, M. C., & Evans, D. A. (2003). Cognitive activity and cognitive decline in a biracial community population. *Neurology*, *61*, 812–816.

Wimmer-Greinecker, G., Matheis, G., Brieden, M., Dietrich, M., Oremek, G., Westphal, K., et al. (1998). Neuropsychological changes after cardiopulmonary bypass for coronary artery bypass grafting. *Thoracic Cardiovascular Surgery*, *46*, 207–212.

7 The impact of cognitive reserve on neuropsychological measures in clinical trials

Linas A. Bieliauskas and Ami Antonucci

Individual differences in risk morbidity are a well-recognized factor in clinical practice. However, medical research has yet to routinely incorporate the concept of cognitive reserve (CR) in understanding how the brain accommodates, copes and changes in the presence of pathology. Broadly defined, cognitive reserve refers to the discrepancy between the degree of pathology and the degree of functional impairment evidenced across individuals with the same disorder. The construct of cognitive reserve has been posited as a potential explanation for individual susceptibility to disease states and the variable levels of disruption in functional performance.

The causes of individual variability have been linked to both genetic and experiential environments (Lee, 2003) and two main models of CR have been proposed. Threshold theory, reviewed by Satz (1993), revolves around the hypothetical construct of "brain reserve capacity," in which a critical threshold must be surpassed before functional deficits emerge. This model supposes differences in brain anatomy as opposed to more active models of CR (Stern, 2003), which focus on the brain's ability to adapt to a changing environment. This more active perception of CR is seen as a normal process used by both healthy and brain damaged individuals as a means of dealing with ever-changing task demands. Thus, in comparison to individuals with low CR, individuals with higher CR process information in a more efficient and flexible manner. Stern (2003) further proposes that CR be limited to the variability observed in normal cognitive function, and that the concept of compensation be reserved for a specific response to brain dysfunction in the face of brain damage. In addition, Paradee, Rapport, Hanks, and Levy (2005) posit the likelihood that person by environment interactions may influence the utilization of cognitive reserve in compensating for limitations in the face of brain damage. As such, the threshold theory is a more passive view of brain capacity whereas the active model highlights the role of efficiency. However, regardless of the model utilized, innate differences in susceptibility and ability are likely to influence both the capacity and the efficiency of brain functioning.

Cognitive reserve has been operationalized in a variety of ways. Brain reserve capacity utilizes neuroanatomical and neurophysiological underpinnings as an anchor, such as head circumference and brain metabolism. Active models of CR utilize a more functional definition assessing several domains of neuropsychological traits. This chapter focuses on the latter.

Proxy measures of CR most often include demographic variables, such as intelligence and level of education. It is widely accepted that intelligence and education have profound effects on both psychological and physical health. As such, these two variables should be viewed more as risk factors than as confounders (Satz et al., 1993). Education levels below high school are clearly associated with significantly poorer levels of performance on common neuropsychological tests (Richardson & Marotolli, 1999). Premorbid intelligence usually serves as a general indicator of expected performance across cognitive domains (Tremont, Hoffman, Scott & Adams, 1998). Patients with above average intelligence are expected to perform better than those with average IQ, and in turn these individuals are expected to outperform those with below average intelligence. This has been demonstrated for measures as broad as the Halstead-Reitan Neuropsychological Test Battery (Warner, Ernst, & Townes, 1987) and as narrow as the Mini Mental State Exam (Bieliauskas, Depp, Kauszler, Steinberg, & Lacy, 2000). When compared to the influence of education, measures of IQ account for much more of the variance in neuropsychological test performance (Steinberg, Bieliauskas, Malec, Smith, Langellotti, & Ivnik, 2005a; Steinberg, Bieliauskas, Malec, Smith, & Ivnick, 2005b, 2005c, 2005d). Corral, Rodriquez, Amenedo, Sanchez, and Diaz (2006) report that individuals with lower cognitive reserve, as measured by IQ estimates, show an increased likelihood of deficient neuropsychological test scores for measures of attention, memory, and global functioning.

A less-frequently reported confound, which is seen when evaluating cognitive decline among high-functioning elders, is the failure of standardized neuropsychological tests to demonstrate cognitive decline when these patients themselves report subjective changes in cognitive efficiency. Rentz, Calvo, Scinto, Sperling, Budson, and Daffner (2000) have suggested that when IQ estimates are below 120, then conventional norms can be used, but added adjustments based on standard deviation are appropriate when estimated IQs are higher. This is supported by Diaz-Asper, Schretlen, and Pearlson (2004) who suggest that while IQ is good for predicting neuropsychological test scores for persons of average intelligence, it is less predictive for those who have above average IQs.

It is therefore surprising that in many large-scale studies, including clinical trials, CR is not taken into account when estimating rates of impairment. It is necessary to guard against attributing "impaired" test performance to a disease state or treatment status when, instead, poor performance may reflect naturally occurring variability. Even with a normal college student population, there have been reports of base rates of "impaired" performance as high as 15% on a standard neuropsychological test battery (Axelrod and Wall, 2003). On the other hand, it is also possible that individuals with lower CR may be more susceptible to disease state or treatment status than individuals with higher CR, and this may be highly relevant to estimating prevalence rates of cognitive impact across differentially vulnerable populations. Data regarding the influence of premorbid functioning on disease progression have been accumulating for some time and it is the purpose of this review to summarize available evidence among various disease domains.

Cardiovascular disease

Patients with cerebrovascular disease can present with mild cognitive deficits. Lopez and colleagues (2003a) examined the risk factors for mild cognitive impairment (MCI) in a longitudinal population study, the Cardiovascular Health Study Cognition Study. The overall prevalence of MCI in a sample of 2470 participants was 19% for those under age 75. The prevalence of MCI increased to 29% in those older than 85. Further analysis of the data revealed that MCI was associated with race and educational level, in addition to depression and other co-morbid illnesses (Lopez et al., 2003b), implicating the influence of cognitive reserve on classification of cognitive deficits.

Chronic obstructive pulmonary disease (COPD)

In a study by Stuss, Peterkin, Guzman, Guzman, and Troyer (1997), 18 patients with COPD were administered a series of pulmonary, neurological, and neuropsychological measures to test if there was an effect of COPD on neurological and cognitive functioning. Overall, there was no evidence of general dementia in this sample. Measures of immediate and delayed memory, complex attention, and speed of information processing correlated highly with arterial carbon dioxide partial pressure and, to a lesser extent, with oxygen partial pressure. Measures of language abilities, perceptual-motor functioning, and simple attention generally were not related to arterial gas pressures. A similar pattern of findings was obtained when group differences were examined between participants classified as severely hypoxic or mildly hypoxic, although group differences were mitigated by premorbid IQ differences. Hypoxia in COPD results in a relatively focused pattern of impairment in measures of memory function and tasks requiring attention allocation. The memory dysfunction may be related to involvement of limbic memory regions necessary for explicit memory. The attentional deficits were attributed to diffuse brain involvement resulting in reduced resource allocation. Early diagnosis and treatment of the hypoxia is essential.

Dementia

Alexander et al. (1997) investigated the relation between premorbid intellectual function and cerebral glucose metabolism in patients with Alzheimer's disease (AD). Premorbid intellectual ability was measured in three ways:

years of education; a demographics-based IQ estimate based on a regression formula incorporating age, gender, education, race and occupational history; and performance on the reading subtest of the Wide Range Achievement Test (WRAT). The findings support the hypothesis that higher levels of pre-morbid ability are associated with greater pathophysiologic effects of AD among patients of similar dementia severity. The association of premorbid ability with cerebral metabolic deficits was strongest in the prefrontal and premotor association areas. Furthermore, metabolism in these areas was related to all the measures of premorbid ability, with the WRAT reading score being the most sensitive. The authors suggest that higher levels of pre-morbid functioning may serve to delay or diminish the clinical presentation of dementia while the neuropathological effects of the disease continue. This finding was further substantiated by Wilson et al. (2004). Using mixed models that allowed for linear and nonlinear decline, and adjusting for age and edu-cation on cognitive decline, the authors showed that individuals with higher levels of education had a higher baseline of cognitive function with a similar early rate of decline to those with lower education. However, the authors also reported that individuals with higher education also had a somewhat greater rate of decline later in the course of the disease.

As mentioned above, neuropsychologists are also often faced with dif-ficulty measuring cognitive decline among elderly patients who are higher functioning. Rentz et al. (2004) provided IQ-based norms to detect cognitive decline among highly intelligent adults. They found that when IQ-adjusted norms were used, half of the individuals who showed memory impairment on that basis converted to mild cognitive impairment over a three and a half year period. IQ can thus certainly be considered as one proxy for CR in studies of dementia and cognitive decline with aging. Satz et al. (1993) also suggested that educational level can be used as a proxy for CR. When Powell and Whitla (1994, p. 71) compared generalized cognitive performance in a large group of physicians against a group of individuals (average of 14 years of education) by age, they found that though the less well-educated group reached lower levels of cognitive efficiency at younger ages, the slope of decline with aging was similar in the two groups. This would support the suggestions of Rentz et al. that higher IQ (i.e., CR) can effectively mask early age-related cognitive decline, though the rate of decline among individuals with lower and higher CR may be similar.

Finally, it has been reported that IQ estimates of CR can have effects not only on more complex neuropsychological measures, but on simpler measures such as the Mini-Mental State Examination (MMSE; Folstein, Folstein, and McHugh, 1975). Bieliauskas et al. (2000) reported that when individuals have an estimated IQ which is below average (i.e., lower than 85), the traditional MMSE cutoff score of 23 must be lowered to accurately classify dementia-related impairment.

The above observations lead to an interesting potential relationship between CR and cognitive changes in dementing conditions. When defining

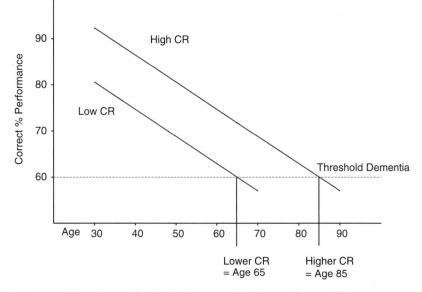

Figure 7.1 CR and cognitive decline in potentially dementing conditions.

the presence or absence of dementia, an arbitrary level of performance on cognitive tasks is often employed as a parameter of dementia. For example, as mentioned above, a score below 24 on the MMSE is the standard among clinicians for designating an individual as being cognitively impaired consistent with dementia. Thus if it is postulated that individuals with lower CR will show cognitive impairment or dementia at an earlier age than individuals with higher CR, the interaction between CR and cognitive impairment would look something like that seen in Figure 7.1. In that figure, the horizontal dashed line would reflect the arbitrary definition of impairment, or dementia, and one can see that even though rates of decline are similar, individuals with higher CR reach the definition point for dementia at a later age. This would support the threshold theory espoused by Satz (1993).

Hepatitis C virus (HCV)

In an initial report on baseline levels of cognitive functioning in patients infected with HCV who were entering a treatment trial with interferon, Fontana et al. (2005) found that 33% met a criterion for impairment (four or more cognitive tests one standard deviation below the mean). In a follow-up study of the same population, Bieliauskas et al. (in press) reported that standard scores could be used to calculate a global deficit score that was closely related to functional clinician ratings of impairment, resulting in classifying 40% and 44% of a subset of these patients as being cognitively impaired, respectively. IQ scores were estimated for that population by using the Shipley Institute of Living Scale (Shipley; Zachary, 1991). Despite having a normal distribution of IQ in their study population, Fontana et al. found the Shipley IQ was the strongest and most consistent correlate of all the neuropsychological standard scores and was strongly related to educational and occupational levels. They speculate that CR may have a significant influence on impairment classification and the degree to which this interacts with disease processes is currently being explored.

Human immunodeficiency virus (HIV)

There have been reports of a relationship between CR disease or treatment-specific interactions. In patients infected with HIV, Stern, Silva, Chaisson, and Evans (1996) calculated CR scores using a combination of the Shipley Vocabulary subtest, educational level, and occupational level. They reported that HIV-1 seropositive subjects with low CR scores exhibited significantly greater deficits than did HIV-1 seropositive subjects with high CR scores. This is similar to the earlier report of Satz et al. (1993), which suggested that low education might reflect lowered CR, which in turn lowered the threshold for neuropsychological abnormalities in cases of early HIV-1 infection.

In addition, over a 1-year period, Basso and Bornstein (2000) studied whether estimated premorbid intelligence would moderate worsening neuro-behavioral dysfunction in HIV infection in 155 homosexual men with stable disease status. These men (54 controls, 49 HIV+ asymptomatic, 24 HIV+ symptomatic, 28 AIDS) were tested on measures of executive function at baseline and 12-month follow-up. Regardless of disease status, men with above-average IQ showed no declines on measures of executive function across the two time points. However, those in the symptomatic groups with average IQ showed declines. No decline was evident in the asymptomatic group. The findings support the hypothesis that estimated premorbid intelligence mediates declines in neuropsychological function in patients with stable HIV status.

Most recently, using reading and education level as proxies for CR, Ryan et al. (2005) found that discrepancies between reading and educational levels were associated with worse neuropsychological test performance in patients infected with HIV, while racial and ethnic minority status was not. They caution that use of standard norms based on education alone may overestimate cognitive impairment among ethnic and racial minorities.

Lupus/auto-immune disease

Systemic lupus erythematosus (SLE) is a chronic autoimmune disease in which patients manifest neurologic and/or psychiatric deficits, such as cranial neuropathy, cerebrovascular disease and depression. Monastero et al. (2001) reported cognitive impairment in 26.9% of SLE patients without overt neuro-psychiatric manifestations. In comparison, cognitive deficits were reported in 52.2% of SLE patients with neuropsychiatric manifestations, with particular deficits in visuospatial memory. Cognitive impairment was evident in both groups on tasks of long-term memory and visuo-constructional ability. Mulherin, Doherty, O'Connell, and Bresnihan (1993) reported on the value of estimating premorbid intelligence as a means of screening for subclinical cognitive dysfunction. Sixteen female patients with clinically quiescent SLE underwent neuropsychological examination, which included measurement of full-scale intelligence quotient, verbal and performance IQ, and verbal and visual memories. These patients were assessed at baseline with a measure of premorbid IQ and then again 1 year later. A comparison of measured full-scale IQ with the estimated premorbid intelligence identified a subgroup of patients who demonstrated a significant reduction in intelligence, suggesting a disease/CR interaction.

Conclusions and recommendations

From this brief review, two things become apparent. First, few large-scale studies of diseases or clinical trials for their treatment control for the influence of CR. Second, accounting for the influence of CR is important and failure to do so may lead to overestimates of the influence of disease or treatment on changes in cognitive efficiency. This would include overestimates of impairment in ethnic/minority populations.

The primary consideration is to obtain an estimate of CR for all participants in the study. Stern et al. (1996) have proposed one such method, as mentioned above. In addition to levels of occupation and education, they used the Vocabulary subtest of the Shipley to estimate general, longstanding knowledge of vocabulary as a proxy for CR. Another potential test for estimating longstanding knowledge as a proxy for CR is the Peabody Picture Vocabulary Test-III (Dunn and Dunn, 1997). Snitz, Bieliauskas, Crosslands, Basso, and Roper (2000) found that an earlier version of this test is a good estimate of premorbid levels of general intellectual functioning, especially for individuals with high school educations or better. Another estimate of CR, as suggested by Ryan et al. (2005) is to estimate reading level. They used the reading score from the Wide Range Achievement Test-3 (Wilkinson, 1993). Two additional methods for estimating proxies for CR are administration instruments such as the American National Adult Reading Test (Grober and Sliwinski, 1991) or calculation of an estimated IQ using demographic methods (Barona, Reynolds, & Chastain, 1984). Snitz et al., however, suggest these latter two types of estimates may overestimate longstanding IQ. A more exhaustive treatment of estimating IQ as a proxy for CR can be found in Strauss, Sherman, and Spreen (2006).

In large-scale disease or treatment clinical trials, a method of estimating longstanding CR should be administered to each patient at baseline. Of importance when selecting from any of the above methods or another, is that an attempt be made to choose an estimate that is as independent as possible from factors that affect performance on other cognitive measures of interest. The methods already indicated attempt to do so and are often described as measures of crystallized vs. fluid general intellectual abilities (Hochandel and Kaplan, 1984). That is, tests of "crystallized intelligence," which are relatively unaffected by disease or injury unless very severe, as opposed to tests of "fluid intelligence," which are susceptible to disease and injury effects.

Whichever method is used to estimate CR, the ideal large-scale study would include a control group, matched to study subjects by age, education, gender, and ethnic/minority makeup. The control group would be administered the same tests and estimate of CR. The patient and control groups can then be compared by level of CR to see how neuropsychological tests are affected and for rates of classification of impairment. The difference between groups would presumably reflect the independent effects of disease, injury, or treatment.

Unfortunately, funding for large-scale clinical trials often does not include measures in appropriate control groups. In these instances, effects of disease, injury, or treatment may be estimated by controlling for the influence of CR by statistical methods. Linear regression methods may be used to measure the degree of variance remaining after the effect of CR is removed. Patient groups can also be broken down into high vs. low CR and the degrees of impairment noted. If the prevalence of impairment in the high CR group is similar to that reported for normal populations, while the prevalence of impairment in the low CR group is higher, than an adverse CR × disease, treatment, or injury state effect might be inferred. If the prevalence of impairment in the high CR group is higher than in a referent normal population, than a disease, treatment, or injury effect across the entire patient group might be inferred. Unfortunately, these statistical methods are inferential and do not directly answer the question of direct CR influence on test performance as would the inclusion of a control group.

Following the proposals of Satz (1993) and Stern (2003), and the many studies supporting, not just an influence, but a very strong influence of CR on neuropsychological test performance, it is strongly recommended that measures of CR be included in all large-scale clinical trials and methods of analysis of its influence be incorporated into any such study design. If untoward cognitive effects of disease, injury, or treatment are overestimated, not only is their impact difficult to assess accurately, but patients may be unnecessarily discouraged and pessimistic about their described quality of life, with associated emotional distress.

References

Alexander, G., Furey, M., Grady, C., Pietrini, P., Brady. D., et al. (1997). Association of premorbid intellectual function with cerebral metabolism in Alzheimer's disease: Implications for the cognitive reserve hypothesis. *American Journal of Psychiatry*, *154* (2): 165–172.

Axelrod, B. N., & Wall, J. R. (2003). Specificity of the Halstead-Reitan Neuropsychological Test Battery [Abstract]. *The Clinical Neuropsychologist, 17*, 101.

Barona, A., Reynolds, C. R., & Chastain, R. (1984). A demographically based index of premorbid intelligence for the WAIS-R. *Journal of Consulting and Clinical Psychology, 52*, 885–887.

Basso, M., & Bornstein, R. (2000). Estimated premorbid intelligence mediates neurobehavioral change in individuals infected with HIV across 12 months. *Journal of Clinical and Experimental Neuropsychology, 22* (2), 208–218.

Bieliauskas, L. A., Back-Madruga, C., Lindsay, K. L., Snow, K. K., Kronfol, Z., Lok, A. S., et al. & the HALT-C Trial Group (in press). *Journal of Clinical and Experimental Neuropsychology.*

Bieliauskas, L. A., Depp, C., Kauszler, M. L., Steinberg, B. A., & Lacy, M. (2000). I.Q. and Scores on the Mini-Mental State Exam (MMSE). *Aging, Neuropsychology, and Cognition, 7*, 227–229.

Corral, M., Rodriquez, M., Amenedo, E., Sanchez, J. L., & Diaz, F. (2006). Cognitive reserve, age, and neuropsychological performance in healthy participants. *Developmental Neuropsychology, 29*, 479–491.

Diaz-Asper, C. M., Schretlen, D. J., & Pearlson, G. D. (2004). How well does IQ predict neuropsychological test performance in normal adults? *Journal of the International Neuropsychological Society, 10*, 82–90.

Folstein, M. F., Folstein, S. E., & McHugh, P. R. (1975). Mini-Mental State: A practical method for grading the cognitive state of patients for clinicians. *Journal of Psychiatric Research, 12*, 189–198.

Dunn, L. M. & Dunn, L. M. (1997). *Examiner's manual for the Peabody Picture Vocabulary Test third edition.* Circle Pine, MN: American Guidance Service.

Fontana, R. J., Bieliauskas, L. A., Back-Madruga, C., Lindsay, K. L., Kronfol, Z., Lok, A. S., et al., & the HALT-C Trial Group (2005). Cognitive function in hepatitis C patients with advanced fibrosis enrolled in the HALT-C trial. *Journal of Hepatology, 43*, 614–622.

Grober, E., & Sliwinski, M. (1991). Development and validation of a model for estimating premorbid verbal intelligence in the elderly. *Journal of Clinical and Experimental Neuropsychology, 13*, 933–949.

Hochandel, G., & Kaplan, E. (1984). Neuropsychology of normal aging. In J. L. Albert (Ed.), *Clinical neurology of aging.* New York: Oxford University Press.

Lee, J. (2003). Genetic evidence for cognitive reserve: Variations in memory and related cognitive functions. *Journal of Clinical and Experimental Neuropsychology, 25* (5), 594–613.

Lopez, O. L., Jagust, W. J., DeKosky, S. T., Becker, J. T., Fitzpatrick, A., Dulberg, C., et al. (2003a). Prevalence and classification of mild cognitive impairment in the Cardiovascular Health Study Cognition Study: Part 1. *Archives of Neurology, 60*, 1385–1389.

Lopez, O. L., Jagust, W. J., Dulberg, C., Becker, J. T., DeKosky, S. T., Fitzpatrick, A., et al. (2003b). Risk factors for mild cognitive impairment in the Cardiovascular Health Study Cognition Study: Part 2. *Archives of Neurology, 60*, 1394–1399.

Monastero, R., Bettini, P., Del Zotto, E., Cottini, E., Tincani, A., et al. (2001). Prevalence and pattern of impairment in systemic lupus erythematosus patients with and without overt neuropsychiatric manifestations. *Journal of the Neurological Sciences, 184*, 33–39.

Mulherin, D., Doherty, E., O'Connell, A., & Bresnihan, B. (1993). Assessment of cognitive function in patients with systemic lupus erythematosus. *Irish Journal of Medical Science, 162* (1), 9–12.

Paradee, C. V., Rapport, L. J., Hanks, R. A., & Levy, J. A. (2005). Circadian preference and cognitive functioning among rehabilitation inpatients. *The Clinical Neuropsychologist, 19*, 55–72.

Powell, D. H., & Whitla, D. K. (1994). *Profiles in cognitive aging.* Cambridge, MA: Harvard University Press.

Rentz, D. M., Calvo, V. L., Scinto, L. F. M., Sperling, R. A., Budson, A. E., & Daffner, K. R. (2000). Detecting early cognitive decline in high-functioning elders. *Journal of Geriatric Psychiatry, 33*, 27–48.

Rentz, D. M., Huh, T. J., Faust, R. R., Budson, A. E., Scinto, L. F., Sperling, R. A., et al. (2004). Use of IQ-adjusted norms to predict progressive cognitive decline in highly intelligent older individuals. *Neuropsychology, 18* (1), 38–49.

Richardson, E. D., & Marottoli, R. A. (1999). Education-specific normative data on common neuropsychological indices for individuals older than 75 years. *The Clinical Neuropsychologist, 10*, 375–381.

Ryan, E. L., Baird, R., Mindt, M. R., Byrd, D., Monzones, J., & Morgello, S. for the Manhattan HIV Brain Bank (2005). Neuropsychological impairment in racial/ethnic minorities with HIV infection and low literacy levels: Effects of education and reading level in participant characterization. *Journal of the International Neuropsychological Society, 11*, 889–898.

Satz, P. (1993). Brain reserve capacity on symptoms onset after brain injury: A formulation and review of evidence for threshold theory. *Neuropsychology, 7* (3), 273–295.

Satz, P., Morgenstern, H., Miller, E. N., Selnes, O. A., McArthur, J. C., Cohen, B. A., et al. (1993). Low education as a possible risk factor for early cognitive abnormalities in HIV-1: Findings from the Multicenter AIDS Cohort Study (MACS). *Journal of Acquired Immune Deficiency Syndrome, 6*, 503–511.

Snitz, B. E., Bieliauskas, L. A., Crosslands, A., Basso, M. R., & Roper, B. (2000). The PPVT-R as an estimate of premorbid intelligence in older adults. *The Clinical Neuropsychologist, 14*, 181–186.

Steinberg, B. A., Bieliauskas, L. A., Malec, J. F., Smith, G. E., Langellotti, C., and Ivnik, R. J. (2005a). Mayo's Older Americans Normative Studies: Age- and IQ-adjusted norms for the Boston Naming Test, the MAE Token Test, and the Judgment of Line Orientation Test. *The Clinical Neuropsychologist, 19*, 280–328.

Steinberg, B. A., Bieliauskas, L. A., Malec, J. F., Smith, G. E. and Ivnik, R. J. (2005b). Mayo's Older Americans Normative Studies: Age- and IQ-adjusted norms for the Boston Naming Test, the Trail-Making Test, the Stroop Test, and MAE Controlled Oral Word Association Test. *The Clinical Neuropsychologist, 19*, 329–377.

Steinberg, B. A., Bieliauskas, L. A., Malec, J. F., Smith, G. E., and Ivnik, R. J. (2005c). Mayo's Older Americans Normative Studies: Age- and IQ-adjusted norms for the Wechsler Memory Scale-Revised. *The Clinical Neuropsychologist, 19*, 378–463.

Steinberg, B. A., Bieliauskas, L. A., Malec, J. F., Smith, G. E., and Ivnik, R. J. (2005d). Mayo's Older Americans Normative Studies: Age- and IQ-adjusted norms for the Auditory Verbal Learning Test and the Visual Spatial Learning Test. *The Clinical Neuropsychologist, 19*, 464–523.

Stern, R. A., Silva, S. G., Chaisson, N., & Evans, D. L. (1996). Influence of cognitive reserve on neuropsychological functioning in asymptomatic human immunodeficiency virus-1 infection. *Archives of Neurology, 53*, 148–153.

Stern, Y. (2003). The concept of cognitive reserve: A catalyst for research. *Journal of Clinical and Experimental Neuropsychology, 25* (5), 589–593.

Strauss, E., Sherman, E. M. S., & Spreen, O. (2006). General cognitive functioning, neuropsychological batteries, and assessment of premorbid intelligence. In *A compendium of neuropsychological tests: Administration, norms, and commentary* (pp. 98–362). New York: Oxford University Press.

Stuss, D., Peterkin, I., Guzman, D., Guzman, C. & Troyer, A. (1997). Chronic obstructive pulmonary disease: Effects of hypoxia on neurological and neuro-psychological measures. *Journal of Clinical and Experimental Neuropsychology, 19* (4), 515–524.

Tremont, G., Hoffman, R., Scott, J., & Adams, R. (1998). Effect of intellectual level on neuropsychological performance: A response to Dodrill (1997). *Clinical Neuropsychologist, 12* (4), 560–567.

Warner, M., Ernst, J., & Townes, B.D. (1987). Relationships between IQ and neuro-psychological measures in neuropsychiatric populations: Within-laboratory and cross-cultural replications using WAIS and WAIS-R. *Journal of Clinical and Experimental Neuropsychology, 9*, 545–562.

Wilkinson, G. (1993). *Wide Range Achievement Test* (3rd ed.). *Administration manual.* Wilmington, DE: Wide Range, Inc.

Wilson, R., Li, Y., Aggarwal, N., Barnes, L., McCann, J., et al. (2004). Education and the course of cognitive decline in Alzheimer disease. *Neurology, 63*, 1198–1202.

Zachary, R. A. (1991). *Shipley Institute of Living Scale.* Los Angeles, CA: Western Psychological Services.

8 Association between early life physical activity and late-life cognition: Evidence for cognitive reserve

Miranda G. Dik, Dorly J. H. Deeg,
Marjolein Visser, and Cees Jonker

Physical activity has shown to be inversely associated with cognitive decline in older people. Whether this association is already present in early life is investigated and discussed in this chapter. The association between early life physical activity and cognition was studied in 1241 subjects aged 62–85 years, in a prospective population-based study. Physical activity between ages 15–25 years was asked retrospectively. The findings suggest a positive association between regular physical activity early in life and level of information processing speed at older age in men, not in women. The association could not be explained by current physical activity or other lifestyle factors. This finding supports the cognitive reserve hypothesis, and might suggest that early life physical activity may delay late-life cognitive deficits.

Introduction

There is a growing body of literature showing that physical activity is positively associated with cognition in older persons. Intervention studies have shown beneficial effects of aerobic fitness on cognition (Colcombe & Kramer, 2003; Fabre, Chamari, Mucci, Masse-Biron, & Prefaut, 2002), and also longitudinal population-based studies increasingly show inverse associations with cognitive decline and dementia (Abbott, White, Ross, Masaki, Curb, & Petrovich, 2004; Laurin, Verreault, Lindsay, MacPherson, & Rockwood, 2001; van Gelder, Tijhuis, Kalmijn, Giampaoli, Nissinen, & Kromhout, 2004; Weuve, Kang, Manson, Breteler, Ware, & Grodstein, 2004; Yaffe, Barnes, Nevitt, Lui, & Covinsky, 2001).

Animal studies have shown that physical activity directly stimulates neurogenesis in the hippocampus (Cotman & Berchtold, 2002; Gómez-Pinilla, So, & Kesslak, 1998; van Praag, Christie, Sejnowski, & Gage, 1999), providing reserve against later cognitive decline and dementia. Also in aging humans, aerobic fitness has been shown to be associated with reduced brain tissue loss in the frontal, parietal, and temporal cortices (Colcombe et al., 2003), suggesting beneficial effects of physical activity on brain volume. Evidence from animal models suggest that physical activity may be most beneficial at a young age because it enables optimal neural development, resulting in a neural reserve that can be drawn on in old age (Black, Isaacs, & Greenough, 1991). Long-term environmental enrichment has been shown to induce sustained effects on brain plasticity in active mice (Kempermann, Gast, & Gage, 2002). In humans, studies on socioeconomic status and education also suggest that early life factors are important for late-life cognitive impairment and dementia (Breteler, 2001; Moceri et al., 2001; Stern, Gurland, Tatemichi, Tang, Widler, & Mayeux, 1994; Geerlings, Schmand, Jonker, Lindeboom, & Bouter, 1999). To our knowledge, no previous study has explored the association between early life physical activity and cognitive decline in aging humans. It is important to gain more insight into the possible association between early life physical activity and cognitive decline, because physical activity can be used in prevention strategies starting at a young age. Prevention of cognitive decline has high priority because of the growing number of elderly with cognitive decline in the community.

Therefore, in a prospective population-based study, we explored the association between early life physical activity and cognition in older persons.

Method

Study sample

Subjects were participants in the Longitudinal Aging Study Amsterdam (LASA), a population-based study among 3107 subjects aged 55 to 85 years (Deeg & Westendorp-de Serière, 1994). The sampling and data collection procedures have been described elsewhere in detail (Van den Heuvel, Smits, Deeg, & Beekman, 1996; Smit, de Vries, & Poppelaars, 1998). In summary, a random sample stratified by age and sex was drawn from the population registries in three geographic areas of the Netherlands. Sample selection was stratified by age and sex according to expected 5-year mortality to ensure sufficient sample sizes for longitudinal analyses within age and sex strata. Subjects were interviewed and tested at home by trained interviewers. Approval for the study was given by the local medical ethics committee and all respondents gave informed consent at the start of the study.

The LASA study started in 1992/1993, and includes follow-up measurements after 3 and 6 years. For the present study, the design involved additional cognitive testing in subjects aged 62 years and over ($n = 2064$). The data on early life physical activity were recorded at the second data collection cycle, 3 years after baseline, and were available for 1385 subjects (67.1%). Loss to follow-up between the first and the second data collection was mainly due to mortality (Smit et al., 1998). Subjects who were lost to follow-up (679 of 2064 subjects; 32.9%) were significantly older, more often men, and had lower cognition scores (all $p < .01$) than subjects who participated in the second data collection. We excluded subjects with cognitive impairment at the second measurement, using a Mini-Mental State Examination (MMSE) score of less than 24, to lower the probability of errors in the early life physical activity recall. This resulted in a total sample of 1241 subjects included in this study.

Of these 1241 subjects, 256 (20.6%) were lost to follow-up at the third measurement, leaving 985 (79.4%) with measurements on three occasions. Again, loss to follow-up between the second and the third measurement was mainly due to mortality (11.4%). Other reasons that subjects did not participate in the third measurement were that they were too ill to be interviewed (1.6%), refused (2.4%), could not be contacted (0.3%), had a short interview by phone (3.1%), or for 1.8% the reason was unknown. Subjects with data at the first and second measurement had reported higher early life activity levels than subjects with complete data on all three measurements ($\chi^2 = 14.5$; $p < .01$).

Cognitive functioning

General cognitive function was measured with the MMSE (Folstein, Folstein, & McHugh, 1975). This is a widely-used, brief, global cognitive function test designed as a screening instrument for cognitive impairment. Scores range from 0 to 30, with a higher score indicating better performance.

Information processing speed was measured with an adapted version of a letter substitution task, the Alphabet Coding Task-15 (Piccinin & Rabbitt, 1999). This is a timed task in which the respondent has to combine as many characters as possible, according to a given example. The example shows 15 combinations of two characters in a row of double boxes (the substitution key). The test itself shows rows of double boxes, in which only the upper box contains characters and the lower box is empty. The respondent has to name the missing characters corresponding to the characters in the upper box (using the substitution key) as quickly and accurately as possible. The task consists of three identical 1-minute trials. The score on each trial consists of the number of completed characters. The mean score of the three trials was used in the analyses.

Early life physical activity

Respondents were asked retrospectively whether they had participated in sports or any other physical activity that caused them to sweat or that made them exhausted, between the age of 15 to 25 years. Physical activity was categorized into four groups based on total time per week: (1) no regular physical activity (never or sometimes); (2) low (less than 1 to 2 hours per week); (3) moderate (3 to 9 hours per week), and (4) high (10 hours or more per week).

Potential confounders

The potential confounders that were included in the analyses were age, sex, verbal intelligence, socioeconomic status (SES), lifestyle (early life physical work demands, current physical activity level, smoking status, alcohol consumption), and health indicators (diabetes mellitus, cardiac disease, depression).

Verbal intelligence was measured with a Dutch vocabulary test (Luteijn & van der Ploeg, 1983), and is a more reliable measure for premorbid intelligence than the level of education (Lezak, 1995). Socioeconomic status was a composite score including education, income, and occupational prestige (Sixma & Ultee, 1983). Early life physical work demands were assessed by asking for the highest physical demand that the respondent had performed almost daily between 15 and 25 years of age. Answers were coded as "low to moderate" and "high to very high." Current physical activity was assessed with the Lasa Physical Activity Questionnaire (LAPAQ) (Stel, Smit, Pluijm, Visser, Deeg, & Lips, 2004). Because predominantly high-intensity activities have previously been associated with cognition (Chodzko-Zajko & Moore, 1994), we selected only medium-to-high-intensity activities, with MET scores of 4.0 or higher (Ainsworth et al., 1993, 2000), such as bicycling, gardening, heavy housework, and sports activities. Respondents were asked how often and for how long during the previous 2 weeks they had engaged in these activities. These scores were converted to the time spent on physical activity in minutes per day. Smoking status was classified as never, former, and current smokers. Alcohol consumption was assessed by asking for the number of alcoholic units per week over the past year. Diabetes mellitus and cardiac disease were assessed by self-report. These diseases are likely to be associated with early life physical activity and cognition. Depression was assessed with the Center for Epidemiologic Studies Depression Scale (CES-D), using the generally applied cutoff score ≥ 16 to identify clinically relevant depressive subjects (Radloff, 1977; Beekman, Deeg, Van Limbeek, Braam, De Vries, & Van Tilburg, 1997).

Data analysis

Characteristics of the study sample were compared using χ^2 tests or Student's *t*-tests for independent samples.

Associations between early life physical activity and cognition at older age were analyzed using generalized estimating equations (GEE) (Zeger & Liang, 1986; Twisk, 1997). This method of longitudinal analysis uses the continuous scores from all three measurements, and includes subjects regardless of missing values. Thus even subjects who were lost to follow-up after two measurements were included in the analysis, to reduce bias that might have arisen from a differential loss to follow-up of more cognitively impaired elderly. The dependency of the repeated observations within persons was defined by an exchangeable correlation structure, meaning that the correlation was constant between any two cognitive scores for a person. The physical activity levels were entered as dummies, and the inactive category was used as the reference group. The analyses were adjusted for time (model 1), adjusted for age, sex, and verbal intelligence (model 2), and additionally adjusted for SES, lifestyle and health indicators (model 3). Effect modification by sex was investigated using interaction terms. Whether physical activity was significantly associated with 6-year cognitive decline was evaluated by including the product terms of cognition with time in the models. The associations were tested at the .05 level of significance, and the interaction terms at the .10 level of significance.

Results

Almost 65 percent of the elderly were physically inactive during adolescence and young adulthood, 12 percent were regularly physically active at low frequency, 16 percent were moderately, and 8 percent highly frequently active. These proportions differed significantly between men and women, with 52 percent inactive young men compared with 76 percent inactive young women (Table 8.1). Among men were higher proportions of moderately and highly active subjects. Furthermore, men and women differed in verbal intelligence, SES, early life physical work demands, current physical activity, smoking, alcohol, cardiac disease and depression (all $p < .001$). Men and women did not differ significantly in the cognitive scores.

Table 8.2 shows the characteristics of the study sample by physical activity level. The proportion of men increased significantly by increasing physical activity level. Verbal intelligence and SES differed significantly between the physical activity groups, with the lowest levels of verbal intelligence and SES in both the inactive and the highly active groups. The proportion of high-to-very high early life physical work demands was lowest (36%) in the low physical activity group, and highest (82%) in the high physical activity group. The proportion of former and current smokers increased significantly with increasing physical activity level. Age, current physical activity, alcohol consumption, the health indicators, and scores on general cognition (MMSE) did not differ significantly between the groups. Scores on information processing speed did differ significantly by physical activity level, with the lowest scores in both the inactive and highly active groups.

Table 8.3 shows the results of the longitudinal analyses. The associations between early life physical activity and general cognition were not significant, except for low physical activity, showing a positive association with general cognition (beta = 0.38; model 1). This beta of 0.38 indicates that low physically active subjects scored on average 0.38 points higher on MMSE compared with inactive subjects (= reference group) during 6 years follow-up. After adjustment for age and verbal intelligence, and the other confounding factors, this association was no longer significant (models 2 and 3). On

Table 8.1 Characteristics of the study sample (*n* = 1241)[a]

Characteristic	Total study sample	Men (*n* = 604)	Women (*n* = 637)
Men, % (*n*)	48.7 (604)		
Age, year, M (SD)	74.9 (6.4)	74.9 (6.4)	74.9 (6.4)
Verbal intelligence, M (SD)[b]	13.2 (3.7)	13.8 (3.7)	12.7 (3.7)**
Socioeconomic status, M (SD)[c]	36.3 (19.2)	39.9 (18.3)	33.0 (19.4)**
Early life physical activity, % (*n*)			
None	64.1 (795)	51.5 (311)	76.0 (484)**
Low	12.0 (149)	12.9 (78)	11.1 (71)
Moderate	15.9 (197)	23.0 (139)	9.1 (58)
High	8.1 (100)	12.6 (76)	3.8 (24)
Early life physical work demands, % (*n*)			
High-to-very high	52.7 (653)	58.6 (354)	47.0 (299)**
Current physical activity, M (SD)[d]	43.4 (61.3)	51.5 (70.8)	35.8 (49.7)**
Smoking status, % (*n*)			
Never	34.2 (424)	9.4 (57)	57.6 (367)**
Former smoker	47.1 (584)	65.9 (398)	29.2 (186)
Current smoker	18.8 (233)	24.7 (149)	13.2 (84)
Alcohol consumption, % (*n*)[d]			
None	22.9 (284)	14.2 (86)	31.1 (198)**
Modest	50.8 (631)	48.0 (290)	53.6 (341)
Moderate	19.8 (246)	27.5 (166)	12.6 (80)
Heavy	4.4 (54)	7.0 (42)	1.9 (12)
Excessive	2.0 (25)	3.3 (20)	0.8 (5)
Diabetes mellitus, % (*n*)	7.3 (90)	6.8 (41)	7.7 (49)
Cardiac disease, % (*n*)	26.3 (327)	32.3 (195)	20.7 (132)**
Depression, % (*n*)[d]	13.9 (173)	7.3 (44)	20.3 (129)**
MMSE, M (SD)[e]	27.6 (1.6)	27.6 (1.7)	27.7 (1.6)
Information processing speed, M (SD)[f]	23.8 (6.8)	23.7 (6.7)	23.9 (7.0)

Notes: [a] Data at second data collection cycle. [b] Range, 0–20. [c] Range, 4–100. [d] Missing values for some subjects. [e] Range, 24–30. [f] Range, 1.0–42.7.
* *p* < .05. ** *p* < .001. MMSE = Mini-Mental State Examination.

information processing speed, low and moderate physical activity were significantly associated with higher speed (model 1). Low active subjects scored 2.62 points higher on information processing, and moderately active subjects scored 1.16 points higher on information processing than inactive subjects. After adjustment for confounding factors (models 2 and 3), low physical activity remained significantly associated with information processing speed (beta = 0.97). Furthermore, including the interaction term with sex in the model revealed that the associations between early life physical activity and information processing speed were significantly modified by sex. Therefore, these associations were analyzed separately for men and women (Table 8.4).

The results show that the associations were only significant in men. Men who were physically active at low or moderate level had significantly higher scores in older age than inactive men (models 1 and 2). This association remained significant after adjustment for all confounders (model 3).

Table 8.2 Characteristics of the study sample by early life physical activity (n = 1241)[a]

Characteristic	Early life physical activity			
	None (n = 795)	Low (n = 149)	Moderate (n = 197)	High (n = 100)
Men, % (n)	39.1 (311)	52.3 (78)	70.6 (139)	76.0 (76)**
Age, year, M (SD)	75.1 (6.4)	74.1 (6.2)	75.0 (6.2)	74.6 (6.7)
Verbal intelligence, M (SD)[b]	12.9 (3.7)	14.3 (3.5)	13.9 (3.8)	12.9 (4.1)**
Socioeconomic status, M (SD)[c]	34.8 (19.2)	41.1 (20.3)	40.1 (18.8)	33.5 (16.0)**
Early life physical work demands, % (n)				
High-to-very high	51.1 (406)	36.2 (54)	56.3 (111)	82.0 (82)**
Current physical activity, M (SD)[d]	39.2 (55.2)	50.1 (63.6)	50.4 (75.6)	53.5 (70.8)*
Smoking status, % (n)				
Never	39.0 (310)	27.5 (41)	25.4 (50)	23.0 (23)**
Former smoker	42.5 (338)	53.7 (80)	55.8 (110)	56.0 (56)
Current smoker	18.5 (147)	18.8 (28)	18.8 (37)	21.0 (21)
Alcohol consumption, % (n)[d]				
None	23.8 (189)	18.8 (28)	20.8 (41)	26.0 (26)
Modest	51.3 (408)	55.0 (82)	46.7 (92)	49.0 (49)
Moderate	19.4 (154)	18.8 (28)	22.8 (45)	19.0 (19)
Heavy	3.9 (31)	6.7 (10)	5.6 (11)	2.0 (2)
Excessive	1.5 (12)	0.7 (1)	4.1 (8)	4.0 (4)
Diabetes mellitus, % (n)	7.7 (61)	3.4 (5)	9.1 (18)	6.0 (6)
Cardiac disease, % (n)	25.4 (202)	24.2 (36)	28.9 (57)	32.0 (32)
Depression, % (n)[d]	14.3 (114)	13.4 (20)	13.2 (26)	13.0 (13)
MMSE, M (SD)[e]	27.6 (1.6)	27.9 (1.6)	27.5 (1.8)	27.6 (1.7)
Information processing speed, M (SD)[f]	23.3 (6.7)	26.0 (6.9)	24.8 (7.0)	22.2 (6.5)**

Notes: [a] Data at second data collection cycle. [b] Range, 0–20. [c] Range, 4–100. [d] Missing values for some subjects. [e] Range, 24–30. [f] Range, 1.0–42.7.
* $p < .05$. ** $p < .001$. MMSE = Mini-Mental State Examination.

Table 8.3 Associations between early life physical activity and cognition for the total study sample (*n* = 1241)

	Model 1	Model 2	Model 3
MMSE[a]			
Early life physical activity			
None (= reference)	0	0	0
Low	0.38*	0.07	0.06
Moderate	−0.02	−0.13	−0.11
High	0.05	0.11	0.15
Information processing speed[b]			
Early life physical activity			
None (= reference)	0	0	0
Low	2.62*	1.20*	0.97*
Moderate	1.16*	0.70	0.67
High	−1.10	−0.76	−0.34

Notes: Model 1: time adjusted. Model 2: adjusted for age, sex, verbal intelligence. Model 3: additionally adjusted for socioeconomic status, early life physical work demands, current physical activity, smoking, alcohol, diabetes mellitus, cardiac disease, depression.
[a] Values are betas (0–30 points). [b] Values are betas (0–43 points).
* $p < .05$.

Table 8.4 Associations between early life physical activity and cognition, separately for men (*n* = 604) and women (*n* = 637)

	Men			Women		
	Model 1	Model 2	Model 3	Model 1	Model 2	Model 3
MMSE[a]						
Early life physical activity						
None (= reference)	0	0	0	0	0	0
Low	0.36	0.13	0.10	0.40*	0.02	0.03
Moderate	−0.05	−0.06	−0.08	0.08	−0.25	−0.15
High	0.03	0.07	0.11	0.10	0.25	0.29
Information processing speed[b]						
Early life physical activity						
None (= reference)	0	0	0	0	0	0
Low	2.35*	1.36*	1.24*	3.00*	1.05	0.73
Moderate	1.29*	1.24[c]*	1.07[d]*	1.15	−0.43[c]	−0.41[d]
High	−1.33	1.20*	−1.04[e]	0.10	0.82	1.85[e]

Notes: Model 1: time adjusted. Model 2: adjusted for age, verbal intelligence. Model 3: additionally adjusted for socioeconomic status, early life physical work demands, current physical activity, smoking, alcohol, diabetes mellitus, cardiac disease, depression.
[a] Values are betas (0–30 points). [b] Values are betas (0–43 points). [c] Significant interaction "early life physical activity*sex" ($p = .04$). [d] Significant interaction "early life physical activity*sex" ($p = .07$). [e] Significant interaction "early life physical activity*sex" ($p = .07$).
* $p < .05$.

Physically active men at low and moderate level scored respectively 1.24 points and 1.07 points higher on information processing than inactive men. However, men who were physically active at the highest level (10 hours or more per week) had lower scores on information processing speed. This association was significant after adjustment for age and verbal intelligence, but not significant after full adjustment (beta = −1.04). Additional data in this high activity group showed that a high proportion (54%) were physically active during work—e.g. while working as a farmer, construction worker, or loader/unloader of heavy loads—compared with 46 percent who were active in sports. Separate analyses for work- and sports-related activities revealed that the negative association with information processing speed in men could be attributed to work-related activities (adjusted beta = −1.44, p = .04 for work, versus −0.46, p = .53 for sports activities). In women, only unadjusted scores of low physical activity were significant, both for the MMSE and information processing speed. After adjustment for confounders, the associations were not significant in women. The cognition-by-time interactions were not significant, suggesting that early life physical activity was not associated with the rate of decline during 6-year follow-up, but with the level of cognitive functioning.

Discussion

This population-based study showed, independent of current physical activity, a significant association of early life physical activity with information processing speed, but not with general cognitive impairment (MMSE). The association was only significant in men. Second, early life physical activity was associated with the level of information processing speed, not with the rate of decline.

Physical activity early in life was associated with information processing speed only. This is in line with exercise intervention studies, showing most robust exercise effects on tasks measuring reaction time, both in elderly and in young adults (Chodzko-Zajko & Moore, 1994; Spirduso, 1980). Information processing speed declines rapidly with aging, and is supposed to be the basic component of most cognitive functions (Salthouse, 1996). Therefore, a high speed of information processing seems important also to maintain a high level of higher-order cognitive functions, such as memory and reasoning (Dik, Deeg, Bouter, Corder, Kok, & Jonker, 2000). The positive association between regular early life physical activity and information processing speed was observed in men only. This may be accounted for by differences between men and women in total time spent in activities, intensity of the activities, or recall of the activities. Lack of association in women might be attributed to lower intensity of the activities or insufficient power of the study design, or both.

We investigated high intensity physical activities that caused subjects to sweat or that made them exhausted. Exercise intervention studies have shown that cognitive benefits are associated with endurance activities (e.g., running) rather than with static activities (stretching and toning) (Kramer et al., 1999). Over 50 percent of the subjects in the high activity group (>10 hours per week) were physically active during work. Performing work with high physical load may be associated with poor working conditions—e.g. exposure to chemicals or pesticides—or other unknown socioeconomic or lifestyle factors, which may explain the negative association with cognition in this group (Bosma, van Boxtel, Ponds, Houx, & Jolles, 2000). Moreover, the types of activities performed during work are static, so mainly anaerobic, and these types have been shown to be unrelated to cognition (Chodzko-Zajko & Moore, 1994).

Early life physical activity may be positively associated with late-life cognition through a higher brain reserve capacity (BRC) in those subjects who had been physically active early in life. A potential biological mechanism by which physical activity may increase BRC is the stimulation of trophic factors and neurogenesis (Gómez-Pinilla et al., 1998; van Praag et al., 1999; Neeper, Gómez-Pinilla, Choi, & Cotman, 1995). Physical exercise can raise brain-derived neurotrophic factor (BDNF) gene expression in the hippo-campus (Neeper et al., 1995). In a previous study, we have shown that the trophic factor Insulin-like Growth Factor I (IGF-I) was associated with decline and level of performance on information processing speed, but not on other cognitive tasks (Dik, Pluijm, Jonker, Deeg, Lomecky, & Lips, 2003), which is in line with the findings in the present study. Also, physical activity may stimulate cerebral circulation by increasing the vascularization of the brain, resulting in enhanced oxygen transportation to the brain (Rogers, Meyer, & Mortel, 1990). In addition to these structural changes in the brain (brain reserve), early life physical activity may enhance the functional capacity of the brain (cognitive reserve) by increasing the neural efficiency. Our study suggests that subjects who were physically active early in life may benefit from it in terms of a higher level of information processing speed at older age. The finding that early life physical activity was associated with *level* of processing speed rather than with *rate of decline*, supports the idea that a higher reserve (either brain or cognitive) may have been achieved early in life.

The long-term consequences of early life experiences are demonstrated in rats, showing altered brain neurotrophin levels and cognition during adulthood after exposure to psychological stress during childhood (Zhu, Winblad, Mohammed, Bettschen, Feldon, & Pryce, 2002). The cerebral effects of training in young animals develop somewhat more rapidly than in older animals, and the magnitude of the effects is often larger in the younger animals (Rosenzweig & Bennett, 1996). This suggests that physical activity may be most beneficial early in life, because neural plasticity is greatest early in life, which may set the level for later use and maintenance of the brain (Rosenzweig & Bennett, 1996; Mattson, 2001). Also epidemiological evidence is increasing on the importance of early life factors for late-life cognition and dementia. Several early life factors have been associated with cognitive decline and dementia, including education (Stern et al., 1994; Geerlings et al., 1999; Coffey, Saxton, Ratcliff, Bryan, & Lucke, 1999), socioeconomic status, childhood environment, father's occupation (Moceri et al., 2001), young-adult cognitive performance (Snowdon, Kemper, Mortimer, Greiner, Wekstein, & Markesbery, 1996; Whalley, Starr, Athawes, Hunter, Pattie, & Deary, 2000), and head circumference (Graves, Mortimer, Larson, Wenzlow, Bowen, & McCormick, 1996; Schofield, Logroscino, Andrews, Albert, & Stern, 1997). These findings may support the cognitive reserve hypothesis for Alzheimer's disease, because a higher reserve could have been created, starting early in life.

Several studies have found an association between physical activity and cognition in later life (Abbott et al., 2004; Laurin et al., 2001; van Gelder et al., 2004; Weuve et al., 2004; Yaffe et al., 2001), whereas others have not (Verghese et al., 2003). Since early life physical activity may be associated with an active lifestyle later in life (tracking) (Malina, 1996), the association between early life activity and cognition may also originate from an indirect pathway via late-life activity. However, in our study early life physical activity was associated with cognition independent of current physical activity level, whereas current physical activity was not independently associated with cognition. This suggests that the positive association with late-life cognition was achieved earlier in life, but this needs further investigation.

Several limitations of our study should be discussed. First, early life physical activity was established retrospectively by asking one single question. The level of physical activity was estimated over a 10-year period many years ago, and it is likely that information bias occurred. However, to reduce the probability of incorrect recall to this question, we excluded subjects with cognitive impairment (Cumming & Klineberg, 1994). Probable misclassification of the physical activity levels in the cognitively normal elderly in this study may be non-differential (Falkner, McCann, & Trevisan, 2001), leading to probable underestimation of the associations. Second, early life physical activity included both sports and occupational activities. The negative association with information processing speed in the high activity group could be attributed to the high proportion of occupational activities in this group. For the low and moderate activity groups, sports and occupational activities could not be separated, and inclusion of occupational activities may have weakened the associations with cognition in these groups. Finally, although we adjusted for several potential confounders such as socioeconomic status, early life physical work demands and lifestyle variables, early life physical activity may be associated with other unknown or latent factors that could be linked with cognition.

To our knowledge, this is the first study that has investigated the association between early life physical activity and late-life cognition. We studied the duration of high-intensity physical activity at a young age in a large sample of older men and women. Cognition was assessed at 62 to 85 years of age, with repeated objective cognitive tests 3 years apart. In addition to general cognition, information processing speed was measured, which is shown to be sensitive to both aging and physical activity. In conclusion, our study suggests a positive association between regular physical activity early in life and information processing speed at older age in men. This association could not be explained by current physical activity or lifestyle factors such as smoking and alcohol. However, further longitudinal research is warranted, using more extensive measures of early life physical activity that enable the distinction to be made between recreational and occupational activities.

Acknowledgments

The Longitudinal Aging Study Amsterdam (LASA) is funded by the Dutch Ministry of Health, Welfare and Sports, and the Vrije Universiteit. The study on cognitive decline was supported by grant number 940-90-001 of the Dutch Organization for Scientific Research (NWO-MW).

References

Abbott, R. D., White, L. R., Ross, G. W., Masaki, K. H., Curb, J. D., & Petrovitch, H. (2004). Walking and dementia in physically capable elderly men. *Journal of the American Medical Association, 292*, 1447–1453.

Ainsworth, B. E., Haskell, W. L., Leon, A. S., Jacobs, D. R. Jr., Montoye, H. J., Sallis, J. F., et al. (1993). Compendium of physical activities: Classification of energy costs of human physical activities. *Medicine and Science in Sports and Exercise, 25*, 71–80.

Ainsworth, B. E., Haskell, W. L., Whitt, M. C., Irwin, M. L., Swartz, A. M., Strath, S. J., et al. (2000). Compendium of physical activities: An update of activity codes and MET intensities. *Medicine and Science in Sports and Exercise, 32* (Suppl. 9), S498–504.

Beekman, A. T. F., Deeg, D. J. H., Van Limbeek, J., Braam, A. W., De Vries, M., & Van Tilburg, W. (1997). Criterion validity of the Center for Epidemiologic Studies Depression scale (CES-D): Results from a community-based sample of older subjects in The Netherlands. *Psychological Medicine, 27*, 231–235.

Black, J. E., Isaacs, K. R., & Greenough, W. T. (1991). Usual versus succesful aging: Some notes on experiential factors. *Neurobiology of Aging, 12*, 325–328.

Bosma, H., van Boxtel, M. P., Ponds, R. W., Houx, P. J., & Jolles, J. (2000). Pesticide exposure and risk of mild cognitive dysfunction. *Lancet, 356*, 912–913.

Breteler, M. M. (2001). Early life circumstances and late life Alzheimer's disease. *Epidemiology, 12*, 378–379.

Chodzko-Zajko, W. J., & Moore, K. A. (1994). Physical fitness and cognitive functioning in aging. *Exercise and Sport Sciences Reviews, 22*, 195–220.

Coffey, C. E., Saxton, J. A., Ratcliff, G., Bryan, R. N., & Lucke, J. F. (1999). Relation of education to brain size in normal aging: Implications for the reserve hypothesis. *Neurology, 53*, 189–196.

Colcombe, S., & Kramer, A. F. (2003). Fitness effects on the cognitive function of older adults: A meta-analytic study. *Psychological Sciences, 14*, 125–130.

Colcombe, S. J., Erickson, K. I., Raz, N., Webb, A. G., Cohen, N. J., McAuley, E., et al. (2003). Aerobic fitness reduces brain tissue loss in aging humans. *The Journals of Gerontology: Series A. Biological Sciences and Medical Sciences, 58*, 176–180.

Cotman, C. W., & Berchtold, N. C. (2002). Exercise: A behavioral intervention to enhance brain health and plasticity. *Trends in Neuroscience, 25*, 295–301.

Cumming, R. G., & Klineberg, R. J. (1994). A study of the reproducibility of long-term recall in the elderly. *Epidemiology, 5*, 116–119.

Deeg, D. J. H., & Westendorp-de Serière, M. (Eds.) (1994). *Autonomy and well-being in the aging population I: Report from the Longitudinal Aging Study Amsterdam 1992–1993.* Amsterdam: VU University Press.

Dik, M. G., Deeg, D. J. H., Bouter, L. M., Corder, E. H., Kok, A., & Jonker, C. (2000). Stroke and apolipoprotein E ε4 are independent risk factors for cognitive decline: A population-based study. *Stroke, 31*, 2431–2436.

Dik, M. G., Pluijm, S. M. F., Jonker, C., Deeg, D. J. H., Lomecky, M. Z., Lips, P. (2003). Insulin-like growth factor I (IGF-I) and cognitive decline in older persons. *Neurobiology of Aging, 24*, 573–581.

Fabre, C., Chamari, K., Mucci, P., Masse-Biron, J., & Prefaut, C. (2002). Improvement of cognitive function by mental and/or individualized aerobic training in healthy elderly subjects. *International Journal of Sports Medicine, 23*, 415–421.

Falkner, K. L., McCann, S. E, & Trevisan, M. (2001). Participants' characteristics and quality of recall of physical activity in the distant past. *American Journal of Epidemiology, 154*, 865–872.

Folstein, M. F., Folstein, S. E., & McHugh, P. R. (1975). "Mini-Mental State." A practical method for grading the cognitive state of patients for the clinician. *Journal of Psychiatric Research, 12*, 189–198.

Geerlings, M. I., Schmand, B., Jonker, C., Lindeboom, J., & Bouter, L. M. (1999). Education and incident Alzheimer's disease: A biased association due to selective attrition and use of a two-step diagnostic procedure? *International Journal of Epidemiology, 28*, 492–497.

Gómez-Pinilla, F., So, V., & Kesslak, J. P. (1998). Spatial learning and physical activity contribute to the induction of fibroblast growth factor: Neural substrates for increased cognition associated with exercise. *Neuroscience, 85*, 53–61.

Graves, A. B., Mortimer, J. A., Larson, E. B., Wenzlow, A., Bowen, J. D., McCormick, W. C. (1996). Head circumference as a measure of cognitive reserve associated with severity of impairment in Alzheimer's disease. *British Journal of Psychiatry, 169*, 86–92.

Kempermann, G., Gast, D., & Gage, F. H. (2002). Neuroplasticity in old age: Sustained fivefold induction of hippocampal neurogenesis by long-term environmental enrichment. *Annals of Neurology, 52*, 135–143.

Kramer, A. F., Hahn, S., Cohen, N. J., Banich, M. T., McAuley, E., Harrison, C. R., et al. (1999). Ageing, fitness and neurocognitive function. *Nature, 400*, 418–419.

Laurin, D., Verreault, R., Lindsay, J., MacPherson, K., & Rockwood, K. (2001). Physical activity and risk of cognitive impairment and dementia in elderly persons. *Archives of Neurology, 58*, 498–504.

Lezak, M. D. (1995). *Neuropsychological assessment* (3rd ed.). New York: Oxford University Press.

Luteijn, F., & van der Ploeg, F. A. E. (1983). *Groninger Inteligentie Test. Handleiding.* [*Groninger Intelligence Test. Manual.*] Lisse, The Netherlands: Swets & Zeitlinger BV.

Malina, R. M. (1996). Tracking of physical activity and physical fitness across the lifespan. *Research Quarterly for Exercise and Sport, 67* (Suppl. 3), S48–S57.

Mattson, M. P. (2001). Neuroplasticity and how the brain adapts to aging. *Geriatrics and Aging, 4*, available at http://www.geriatricsandaging.ca/.

Moceri, V. M., Kukull, W. A., Emanual, I., van Belle, G., Starr, J. R., Schellenberg, G. D., et al. (2001). Using census data and birth certificates to reconstruct the early-life socioeconomic environment and the relation to the development of Alzheimer's disease. *Epidemiology, 12*, 383–389.

Neeper, S. A., Gómez-Pinilla, F., Choi, J., & Cotman, C. (1995). Exercise and brain neurotrophins. *Nature, 373*, 109.

Piccinin, A. M., & Rabbitt, P. M. A. (1999). Contribution of cognitive abilities to performance and improvement on a substitution coding task. *Psychology and Aging, 4*, 539–551.

Radloff, L. S. (1977). The CES-D scale: A self-report depression scale for research in the general population. *Applied Psychological Measures, 1*, 385–401.

Rogers, R. L., Meyer, J. S., & Mortel, K. F. (1990). After reaching retirement age physical activity sustains cerebral perfusion and cognition. *Journal of the American Geriatric Society, 38*, 123–128.

Rosenzweig, M. R., & Bennett, E. L. (1996). Psychobiology of plasticity: Effects of training and experience on brain and behavior. *Behaviour and Brain Research, 78*, 57–65.

Salthouse, T. A. (1996). The processing-speed theory of adult age differences in cognition. *Psychological Reviews, 103*, 403–428.

Schofield, P. W., Logroscino, G., Andrews, H. F., Albert, S., & Stern, Y. (1997). An association between head circumference and Alzheimer's disease in a population-based study of aging and dementia. *Neurology, 49*, 30–37.

Sixma, H., & Ultee, W. C. (1983). Een beroepsprestigeschaal voor Nederland in de jaren tachtig. [An occupational prestige scale for the Netherlands in the 1980s]. *Mens en Maatschappij, 58*, 360–382.

Smit, J. H., de Vries, M. Z., & Poppelaars, J. L. (1998). Data-collection and fieldwork procedures. In D. J. H. Deeg, A. T. F. Beekman, D. M. W. Kriegsman, & M. Westendorp-de Serière (Eds.), *Autonomy and well-being in the aging population II: Report from the Longitudinal Aging Study Amsterdam 1992–1996* (pp. 9–20). Amsterdam: VU University Press.

Snowdon, D. A., Kemper, S. J., Mortimer, J. A., Greiner, L. H., Wekstein, D. R., Markesbery, W. R. (1996). Linguistic ability in early life and cognitive function and Alzheimer's in late life: Findings from the Nun Study. *Journal of the American Medical Association, 275*, 528–532.

Spirduso, W. W. (1980). Physical fitness, aging, and psychomotor speed: A review. *Journal of Gerontology, 35*, 850–865.

Stel, V. S., Smit, J. H., Pluijm, S. M. F., Visser, M., Deeg, D. J. H., & Lips, P. (2004). Comparison of the LASA physical activity questionnaire with a 7-day diary and pedometer. *Journal of Clinical Epidemiology, 57*, 252–258.

Stern, Y. (2002). What is cognitive reserve? Theory and research application of the reserve concept. *Journal of the International Neuropsychological Society, 8*, 448–460.

Stern, Y., Gurland, B., Tatemichi, T. K., Tang, M. X., Widler, D., & Mayeux, R. (1994). Influence of education and occupation on the incidence of Alzheimer's disease. *Journal of the American Medical Association, 13*, 1004–1010.

Twisk, J. (1997). Different statistical models to analyze epidemiological observational longitudinal data: An example from the Amsterdam growth and health study. *International Journal of Sports Medicine, 18* (Suppl. 3), S216–S224.

Van den Heuvel, N., Smits, C. H. M., Deeg, D. J. H., & Beekman, A. T. F. (1996). Personality: A moderator of the relation between cognitive functioning and depression in adults aged 55–85? *Journal of Affective Disorders, 41,* 229–240.

van Gelder, B. M., Tijhuis, M. A., Kalmijn, S., Giampaoli, S., Nissinen, A., & Kromhout, D. (2004). Physical activity in relation to cognitive decline in elderly men: The FINE Study. *Neurology, 63,* 2316–2321.

van Praag, H., Christie, B. R., Sejnowski, T. J., & Gage, F. H. (1999). Running enhances neurogenesis, learning, and long-term potentiation in mice. *Proceedings of the National Academy of Sciences of the USA, 96,* 13427–13431.

Verghese, J., Lipton, R. B., Katz, M. J., Hall, C. B., Derby, C. A., Kuslansky, G., et al. (2003). Leisure activities and the risk of dementia in the elderly. *New England Journal of Medicine, 348,* 2508–2516.

Weuve, J., Kang, J. H., Manson, J. E., Breteler, M. M., Ware, J. H., & Grodstein, F. (2004). Physical activity, including walking, and cognitive function in older women. *Journal of the American Medical Association, 292,* 1454–1461.

Whalley, L. J., Starr, J. M., Athawes, R., Hunter, D., Pattie, A., & Deary, I. J. (2000). Childhood mental ability and dementia. *Neurology, 55,* 1455–1459.

Yaffe, K., Barnes, D., Nevitt, M., Lui, L. Y., & Covinsky, K. (2001). A prospective study of physical activity and cognitive decline in elderly women: Women who walk. *Archives of Internal Medicine, 161,* 1703–1708.

Zeger, S. L., & Liang, K. (1986). Longitudinal data analysis for discrete and continuous outcomes. *Biometrics, 42,* 121–130.

Zhu, S. W., Winblad, B., Mohammed, A. H., Bettschen, D., Feldon, J., & Pryce, C. (2002). Early life events alter cognitive function and brain neurotrophin levels in middle aged rats. *Neurobiology of Aging, 23* (Suppl. 1), S530–S531.

9 Assessment of lifetime participation in cognitively stimulating activities

Robert S. Wilson, Lisa L. Barnes, and David A. Bennett

Cognitive activity and neural reserve

Age-related dementia and cognitive decline are substantial public health problems that are projected to increase in the first half of this century as the proportion of older persons in the U.S. population increases (Hebert, Scherr, Bienias, Bennett, & Evans, 2003). Loss of cognitive ability in old age is thought to arise from the interaction of experiential and genetic risk factors with multiple age-related pathologic changes in the brain. On post-mortem examination, late life dementia has been associated with the pathology of Alzheimer's disease (i.e., amyloid deposition, neurofibrillary changes), stroke (i.e., cerebral infarction), and Parkinson's disease (i.e., Lewy bodies). These pathologic changes are also seen in the brains of older people who die without dementia, however, albeit to a lesser degree, suggesting that people differ in their capacity to tolerate the deleterious effects of age-related neuropathology. This ability to maintain function despite the accumulation of pathology in the brain is referred to as neural reserve capacity. Factors are thought to influence risk of late life dementia either by affecting the accumulation of neuropathology or by affecting the brain's ability to function in the presence of such pathology.

The neural reserve hypothesis was originally proposed to account for the observation that risk of late life dementia was reduced in persons with higher levels of educational attainment compared to those with lower levels (Friedland, 1993; Katzman, 1993). Because education does not appear to be related to the accumulation of cortical plaques and tangles (Bennett et al., 2003; Del Ser, Hachinski, Merskey, & Munoz, 1999), the leading cause of late life dementia, its apparently protective effect is assumed to operate through an association with neural reserve.

Support for this hypothesis comes from the Rush Religious Orders Study, a longitudinal clinical-pathological investigation of aging and Alzheimer's disease in older Catholic nuns, priests, and brothers (Wilson, Bienias, Evans, & Bennett, 2004). In this cohort, education was shown to modify the association of Alzheimer's disease pathology with level of cognitive function proximate to death such that the deleterious effects of pathology on cognitive function were substantially greater in those with less education compared to those with more education (Bennett et al., 2003). This effect was seen with summary measures of neuritic plaques and diffuse plaques but not of neurofibrillary tangles.

One possible explanation for the relation of education to risk of dementia is that education is an indicator for time spent in cognitively stimulating activities (Bennett et al., 2003; Evans et al., 1997; Stern, Gurland, Tatemichi, Tang, Wilder, & Mayeux, 1994). That is, frequent cognitive stimulation might enhance the efficiency and flexibility of neural systems underlying cognitive function, eventually making it more difficult for pathologic lesions to disrupt these systems (Stern, 2002; Wilson & Bennett, 2003). Support for this idea comes from a population-based study of older persons in which the associations of educational and occupational attainment with risk of dementia were eliminated after controlling for how frequently people reported engaging in cognitively stimulating activities (Wilson, Bennett et al., 2002).

These findings suggest that level of participation in cognitively stimulating activities might provide an indirect indicator of individual differences in neural reserve capacity. In the remainder of this chapter, we examine attempts to measure cognitive activity and review the relation of cognitive activity with cognition and dementia. We then discuss assessment of lifetime cognitive activity and its relation to neural reserve theory.

Assessment of cognitive activity

The first step in assessing cognitive activity is to define it. Our definition is that cognitive activities are those in which seeking or processing information is central to participation in the activity (Wilson et al., 1999; Wilson, Barnes, & Bennett, 2003; Wilson, Barnes, Kreuger, Hoganson, Bienias, & Bennett, 2005). To this basic idea, we have added two stipulations. First, we have tried to avoid cognitive activities with substantial physical or social barriers to participation. For example, playing contract bridge is a cognitive activity but participation depends in part on other people. Second, we have tried to focus on activities that are relatively common in the general population and to avoid more esoteric cognitive activities like solving differential equations.

Most attempts to quantify cognitive activity have focused on frequency of participation. Typically this has involved preparing a list of activities thought to be cognitively stimulating and asking the participant how often each activity was performed within some fixed time period. Alternatively, people have been asked to keep a diary of activities they engaged in at fixed intervals during a day (Christensen & Mackinnon, 1993) or at psuedorandom times when alerted by a beeper (Salthouse, Berish, & Miles, 2002). Another approach, which is not mutually exclusive, has been to quantify features of the home environment that may stimulate or otherwise support cognitive activity, like an encyclopedia, newspaper subscription, or library card

(Wilson, Barnes et al., 2003; Wilson, Barnes et al., 2005; Barnes, Wilson, Mendes de Leon, & Bennett, in press).

Another consideration is whether to simply total the number of cognitive activities performed or to weight participation by how frequently it occurs and/or by how cognitively demanding or intense the activity is. The most common approach has been to incorporate information on the frequency with which an activity is performed (Christensen & Mackinnon, 1993; Hultsch, Hammer, & Small, 1993; Wilson et al., 1999; Wilson, Barnes et al., 2003; Wilson, Barnes et al., 2005). For the most part, measures based on the product of frequency and intensity of cognitive activities have had very high correlations with measures based on frequency alone (Arbuckle, Gold, & Andres, 1986; Wilson et al., 1999). As a result, information on intensity has not typically been incorporated into cognitive activity measures, except in studies with diverse categories of activity in which multidimensional ratings are used to quantify frequency of different forms (e.g., cognitive, social) of activity (Christensen & Mackinnon, 1993).

Validation of cognitive activity measures has primarily relied on two criteria. First, level of cognitive activity ought to be related to level of education, which can be thought of as the prototypic example of cognitive activity. Second, and perhaps more critically, cognitive activity ought to be related to level of cognitive function even after controlling for level of education. That is, a useful measure of cognitive activity ought to account for variation in cognition beyond that attributable to educational attainment.

Cognitive activity and loss of cognitive function

If level of cognitive activity is an indirect indicator of neural reserve capacity, and if neural reserve protects against the development of dementia, then cognitively active older persons should be less likely to develop dementia than their less cognitively active peers. This hypothesis has now been examined in several large prospective studies. In the Rush Religious Orders Study (Wilson, Mendes de Leon et al., 2002), older Catholic clergy members without dementia rated their current frequency of participation in seven cognitive activities (e.g., reading a magazine). Those reporting more frequent cognitive activity were about half as likely to develop Alzheimer's disease during a mean of about 5 years of observation compared to participants reporting less frequent activity in analyses that controlled for age, sex, education, and baseline level of cognitive function. This association of more frequent cognitive activity with reduced risk of incident dementia or Alzheimer's disease has been confirmed in other studies of selected (Verghese et al., 2003) and population-based (Scarmeas, Levy, Tang, Manly, & Stern, 2001; Wang, Karp, Winblad, & Fratiglioni, 2002; Wilson, Bennett et al., 2002) cohorts.

The association of cognitive activity with risk of dementia is likely due in part to the positive correlation between level of cognitive activity and level of cognitive function (Christensen & Mackinnon, 1993; Hultsch et al., 1993;

Wilson et al., 1999). That is, cognitively active persons are apt to begin old age with a higher level of cognitive function than less active persons and so would need to experience relatively more cognitive decline to reach a level of impairment consistent with dementia. In a strong version of the neural reserve hypothesis (Wilson & Bennett, 2003), however, frequent cognitive activity should be associated not only with a higher level of cognitive function but also with a reduced rate of cognitive decline, and longitudinal studies have supported this (Hultsch, Hertzog, Small, & Dixon, 1999; Wilson, Bennett, Bienias, Mendes de Leon, Morris, & Evans, 2003; Wilson, Mendes de Leon et al., 2002).

Higher levels of physical and social activity have also been associated with reduced cognitive decline and risk of dementia (Barnes, Mendes de Leon, Wilson, Bienias, & Evans, 2004; Fratiglioni, Wang, Ericsson, Maytan, & Winbald, 2000; Laurin, Verreault, Lindsay, MacPherson, & Rockwood, 2001; Scarmeas et al., 2001; Wang et al., 2002; Weuve, Kang, Manson, Breteler, Ware, & Grodstein, 2004). The relation of social engagement to cognitive decline appears to be independent of cognitive activity (Barnes et al., 2004), but there is some evidence that the association of physical activity with cognitive decline may be partly explained by the association of each with frequency of participation in cognitively stimulating activities (Sturman, Morris, Mendes de Leon, Bienias, Wilson, & Evans, in press).

If cognitive activity reduces risk of dementia by contributing to neural reserve capacity, then among persons with clinically evident Alzheimer's disease, those with relatively higher levels of premorbid cognitive activity ought to have a higher burden of Alzheimer's disease pathology. Further, if the protective effect of neural reserve is reduced as the burden of pathology increases, as is widely assumed (Cummings, Vinters, Cole, & Khachaturian, 1998), then frequent premorbid activity ought to be associated with more rapid decline among persons with manifest dementia. Empirical support for this corollary of the neural reserve hypothesis comes from a 4-year study of about 400 persons with clinically diagnosed Alzheimer's disease (Wilson, Bennett, Gilley, Beckett, Barnes, & Evans, 2000). Those with a higher level of reading activity prior to dementia onset, as assessed by an informant-report scale, had more rapid global cognitive decline relative to those with less premorbid reading activity. Further, reading activity was related to decline in verbal cognitive abilities but not to decline in nonverbal cognitive abilities, suggesting that the effects of cognitive activity are specific to the skills involved in that activity.

If the protective effect of neural reserve in those with clinically manifest Alzheimer's disease decreases as Alzheimer's disease pathology accumulates in the brain, then the association of neural reserve with more rapid cognitive decline ought to be most evident late in the natural history of the disease. Support for this idea comes from a 3-year longitudinal study of more than 400 persons with clinically diagnosed Alzheimer's disease (Wilson, Li et al., 2004). In this study, global cognitive decline had linear and nonlinear components, with the mean trajectory showing a gradually accelerating rate of cognitive decline. In mixed-effects models adjusted for age, sex, and race, higher educational attainment was not associated with the linear component of cognitive decline but was negatively associated with the accelerating nonlinear component, consistent with the idea that education is associated with more rapid decline late in the disease course. To further examine this idea, we re-analyzed the association between premorbid reading activity and change in global cognition described by Wilson et al. (2000) with the addition of a quadratic term for time to allow for nonlinear in addition to linear decline. In this analysis, premorbid reading activity was not related to linear cognitive decline but was robustly related to nonlinear decline, with greater acceleration of global cognitive decline associated with higher level of premorbid reading activity.

These data suggest that frequent cognitive activity is associated with a compression of the course of Alzheimer's disease. That is, a cognitively active lifestyle is associated with a later onset of dementia and, once dementia is present, with a more rapid clinical course so that the overall duration of dementia is reduced, thereby reducing the proportion of the life span spent in a diseased state and so the overall burden of the disease.

Cognitive activity during the life span

We suggest two mechanisms that may contribute to individual differences in neural reserve capacity. First, as the central nervous system develops, excess neurons, synapses, and dendrites are generated, and neural activity during this time plays an important role in determining the survival of these cellular and subcellular units (Katz & Shatz, 1996; Penn & Shatz, 1999; Singer, 1995). Thus rearing animals in environments that vary in complexity can alter the number of neurons, synapses, and dendrites in selected brain regions, including the neocortex and hippocampal formation (Beaulieu & Colonnier, 1989; Comery, Stamoudis, Irwin, & Greenough, 1996; Greenough, Hwang, & Gorman, 1985). Development in humans is prolonged, and there is evidence of experience-dependent changes in the human brain through the second decade of life (Benes, Turtle, Kahn, & Farol, 1994; Paus et al., 1999; Pfefferbaum, Mathalon, Sullivan, Rawles, Zipursky, & Lim, 1994; Steen, Ogg, Reddick, & Kingsley, 1997). Second, even after development is complete, the nervous system continues to adapt to changes in the environment, a process referred to as neural plasticity. Changes in neurons, synapses, and dendrites have been documented in adult animals following learning and environmental manipulation (Jones, Klintsova, Kilman, Sirevaag, & Greenough, 1997; Kempermann, Kuhn, & Gage, 1997; Kornack & Rakic, 1999). In the adult human brain, recovery from stroke (Nudo, Wise, SiFuentes, & Milliken, 1996; Seil, 1997) and neurogenesis (Ericksson et al., 1998) provide examples of plasticity. Thus, in humans as well as animals, experience during development and during adulthood and old age appears to contribute to structural and functional changes in the nervous system.

If nervous system function and structure are partially activity dependent, and if activities exert their impact both during and following development, then assessment of patterns of activity across the life span might provide an indirect measure of the capacity of the nervous system to support such activities. Research on patterns of cognitive activity, however, has focused mainly on current activity (Christensen & Mackinnon, 1993; Hultsch et al., 1993; Schinka, McBride, Vanderploeg, Tennyson, Bornstein, & Mortimer, 2005; Wilson et al., 1999) or on past activity (Friedland et al., 2001; Wilson et al., 2000). These considerations led us to construct a lifetime cognitive activity scale to facilitate research on neural reserve (Barnes et al., in press; Wilson, Barnes et al. 2003; Wilson, Barnes et al., 2005).

The initial version of the lifetime cognitive activity scale contained 25 items, three about activities at age 6, six about activities at age 12, six about age 18, five about age 40, and five about current age (Wilson, Barnes et al., 2003). For each item, the person rated how often they participated in the activity at a given age on a 5-point scale, with a score of 1 indicating once a year or less, 2 for several times a year, 3 for several times a month, 4 for several times a week, and 5 for every day or about every day.

We administered the scale to 141 older persons without dementia from the Rush Memory and Aging Project, an ongoing clinicopathologic study of neurobiologic mechanisms linking experiential and genetic risk factors to common chronic health problems in old age (Bennett, Schneider, Buchman, Mendes de Leon, & Wilson, in press). They had a mean age of 83.5 (standard deviation (SD) = 5.5), mean education of 14.7 (SD = 3.0), and a mean Mini-Mental State Examination (Folstein, Folstein, & McHugh, 1975) score of 28.3 (SD = 1.6), with 73.8% women and 95.0% white and non-Hispanic.

Because Cronbach's coefficient alpha for the 25-item scale was .88, indicating a high degree of internal consistency, we constructed a composite measure of lifetime cognitive activity frequency by computing the average score for the 25 items. It ranged from 1.91 to 4.34 (mean = 3.25, SD = 0.53) and had an approximately normal distribution. To assess its short-term temporal stability, we administered it to a separate subset of 23 participants in the Memory and Aging Project and then re-administered it 4 weeks later. The mean score from the two administrations did not differ and the test–retest correlation was .79, indicating adequate temporal stability.

Cognitive activity score accounted for about 6% of the variance in educational attainment, supporting the construct validity of the scale. In analyses controlling for age, sex, and education, a higher level of lifetime cognitive activity was associated with a higher level of semantic memory, perceptual speed, and visuospatial ability, further supporting the validity of the measure.

We subsequently revised the scale in two ways (Barnes et al., in press; Wilson, Barnes et al., 2005). First, we added questions about frequency of participation in cognitively stimulating activities at ages 12, 18, 40, and current age. The full 43-item scale is presented in Table 9.1. Second, given evidence that features of the home intellectual environment are related to cognitive and academic performance in childhood (Bradley et al., 1989), we

Table 9.1 Lifetime cognitive activity scale

Item #	Reference age	Item	Response option
1	6	How often did you play games like tic-tac-toe, checkers or other board games, cards, or word games?	Daily to < 1 per year
2	6	How often did someone in your home read to you?	Daily to < 1 per year
3	6	How often did someone in your home tell you stories?	Daily to < 1 per year
4	12	About how much time did you spend reading each day?	None to < 3 hours
5	12	How often did you visit a library?	Daily to < 1 per year
6	12	How often did you read newspapers?	Daily to < 1 per year
7	12	How often did you read magazines?	Daily to < 1 per year
8	12	How often did you read books?	Daily to < 1 per year
9	12	How often did you write letters?	Daily to < 1 per year
10	12	How often did you play games like checkers or other board games, cards, puzzles, word games, mind teasers, or any other similar games?	Daily to < 1 per year
11a	18	Had you received any instruction in a foreign language?	Yes, No
11b	18	[If yes] How many years?	Total number of years
12a	18	Had you taken any music lessons?	Yes, No
12b	18	[If yes] How many years?	Total number of years
13a	18	Had you taken any art, dance, or theater lessons?	Yes, No
13b	18	[If yes] How many years?	Total number of years
14a	18	Had you ever kept a diary or journal?	Yes, No
14b	18	[If yes] How many years?	Total number of years
15	18	How many times had you visited a museum?	Never to > 20
16	18	How many times had you attended a concert, play, or musical?	Never to > 20
17	18	About how much time did you spend reading each day?	None to > 3 hours
18	18	How often did you visit a library?	Daily to < 1 per year
19	18	How often did you read newspapers?	Daily to < 1 per year
20	18	How often did you read magazines?	Daily to < 1 per year

Continued

Table 9.1 (continued)

Item #	Reference age	Item	Response option
21	18	How often did you read books?	Daily to < 1 per year
22	18	How often did you write letters?	Daily to < 1 per year
23	18	How often did you play games like checkers or other board games, cards, puzzles, word games, mind teasers, or any other similar games?	Daily to < 1 per year
24	40	About how much time did you spend reading each day?	None to > 3 hours
25a	30–40	Had you ever kept a diary or journal?	Yes, No
25b	30–40	[If yes] How many years?	Total number of years
26	30–40	How many times had you visited a museum?	Never to > 20
27	30–40	How many times had you attended a concert, play, or musical?	Never to > 20
28	30–40	How often did you visit a library?	Daily to < 1 per year
29	40	How often did you read newspapers?	Daily to < 1 per year
30	40	How often did you read magazines?	Daily to < 1 per year
31	40	How often did you read books?	Daily to < 1 per year
32	40	How often did you write letters?	Daily to < 1 per year
33	40	How often did you play games like checkers or other board games, cards, puzzles, word games, mind teasers, or any other similar games?	Daily to < 1 per year
34	present	About how much time do you spend reading each day?	None to > 3 hours
35a	present	In the last ten years, did you ever keep a diary or journal?	Yes, No
35b	present	[If yes] How many years?	Total number of years
36	present	In the last ten years, how many times did you visit a museum?	Never to > 20
37	present	In the last ten years, how many times did you attend a concert, play or musical?	Never to > 20
38	present	In the last ten years, how often did you visit a library?	Daily to < 1 per year
39	present	How often do you read newspapers?	Daily to < 1 per year
40	present	How often do you read magazines?	Daily to < 1 per year
41	present	How often do you read books?	Daily to < 1 per year
42	present	How often do you write letters?	Daily to < 1 per year
43	present	How often do you play games like checkers or other board games, cards, puzzles, word games, mind teasers, or any other similar games?	Daily to < 1 per year

also assessed aspects of the home environment that might support cognitive activity. For age 12 and age 40, we asked about the presence in the home of seven items: newpaper subscription, magazine subscription, dictionary, encyclopedia, atlas, globe, and library card, and we assigned one point for each item that was present. We also asked persons to estimate the number of books in the house as less than 20 (for which no points were assigned), 20–49 (0.25 point), 50–100 (0.50 point), 101–250 (0.75 point), or more than 250 (1 point). For both age 12 and age 40, therefore, the score for cognitive resources in the home could vary from 0 to 8.

In our analyses we examined the relation of past cognitive activity to current cognitive activity and the relation of each to current cognitive function in more than 500 older persons participating in the Rush Memory and Aging Project (Wilson, Barnes et al., 2005). For these analyses, we formed measures of cognitive activity frequency in childhood (ages 6 and 12), young adulthood (age 18), middle adulthood (age 40), and old age. These measures had adequate levels of internal consistency (coefficient alpha range: .71 to .77) and were moderately correlated with one another (range of correlations: .43 to .69). With few exceptions, each of these measures was positively related to current level of cognitive function, but the associations tended to be stronger for current than for past cognitive activity, and for measures of semantic memory and perceptual speed compared to measures of episodic memory, working memory, and visuospatial ability. When we made a composite measure of past activity based on childhood, young adulthood, and middle adulthood and analyzed it in conjunction with current cognitive activity, current activity maintained a robust association with all domains of cognitive function, whereas past activity had modest associations with episodic and semantic memory but was not related to other cognitive functions. Past cognitive activity accounted for about one quarter of the variance in current cognitive activity.

The measures of cognitive resources in the home at age 12 and at age 40 were each related to current level of cognitive function, but the effects for resources at age 12 were less robust and were substantially reduced after controlling for age 40 resources. When both resource measures, past activity, and current activity were entered in the same model, they accounted for between 5% (in working memory) and 20% (in semantic memory) of the variance in different cognitive functions, with the effects primarily due to age 40 cognitive resources and current cognitive activity frequency. Overall, these data suggest that past cognitive activity contributes to level of cognitive function in old age primarily through its association with late life level of cognitive activity.

Because knowledge about cognitive activity patterns in racial or ethnic minorities is limited (Wilson et al., 1999), we administered the lifetime cognitive activity scale to a selected group of 108 older African Americans (Barnes et al., in press). In this study, composite measures of frequency of cognitive activity and level of cognitive resources in the home each had positive correlations with level of education and with a measure of global cognitive function, supporting the validity of the measures in older African Americans.

Conclusions

Higher levels of cognitive activity and educational attainment are associated with higher level of cognition, reduced cognitive decline, and reduced risk of dementia in old age. Cognitive activity and education do not appear to affect the accumulation of age-related neuropathology but rather appear to bolster the brain's ability to tolerate that pathology.

Most people finish formal schooling in adolescence or early adulthood, but education contributes strongly to occupational experiences, and both education and occupation are related to patterns of cognitive activity throughout adulthood (Wilson, Bennett et al., 2002). We found that retrospective estimates of level of cognitive activity across the life span were robustly related to late life level of cognitive function, but the association was strongest for late life cognitive activity (Wilson, Barnes et al., 2005). Thus cognitive activity in early life, along with early life socioeconomic conditions (Everson-Rose, Mendes de Leon, Bienias, Wilson, & Evans, 2003; Wilson, Scherr, Hoganson, Bienias, Evans, & Bennett, 2005; Wilson, Scherr et al., 2005) appear to affect late life cognitive function in part by affecting cognitive lifestyle activities throughout adulthood and old age.

Further research is needed to clarify the structural, biochemical, and molecular mechanisms contributing to neural reserve in old age. Progress is likely to require large-scale longitudinal clinical-pathological and clinical-radiological studies of older persons in whom cognitive experiences at different points in the life span have been systematically quantified, along with negative experiences like chronic psychological distress which may affect dementia risk by reducing neural reserve capacity (Wilson, Evans, Bienias, Mendes de Leon, Schneider, & Bennett, 2003; Wilson, Barnes et al., 2005). The Rush Religious Orders Study (Wilson, Bienias et al., 2004) and the Rush Memory and Aging Project (Bennett et al., in press) are longitudinal clinical-pathological studies that were designed to elucidate the neuro-biological mechanisms linking life experiences to neural reserve. Understanding the neurobiological mechanisms through which positive and negative life experiences affect the brain's ability to tolerate age-related pathology may suggest new strategies for preventing or delaying dementia in old age and thereby help reduce disability in old age.

Acknowledgments

This research was supported by National Institute on Aging grants R01 AG179917, R01 AG15819, R01 AG022018, and P30 AG10161.

References

Arbuckle, T., Gold, D., & Andres, D. (1986). Cognitive functioning of older people in relation to social and personality variables. *Psychology and Aging, 1,* 55–62.

Barnes, L. L., Mendes de Leon, C. F., Wilson, R. S., Bienias, J. L., & Evans, D. A. (2004). Social resources and cognitive decline in a population of older African Americans and whites. *Neurology, 63,* 2332–2326.

Barnes, L. L., Wilson, R. S., Mendes de Leon, C. F., & Bennett, D. A. (in press). The relation of lifetime cognitive activity and lifetime access to resources to late-life cognitive function in older African Americans. *Aging Neuropsychology and Cognition.*

Beaulieu, C., & Colonnier, M. (1989). Number and size of neurons and synapses in the motor cortex of cats raised in different environmental complexities. *Journal of Comparative Neurology, 289,* 178–181.

Benes, F. M., Turtle, M., Kahn, Y., & Farol, P. (1994). Myelination of a key relay zone in the hippocampal formation occurs in the human brain during childhood, adolescence, and adulthood. *Archives of General Psychiatry, 51,* 477–484.

Bennett, D. A., Schneider, J. A., Buchman, A. S., Mendes de Leon, C. F., & Wilson, R. S. (in press). The Rush Memory and Aging Project: Study design and baseline characteristics of the study cohort. *Neuroepidemiology.*

Bennett, D. A., Wilson, R. S., Schneider, J. A., Evans, D. A., Mendes de Leon, C. F., Arnold, S. E., et al. (2003). Education modifies the relation of AD pathology to level of cognitive function in older persons. *Neurology, 60,* 1909–1915.

Bradley, R. H., Caldwell, B. M., Rock, S. L., Barnard, K. E., Gray, C., Hammond, M. A., et al. (1989). Home environment and cognitive development in the first 3 years of life: A collaborative study involving six sites and three ethnic groups in North America. *Developmental Psychology, 28,* 217–235.

Christensen, H., & Mackinnon, A. (1993). The association between mental, social, and physical activity and cognitive performance in young and old subjects. *Age and Ageing, 22,* 175–182.

Comery, T. A., Stamoudis, C. X., Irwin, S. A., & Greenough, W. T. (1996). Increased density of multiple-head dendritic spines on medium-sized spiny neurons of the striatum in rats reared in a complex environment. *Neurobiology of Learning and Memory, 66,* 93–96.

Cummings, J., Vinters, H., Cole, G., & Khachaturian, Z. (1998). Alzheimer's disease: Etiology, pathophysiology, cognitive reserve, and treatment opportunities. *Neurology, 51* (Suppl. 1), S2–S17.

Del Ser, T., Hachinski, V., Merskey, H., & Munoz, D. G. (1999). An autopsy-verified study of the effects of education on degenerative dementia. *Brain, 122,* 2309–2319.

Eriksson, P. S., Perfilieva E., Bjork-Eriksson, T., Alborn, A. M., Nordborg, C., Peterson, D. A., et al. (1998). Neurogenesis in the adult human hippocampus. *Nature Medicine, 4,* 1313–1317.

Evans, D. A., Hebert, L. E., Beckett, L. A., Scherr, P. A., Albert, M. A., Chown, M. J., et al. (1997). Education and other measures of socioeconomic status and risk of incident Alzheimer's disease in a defined population of older persons. *Archives of Neurology, 54,* 1399–1405.

Everson-Rose, S. A., Mendes de Leon, C. F., Bienias, J. L., Wilson, R. S., & Evans, D. A. (2003). Early life conditions and cognitive functioning in later life. *American Journal of Epidemiology, 158,* 1083–1089.

Folstein, M., Folstein, S., & McHugh, P. (1975). Mental-mental state: A practical method for grading the mental state of patients for the clinician. *Journal of Psychiatric Research, 12*, 189–198.

Fratiglioni, L., Wang, H.-X., Ericsson, K., Maytan, M., & Winblad, B. (2000). Influence of social network on occurence of dementia: A community-based longitudinal study. *Lancet, 355*, 1315–1319.

Friedland, R. P. (1993). Epidemiology, education, and the ecology of Alzheimer's disease. *Neurology, 43*, 246–249.

Friedland, R. P., Fritsch, T., Smyth, K. A., Koss, E., Lerner, A. J., Chen, C. H., et al. (2001). Patients with Alzheimer's disease have reduced activities in midlife compared with healthy control-group members. *Proceedings of the National Academy of Science, USA, 98*, 3440–3445.

Greenough, W. T., Hwang, H. M., & Gorman, C. (1985). Evidence for active synapse formation or altered postsynaptic metabolism in visual cortex of rats reared in complex environments. *Proceedings of the National Academy of Science, USA, 82*, 4549–4552.

Hebert, L. E., Scherr, P. A., Bienias, J. L., Bennett, D. A., & Evans, D. A. (2003). State-specific projections through 2025 of Alzheimer's disease prevalence. *Neurology, 62*, 1645.

Hultsch, D., Hammer, M., & Small, B. (1993). Age difference in cognitive performance in later life: Relationships to self-reported health and activity life style. *Journal of Gerontology: Psychological Sciences, 48*, P1–P11.

Hultsch, D., Hertzog, C., Small, B., & Dixon, R. (1999). Use it or lose it: Engaged lifestyle as a buffer of cognitive decline in aging? *Psychology and Aging, 14*, 245–263.

Jones, T. A., Klintsova, A. Y., Kilman, V. L., Sirevaag, A. M., & Greenough, W. T. (1997). Induction of multiple synapses by experience in the visual cortex of adult rats. *Neurobiology of Learning and Memory, 68*, 13–20.

Katz, L. C., & Shatz, C. J. (1996). Synaptic activity and construction of cortical circuits. *Science, 274*, 1133–1138.

Katzman, R. (1993). Education and the prevalence of dementia and Alzheimer's disease. *Neurology, 43*, 13–20.

Kempermann, G., Kuhn, H. G., & Gage, F. H. (1997). More hippocampal neurons in adult mice living in an enriched environment. *Nature, 386*, 493–495.

Kornack, D. R., & Rakic, P. (1999). Continuation of neurogenesis in the hippocampus of the adult macaque monkey. *Proceedings of the National Academy of Science, USA, 96*, 5768–5773.

Laurin, D., Verreault, R., Lindsay, J., MacPherson, K., & Rockwood, K. (2001). Physical activity and risk of cognitive impairment and dementia in elderly persons. *Archives of Neurology, 58*, 498–504.

Nudo, R. J., Wise, B. M., SiFuentes, F., & Milliken, G. W. (1996). Neural substrates for the effects of rehabilitative training on motor recovery after ischemic infarct. *Science, 272*, 1791–1794.

Paus, T., Zijdenbos A., Worsley K., Collins, D. L., Blumenthal, J., Giedd, J. N., et al. (1999). Structural maturation of neural pathways in children and adolescents: In vivo study. *Science, 283*, 1908–1911.

Penn, A. A., & Shatz, C. J. (1999). Brain waves and brain wiring: The role of endogenous and sensory-driven neural activity in development. *Pediatric Research, 45*, 447–458.

Pfefferbaum, A., Mathalon, D. H., Sullivan, E. V., Rawles, J. M., Zipursky, R. B., & Lim, K. O. (1994). A quantitative magnetic resonance imaging study of changes in brain morphology from infancy to late adulthood. *Archives of Neurology, 51,* 874–887.

Salthouse, T. A., Berish, T. E., & Miles, J. D. (2002). The role of cognitive stimulation on the relations between age and cognitive functioning. *Psychology and Aging, 17,* 548–557.

Scarmeas, N., Levy, G., Tang, M.-X., Manly, J., & Stern, Y. (2001). Influence of leisure activity on the incidence of Alzheimer's disease. *Neurology, 57,* 2236–2242.

Schinka, J. A., McBride, A., Vanderploeg, R. D., Tennyson, K., Bornstein, A. R., & Mortimer, J. A. (2005). Florida Cognitive Activities Scale: Initial development and validation. *Journal of the International Neuropsychological Society, 11,* 108–116.

Seil, F. J. (1997). Recovery and repair issues after stroke from the scientific perspective. *Current Opinions in Neurobiology, 10,* 49–51.

Singer, W. (1995). Development and plasticity of cortical processing architectures. *Science, 270,* 758–764.

Steen, R. G., Ogg, R. J., Reddick, W. E., & Kingsley, P. B. (1997). Age-related changes in the pediatric brain: Quantitative MR evidence of maturational changes during adolescence. *American Journal of Neuroradiology, 18,* 819–828.

Stern, Y. (2002). What is cognitive reserve? Theory and research application of the reserve concept. *Journal of the International Neuropsychological Society, 8,* 448–460.

Stern, Y., Gurland, B., Tatemichi, T., Tang, M.-X., Wilder, D., & Mayeux, R. (1994). Influence of education and occupation on the incidence of Alzheimer's disease. *Journal of the American Medical Association, 271,* 1004–1010.

Sturman, M. T., Morris, M. C., Mendes de Leon, C. F., Bienias, J. L., Wilson, R. S., & Evans, D. A. (in press). Physical activity, cognitive activity, and cognitive decline in a biracial population. *Archives of Neurology.*

Verghese, J., Lipton, R. B., Hall, C. B., Derby, C. A., Kuslansky, G., Ambronse, A. F., et al. (2003). Leisure activities and the risk of dementia in the elderly. *New England Journal of Medicine, 348,* 2508–2516.

Wang, H.-X., Karp, A., Winblad, B., & Fratiglioni, L. (2002). Late-life engagement in social and leisure activities is associated with a decreased risk of dementia: A longitudinal study from the Kungsholmen Project. *American Journal of Epidemiology, 155,* 1081–1087.

Weuve, J., Kang, J. H., Manson, J. E., Breteler, M. M., Ware, J. H., & Grodstein, F. (2004). Physical activity, including walking, and cognitive function in older women. *Journal of the American Medical Association, 292,* 1454–1461.

Wilson, R. S., Barnes, L. L., & Bennett, D. A. (2003). Assessment of lifetime participation in cognitively stimulating activities. *Journal of Clinical and Experimental Neuropsychology, 25,* 634–642.

Wilson, R. S., Barnes, L. L., Bennett, D. A., Li, Y., Bienias, J. L., Mendes de Leon, C. F., et al. (2005). Proneness to psychological distress and risk of Alzheimer's disease in a biracial community. *Neurology, 64,* 380–382.

Wilson, R. S., Barnes, L. L., Krueger, K. R., Hoganson, G., Bienias, J. L., & Bennett, D. A. (2005). Early and late life cognitive activity and cognitive systems in old age. *Journal of the International Neuropsychological Society, 11,* 400–407.

Wilson, R. S., & Bennett, D. A. (2003). Cognitive activity and risk of Alzheimer's disease. *Current Directions in Psychological Science, 12,* 87–91.

Wilson, R. S., Bennett, D. A, Beckett, L. A., Morris, M. C., Gilley, D. W., Bienias, J. L., et al. (1999). Cognitive activity in older persons from a geographically defined population. *Journal of Gerontology: Psychological Sciences, 54B,* P155–P160.

Wilson, R. S., Bennett, D. A., Bienias, J. L., Aggarwal, N. T., Mendes de Leon, C. F., Morris, M. C., et al. (2002). Cognitive activity and incident AD in a population-based sample of older persons. *Neurology, 59,* 1910–1914.

Wilson, R. S., Bennett, D. A., Bienias, J. A., Mendes de Leon, C. F., Morris, M. C., & Evans, D. A. (2003). Cognitive activity and cognitive decline in a biracial community population. *Neurology, 61,* 812–816.

Wilson, R. S., Bennett, D. A., Gilley, D. W., Beckett, L. A., Barnes, L. L., & Evans, D. A. (2000). Premorbid reading activity and patterns of cognitive decline in Alzheimer's disease. *Archives of Neurology, 57,* 1718–1723.

Wilson, R. S., Bienias, J. L., Evans, D. A., & Bennett, D. A. (2004). Religious Orders Study: Overview and change in cognitive and motor speed. *Aging Neuropsychology and Cognition, 11,* 280–303.

Wilson, R. S., Evans, D. A., Bienias, J. L., Mendes de Leon, C. F., Schneider, J. A., & Bennett, D. A. (2003). Proneness to psychological distress is associated with risk of Alzheimer's disease. *Neurology, 61,* 1479–1485.

Wilson, R. S., Li, Y., Aggarwal, N. T., Barnes, L. L., McCann, J. J., Gilley, D. W., et al. (2004). Education and the course of cognitive decline in Alzheimer's disease. *Neurology, 63,* 1198–1202.

Wilson, R. S., Mendes de Leon, C. F., Barnes, L. L., Schneider, J. A., Bienias, J. L., Evans, D. A., et al. (2002). Participation in cognitively stimulating activities and risk of incident Alzheimer's disease. *Journal of the American Medical Association, 287,* 742–748.

Wilson, R. S., Scherr, P. A., Bienias, J. L., Mendes de Leon, C. F., Everson-Rose, S. A., Bennett, D. A., et al. (2005). Socioeconomic characteristics of the community in childhood and cognition in old age. *Experimental Aging Research, 31,* 393–407.

Wilson, R. S., Scherr, P. A., Hoganson, G., Bienias, J. L., Evans, D. A., & Bennett, D. A. (2005). Early life socioeconomic statues and late life risk of Alzheimer's disease. *Neuroepidemiology, 25,* 8–14.

10 Lifestyle activities and late-life changes in cognitive performance

Brent J. Small, Tiffany F. Hughes,
David F. Hultsch, and Roger A. Dixon

A considerable body of research indicates that multiple cognitive abilities decline as we grow older (see Craik & Salthouse, 2000; Dixon, Bäckman, & Nilsson, 2004 for reviews). At the same time, a growing body of research on cognitive performance suggests that older adults who participate in a variety of intellectually engaging activities outperform their coevals who are less engaged in such activities (see Anstey & Christensen, 2000; Kramer, Bherer, Colcombe, Dong, & Greenough, 2004, for reviews). Furthermore, some studies have even suggested that participation in intellectually demanding leisure activities may protect against the occurrence of dementing diseases such as Alzheimer's disease (see Fratiglioni, Paillard-Borg, & Winblad, 2004 for a review). Taken at face value, such results would suggest that late-life lifestyles featuring intellectual activities might buffer cognitive decline—an effect often referred to as "use it or lose it." However, despite these promising results and the intuitive appeal of a "use it or lose it" explanation for adult age differences in cognitive functioning, the full literature on this topic is mixed.

In the current chapter, we examine the relationship between cognitive performance and participation in lifestyle activities among healthy older adults. We begin by describing two dominant theoretical perspectives, cognitive reserve and substantive complexity, and discuss their implications in terms of the ability of older adults to improve, maintain, or repair their cognitive abilities. Next we review cross-sectional and longitudinal evidence regarding a possible relationship between lifestyle activities and cognitive abilities. We then identify two challenges to the study of this relationship, including the adequate conceptualization of lifestyle activities, and the proper statistical analysis of the temporal relationship among changes in lifestyle activities and changes in cognitive functioning.

Theoretical foundations: Cognitive reserve and substantive complexity

The concept of cognitive reserve is intended to account for the fact of considerable cognitive and behavioral heterogeneity in both healthy individuals and patients with brain pathology or damage. Moreover, it is designed to link this behavioral heterogeneity with the underlying neurological substrate. Related concepts such as the threshold model, neuronal or brain reserve, and compensation have also emerged from the study of this heterogeneity (Stern, 2002). Stern proposes from these models that the concept of cognitive reserve can be further delineated as passive or active reserve. It is likely that a combination of both types of cognitive reserve will provide the most comprehensive explanation of the cognitive variation between individuals at the neurophysiologic level.

The passive model of reserve includes the threshold model (Statz, 1993) and the brain and neuronal reserve models (Katzman et al., 1989, Mortimer, Schuman, & French, 1981). These models suggest that the basis for cognitive reserve is provided by neuron and synapse number or brain size and volume. Consequently, passive reserve is determined primarily by genetics, although it also may be influenced to some degree by environment. The passive model is essentially a quantitative model of reserve and assumes that there is some fixed cut-off or threshold at which functional impairment will occur for everyone (Stern, 2002). This model does not address the qualitative differences in brain damage and/or pathology and is unable to account for individual differences in cognitive processing or performance (Stern, 2002).

The active model of reserve is concerned more with neural processing and synaptic organization than sheer neuroanatomical characteristics and differences. The construct of compensation is a type of active reserve where different brain structures or networks become active following brain pathology or damage (see also Dixon & Bäckman, 1999). Similarly, the active model of reserve can also include situations where normal individuals recruit additional or different brain networks when faced with increasing task demands. Neural processing and synaptic organization are more sensitive to environmental influences; therefore, it is these changes that provide the greatest potential for increasing reserve. Essentially, the active model of reserve posits that cognitive reserve is provided less by quantity of available neural substrate, and more by the efficiency and adaptability (plasticity) of its processing.

Both the active and passive versions of the cognitive reserve hypothesis are potentially relevant for changes that accompany advancing age. For example, Raz (2000) nicely demonstrated a relationship between select brain volumes and participant age. Although his data showed that the correlation between age and hippocampal volume is relatively modest ($r = -.30$), the relationship between the volume of the prefrontal cortex and age was slightly stronger ($r = -.55$). In both cases, increasing age being was associated with reductions in volume. Given the importance of these brain structures for episodic memory and executive functioning, which are two abilities that demonstrate robust age-related changes (e.g., Bäckman, Small, & Wahlin, 2001; West, 1996), decreases in the volume of these brain structures may affect an individual's cognitive reserve, as well as overall cognitive functioning.

Evidence demonstrating an effect of active reserve and aging may be found in the work of Cabeza, Anderson, Locantore, and McIntosh (2002; see also Buckner, 2004). In Cabeza et al.'s study, high- and low-performing older adults were identified on the basis of a composite measure of episodic memory task. Using fMRI analysis of performance on a source memory test, these investigators noticed a difference in the areas of activation for the high-performing group, as compared to the low-performing group. Specifically, the high-performing older adult group exhibited bilateral activation of the prefrontal cortex (PFC) during task performance, whereas the low-performing older adults, as well as the younger control group, exhibited only activation of the left PFC. Cabeza and colleagues interpreted this as indicating that the older high-performing group exhibited compensation, in the form of bilateral activation of the PFC during task performance. This compensatory action resulted in cognitive functioning levels that were comparable to the younger control group.

Research on environmental complexity provides another theoretical perspective that is relevant to the study of lifestyle activities and cognitive performance (Schooler, 1984, 1989). This theory, which operates at a very different level of analysis, originated from a program of research that examined the link between occupational demands and intellectual flexibility (Kohn & Schooler, 1983). In this view, the complexity of an environment is defined by the stimulus and demand characteristics. Complex environments are characterized by a diversity of stimuli, large numbers of decisions, multiple factors to be considered in making decisions, and ill-defined and apparently contradictory contingencies resulting from decisions. To the extent that environments with characteristics such as these reward cognitive effort, persons would be motivated to develop their cognitive abilities and generalize them to other environments. On the other hand, environments that offer relatively little complexity may not provide sufficient support for the maintenance and enhancement of cognitive functioning.

Evidence in support of this theory has come from several sources. For example, Schooler, Mulatu, and Oates (1999) found that substantive complexity in a work environment, defined by objective measures of occupational complexity from the United States Department of Labor *Dictionary of Occupational Titles* (1965), was significantly related to a composite measure of intellectual functioning. Further, these effects were reciprocal, in that the complexity of the work environment predicted cognitive performance, but was also affected by a person's intellectual flexibility. Similarly, research from the Seattle Longitudinal Study (Schaie, 1996) has shown that persons who retired from complex occupations exhibited significantly greater declines on tests of intelligence as compared to persons who retired from less complex, or more routinized, occupations. Presumably, changes in the complexity of environments following retirement may have affected subsequent cognitive performance. Finally, experimental animal work has suggested that exposure to complex environments positively influences many brain structures including "glial cells, blood vessels, as well as neurons and their synaptic connections" (Kramer et al., 2004, p. 946).

The theoretical formulations of cognitive reserve and environmental complexity originated from different empirical roots—brain injury and the sociology of work, respectively. When considered together, however, they may provide a more complete understanding of the potential mechanisms through which lifestyle activities may influence late-life cognitive performance. That is, the environmental complexity model may allow us to identify settings or environments that are conducive to the development and maintenance of cognitive abilities. Following exposure to these enriched settings, the cognitive reserve theory may provide a mechanism of action for improvements or maintenance of functioning. These could appear in the form of the development of compensatory brain pathways (e.g., Cabeza et al., 2002) or through structural changes in specific regions of the brain (e.g., Kemperman, Gast, & Gage, 2002; Kozorovitsky & Gould, 2003). Thus both theories are relevant and complementary to the study of how participation in lifestyle activities may lessen normative age-related changes in cognitive functioning. Evidence relevant to this issue is reviewed next.

Lifestyle activities and cognitive performance in late life

In this section, we provide a selective review of studies that have examined the relationship between cognitive performance and lifestyle activities among older adults (see also Anstey & Christensen, 2000). These studies can largely be divided into two classes. The first represents studies that examine the relationship between cross-sectional differences in activity participation in relation to age-related differences in cognitive functioning, or subsequent longitudinal changes in performance. The second, and smaller group of studies, are those that examine longitudinal changes in both activity participation and cognitive performance.

Age-related differences in lifestyle activities and cognitive performance

Hultsch, Hammer, and Small (1993) examined the relationship between life-style activities and multiple domains of cognitive performance in a sample of 484 adults between the ages of 55 and 86. The results indicated that higher scores on an active lifestyle factor, comprising measures of cognitive and physical activity, was related to performance on tests of processing speed, vocabulary, and episodic memory. Further, age was found to modify the strength of this relationship, such that for the oldest group (75–85 years) the relationship between activity participation and cognitive performance was greater than when compared to the younger group (55–64 years). This result indicated that the participation in lifestyle activities may be more beneficial to older cohorts of adults than young-old adults.

Wilson, Bennett, Bienias, Mendes de Leon, Morris, and Evans (2003)

examined longitudinal changes in a composite measure of cognitive performance in relation to self-reports of the frequency of cognitively stimulating
activities at baseline. The composite cognitive measure included tests of
global cognitive functioning (i.e., Mini-Mental State Examination, MMSE),
perceptual speed (i.e., Digit Symbol Substitution), and episodic memory
(i.e., immediate and delayed text recall from the Wechsler Memory Scale).
Participants were followed at 3-year intervals with a mean of 2.6 interviews
per person. The results indicated that persons who were cognitively active
at baseline experienced fewer longitudinal declines, as compared to those
who were less active. Specifically, "persons with frequent cognitive activity
(90th percentile) experienced about 35% less cognitive decline than persons
with infrequent cognitive activity (10th percentile)" (Wilson et al., 2003,
p. 814).

However, several studies have failed to observe a relationship between
participation in lifestyle activities and cognitive performance. For example,
Aartsen, Smits, van Tillburg, Knipscheer, and Deeg (2002) examined the
relationship between several dimensions of lifestyle activities and changes in
cognitive functioning across a 6-year follow-up period. The authors observed
no significant relationship between social activity (e.g., visiting neighborhood
associations), experiential activity (e.g., visiting a cultural institution), or
developmental activity (e.g., following an educational course) on subsequent
changes in a measure of global cognitive functioning (i.e., MMSE) or tests
of episodic memory, verbal intelligence, or processing speed. Moreover the
authors reported that baseline cognitive functioning, in this case processing
speed, was significantly associated with changes in developmental activity,
thus suggesting that reductions in cognitive processes may precede changes in
lifestyle activities.

Salthouse, Berish, and Miles (2002) also found little evidence for a relationship between cognitive stimulation, indexed by a composite measure of
the frequency and cognitive demand associated with 22 common activities
(e.g., reading, preparing meals), and multiple measures of cognitive performance. In this case, cognitive functioning was indexed by two composite
measures of fluid intelligence, one composite measure of vocabulary, and
one composite measure of episodic memory. Using a sample of 204 adults
ranging from 20 to 91 years of age, Salthouse and colleagues sought to
examine whether participation in cognitively stimulating activities mediated
age-related differences in cognitive performance. They reported that controlling for participation in cognitively demanding activities did little to
modify the age-related deficits in cognitive performance. Obviously, this
result leaves unsupported the notion that people who remain mentally active
also stave off age-related differences in functioning. Conceivably, however,
the inclusion of younger adults in the sample may have reduced the
opportunity to observe a diminution of aging-related differences. That is,
younger adults may exhibit less variability in both cognitive performance and
participation in cognitively stimulating activities, a characteristic that could

restrict the possibility of observing a reduction in aging-related differences in performance.

Although some of the studies reviewed above suggest a relationship between lifestyle activities and cognitive performance, a critical issue is the directionality of such effects. For example, bright well-educated older adults not only perform better on tests of cognitive performance, as compared to their more poorly educated counterparts, but they also tend to engage in more lifestyle activities. As such, the relationships that are observed cross-sectionally may be confounded with initial level of performance. Moreover, one could conceive of individuals who maintain or increase lifestyle activities as benefiting cognitively, but the opposite may also be true, in that persons who are experiencing cognitive declines may choose to limit their participation in lifestyle activities. As such, with cross-sectional data we are unable to determine the legitimacy of either explanation. However, several studies have now examined how changes in lifestyle activities relate to changes in cognitive performance and these are reviewed next.

Age-related changes in lifestyle activities and cognitive performance

In this section, we review several studies that have examined whether changes in lifestyle activities are associated with changes in cognitive performance. Studies such as these are important for determining the temporal relationship between cognitive functioning and engagement in lifestyle activities.

Building on their past research, Schooler and Mulatu (2001) examined the relationship between 20-year changes in intellectual flexibility and changes in cognitively oriented leisure time activities. Intellectual flexibility was measured with a combination of items that were initially assessed at baseline. These items comprised mainly subjective ratings of an individual's intellectual competence, along with a few objective cognitive tasks. At the follow-up assessment, six new standard psychometric instruments were added to the battery to evaluate cognitive performance. Cognitive leisure activity was measured at both times of assessment with six questions that examined the number of books and magazines read, including ratings of the intellectual level of this material; the frequency of visits to fine arts institutions or museums; as well as the number of special interests and hobbies and the number of hours spent per month on all of these activities. In addition, at the follow-up assessment a new set of measures were used to index complexity of leisure time activities. These measures included standardized ratings (based on the *Dictionary of Occupational Titles*; United States Department of Labor, 1965) of the complexity of leisure time activities in relation to data, things, and special interests. Schooler and Mulatu also used the number of hours spent on leisure time activities with data and with things as a measure of this domain.

Using structural equation modeling, Schooler and Mulatu (2001) examined the reciprocal relationship between changes in intellectual flexibility and changes in cognitive leisure activity, independent of such potentially confounding variables as age, race, gender, and socioeconomic status. In all analyses, the authors found that changes in leisure time activities were associated with changes in cognitive performance, such that persons who declined in activity participation also declined cognitively. However, the authors also demonstrated that changes in cognitive performance predicted changes in lifestyle activities. Although it may not be surprising that an individual's cognitive ability influences the lifestyle activities they pursue, in many of the statistical analyses the magnitude of the relationships between changes in activities and changes in intellectual flexibility were comparable. Thus it may be that a person's cognitive ability level is just as important as the activities they pursue, in terms of longitudinal changes in cognitive functioning.

Mackinnon, Christensen, Hofer, Korten, and Jorm (2003) examined changes in several domains of cognitive performance, including memory, speed of processing, and crystallized intelligence and changes in lifestyle activities. Participants who initially ranged between 70 and 93 years of age were tested on three occasions across a 7-year follow-up period. Activity was indexed by the frequency of participation in six common activities (e.g., reading a newspaper, engaging in physical activities). The activity inventory was designed to provide an adequate representation of activities that were common enough so that they would reflect the daily activity patterns of most adults. The results indicated that statistically significant change was observed for the three domains of cognitive performance and for the activities measure; all indicators demonstrated decline over time. Mackinnon and colleagues also examined the relationship between changes in activities and changes in cognitive performance. They found that decline in activity frequency was mirrored by decline in cognitive functioning. However, when participants were dichotomized into those who maintained their level of activity and those who demonstrated significant decline in activity participation over time, no statistically significant differences were observed in terms of the magnitude of the decrements in cognitive functioning between each group. Although decrements in activity frequency and cognitive performance were in synchrony, the persons who maintained or declined in activity frequency showed no differences in the magnitude of change in cognitive performance over time, and Mackinnon and colleagues concluded that "the naturalistic maintenance of activities offers no protection against cognitive decline" (2003, p. 225).

We (Hultsch, Hertzog, Small, & Dixon, 1999) have also examined how changes in several dimensions of lifestyle activities affect 6-year changes across multiple domains of cognitive performance. Participants consisted of 250 adults, initially 55 to 85 years of age, who were tested on three occasions across the 6-year follow-up interval. Participants rated their typical frequency of participation on a 9-point scale, ranging from never to daily, in 64 lifestyle activities that coalesced into six broad domains of activity. These were (with exemplar activities in parentheses): physical activity (jogging), self-maintenance (shopping), social activities (visiting friends), hobbies or home maintenance (repairing mechanical items), passive cognitive activities (listening to the radio), and novel cognitive activities (playing bridge). Further evaluation with confirmatory factor analysis indicated that two latent variables emerged. These corresponded to active lifestyle (physical activity, social activity, hobbies), and a factor indexing novel information processing. Cognitive performance was indexed by multiple ability domains corresponding to processing speed, working memory, episodic memory, semantic memory, and verbal ability. The results indicated that changes in novel information processing, as well as baseline participation in these types of activities, were significantly associated with changes in working memory performance. Thus this analysis provided evidence suggesting that the frequency of activity participation at baseline, as well as changes in this measure, were significantly associated with subsequent changes in working memory performance. None of the relationships between changes in active lifestyle and cognitive performance was statistically significant. Although the results for the novel information processing measure were suggestive of a mediating effect of activity participation on cognitive decline, one final model was estimated in which a latent variable defining change in general cognitive abilities was used to predict changes in the frequency of changes in novel information processing activities. This model also provided a good fit to the data and thus the hypothesis that changes in cognitive performance precipitate changes in lifestyle activities also received some support here.

The key advantage of the selected longitudinal studies reviewed here is the ability to evaluate changes in lifestyle activities in relation to changes in the cognitive outcomes. This ability allows researchers to address issues of temporal order, as well as to minimize the effect of potential confounding factors (e.g., education, socioeconomic status) because individuals act as their own controls. Nevertheless, the evidence reviewed above provides a mixed picture of the importance of maintaining an active lifestyle, in relation to maintaining cognitive functioning. In all cases, there was some evidence for the idea that changes in cognitive functioning may predate changes in the participation in lifestyle activities, in addition to evidence suggesting that changes in lifestyle activities were the driving force.

Future directions

Thus far, we have documented that there does seem to be some potential for participation in lifestyle activities to mediate late-life cognitive decline, but that this conclusion is far from certain. Partly this ambiguity reflects that different methods and measures have been used to assess these relationships. In this section we outline two specific challenges to resolving this conundrum. These challenges include the adequate conceptualization of lifestyle activities, especially those that are relevant to cognitive functioning, and the appropriate analysis of longitudinal data in order to establish the temporal relationship between changes in activities and changes in cognitive performance.

Conceptualizing lifestyle activities

There is substantial variability in the literature in terms of how participation in lifestyle activities is conceptualized across multiple studies. Most commonly, participants are presented with a list of common activities and are asked to indicate their frequency of participation. However, the potential of different types of activities to influence cognitive performance varies greatly. For example, Mackinnon and colleagues (2003) evaluated six items that were selected because they represented "day-to-day activities of all participants irrespective of educational and social status" (p. 217). Notably, however, two of the items asked participants about frequency of daily naps, as well as how much time they spent sitting around without doing very much. Clearly the cognitive demands of such activities are minimal.

Several investigators have distinguished among types of activities before evaluating the relationship to cognitive performance. Hultsch and colleagues (1993) used factor analysis to reduce 70 everyday activities into six broad domains of performance. In this case, those activities that were more demanding, either physically or cognitively, were found to be more strongly associated with age differences in cognitive performance, as compared to activities that posed fewer demands, such as self-maintenance activities. Similarly, Schinka, McBride, Vanderploeg, Tennyson, Borenstein, and Mortimer (2005) used psychometric test development procedures to create the Florida Cognitive Activities Scale, which was designed to index the frequency and duration of activities that differed in terms of their cognitive demands. Further, the items were shown to coalesce into a dimension of higher cognitive activities (e.g., playing chess or bridge), as well as a dimension of frequent cognitive activities (e.g., reading the newspaper). The analyses also revealed that each dimension was significantly associated with measures of episodic memory, executive functioning, and attention. Aartsen and colleagues (2002) classified 11 everyday activities as social, experimental, or developmental. The expectation was that developmental activities, such as following an educational course or study during the past 6 months, would be the most cognitively demanding. Although developmental activities were clearly demanding, this type of activity can hardly be considered an "everyday" activity of older adults. A slightly different method was used by Salthouse and colleagues (2002). In this case, not only did the investigators ask individuals to rate the frequency of participation in each activity, participants were also asked to self-rate the demand of each activity in which they participated. Although this approach attempted to control for individual differences in the extent to which activities are cognitively demanding, almost all activities were rated as moderately demanding, thus limiting the comparison between the effects of more or less demanding activity participation on cognitive performance.

Finally, another critical issue when examining the relationship between leisure activities and cognitive performance may be the match between the activity domains that are evaluated and the cognitive tests that are examined. For example, results from the ACTIVE cognitive intervention trial indicated that there was little transfer of gains from training between cognitive domains that were trained versus those that were not (Ball et al., 2002; see also Kramer & Willis, 2002). Thus, if some lifestyle activities promote skills that are subsequently not evaluated in standardized tests of cognitive performance, the potential beneficial aspects of the leisure activity on cognitive performance may not be observed. As such, future studies should also consider the cognitive components associated with the lifestyle activities included in their analysis in order to demonstrate whether or not participation in lifestyle activities mediates late-life cognitive abilities.

Statistical analysis of longitudinal relationships

The appropriate analysis of the temporal relationships between changes in lifestyle activities and changes in cognitive performance is demanding, both in terms of the number of testing occasions that are necessary to evaluate these relationships, and in terms of the specific statistical techniques that are most appropriate for the research questions at hand. One of the central issues when examining changes in lifestyle activities and changes in cognitive performance is the identification of leading vs. lagging relationships. That is, researchers are interested in the extent to which changes in one variable "leads" changes in another variable. For a relationship between participation in lifestyle activities to be a mediator of cognitive functioning, declines in activity participation would be expected to lead to subsequent declines in cognitive performance. By contrast, if the relationship between lifestyle activities and cognitive performance reflects the fact that persons who are experiencing cognitive declines relinquish leisure activities, then we would expect changes in activity participation to lag behind changes in cognitive performance. In order to evaluate whether a variable is leading or lagging another, three or more times of measurement are necessary. Indeed, there are a number of advantages of having more than two measurement points (Singer & Willet, 2003), including the ability to estimate non-linear relationships, and to describe the lead–lag relationships. Unfortunately, the majority of research that has examined the relationship between changes in lifestyle activities and changes in cognitive performance has only used two measurement points (e.g., Hultsch et al., 1999; Pushkar Gold, Andres, Etezadi, Arbuckle, Schwartzman, & Chaikelson, 1995; Schooler & Mulatu, 2001).

In addition to having multiple waves of data, the statistical analysis requirements of specifying lead–lag relationships are substantial. For example, the statistical analytic approaches that have been used thus far have not been able to truly evaluate the temporal relationships among lifestyle activities and cognitive performance. For example, Schooler and Mulatu's (2001) analysis of the reciprocal relationship between changes in intellectual flexibility and changes in leisure activities actually represented the sum of these effects, as well as the lagged effects of baseline functioning. As such, the authors concluded that "we cannot assess how much of the effect is actually contemporaneous and how much is actually lagged" (2001, p. 471). Thus the parameters that they report represent the direct effect of changes in each construct, as well as the indirect effect of baseline functioning.

The latent change analyses described by Hultsch and colleagues (1999) and Mackinnon and colleagues (2003) are able to evaluate the relationship between changes in performance that are independent of baseline functioning. However, the limitation of this technique is the inability to specifically describe the temporal ordering of these changes, at least in the context of these two studies. For example, Hultsch and colleagues (1999) note that the statistically significant relationship between changes in lifestyle activities and changes in working memory amounts to a "concurrent correlation" (p. 257), and that this cannot adequately describe the true direction of the influence. A similar criticism can be levied against the latent change models described by Mackinnon and colleagues (2003). They too observed significant relationships between changes in activity participation and changes in composite measures of memory, speed, and crystallized intelligence. However, Mackinnon and colleagues also categorized persons in terms of whether activity levels were maintained or declined over the longitudinal interval. They then examined changes in cognitive performance as a function of the two activity groups and failed to observe any statistically significant differences in rate of change over time.

Recent developments in models of longitudinal data analysis may permit a more complete analysis of these relationships. For example, the latent difference score (LDS) approach enables investigators to test hypotheses about the nature of the changes that are present among measures of cognitive performance and activity lifestyle (McArdle, 2001; McArdle & Hamagami, 2001). Specifically the LDS approach allows researchers to directly pose and test models about longitudinal changes in multiple variables over time. Accordingly, researchers can evaluate multiple models corresponding to specific hypotheses. These hypotheses include (a) that there is no relationship between changes in activity lifestyle and changes in cognitive performance; (b) that changes in active lifestyle are a "leading indicator," such that they precede changes in cognitive functioning; (c) that changes in cognitive performance are the "leading indicator" of changes in activity participation; or (d) that a form of "dynamic coupling" exists among both variables, whereby changes in both variables influence changes in the other, although the magnitude of these effects may be different.

Summary

The evidence reviewed here has provided some support for the notion that participation in leisure activities may mediate some of the age-related changes in cognitive performance seen in late life. However, what should also be clear from this review is that this conclusion is far from certain. Issues associated with properly conceptualizing participation in leisure pursuits, as well as being able to adequately describe the changes statistically, represent specific challenges to better understanding of these issues. Finally, although much attention has been directed at describing the relationship between life-style activities and cognitive performance, very little attention has been paid to better understanding the potential mechanism of this action. Information about the types of activities that elicit greatest gains in cognitive functioning, as well as implications for the cognitive reserve hypothesis, may allow us to design effective interventions that allow older adults to optimize their cognitive functioning in late life.

Acknowledgments

The support of the National Institute on Aging through grants to Brent Small (R03 AG024082) and Roger Dixon (R01 AG08235) during preparation of this chapter is gratefully acknowledged.

References

Aartsen, M. J., Smits, C. H. M., van Tillburg, T., Knipscheer, K. C. P. M., & Deeg, D. J. H. (2002). Activity in older adults: Cause or consequence of cognitive functioning? A longitudinal study on everyday activities and cognitive performance in older adults. *Journal of Gerontology: Psychological Sciences, 57B*, 153–162.

Anstey, K., & Christensen, H. (2000). Education, activity, health, blood pressure, and Apolipoprotein E as predictors of cognitive change in old age: A review. *Gerontology, 46*, 163–177.

Bäckman, L., Small, B. J., & Wahlin, Å. (2001). Aging and Memory: Cognitive and biological perspectives. In J. E. Birren & K. W. Schaie (Eds.), *Handbook of the psychology of aging* (5th ed., pp. 349–377). San Diego, CA: Academic Press.

Ball, K., Berch, D. B., Helmers, K. F., Jobe, J. B., Leveck, M. D., Marsiske, M., et al. (2002). Effects of cognitive training interventions with older adults: A randomized controlled trial. *Journal of the American Medical Association, 288*, 2271–2281.

Buckner, R. L. (2004). Memory and executive function in aging and AD: Multiple factors that cause decline and reserve factors that compensate. *Neuron, 44*, 195–208.

Cabeza, R., Anderson, N. D., Locantore, J. K., & McIntosh, A. R. (2002). Aging gracefully: Compensatory brain activity in high-performing older adults. *Neuroimage, 17*, 1394–1402.

Craik, F. I. M., & Salthouse, T. A. (2000). *The handbook of aging and cognition* (2nd ed.). Mahwah, NJ: Lawrence Erlbaum Associates, Inc.

Dixon, R. A., & Bäckman, L. (1999). Principles of compensation in cognitive neurorehabilitation. In D. T. Stuss, G. Winocur, & I. H. Robertson (Eds.), *Cognitive neurorehabilitation* (pp. 59–72). New York: Cambridge University Press.

Dixon. R. A., Bäckman, L., & Nilsson, L.-G. (2004). *New frontiers in cognitive aging.* New York: Oxford University Press.

Fratiglioni, L., Paillard-Borg, S., & Winblad, B. (2004). An active and socially inte-grated lifestyle in late life may protect against dementia. *The Lancet Neurology, 3*, 343–353.

Hultsch, D. F., Hammer, M., & Small, B. J. (1993). Age differences in cognitive per-formance in later life: Relationships to self-reported health and activity life-style. *Journal of Gerontology: Psychological Sciences, 48*, 1–11.

Hultsch, D. F., Hertzog, C., Small, B. J., & Dixon, R. A. (1999). Use it or lose it: Engaged lifestyle as a buffer of cognitive decline in aging? *Psychology and Aging, 14*, 245–263.

Katzman, R., Aronson, M., Fuld, P., Kawas, C., Brown, T., Morgenstern, H., et al. (1989). Development of dementing illnesses in an 80-year-old volunteer cohort. *Annals of Neurology, 25*, 317–324.

Kemperman, G., Gast, D., & Gage, F. H. (2002). Neuroplasticity in old age: Sustained fivefold induction of hippocampal neurogenesis by long-term environmental enrichment. *Annals of Neurology, 52*, 135–143.

Kohn, M. L., & Schooler, C., with Miller, J., Miller, K., Schoenbach, C., & Schoenberg, R. (1983). *Work and personality: An inquiry into the impact of social stratification.* Norwood, NJ: Ablex.

Kozorovitsky, Y., & Gould, E. (2003). Adult neurogenesis: A mechanism for brain repair? *Journal of Clinical and Experimental Neuropsychology, 25*, 721–752.

Kramer, A. F., & Willis, S. L. (2002). Enhancing the cognitive vitality of older adults. *Current Directions in Psychological Science, 11*, 173–177.

Kramer, A. F., Bherer, L., Colcombe, S. J., Dong, W., & Greenough, W. T. (2004). Environmental influences on cognitive and brain plasticity during aging. *Journal of Gerontology: Medical Sciences, 59A*, 940–957.

Mackinnon, A., Christensen, H., Hofer, S. M., Korten, A. E., & Jorm, A. F. (2003). Use it and still lose it? The association between activity and cognitive performance established using latent growth techniques in a community sample. *Aging, Neuro-psychology, and Cognition, 10*, 215–229.

McArdle, J. J. (2001). A latent difference score approach to longitudinal dynamic structural analysis. In R. Cudeck, S. du Toit, & D. Sörbom (Eds.), *Structural equation modeling: Present and future* (pp. 341–380). Chicago, IL: Scien-tific Software Intenational.

McArdle, J. J., & Hamagami, F. (2001). Latent difference score structural models for linear dynamic analyses with incomplete longitudinal data. In L. M. Collins & A. G. Sayer (Eds.), *New methods for the analysis of change* (pp. 139–175). Washington, DC: American Psychological Association.

Mortimer, J. A., Schuman, L., & French, L. (1981). Epidemiology of dementing illness. In J. A. Mortimer & L. M. Schuman (Eds.), *The epidemiology of dementia: Monographs in epidemiology and biostatistics* (pp. 323–333). New York: Oxford University Press.

Pushkar Gold, D., Andres, D., Etezadi, J., Arbuckle, T., Schwartzman, A., & Chaikel-son, J. (1995). Structural equation model of intellectual change and continuity and predictors of intelligence in elderly men. *Psychology and Aging, 10*, 294–303.

Raz, N. (2000). Aging of the brain and its impact on cognitive performance: Integration of structural and functional findings. In F. I. M. Craik & T. A. Salthouse (Eds.) *Handbook of aging and cognition* (2nd ed., pp. 1–90). Mahwah, NJ: Lawrence Erlbaum Associates, Inc.

Salthouse, T. A., Berish, D. E., & Miles, J. D. (2002). The role of cognitive stimulation on the relations between age and cognitive functioning. *Psychology and Aging, 17,* 548–557.

Satz, P. (1993). Brain reserve capacity on symptom onset after brain injury: A formulation and review of evidence of threshold theory. *Neuropsychology, 7,* 273–295.

Schaie, K. W. (1996). *Intellectual development in adulthood.* New York: Cambridge University Press.

Schinka, J. A., McBride, A., Vanderploeg, R. D., Tennyson, K., Borenstein, A. R., & Mortimer, J. A. (2005). Florida Cognitive Activities Scale: Initial development and validation. *Journal of the International Neuropsychological Society, 11,* 108–116.

Schooler, C. (1984). Psychological effects of complex environments during the life span: A review and theory. *Intelligence, 8,* 259–281.

Schooler, C. (1989). Social structural effects and experimental situations: Mutual lessons of cognitive and social science. In K. W. Schaie & C. Schooler (Eds.), *Social structure and aging: Psychological processes* (pp. 129–147). Hillsdale, NJ: Lawrence Erlbaum Associates, Inc.

Schooler, C., & Mulatu, M. S. (2001). The reciprocal effects of leisure time activities and intellectual functioning in older people. A longitudinal analysis. *Psychology and Aging, 16,* 466–482.

Schooler, C., Mulatu, M. S., & Oates, G. (1999). The continuing effects of substantively complex work on the intellectual functioning of older workers. *Psychology and Aging, 14,* 483–506.

Singer, J. D., & Willett, J. B. (2003). *Applied longitudinal data analysis: Modeling change and event occurrence.* New York: Oxford University Press.

Stern, Y. (2002). What is cognitive reserve? Theory and research application of the reserve concept. *Journal of the International Neuropsychological Society, 8,* 448–460.

U.S. Department of Labor (1965). *Dictionary of occupational titles* (3rd ed.). Washington, DC: U.S. Government Printing Office.

West, R. L. (1996). An application of prefrontal cortex function theory to cognitive aging. *Psychological Bulletin, 120,* 272–292.

Wilson, R. S., Bennett, D. A., Bienias, J. L., Mendes de Leon, C. F., Morris, M. C., & Evans, D. A. (2003). Cognitive activity and cognitive decline in a biracial community population. *Neurology, 61,* 812–816.

11 Lifestyle patterns and cognitive reserve

Nikolaos Scarmeas

The concept of cognitive reserve (CR) suggests that innate intelligence or aspects of life experience such as educational or occupational attainments may supply reserve, in the form of a set of skills or repertoires, that allows some people to cope with progressing Alzheimer's disease (AD) pathology better than others. There is epidemiological evidence that lifestyle characterized by engagement in leisure activities of an intellectual, social and physical nature is associated with slower cognitive decline in healthy elderly and may reduce the risk of incident dementia. The association between such activities and cognitive function is also supported by genetic, structural and functional imaging studies. It is possible that aspects of life experience such as engagement in leisure activities may result in functionally more efficient cognitive networks and therefore provide a CR that delays the onset of clinical manifestations of dementia.

The CR hypothesis suggests that there are individual differences in the ability to cope with AD pathology (Stern, 2002). For example, Katzman et al. (1989) described cases of cognitively normal, elderly women who were discovered to have advanced AD pathology in their brains at death. They speculated these women did not express the clinical features of AD because their brains were larger than average. About 25–67% of subjects who during autopsy fulfilled pathologic criteria for AD and were assessed and followed in well-characterized cohorts were clinically intact during life (Crystal et al., 1988; Ince, 2001; Morris et al., 1996; Mortimer, Snowdon, & Markesbery, 2003). Similarly, most clinicians are aware of the fact that a stroke of a given magnitude can produce profound impairment in one patient while having minimal effect on another. Something must account for the disjunction between the degree of brain damage and its outcome, and the concept of reserve has been proposed to serve this purpose.

Innate intelligence or aspects of life experience like educational or occupational attainment may supply reserve, in the form of a set of skills or repertoires that allows some people to cope with pathology better than others. Epidemiological data supporting the CR hypothesis include observations that lower educational and occupational attainment is associated with increased risk for incident dementia (Stern, Gurland, Tatemichi, Tang,

Wilder, & Mayeux, 1994). Similarly, lower linguistic ability (as expressed by idea density and grammatical complexity) in early life and childhood mental ability scores are strong predictors of poor cognitive function and dementia in late life (Snowdon Greiner, Mortimer, Riley, Greiner, & Markesbery, 1997; Whalley, Starr, Athawes, Hunter, Pattie, & Deary, 2000). This is consistent with the prediction that people with more reserve can cope with advancing AD pathology longer before it is expressed clinically. In addition it has been shown that AD patients with higher educational and occupational attainment have more rapid cognitive decline than those with lower attainment, consistent with the idea that, at any level of clinical severity, the underlying AD pathology is more advanced in patients with more CR (Stern, Tang, Denaro, & Mayeux, 1995).

Nature of activities

Factors other than IQ, education and occupation might also provide reserve and influence the incidence of AD. In this review we will examine some of the environmental factors and lifestyle activities that affect CR and therefore may alter the risk for cognitive decline or clinical AD. For economy of size, we will not discuss education, occupation and non-environmental factors affecting CR such as genetics or head size (although perinatal environment may also affect head size), or some other environmental factors such as nutrition. It should be noted here that although some life experience factors that affect CR are considered environmental, it is possible that they may to some extent reflect genetic effects. In addition, these factors are not independent but are related both to each other and to other parameters such as education, occupation, and so on.

It has been theorized that changes in everyday experiences and activity patterns may result in disuse and consequent atrophy of cognitive processes and skills (a view captured in the adage "use it or lose it") (Salthouse, 1991). Taking into account the considerable plasticity of cognitive abilities of older adults, one might predict that deliberate practice of such skills would at least result in stable performance or may even reverse age-related changes. Does the stimulation provided by typical everyday activities facilitate the maintenance and improvement of general cognitive skills via exposure to cognitive training (Hultsch, Hertzog, Small, & Dixon, 1999)? In other words, could everyday experience affect cognition in a manner that is analogous to physical exercise for musculosceletal and cardiovascular functions?

Although it makes intuitive sense that only cognitively or socially challenging activities might be related to risk for dementia there is also evidence for protection even for non-cognitive activities. There is basic research evidence that environmental enrichment in the form of voluntary wheel running is associated with enhanced neurogenesis in the adult mouse dentate gyrus (van Praag, Kempermann, & Gage, 1999). It has also been shown that physical activity sustains cerebral blood flow (Rogers, Meyer, & Mortel,

1990), may improve aerobic capacity and cerebral nutrient supply (Dustman et al., 1984; Spirduso, 1980), may enhance cortical high-affinity choline uptake and dopamine receptor density (Fordyce & Farrar, 1991), may stimulate trophic factors and neuronal growth (Gomez-Pinilla, So, & Kesslak, 1998), and can upregulate brain-derived neurotrophic factor gene expression (Cotman & Engesser-Cesar, 2002; Neeper, Gomez-Pinilla, Choi, & Cotman, 1995). Therefore, although it is conceivable that physical activity may merely be a non-specific marker of good health indirectly related to dementia (or even not related to dementia at all), it is also possible that it has a direct physiological association with brain disease. Given the above, we review leisure activity data, including life habits of either cognitive, social or physical nature.

Healthy adults

Many cross-sectional studies have investigated the association between level of participation in activities and performance on various cognitive tasks in healthy adults (Arbuckle, Gold, & Andres, 1986; Christensen, Korten, Jorm, Henderson, Scott, & Mackinnon, 1996; Craik, Byrd, & Swanson, 1987; Erber & Szuchman, 1996; Hill, Wahlin, Winblad, & Backman, 1995; Hultsch, Hammer, & Small, 1993; Luszcz, Bryan, & Kent, 1997; van Boxtel, Langerak, Houx, & Jolles, 1996). In general, these studies have reported that there is a positive association between participation in intellectual, social and physical activities and performance on a wide range of cognitive tasks.

Nevertheless, the lack of temporal depth of cross-sectional studies raises concerns over issues of causal directionality. Does participation in stimulating activities promote cognitive performance, or is it that better performing cognitively capable subjects tend to participate in more intellectual, social and physical activities? Longitudinal data can offer a partial resolution of this conundrum.

At least three studies have used structural equation modeling in longitudinal data to address this question. Schooler and Mulatu (2001) reported that initial high levels of intellectual functioning lead to high levels of environmental complexity, which in turn raise the levels of intellectual functioning over a 20-year period. Gold, Andres, Etezadi, Arbuckle, Schwartzman, and Chaikelson (1995) reported that individuals with higher levels of intellectual ability, education and socioeconomic status are more likely to develop an engaged lifestyle, which in turn contributes to the maintenance of verbal intelligence in later life. Similar observations were reported in a 250-individual sample tested three times over 6 years: intellectually engaging activities seemed to buffer against decline in cognitive functioning (Hultsch et al., 1999). Nevertheless, an alternative model in this study suggested that findings were also consistent with the hypothesis that high-ability individuals lead intellectually active lives until cognitive decline in old age limits their activities.

In another study, individuals with high socioeconomic status who were fully engaged with their environment had the least intellectual decline over 7 and 14 years (K. Schaie, 1984; K. W. Schaie, 1996). In this study it was widowed women who had never been in the workforce and who exhibited a disengaged lifestyle that exhibited the greatest decline. According to another report, participation in intellectual activities was related to maintenance of intellectual performance in a sample of Second World War veterans tested twice over a 40-year period (Arbuckle, Gold, Andres, Schwartzman, & Chaikelson, 1992).

Frequent participation in cognitively stimulating activities was associated with reduced cognitive decline (assessments every 3 years) in a study of 4000 elderly community residents followed for an average of 5.3 years (Wilson, Bennett, Bienias, Mendes de Leon, Morris, & Evans, 2003). Finally, a variety of spare-time mental and social activities at age 36 for subjects of the British 1946 birth cohort were positively associated with memory performance at age 43 (Richards, Hardy, & Wadsworth, 2003; Richards & Sacker, 2003).

In a study of 5925 community dwelling women aged over 65, higher levels of physical activity at baseline (blocks walked and stairs climbed) was associated with lower risk of cognitive decline, irrespective of baseline function or health status (Yaffe, Barnes, Nevitt, Lui, & Covinsky, 2001). In a cohort of 347 elderly Dutch men increased physical activity was associated with lower risk of cognitive decline (Schuit, Feskens, Launer, & Kromhout, 2001). In another population sample of 1261 subjects 62–85 years old in the Netherlands, there was a significant association between physical activity at ages 15 and 25 and faster information processing speed at older age for men, but not for women (Dik, Deeg, Visser, & Jonker, 2003). In a study of 1919 subjects from the 1936 British birth cohort, physical activity at age 36 was associated with both memory performance at age 46 and significantly slower rate of decline in memory from age 43 to age 53 (Richards et al., 2003). In the Nurses' Health Study, including 18,766 US women aged 70 to 81 years, participation in physical activities (as assessed by biennial mailed questionnaires) was associated both with better cognitive performance at baseline and with slower cognitive decline over time (Weuve, Kang, Manson, Breteler, Ware, & Grodstein, 2004). Finally, analyses from other cohorts also suggest that physical activities provide protection for future cognitive decline (Albert et al., 1995; Carmelli, Swan, LaRue, & Eslinger, 1997; Rogers et al., 1990).

Cognitive training in healthy adults

There is a sizeable body of literature documenting that different types of cognitive training programs have large and durable effects on cognitive functioning of older adults not only under laboratory or small-scale field conditions (Ball, Beard, Roenker, Miller, & Griggs, 1988; Baltes, 1991; Baltes & Willis, 1982; Edwards, Wadley, Myers, Roenker, Cisell, & Ball, 2002; Greenberg & Powers, 1987; Kliegl, Smith, & Baltes, 1990; Rasmusson,

Rebok, Bylsma, & Brandt, 1999; Rebok & Balcerak, 1989; Willis, 1987; Willis & Nesselroade, 1990; Willis & Schaie, 1986; Yesavage, 1985) but also in a large randomized controlled trial with long follow-up (Ball et al., 2002).

Some intervention studies examining the role of exercise (for reviews see Churchill, Galvez, Colcombe, Swain, Kramer, & Greenough, 2002 and Colcombe & Kramer, 2003) have failed to observe improvements in cognitive function of non-demented elderly (Blumenthal & Madden, 1988; Hill, Storandt, & Malley, 1993; Madden, Blumenthal, Allen, & Emery, 1989; Normand, Kerr, & Metivier, 1987; Panton, Graves, Pollock, Hagberg, & Chen, 1990). However, many other trials have found improvements in cognitive function with physical fitness training (Chodzko-Zajko & Moore, 1994; Dustman et al., 1984; Emery, Schein, Hauck, & MacIntyre, 1998; Hawkins, Kramer, & Capaldi, 1992; Kramer et al., 1999; Moul, Goldman, & Warren, 1995; Rikli & Edwards, 1991; Williams & Lord, 1997). There is evidence that aerobically trained individuals have outperformed non-aerobic control subjects on a variety of cognitive tasks (Dustman et al., 1984; Hawkins et al., 1992; Rikli & Edwards, 1991).

In a meta-analysis of 18 aerobic fitness training intervention studies for healthy elderly, exercise had the greatest effects for executive function, but other cognitive domains also improved (Colcombe & Kramer, 2003). Physical intervention characteristics that provided maximum benefit included combined strength and aerobic training, sessions of moderate duration (no shorter than 30 minutes), overall training program of long duration (6 months or more), higher percentage of female participants, and "mid-old" participants (not younger than 65, not older than 70) (Colcombe & Kramer, 2003).

Alzheimer's disease

Although educational and occupational attainments have been extensively studied, there are very few reports examining the influence of socially and intellectually engaged lifestyle on dementia. One case control study of AD in Japan (Kondo, Niino, & Shido, 1994) (60 patients), reported that cases were significantly less active in various uses of leisure time, hobbies and psychosocial behaviors. Another case-control study examined the presence of non-occupational activities during midlife in 193 subjects with possible and probable AD (Friedland et al., 2001). When activity patterns were classified into intellectual, passive and physical, cases were less likely to have participated in intellectual activities. In the Canadian Study of Health and Aging, a nationwide, population-based study, 194 incident AD cases were compared with 3894 cognitively normal controls (Lindsay et al., 2002). Regular physical activity was associated with a reduced risk of AD. Another case-control study examined differences in mental, physical and social occupational demands (across four decades of life; 20s, 30s, 40s, and 50s) of 122 AD cases and 235 controls. Social demands did not differ, and physical demands were higher for AD cases (Smyth, Fritsch, Cook, McClendon, Santillan, & Friedland, 2004). Mental occupational demands were lower for AD cases in later decades, which was interpreted either as early influence of AD neuropathology on capacity to pursue mentally demanding occupations, or as mentally demanding occupation having a protective influence on development of AD neuropathology for the controls.

There have been some prospective longitudinal studies examining the influence of socially and intellectually engaged lifestyle on incident dementia. These studies can better approach the issue of temporal order, which relates to causal directionality: does lack of participation in stimulating activities represent a true risk factor or is it that already mildly subclinically affected subjects tend to participate in less intellectual, social and physical activities as a result of their disease? There are also concerns that case-control studies may suffer from misclassification of exposure (i.e., AD subjects or their family may have a tendency to under-report CR-associated activities that they may consider as potentially protective for the disease), decreased accuracy of exposure reporting as a result of using surrogate respondents (Debanne et al., 2001), and recall bias (Lissner, Potischman, Troiano, & Bengtsson, 2004). For example, in data from a 32-year follow-up of a prospective population study of women in Goteborg, Sweden, systematic errors were observed in remote physical activity reports. Most elderly women generally remembered being more active 32 years earlier than they had originally reported (Lissner et al., 2004). Finally, longitudinal studies provide more confidence in dementia diagnosis, since documentation of cognitive change is of real (rather than historical) nature. The need for prospective studies is exemplified by associations (between dementia diagnosis and occupation, for example) noted in cross-sectional studies that were refuted when the data were inspected longitudinally (Dartigues et al., 1992; Helmer et al., 2001; Jorm et al., 1998).

In a survey sample of 422 elderly subjects the relation of various indicators of socioeconomic status to incident dementia was investigated (Bickel & Cooper, 1994). Only poor quality living accommodation was associated with increased risk of incident dementia, while indicators of social isolation such as low frequency of social contacts within and outside the family circle, low standard of social support and living in single person households did not prove to be significant. In a population study of 327 elderly from Sydney, there was no association between physical exercise and risk of incident AD or dementia (Broe et al., 1998). Another study evaluated social and leisure activity data in 2040 non-demented elderly community residents from the Gironde (France) and recorded incident dementia on follow-up visits (Fabrigoule, Letenneur, Dartigues, Zarrouk, Commenges, & Barberger-Gateau, 1995). Traveling, doing odd jobs and knitting were associated with lower risk of incident dementia when occupational status was controlled for. Community activities and gardening have also been shown to be protective for incident dementia in another study performed in China (Zhang, Li, & Zhang, 1999).

A longitudinal study in Sweden reported that having an extensive social network was protective for development of incident dementia (Fratiglioni, Wang, Ericsson, Maytan, & Winblad, 2000). The same group also reported that both social interaction and intellectual stimulation may help preserve mental function in the elderly, since engagement in mental, social and productive activities was associated with decreased risk for incident dementia (Wang, Karp, Winblad, & Fratiglioni, 2002). There was no association between physical activity and dementia risk. In the Honolulu-Asia Aging Study distance walked per day in 2257 physically capable men 71–93 years old was recorded and cognitive assessments and clinical evaluations were performed over time (Abbott, White, Ross, Masaki, Curb, & Petrovich, 2004). Men who walked less than 0.25 miles per day experienced a 1.8-fold higher risk for dementia as compared to those who walked more than 2 miles per day.

We studied a total of 1772 non-demented individuals aged 65 years or older, living in Northern Manhattan, New York who were identified and followed longitudinally in a community based cohort incidence study for up to 7 years (mean 2.9 years) (Scarmeas, Levy, Tang, Manly, & Stern, 2001). In the initial visit, an interview elicited self-reported participation in a variety of leisure activities of an intellectual (reading magazines or newspapers or books, playing cards or games or bingo, going to classes, etc.), social (visiting or being visited by friends or relatives, etc.), and even physical (walking for pleasure or excursion, physical conditioning, etc.) nature. Even when factors like ethnic group, education and occupation were controlled for, subjects with high leisure activity had 38% less risk of developing dementia. The risk of incident dementia was reduced by approximately 12% for each additional leisure activity adopted. The effect of leisure activities on incident dementia was still present even when baseline cognitive performance, health limitations interfering with social activities, cerebrovascular disease, and depression were considered. In another cohort from New York, participation in leisure activities (in particular reading, playing board games, musical instruments and dancing) was associated with a reduced risk for incident dementia (Verghese et al., 2003). Increased participation in cognitive activities was also associated with reduced rates of decline in memory in this study. Higher physical activity was not protective.

In another prospective study, frequency of participation in common cognitive activities (i.e., reading a newspaper, magazine, books) was assessed at baseline for 801 elderly Catholic nuns, priests and brothers without dementia (Wilson, Mendes de Leon et al., 2002). During a mean follow-up of 4.5 years, a 1-point increase in the cognitive activity score was associated with a 33% reduction in the risk for AD. Additionally, engagement in cognitive activities was also associated with slower rates of cognitive decline. The results held even when many potential confounders were controlled for, and even when subjects with memory impairment at baseline evaluation were excluded from the analyses. Similar associations were found by the same group in another biracial cohort of 842 dementia free participants aged 65 years and older in Chicago. Frequency of participation in seven cognitive activities (e.g., reading a newspaper) and nine physical activities (e.g., walking for exercise) was assessed and composite measures of cognitive and physical activity frequency were derived (Wilson, Bennett et al., 2002). Increased frequency of participation in cognitively stimulating activities, but not weekly hours of physical activity, were associated with reduced risk of AD.

Lifestyle activities and AD course

In contrast to previous studies that were investigating risk for incident dementia, another study by the same group has explored the rate of cognitive decline in relation to premorbid reading activity in subjects who had already manifested the disease. In a cohort of 410 persons with AD followed for a 4-year period, higher levels of premorbid reading activity were associated with more rapid decline in the global cognitive and verbal measures (Wilson et al., 2000). Although counterintuitive at first glance, the results are consistent with the hypothesis that intellectual activities may enhance the brain's reserve capacity and that at any level of clinical severity, the underlying AD pathology is more advanced in patients with more CR. Therefore, although subjects with higher CR (compared to ones with lower CR) may manifest dementia symptomatology later in life, they may decline faster after dementia onset. These results for reading activity parallel previous similar ones for education and occupation (Stern, Tang et al., 1995; Scarmeas et al., 2006).

Genetics

To what extent are both participation in stimulating activities and superior cognitive performance markers of innate or genetic capacities? Or is it that increased participation in intellectual, social and physical activities exerts a true environmental influence improving genetically planned cognitive performance? Genetic studies can offer relative estimates of genetic contributions to examined phenotypes. A twin study examined 107 same-sex twin pairs discordant for dementia and for whom information on leisure activities was self-reported more than 20 years prior to clinical evaluation (Crowe, Andel, Pedersen, Johansson, & Gatz, 2003). Controlling for level of education, participation in a greater overall number of leisure activities was associated with lower risk of both AD and dementia in general. Greater participation in intellectual-cultural activities was associated with lower risk of AD for women in particular. These results argue for an environmental, non-genetic effect of leisure activities on cognitive performance.

Imaging

Physiologic data from imaging studies have served as an indirect affirmation of the CR hypothesis and have provided the first attempts to investigate the neural correlate of CR.

Structural imaging

According to the CR hypothesis, among subjects with similar degrees of pathology, those with higher CR would be expected to demonstrate less cognitive impairment. Stated differently, among subjects with similar cognitive status, those with more CR would have (or be able to tolerate) more severe degrees of pathology. In order to test this hypothesis, some imaging studies have used brain atrophy as a surrogate for pathology. Aerobic fitness training has been associated with reduced brain tissue loss in healthy older adults (Colcombe et al., 2003). Although limited by its cross-sectional and observational (i.e., non-randomized) character, this study provides empirical suggestion and a biologic basis for the association between physical fitness and brain tissue density. According to another study, London taxi drivers, who are required to undertake an intensive navigational study of the city as part of their training, manifest significantly larger posterior hippocampi than controls, the size of which correlates with the amount of their occupational experience (Maguire et al., 2000).

Functional imaging

Given the regional correlation between PET cerebral blood flow (CBF) deficits and histologically confirmed post-mortem dementia changes, CBF has been used as an indirect surrogate measure of disease pathology (lower CBF indicating more advanced pathology). It has been shown that patients with higher educational (Stern, Alexander, Prohovnik, & Mayeux, 1992), or occupational (Stern, Alexander et al., 1995) attainment, as well as those with higher premorbid IQ (Alexander et al., 1997) have more prominent flow deficits (and hence more pathology) when controlling for clinical severity. These observations support the prediction that individuals with more reserve can tolerate more pathology.

Results from a recent study involving leisure activities seem to parallel those for education, occupation and IQ. We evaluated leisure (intellectual, social, and physical) activities in 9 patients with early AD and 16 healthy elderly who underwent brain $H_2^{15}O$ PET (Scarmeas et al., 2003a). In a voxel-wise multiple regression analysis that controlled for clinical severity, there was a negative correlation between leisure activity score and CBF. When education, estimates of premorbid IQ or both were added as covariates in the same model, a higher leisure activities score was still associated with more prominent CBF deficits. These results corroborate the hypothesis that at any given level of clinical disease severity, more severe AD pathology can be tolerated by patients with high leisure activities, even when education and IQ are taken into account.

Theoretical considerations

The association between engaged lifestyle and dementia risk could be either mediated or confounded by abilities like IQ, education and occupation. If this is the case then it could be that either IQ or education represent the true causal links with dementia or that subjects with higher IQ or education tend to adopt lifestyles which themselves causally reduce the risk of dementia (such as exercise, diet, etc.). Nevertheless, in studies where education or occupation (Scarmeas et al., 2001) were controlled for, the association between leisure activities and dementia risk was still there.

Another explanation for the findings could be that borderline dementia subjects might have lower leisure activity as a result of early disease. The consequence of such a premise would be that low leisure activity as recorded in epidemiological studies represents a manifestation of early dementia rather than a premorbid risk factor per se. Some studies attempted to partially address this possibility by excluding from the analyses subjects with memory impairment at baseline evaluation or by considering baseline cognitive performance in the analyses (Scarmeas et al., 2001; Verghese et al., 2003; Wilson et al., 2002). Although the protective effect of leisure activities remained unchanged in these studies, the activities were recorded only a few years before dementia incidence. The longer the interval between assessment of such activities and dementia diagnosis, the more confident one can be about the temporality and causality of the relation. Nevertheless, the fact that the association between lifestyle and dementia risk has been noted, even in a twin study that recorded activities more than 20 years prior to clinical evaluation for dementia, provides some reassurance. Overall, given the current literature, the scenario of lifestyle being affected by subtle, incipient cerebral disease cannot be completely excluded.

Finally, one should also entertain the possibility that there is another not yet identified causal factor characteristic that confounds or mediates the inverse association between engaged lifestyle and incident dementia.

Overall, the accumulated data seem to make a case for a protective effect of physical, intellectual and social activities for cognitive decline and dementia. But how is this protection imparted? In other words, if this association is truly present, what could be the biological nature of the final common pathway of CR's protection against cognitive decline?

Possible neural correlates (Scarmeas & Stern, 2003, 2004; Stern, 2002)

1. Passive or hardware: bigger brains tolerate more loss before exhibiting impaired function because of the higher number of healthy synapses or neurons resulting in an increased number of them remaining available when a certain percentage is affected by a pathologic process (Katzman et al., 1988). Intellectually and socially engaged lifestyle may increase synaptic density in neocortical association cortex (on the

basis of stimulation; Katzman, 1993), which may result in more efficient cognitive functioning of unaffected neurons that might be able to compensate for loss of function of affected brain areas.

2. Active or software: more efficient use of the same brain networks. Even though the number of neurons or synapses might be the same, enhanced synaptic activity or more efficient circuits of synaptic connectivity might exist in subjects exerting more leisure activities.

3. Active or software: more efficient use of alternative brain networks, i.e., more efficient ability to shift operations to alternate circuits. As a concrete example, a trained mathematician or somebody with life-long engagement in mathematical training, might be able to solve a mathematics problem many different ways, while a less experienced individual might have only one possible solution strategy available. The mathematician would have more flexibility in solving the problem if any particular solution strategy was precluded. This built-in redundancy would permit greater resilience in the face of brain damage.

4. Finally, it is conceivable that lifestyle activity factors that affect CR may even result in hindering the development of the disease pathology per se (Lazarov et al., 2005). Involvement in challenging avocations during life may even decrease neurodegeneration, and enhance brain repair and recovery mechanisms, thus slowing the rate of progression.

Possible biological mechanisms

The effect of lifestyle experiences on the brain may materialize via many possible routes. First, it may be mediated by increased training. Increased "brain exercise" may result in alteration of a variety of underlying neurobiological processes (Friedland, 1993), such as enhanced chronic neuronal activation, increased regional cerebral blood flow (Rogers et al., 1990), increased glucose and oxygen metabolism, improved aerobic capacity and cerebral nutrient supply (Dustman et al., 1984; Spirduso, 1980), enhanced cortical high-affinity choline uptake and dopamine receptor density (Fordyce & Farrar, 1991), stimulation of trophic factors and neuronal growth (Gomez-Pinilla et al., 1998), upregulation of brain-derived neurotrophic factor gene expression (Cotman & Engesser-Cesar, 2002; Neeper et al., 1995), higher ability for generation of new neurons into adulthood (Eriksson et al., 1998; Johansson, Svensson, Wallstedt, Janson, & Frisen, 1999; Kempermann, Gast, & Gage, 2002; Kukekov et al., 1999; van Praag et al., 1999), or even via reductions in steady-state levels of cerebral beta amyloid peptides and amyloid deposition and selective upregulation in levels of specific transcripts encoded by genes associated with learning and memory, vasculogenesis, neurogenesis, cell survival pathways, beta amyloid sequestration, and prostaglandin synthesis (Lazarov et al., 2005).

Second, life experiences may affect the brain via differential exposure to neurotoxins. It is possible that the connection between lower socioeconomic status (such as suggested by a less engaged lifestyle) and dementia is through exposure to more environmental insults (such as pollutants, industrial and non-industrial toxins), habits such as drinking, or other factors associated with low income and poverty (such as malnutrition and lower health care quality and access, and higher rates of cerebrovascular disease) (Cohen, 1994; Del Ser, Hachinski, Merskey, & Munoz, 1999; Devitt, 1994) that may result in incipient neurological damage and lower the threshold for the clinical manifestation of dementia. According to this model, higher cognitive capacities in high education and occupation attainment subjects may be mediated through avoidance of potentially neurotoxic factors and behaviors.

Third, although a twin study suggests otherwise (Crowe et al., 2003) lifestyle may not reflect true environmental influences but may be just a marker of innate capacities. "Innate" might refer to either genetic or early life developmental factors, or a combination of these. The innate capacities might in turn lead to higher levels of educational and occupational attainment and increased engagement in stimulating vocational activities. These, in turn, may have no association, but just coexist with a genetically predetermined lower risk for cognitive decline and dementia. For example, it may be that subjects genetically predetermined to become demented have early subclinical cognitive dysfunction since their birth, which in turn leads them to fewer years of schooling, lower performance in literacy tests, lower occupational attainment and a more sedentary lifestyle.

Finally, it is likely that a combination of the different scenarios exists. We consider this as the most likely case. It is known that intellectual, social and physical aspects of lifestyle and other CR-related factors are affected by both genetic and environmental factors (Beunen & Thomis, 1999; Bouchard, McGue, Lykken, & Tellegen, 1999; Duncan, Brooks-Gunn, & Klebanov, 1994; Eaves et al., 1999; Koopmans, Slutske, Heath, Neale, & Boomsma, 1999; Madden et al., 1999; McKeown & Record, 1976; Richards & Sacker, 2003; Sacker, Schoon, & Bartley, 2002; van den Bree, Eaves, & Dwyer, 1999). Also, although clear autosomal dominant genetic contributions have been identified for familial AD, more than 95% of AD is of the sporadic form. Therefore, both less activities on one hand and dementia on the other may be genetically predetermined to a certain degree, but aspects of environmental experience may also exacerbate risk or accelerate dementia onset. This may in turn take effect via a combination of both increased cognitive training and healthier behaviors (that lead to lower neurotoxic exposure). These mechanisms may actually be interactive in many possible combinations. For example, life experiences may have a differential effect on subjects with different innate capacities, or different genetic predispositions for dementia and cognitive training may have a differential effect on subjects with varying levels of exposure to neurotoxins.

Future directions

Inter-individual differences in life experiences may partially mediate the relationship between brain pathology and its clinical manifestation. Presently, the lack of biomarkers for AD is a severe obstacle in further clarification of the biological correlate of CR: for example it is unclear whether an elder's healthy cognitive status is due to absence of disease pathology or due to presence of incipient pathology that is counteracted by CR. When a reliable biomarker is available, then high CR subjects who can counteract pathology could be identified and the nature of factors that provide CR and the mechanism by which is effected can be further investigated.

We are currently lacking scientific data informing the underlying physiological effect of life experiences. Investigations of the nature and specifics of the neural instantiation of CR should be undertaken. Except for animal studies examining the biological effects of life experiences on cerebral circulation, neurotransmitters, neurogenesis, and so on, other approaches such as modern functional brain imaging technology during either rest or cognitive activation tasks in humans may provide useful insight into associations between CR and particular cognitive processes (Scarmeas et al., 2003b; Scarmeas et al., 2004). They can also provide measurable physiological effects of CR, which in turn may help identify which are the most effective and potent types of activities in terms of their effect on cerebral physiology. These types of activities can then be used in pilot clinical trials with the cerebral physiological effects as outcomes. Eventually, larger therapeutic trials may lead to the exciting prospect of suggestions of particular life experience modifications that could affect the risk for dementia.

References

Abbott, R. D., White, L. R., Ross, G. W., Masaki, K. H., Curb, J. D., & Petrovitch, H. (2004). Walking and dementia in physically capable elderly men. *Journal of the American Medical Association, 292*(12), 1447–1453.

Albert, M. S., Jones, K., Savage, C. R., Berkman, L., Seeman, T., Blazer, D., et al. (1995). Predictors of cognitive change in older persons: MacArthur studies of successful aging. *Psychology and Aging, 10*(4), 578–589.

Alexander, G. E., Furey, M. L., Grady, C. L., Pietrini, P., Brady, D. R., Mentis, M. J., et al. (1997). Association of premorbid intellectual function with cerebral metabolism in Alzheimer's disease: Implications for the cognitive reserve hypothesis. *American Journal of Psychiatry, 154*(2), 165–172.

Arbuckle, T. Y., Gold, D., & Andres, D. (1986). Cognitive functioning of older people in relation to social and personality variables. *Psychology and Aging, 1*(1), 55–62.

Arbuckle, T. Y., Gold, D. P., Andres, D., Schwartzman, A., & Chaikelson, J. (1992). The role of psychosocial context, age, and intelligence in memory performance of older men. *Psychology and Aging, 7*(1), 25–36.

Ball, K., Berch, D. B., Helmers, K. F., Jobe, J. B., Leveck, M. D., Marsiske, M., et al. (2002). Effects of cognitive training interventions with older adults: A randomized controlled trial. *Journal of the American Medical Association, 288*(18), 2271–2281.

Ball, K. K., Beard, B. L., Roenker, D. L., Miller, R. L., & Griggs, D. S. (1988). Age and visual search: Expanding the useful field of view. *Journal of the Optical Society of America, A, 5*, 2210–2219.

Baltes, P. (1991). The many faces of human ageing: Toward a psychological culture of old age. *Psychology and Aging, 21*, 837–854.

Baltes, P. B., & Willis, S. L. (1982). Plasticity and enhancement of intellectual functioning in old age: Penn State's Adult Development and Enrichment Project (ADEPT). In F. I. M. Craik & S. Trehub (Eds.), *Aging and cognitive processes* (pp. 353–390). New York: Plenum Press.

Beunen, G., & Thomis, M. (1999). Genetic determinants of sports participation and daily physical activity. *International Journal of Obesity and Related Metabolic Disorders, 23* (Suppl 3), S55–63.

Bickel, H., & Cooper, B. (1994). Incidence and relative risk of dementia in an urban elderly population: Findings of a prospective field study. *Psycholical Medicine, 24*(1), 179–192.

Blumenthal, J. A., & Madden, D. J. (1988). Effects of aerobic exercise training, age, and physical fitness on memory-search performance. *Psychology and Aging, 3*(3), 280–285.

Bouchard, T. J., Jr., McGue, M., Lykken, D., & Tellegen, A. (1999). Intrinsic and extrinsic religiousness: Genetic and environmental influences and personality correlates. *Twin Research, 2*(2), 88–98.

Broe, G. A., Creasey, H., Jorm, A. F., Bennett, H. P., Casey, B., Waite, L. M., et al. (1998). Health habits and risk of cognitive impairment and dementia in old age: A prospective study on the effects of exercise, smoking and alcohol consumption. *Australian and New Zealand Journal of Public Health, 22*(5), 621–623.

Carmelli, D., Swan, G. E., LaRue, A., & Eslinger, P. J. (1997). Correlates of change in cognitive function in survivors from the Western Collaborative Group Study. *Neuroepidemiology, 16*(6), 285–295.

Chodzko-Zajko, W. J., & Moore, K. A. (1994). Physical fitness and cognitive functioning in aging. *Exercise and Sport Sciences Reviews, 22*, 195–220.

Christensen, H., Korten, A., Jorm, A. F., Henderson, A. S., Scott, R., & Mackinnon, A. J. (1996). Activity levels and cognitive functioning in an elderly community sample. *Age and Ageing, 25*(1), 72–80.

Churchill, J. D., Galvez, R., Colcombe, S., Swain, R. A., Kramer, A. F., & Greenough, W. T. (2002). Exercise, experience and the aging brain. *Neurobiology of Aging, 23*(5), 941–955.

Cohen, C. I. (1994). Education, occupation, and Alzheimer's disease. *Journal of the American Medical Association, 272*(18), 1405; author reply 1406.

Colcombe, S., & Kramer, A. F. (2003). Fitness effects on the cognitive function of older adults: A meta-analytic study. *Psychological Science, 14*(2), 125–130.

Colcombe, S. J., Erickson, K. I., Raz, N., Webb, A. G., Cohen, N. J., McAuley, E., et al. (2003). Aerobic fitness reduces brain tissue loss in aging humans. *Journals of Gerontology Series A: Biological Sciences and Medical Sciences, 58*(2), 176–180.

Cotman, C. W., & Engesser-Cesar, C. (2002). Exercise enhances and protects brain function. *Exercise and Sport Sciences Reviews, 30*(2), 75–79.

Craik, F. I., Byrd, M., & Swanson, J. M. (1987). Patterns of memory loss in three elderly samples. *Psychology and Aging, 2*(1), 79–86.

Crowe, M., Andel, R., Pedersen, N. L., Johansson, B., & Gatz, M. (2003). Does participation in leisure activities lead to reduced risk of Alzheimer's disease? A prospective study of Swedish twins. *Journals of Gerontology Series B: Psychological Sciences and Social Sciences, 58*(5), 249–255.

Crystal, H., Dickson, D., Fuld, P., Masur, D., Scott, R., Mehler, M., et al. (1988). Clinico-pathologic studies in dementia: Nondemented subjects with pathologically confirmed Alzheimer's disease. *Neurology, 38*(11), 1682–1687.

Dartigues, J. F., Gagnon, M., Mazaux, J. M., Barberger-Gateau, P., Commenges, D., Letenneur, L., et al. (1992). Occupation during life and memory performance in nondemented French elderly community residents. *Neurology, 42*(9), 1697–1701.

Debanne, S. M., Petot, G. J., Li, J., Koss, E., Lerner, A. J., Riedel, T. M., et al. (2001). On the use of surrogate respondents for controls in a case-control study of Alzheimer's disease. *Journal of the American Geriatric Society, 49*(7), 980–984.

Del Ser, T., Hachinski, V., Merskey, H., & Munoz, D. G. (1999). An autopsy-verified study of the effect of education on degenerative dementia. *Brain, 122* (Pt 12), 2309–2319.

Devitt, N. (1994). Education, occupation, and Alzheimer's disease. *Journal of the American Medical Association, 272*(18), 1405; author reply 1406.

Dik, M., Deeg, D. J., Visser, M., & Jonker, C. (2003). Early life physical activity and cognition at old age. *Journal of Clinical and Experimental Neuropsychology, 25*(5), 643–653.

Duncan, G. J., Brooks-Gunn, J., & Klebanov, P. K. (1994). Economic deprivation and early childhood development. *Child Development, 65*(2), 296–318.

Dustman, R. E., Ruhling, R. O., Russell, E. M., Shearer, D. E., Bonekat, H. W., Shigeoka, J. W., et al. (1984). Aerobic exercise training and improved neuro-psychological function of older individuals. *Neurobiology of Aging, 5*(1), 35–42.

Eaves, L., Heath, A., Martin, N., Maes, H., Neale, M., Kendler, K., et al. (1999). Comparing the biological and cultural inheritance of personality and social attitudes in the Virginia 30,000 study of twins and their relatives. *Twin Research, 2*(2), 62–80.

Edwards, D. J., Wadley, V. G., Myers, R. S., Roenker, D. L., Cissell, G. M., & Ball, K. K. (2002). The transfer of a speed of processing intervention to near and far cognitive functions. *Gerontology, 48*, 329–340.

Emery, C. F., Schein, R. L., Hauck, E. R., & MacIntyre, N. R. (1998). Psychological and cognitive outcomes of a randomized trial of exercise among patients with chronic obstructive pulmonary disease. *Health Psychology, 17*(3), 232–240.

Erber, J. T., & Szuchman, L. T. (1996). Memory performance in relation to age, verbal ability, and activity. *Experimental Aging Research, 22*(1), 59–72.

Eriksson, P. S., Perfilieva, E., Bjork-Eriksson, T., Alborn, A. M., Nordborg, C., Peterson, D. A., et al. (1998). Neurogenesis in the adult human hippocampus. *Nature Medicine, 4*(11), 1313–1317.

Fabrigoule, C., Letenneur, L., Dartigues, J. F., Zarrouk, M., Commenges, D., & Barberger-Gateau, P. (1995). Social and leisure activities and risk of dementia: A prospective longitudinal study. *Journal of the American Geriatric Society, 43*(5), 485–490.

Fordyce, D. E., & Farrar, R. P. (1991). Physical activity effects on hippocampal and parietal cortical cholinergic function and spatial learning in F344 rats. *Behavioural Brain Research, 43*(2), 115–123.

Fratiglioni, L., Wang, H. X., Ericsson, K., Maytan, M., & Winblad, B. (2000). Influence of social network on occurrence of dementia: A community-based longitudinal study. *Lancet, 355*(9212), 1315–1319.

Friedland, R. P. (1993). Epidemiology, education, and the ecology of Alzheimer's disease. *Neurology*, *43*(2), 246–249.

Friedland, R. P., Fritsch, T., Smyth, K. A., Koss, E., Lerner, A. J., Chen, C. H., et al. (2001). Patients with Alzheimer's disease have reduced activities in midlife compared with healthy control-group members. *Proceedings of the National Academy of Science, USA*, *98*(6), 3440–3445.

Gold, D. P., Andres, D., Etezadi, J., Arbuckle, T., Schwartzman, A., & Chaikelson, J. (1995). Structural equation model of intellectual change and continuity and predictors of intelligence in older men [published erratum appears in *Psychology and Aging* (1998) *13*(3), 434]. *Psychology and Aging*, *10*(2), 294–303.

Gomez-Pinilla, F., So, V., & Kesslak, J. P. (1998). Spatial learning and physical activity contribute to the induction of fibroblast growth factor: Neural substrates for increased cognition associated with exercise. *Neuroscience*, *85*(1), 53–61.

Greenberg, C., & Powers, S. M. (1987). Memory improvement among adult learners. *Educational Gerontology*, *12*, 385–394.

Hawkins, H. L., Kramer, A. F., & Capaldi, D. (1992). Aging, exercise, and attention. *Psychology and Aging*, *7*(4), 643–653.

Helmer, C., Letenneur, L., Rouch, I., Richard-Harston, S., Barberger-Gateau, P., Fabrigoule, C., et al. (2001). Occupation during life and risk of dementia in French elderly community residents. *Journal of Neurology, Neurosurgery and Psychiatry*, *71*(3), 303–309.

Hill, R. D., Storandt, M., & Malley, M. (1993). The impact of long-term exercise training on psychological function in older adults. *Journal of Gerontology: Psychological Sciences*, *1*, 12–17.

Hill, R. D., Wahlin, A., Winblad, B., & Backman, L. (1995). The role of demographic and life style variables in utilizing cognitive support for episodic remembering among very old adults. *Journals of Gerontology Series B: Psychological Sciences and Social Sciences*, *50*(4), 219–227.

Hultsch, D. F., Hammer, M., & Small, B. J. (1993). Age differences in cognitive performance in later life: Relationships to self-reported health and activity life style. *Journal of Gerontology*, *48*(1), 1–11.

Hultsch, D. F., Hertzog, C., Small, B. J., & Dixon, R. A. (1999). Use it or lose it: Engaged lifestyle as a buffer of cognitive decline in aging? *Psychology and Aging*, *14*(2), 245–263.

Ince, P. (2001). Pathological correlates of late-onset dementia in a multicenter community-based population in England and Wales. *Lancet*, *357*(9251), 169–175.

Johansson, C. B., Svensson, M., Wallstedt, L., Janson, A. M., & Frisen, J. (1999). Neural stem cells in the adult human brain. *Experimental Cell Research*, *253*(2), 733–736.

Jorm, A. F., Rodgers, B., Henderson, A. S., Korten, A. E., Jacomb, P. A., Christensen, H., et al. (1998). Occupation type as a predictor of cognitive decline and dementia in old age. *Age and Ageing*, *27*(4), 477–483.

Katzman, R. (1993). Education and the prevalence of dementia and Alzheimer's disease. *Neurology*, *43*(1), 13–20.

Katzman, R., Aronson, M., Fuld, P., Kawas, C., Brown, T., Morgenstern, H., et al. (1989). Development of dementing illnesses in an 80-year-old volunteer cohort. *Annals of Neurology*, *25*(4), 317–324.

Katzman, R., Terry, R., DeTeresa, R., Brown, T., Davies, P., Fuld, P., et al. (1988). Clinical, pathological, and neurochemical changes in dementia: A subgroup with preserved mental status and numerous neocortical plaques. *Annals of Neurology*, *23*(2), 138–144.

Kempermann, G., Gast, D., & Gage, F. H. (2002). Neuroplasticity in old age: Sustained fivefold induction of hippocampal neurogenesis by long-term environmental enrichment. *Annals of Neurology*, *52*(2), 135–143.

Kliegl, R., Smith, J., & Baltes, P. B. (1990). On the locus and process of magnification of age differences during mnemonic training. *Developmental Psychology*, *26*, 894–904.

Kondo, K., Niino, M., & Shido, K. (1994). A case-control study of Alzheimer's disease in Japan—significance of life-styles. *Dementia*, *5*(6), 314–326.

Koopmans, J. R., Slutske, W. S., Heath, A. C., Neale, M. C., & Boomsma, D. I. (1999). The genetics of smoking initiation and quantity smoked in Dutch adolescent and young adult twins. *Behavior Genetics*, *29*(6), 383–393.

Kramer, A. F., Hahn, S., Cohen, N. J., Banich, M. T., McAuley, E., Harrison, C. R., et al. (1999). Ageing, fitness and neurocognitive function. *Nature*, *400*(6743), 418–419.

Kukekov, V. G., Laywell, E. D., Suslov, O., Davies, K., Scheffler, B., Thomas, L. B., et al. (1999). Multipotent stem/progenitor cells with similar properties arise from two neurogenic regions of adult human brain. *Experimental Neurology*, *156*(2), 333–344.

Lazarov, O., Robinson, J., Tang, Y. P., Hairston, I., Korade-Mirnics, Z., Lee, V. M., et al. (2005). Environmental enrichment reduces A-beta levels and amyloid deposition in transgenic mice. *Cell*, *120*, 701–713.

Lindsay, J., Laurin, D., Verreault, R., Hebert, R., Helliwell, B., Hill, G. B., et al. (2002). Risk factors for Alzheimer's disease: A prospective analysis from the Canadian Study of Health and Aging. *American Journal of Epidemiology*, *156*(5), 445–453.

Lissner, L., Potischman, N., Troiano, R., & Bengtsson, C. (2004). Recall of physical activity in the distant past: The 32-year follow-up of the prospective population study of women in Goteborg, Sweden. *American Journal of Epidemiology*, *159*(3), 304–307.

Luszcz, M. A., Bryan, J., & Kent, P. (1997). Predicting episodic memory performance of very old men and women: contributions from age, depression, activity, cognitive ability, and speed. *Psychology and Aging*, *12*(2), 340–351.

Madden, D. J., Blumenthal, J. A., Allen, P. A., & Emery, C. F. (1989). Improving aerobic capacity in healthy older adults does not necessarily lead to improved cognitive performance. *Psychology and Aging*, *4*(3), 307–320.

Madden, P. A., Heath, A. C., Pedersen, N. L., Kaprio, J., Koskenvuo, M. J., & Martin, N. G. (1999). The genetics of smoking persistence in men and women: A multicultural study. *Behavior Genetics*, *29*(6), 423–431.

Maguire, E. A., Gadian, D. G., Johnsrude, I. S., Good, C. D., Ashburner, J., Frackowiak, R. S., et al. (2000). Navigation-related structural change in the hippocampi of taxi drivers. *Proceedings of the National Academy of Sciences USA*, *97*(8), 4398–4403.

McKeown, T., & Record, R. G. (1976). Relationship between childhood infections and measured intelligence. *British Journal of Preventive & Social Medicine*, *30*(2), 101–106.

Morris, J. C., Storandt, M., McKeel, D. W., Jr., Rubin, E. H., Price, J. L., Grant, E. A., et al. (1996). Cerebral amyloid deposition and diffuse plaques in "normal" aging:

Evidence for presymptomatic and very mild Alzheimer's disease. *Neurology*, *46*(3), 707–719.

Mortimer, J. A., Snowdon, D. A., & Markesbery, W. R. (2003). Head circumference, education and risk of dementia: Findings from the Nun Study. *Journal of Clinical and Experimental Neuropsychology*, *25*(5), 671–679.

Moul, J., Goldman, B., & Warren, B. (1995). Physical activity and cognitive performance in the older population. *Journal of Aging and Physical Activity*, *3*, 135–145.

Neeper, S. A., Gomez-Pinilla, F., Choi, J., & Cotman, C. (1995). Exercise and brain neurotrophins. *Nature*, *373*(6510), 109.

Normand, R., Kerr, R., & Metivier, G. (1987). Exercise, aging and fine motor performance: An assessment. *Journal of Sports Medicine and Physical Fitness*, *27*(4), 488–496.

Panton, L. B., Graves, M. L., Pollock, J. M., Hagberg, J. M., & Chen, W. (1990). Effect of aerobic and resistance training on fractionated reaction time and speed of improvement. *Journal of Gerontology: Medical Science*, *42*, 26–31.

Rasmusson, D. X., Rebok, G. W., Bylsma, F. W., & Brandt, J. (1999). Effects of three types of memory training in normal elderly. *Aging, Neuropsychology and Cognition*, *6*, 56–66.

Rebok, G. W., & Balcerak, L. J. (1989). Memory self-efficacy and performance differences in young and old adults: The effect of mnemonic training. *Developmental Psychology*, *25*(5), 714–721.

Richards, M., & Sacker, A. (2003). Lifetime antecedents of cognitive reserve. *Journal of Clinical and Experimental Neuropsychology*, *25*(5), 614–624.

Richards, M., Hardy, R., & Wadsworth, M. E. (2003). Does active leisure protect cognition? Evidence from a national birth cohort. *Social Science and Medicine*, *56*(4), 785–792.

Rikli, R. E., & Edwards, D. J. (1991). Effects of a three-year exercise program on motor function and cognitive processing speed in older women. *Research Quarterly for Exercise and Sport*, *62*(1), 61–67.

Rogers, R. L., Meyer, J. S., & Mortel, K. F. (1990). After reaching retirement age physical activity sustains cerebral perfusion and cognition. *Journal of the American Geriatric Society*, *38*(2), 123–128.

Sacker, A., Schoon, I., & Bartley, M. (2002). Social inequality in educational achievement and psychosocial adjustment throughout childhood: Magnitude and mechanisms. *Social Science and Medicine*, *55*(5), 863–880.

Salthouse, T. (1991). *Theoretical perspectives on cognitive aging*. Hillsdale, NJ: Lawrence Erlbaum Associates, Inc.

Scarmeas, N., & Stern, Y. (2003). Cognitive reserve and lifestyle. *Journal of Clinical and Experimental Neuropsychology*, *25*(5), 625–633.

Scarmeas, N., & Stern, Y. (2004). Cognitive reserve: Implications for diagnosis and prevention of Alzheimer's disease. *Current Neurology and Neuroscience Reports*, *4*(5), 374–380.

Scarmeas, N., Albert, S. M., Manly, J. J., & Stern, Y. (2006). Education and rates of cognitive decline in incident Alzheimer's disease. *Journal of Neurology, Neurosurgery, and Psychiatry*, *77*(3), 308–316.

Scarmeas, N., Levy, G., Tang, M., Manly, J., & Stern, Y. (2001). Influence of leisure activity on the incidence of Alzheimer's disease. *Neurology*, *57*(12), 2236–2242.

Scarmeas, N., Zarahn, E., Anderson, K. E., Habeck, C., Hilton, J., Flynn, J., et al. (2003a). Association of life activities with cerebral blood flow in Alzheimer's disease: Implications for the cognitive reserve hypothesis. *Archives of Neurology, 60*(3), 359–365.

Scarmeas, N., Zarahn, E., Anderson, K. E., Hilton, J., Flynn, J., Van Heertum, R. L., et al. (2003b). Cognitive reserve modulates functional brain responses during memory tasks: A PET study in healthy young and elderly subjects. *Neuroimage, 19*(3), 1215–1227.

Scarmeas, N., Zarahn, E., Anderson, K. E., Honig, L. S., Park, A., Hilton, J., et al. (2004). Cognitive reserve-mediated modulation of positron emission tomographic activations during memory tasks in Alzheimer disease. *Archives of Neurology, 61*(1), 73–78.

Schaie, K. (1984). Midlife influences upon intellectual functioning in old age. *International Journal of Behavioral Development, 7*, 463–478.

Schaie, K. W. (1996). *Intellectual development in adulthood: The Seattle longitudinal study*. New York: Cambridge University Press.

Schooler, C., & Mulatu, M. S. (2001). The reciprocal effects of leisure time activities and intellectual functioning in older people: A longitudinal analysis. *Psychology and Aging, 16*(3), 466–482.

Schuit, A. J., Feskens, E. J., Launer, L. J., & Kromhout, D. (2001). Physical activity and cognitive decline, the role of the apolipoprotein e4 allele. *Medical Science and Sports Exercise, 33*(5), 772–777.

Smyth, K. A., Fritsch, T., Cook, T. B., McClendon, M. J., Santillan, C. E., & Friedland, R. P. (2004). Worker functions and traits associated with occupations and the development of AD. *Neurology, 63*(3), 498–503.

Snowdon, D. A., Greiner, L. H., Mortimer, J. A., Riley, K. P., Greiner, P. A., & Markesbery, W. R. (1997). Brain infarction and the clinical expression of Alzheimer disease. The Nun Study. *Journal of the American Medical Association, 277*(10), 813–817.

Spirduso, W. W. (1980). Physical fitness, aging, and psychomotor speed: A review. *Journal of Gerontology, 35*(6), 850–865.

Stern, Y. (2002). What is cognitive reserve? Theory and research application of the reserve concept. *Journal of the International Neuropsychological Society, 8*(3), 448–460.

Stern, Y., Alexander, G. E., Prohovnik, I., & Mayeux, R. (1992). Inverse relationship between education and parietotemporal perfusion deficit in Alzheimer's disease. *Annals of Neurology, 32*(3), 371–375.

Stern, Y., Alexander, G. E., Prohovnik, I., Stricks, L., Link, B., Lennon, M. C., et al. (1995). Relationship between lifetime occupation and parietal flow: Implications for a reserve against Alzheimer's disease pathology. *Neurology, 45*(1), 55–60.

Stern, Y., Gurland, B., Tatemichi, T. K., Tang, M. X., Wilder, D., & Mayeux, R. (1994). Influence of education and occupation on the incidence of Alzheimer's disease. *Journal of the American Medical Association, 271*(13), 1004–1010.

Stern, Y., Tang, M. X., Denaro, J., & Mayeux, R. (1995). Increased risk of mortality in Alzheimer's disease patients with more advanced educational and occupational attainment. *Annals of Neurology, 37*(5), 590–595.

Teri, L., Gibbons, L. E., McCurry, S. M., Logsdon, R. G., Buchner, D. M., Barlow, W. E., et al. (2003). Exercise plus behavioral management in patients with Alzheimer disease: A randomized controlled trial. *Journal of the American Medical Association, 290*(15), 2015–2022.

van Boxtel, M. P., Langerak, K., Houx, P. J., & Jolles, J. (1996). Self-reported physical activity, subjective health, and cognitive performance in older adults. *Experimental Aging Research, 22*(4), 363–379.

van den Bree, M. B., Eaves, L. J., & Dwyer, J. T. (1999). Genetic and environmental influences on eating patterns of twins aged ≥50 y. *American Journal of Clinical Nutrition, 70*(4), 456–465.

van Praag, H., Kempermann, G., & Gage, F. H. (1999). Running increases cell proliferation and neurogenesis in the adult mouse dentate gyrus. *Nature Neuroscience, 2*(3), 266–270.

Verghese, J., Lipton, R. B., Katz, M. J., Hall, C. B., Derby, C. A., Kuslansky, G., et al. (2003). Leisure activities and the risk of dementia in the elderly. *New England Journal of Medicine, 348*(25), 2508–2516.

Wang, H.-X., Karp, A., Winblad, B., & Fratiglioni, L. (2002). Late-life engagement in social and leisure activities is associated with a decreased risk of dementia: A longitudinal study from the Kungsholmen Project. *American Journal of Epidemiology, 155*(12), 1081–1087.

Weuve, J., Kang, J. H., Manson, J. E., Breteler, M. M. B., Ware, J. H., & Grodstein, F. (2004). Physical activity, including walking, and cognitive function in older women. *Journal of the American Medical Association, 292*(12), 1454–1461.

Whalley, L. J., Starr, J. M., Athawes, R., Hunter, D., Pattie, A., & Deary, I. J. (2000). Childhood mental ability and dementia. *Neurology, 55*(10), 1455–1459.

Williams, P., & Lord, S. R. (1997). Effects of group exercise on cognitive functioning and mood in older women. *Australian and New Zealand Journal of Public Health, 21*(1), 45–52.

Willis, S. L. (1987). Cognitive training and everyday competence. In K. W. Schaie (Ed.), *Annual review of gerontology and geriatrics* (Vol. 7). New York: Springer.

Willis, S. L., & Nesselroade, C. S. (1990). Long-term effects of fluid ability training in old-old age. *Developmental Psychology, 26*(6), 905–910.

Willis, S. L., & Schaie, K. W. (1986). Training the elderly on the ability factors of spatial orientation and inductive reasoning. *Psychology and Aging, 1*(3), 239–247.

Wilson, R. S., Bennett, D. A., Bienias, J. L., Aggarwal, N. T., Mendes de Leon, C. F., Morris, M. C., et al. (2002). Cognitive activity and incident AD in a population-based sample of older persons. *Neurology, 59*(12), 1910–1914.

Wilson, R. S., Bennett, D. A., Bienias, J. L., Mendes de Leon, C. F., Morris, M. C., & Evans, D. A. (2003). Cognitive activity and cognitive decline in a biracial community population. *Neurology, 61*(6), 812–816.

Wilson, R. S., Bennett, D. A., Gilley, D. W., Beckett, L. A., Barnes, L. L., & Evans, D. A. (2000). Premorbid reading activity and patterns of cognitive decline in Alzheimer disease. *Archives of Neurology, 57*(12), 1718–1723.

Wilson, R. S., Mendes de Leon, C. F., Barnes, L., Schneider, J. A., Bienias, J. L., Evans, D. A., et al. (2002). Participation in cognitively stimulating activities and risk of incident Alzheimer disease. *Journal of the American Medical Association, 287*(6), 742–748.

Yaffe, K., Barnes, D., Nevitt, M., Lui, L. Y., & Covinsky, K. (2001). A prospective study of physical activity and cognitive decline in elderly women: Women who walk. *Archives of Internal Medicine, 161*(14), 1703–1708.

Yesavage, J. (1985). Nonpharmacologic treatments for memory losses with normal aging. *American Journal of Psychiatry, 142*(5), 600–605.

Zhang, X., Li, C., & Zhang, M. (1999). [Psychosocial risk factors of Alzheimer's disease]. *Zhonghua Yi Xue Za Zhi, 79*(5), 335–338.

12 Brain reserve: HIV morbidity and mortality

*Matthew J. Reinhard, Paul Satz, Ola A. Selnes,
Ned Sacktor, Bruce A. Cohen, James T. Becker,
and Eric N. Miller*

This chapter has two major objectives:

1. To examine the prognostic influence of cognitive and psychosocial risk factors across the spectrum of HIV disease progression. To accomplish this we draw on a previous 13-year prospective study assessing the effect of general intellectual functioning, age, CD4, and emotional distress on HIV morbidity and mortality (Farinpour et al., 2003).
2. In order to further validate the findings and examine the degree to which brain reserve remains an influence for HIV disease progression, a replication study was conducted comprising a 5-year follow-up analysis utilizing the same study sample drawn from the Multicenter AIDS Cohort Study (MACS). The replication study was conducted specifically for the purposes of the present chapter and utilized the same baseline data points as the original study with a new observation period ending September 30, 2004.

Following study participants for an additional 5 years will allow an examination of the effects of highly active antiretroviral therapy (HAART) on HIV disease progression. Of the 13-year prospective study, it was only in the last 2 years from 1996 to 1998 that HAART was introduced. As it is widely known that HAART has had a profound effect on treatment of HIV/AIDS in general, it is also expected that the additional 5 years of data will show the effect of potent antiretroviral medication for the participants of the present study. It is of interest to ascertain whether brain reserve capacity remains a factor in predicting disease progression in the contemporary HAART era.

Objective 1

(*Note*: The following is a summary of the aims, methods, and results of a study by Farinpour et al., 2003. Please refer to the original article for more in-depth discussion of the findings.)

The aim of the Farinpour et al. (2003) study was to examine the prognostic influence of age, general intellectual functioning and emotional distress across the spectrum of HIV disease progression. They predicted that these risk factors at baseline would be associated with a more rapid disease progression (time to AIDS and dementia diagnosis) and shortened survival (time to death) above and beyond the influence of immune functioning and medication therapy.

Several characteristics of the original study made the investigation unique. HIV-seropositive participants were followed for approximately 13 years after baseline testing, which was the longest follow-up period among HIV survival studies. The sample size of 1231 HIV-seropositive men was also one of the largest to be included in a longitudinal study. The time to AIDS onset, dementia onset, and death were evaluated in order to assess disease morbidity as well as mortality.

The sample was drawn from the Multicenter AIDS Cohort Study (MACS), an ongoing prospective cohort study initiated in 1984 to study the natural history of HIV infection. More detailed descriptions of the MACS recruitment, follow-up procedures, and general demographic characteristics have been given previously (Detels et al., 1998; Enger et al., 1996; McArthur et al., 1993).

Intellectual functioning was estimated using the Shipley Institute of Living Scale (Shipley, 1946). The Center for Epidemiologic Studies—Depression Scale (CES-D; Radloff, 1977) was used to assess depressive symptoms. The CES-D was examined as a continuous (CES-D Total scores) and as a binary variable (CES-D Categorial-16). Dichotimization to a binary variable was based on a cut-off score of 16, which has been shown to be indicative of significant depressive symptoms (Radloff, 1977) and has been applied in other HIV survival studies (Burack, Barrett, Stall, Chesney, Ekstrond, & Coates, 1993; Lyketsos et al., 1993). In addition, given research suggesting somatic items on the CES-D may account for much of the variability in HIV samples, they evaluated a CES-D somatic score representing a sum of the somatic items. Participants were followed from baseline (median: August 15, 1987; range: November 8, 1985 to December 29, 1997) until December 15, 1998, the end of the observation period. Cox Proportional Hazards Regression Models were used to test the relative influence of each psychosocial risk variable on the time to reach each of the three outcome measures.

Results from the Farinpour et al. (2003) study indicated Shipley IQ and CES-D Somatic scores were significant predictors of time to AIDS defining illness; all of the psychosocial variables except education were significant predictors of time to dementia; and older age, fewer years of education, lower Shipley IQ, and higher CES-D depression (Categorical-16 and Somatic) were associated with shortened survival, controlling for baseline CD4 use during the observation period.

As cited in Farinpour et al. (2003), lower IQ and fewer years of education are risk factors for HIV cognitive impairments (Arendt, Hefter, Nelles,

Hilperath, & Strohmeyer, 1993; Basso & Bornstein, 2000; Satz et al., 1993; Stern, Silva, Chaisson, & Evans, 1996; Van Gorp et al., 1994). Their results extended these findings by demonstrating that IQ is also associated with time to AIDS and death. However, education was not a significant predictor of disease progression in the study. This finding was unexpected, particularly given the significant and positive correlations they found between education and IQ. Thus they re-examined education effects without covaring IQ, and education remained a non-significant predictor of HIV disease progression. One possible explanation that may account for this null finding is a Type II error (failure to detect a significant effect) as a result of the skewed and restricted range of education in the cohort (mean education was 15.7, SD 2.4). A second and perhaps more plausible explanation is that IQ is a better marker of brain reserve (to be discussed further below), while education may only represent a surrogate marker.

In terms of the influence of depression on HIV morbidity and mortality, they found somatic CES-D scores, but not total CES-D scores, to be significant risk factors of HIV morbidity and mortality. One explanation for this finding is that somatic symptoms of depression may simply be more influential in HIV disease course compared to mood and interpersonal symptoms of depression. The authors indicate that unlike education and IQ, mood is expected to fluctuate over time, particularly in the face of illness progression, and using a baseline measure of mood to predict clinical endpoints up to 13 years later may miss critical changes in mood that occur before clinical endpoints.

Farinpour et al. (2003) utilize the brain reserve capacity model in their discussion of the findings: General intellectual functioning, age and depression reflect biological processes and/or mediate morbidity and mortality through social correlates of disease progression. For example, the brain reserve capacity model (Satz, 1993) suggests differences in biological predisposition and environmental enrichment result in individual differences in brain reserve. Brain reserve capacity can be measured directly by brain weight, size, and dendritic arborizations, or indirectly by behavioral markers of enrichment such as education, intelligence, and age. Applying theoretical distinctions of passive and active models recently outlined by Stern (2002), brain reserve capacity is conceptualized as an active and dynamic synergy between biological and environmental processes that provide the structure for changes in cognitive reserve throughout the lifespan as the nervous system undergoes retraction and expansion with aging and disease. Poor adaptive functioning such as depression or mental inactivity can diminish this reserve, while continued enrichment may increase reserve and provide a protective factor in delaying the onset of disease expression and death (Satz, 1993).

The construct of brain reserve capacity has most often been applied to the study of dementia. Compared with individuals with greater brain reserve, lower reserve (lower premorbid IQ, fewer years of education, and older age) is associated with an earlier onset of clinical symptoms of dementia (Satz,

1993). Similarly, in HIV studies, brain reserve theory has been invoked to explain variable incubation periods for pre-AIDS neurologic symptoms (Stern et al., 1996). The current findings also suggest that brain reserve capacity may influence HIV progression. However, the mechanism by which brain reserve influences HIV progression (i.e., central nervous system integrity, social and economic correlates, or initiative in pursuing optimal health care) remains to be explained (Farinpour et al., 2003, p. 665).

Objective 2

Methods for examining the degree to which brain reserve remains an influence for HIV disease progression were kept identical to those in the original study, and the same study sample from the Multicenter AIDS Cohort Study was utilized. Refer to Farinpour et al. (2003) for an in-depth description of the sample design, subject criteria, risk variables, data analysis, and statistical results. Identical baseline data points were used for each participant (median August 15, 1987). However, the observation period for the 1231 HIV-seropositive participants was updated from the original end date of December 15, 1998 to a new end date of September 30, 2004. In essence, approximately 5 years of additional data were included to assess which predictors continue to influence the outcome measures of HIV disease progression. Outcome measures are identical and include the number of years from baseline testing to (1) first AIDS defining illness, (2) HIV-dementia, and (3) death.

Procedures and statistical analyses

As in the original study, Cox proportional hazards regression models were used to test the influence of each cognitive and psychosocial risk variable on the time to reach each of the three outcome measures, and variables were entered in the identical stepwise fashion. Tables 1 and 4 from the original study were then recreated with the additional 5-year follow-up data imbedded alongside the results from the original study.

Results

Descriptive statistics enabling comparisons between the original study and the additional 5-year follow-up data of HIV morbidity and mortality are presented in Table 12.1. There have been 87 new cases meeting one of three clinical outcomes (35 new HIV-related deaths, 45 new participants diagnosed with an AIDS defining illness other than dementia, and 7 new cases of HIV-related dementia). Results of Cox proportional hazard models indicating the significant predictors of HIV disease progression and survival for the original study as well as the 5-year follow-up data are presented in Table 12.2. The new hazard ratios (HR) for CD4 remained significant: AIDS 1.72 (95% CI, 1.47–2.02), dementia 1.58 (95% CI, 1.18–2.10), and survival 1.87

Table 12.1 Descriptive statistics of HIV morbidity and mortality (with additional 5-year follow-up data)[1]

Outcome	N original data (new data)	Range in years (new data)	Mean (SD) [new data]
Time to HIV-related death			
Died	599 (634)	0.14–12.24 (0.14–17.37)	5.11 (2.66) [5.46 (3.07)]
Alive	632 (597)		
Total cases	1231 (1231)		
Time to first AIDS-defining illness (without dementia)			
AIDS	659 (704)	0.04–12.28 (0.05–17.99)	4.47 (2.79) [4.87 (3.23)]
No AIDS	514 (475)		
Total cases	1173 (1179)*		
Time to dementia (possible + probable)			
Dementia	202 (209)	0.11–11.34 (0.11–14.12)	4.29 (2.61) [4.47 (2.85)]
No dementia	1025 (1018)		
Total cases	1227 (1227)		

Notes: [1] This table corresponds with Table 1 from the original study; * 6 subjects who were excluded from the original study due to missing data were included in the present analysis.

(95% CI, 1.57–2.23), but were all smaller compared to HR results from the original study. The new hazard ratios for Shipley IQ remained significant: AIDS 1.21 (95% CI, 1.09–1.52), dementia 1.48 (95% CI, 1.09–2.01), and survival 1.33 (95% CI, 1.17–1.60). New HR results were larger for AIDS and dementia compared to HR results from the original study. The HR for survival was slightly reduced in the follow-up data as compared to the HR from the original study. Hazard ratios for all CES-D variables on clinical outcomes were no longer significant using a 95% confidence interval in the follow-up analyses.

Discussion

Prescription of protease inhibitors was initiated for the sample between 1996 and 1998 and it was expected that the 5-year follow-up data would reflect the full effect that introducing potent antiretroviral therapy has on disease progression. This effect is probably seen most clearly with the relatively few numbers of new dementia cases ($n = 7$) (see Table 12.1). While the introduction of protease inhibitors likely influenced the relatively low frequency of new cases of dementia, the new cases of AIDS-related deaths may have been due to participants who were already at an advanced stage of the disease by the time HAART was introduced, and were therefore beyond the threshold where HAART could be maximally effective.

Table 12.2 indicates that the hazard ratios for CD4 are smaller in the follow-up analysis as compared to the original study. Considering again that of the 13 years of the original observation period it was only in the last 2

Table 12.2 Results of Cox proportional hazards models, adjusting for concurrent predictors (with additional 5-year follow-up data)[1]

Predictor	HR (95% CL)	[New HR data]	p value (new data) Wald, B
AIDS (without dementia)			
CD4	2.40 (2.04–2.82)	[1.72 (1.47–2.02)]	<.01* (<.01)*
Age	1.12 (.096–1.32)	[1.12 (0.96–1.31)]	.17 (.14)
Education	1.04 (0.87–1.24)	[1.10 (0.93–1.31)]	.69 (.25)
Shipley IQ	1.24 (1.05–1.46)	[1.29 (1.09–1.52)]	<.01* (<.01)*
CES-D Total	1.14 (0.97–1.33)	[1.00 (0.86–1.17)]	.11 (.93)
CES-D Somatic	1.22 (1.04–1.43)	[0.99 (0.85–1.15)]	.01* (.90)
CES-D Categorical-16	1.17 (0.97–1.41)	[0.99 (1.47–2.03)]	.10 (.90)
Dementia			
CD4	1.73 (1.30–2.30)	[1.58 (1.18–2.10)]	<.01* (<.01)*
Age	1.56 (1.16–2.08)	[1.29 (0.97–1.72)]	<.01* (.07)
Education	1.03 (0.75–1.40)	[0.96 (0.71–1.31)]	.87 (.96)
Shipley IQ	1.35 (0.99–1.83)	[1.48 (1.09–2.01)]	.05* (.01)*
CES-D Total	1.57 (1.18–2.08)	[1.11 (0.83–1.48)]	<.01* (.46)
CES-D Somatic	1.62 (1.22–2.16)	[1.29 (0.96–1.74)]	<.01* (.08)
CES-D Categorical-16	1.60 (1.17–2.18)	[1.25 (0.91–1.72)]	<.01* (.16)
Survival			
CD4	2.95 (2.47–3.51)	[1.87 (1.57–2.23)]	<.01* (<.01)*
Age	1.31 (1.11–1.54)	[1.29 (1.09–1.53)]	<.01* (<.01)*
Education	1.11 (0.93–1.34)	[1.05 (0.87–1.27)]	.25 (.57)
Shipley IQ	1.48 (1.24–1.78)	[1.33 (1.17–1.60)]	<.01* (<.01)*
CES-D Total	1.10 (0.94–1.30)	[1.09 (0.93–1.29)]	.24 (.27)
CES-D Somatic	1.25 (1.06–1.47)	[1.09 (0.92–1.28)]	.01* (.29)
CES-D Categorical-16	1.25 (1.04–1.52)	[1.17 (0.97–1.41)]	.02* (.09)

Notes: [1] This table corresponds with Table 4 from the original study; * significant predictor.

years from 1996 to 1998 that HAART was introduced, these new results likely relate to the effect of HAART on CD4 itself. The additional 5 years of CD4 data collected in a post-HAART era probably relate to a reduced rate of CD4 decline. This effect has been substantiated by Detels et al. (1998) using a MACS sample and analyzing different calendar periods associated with different types of therapies being used (i.e., monotherapy, combotherapy, or antiretroviral) showing that when potent antiretroviral therapy was introduced there was a slower CD4 cell count decline.

As discussed in Farinpour et al. (2003), the literature on depression and HIV morbidity and mortality remains controversial. A comparison of Tables 4 and 5 in Farinpour et al. (2003) indicates that symptoms of depression were no longer associated with progression to AIDS or dementia after adjusting for medication variables (monotherapy and combotherapy), and only somatic symptoms of depression remained a predictor of survival (Table 5, original study). As indicated, this may have been related to a reduced number of participants meeting the clinical outcomes in the redefined observation period used for Table 5 (baseline to December 31, 1995), thus decreasing statistical power. We acknowledge that interpretations of the original study results and comparisons with the new follow-up data are speculative at best. However, the lack of putative explanations for differences between Tables 4 and 5 can be considered a weakness of the original study. Aside from (or in addition to) a potential decrease in statistical power, the results of Table 5 may relate to the effect of the therapies themselves on estimates of depression. Similarly, our findings that not even somatic symptoms of depression continue to effect disease progression may be indicative of a primary effect of HAART (see Table 12.2). Considering that in the present analysis the observation period was expanded beyond even the period used for Table 4 (original study), which showed the effect of CES-D on clinical outcomes, and that all available participants were included, an explanation of reduced statistical power is no longer sufficient. It is possible that the somatic complaints related to survival in the limited observation period used to derive Table 5 (original study) were not related to depression as much as they were a physical manifestation of the HIV disease process itself. It is beyond the scope of this chapter to discuss the sources of somatic complaints in HIV/AIDS such as neuropathic pain reflecting injury to the central or peripheral nervous system from direct viral infection. However, it is possible that the introduction of HAART itself relates to a reduced presence of somatic complaints originally considered a part of the depression sequelea as well as the reduced power of somatic complaints to predict clinical outcomes. The effect of HAART on pain symptoms is not well understood, nor is the degree to which iatrogenic pain has been reduced in the HAART era. This remains an area in need of further study now that HIV is evolving into a chronic condition rather than an invariably fatal disease.

The hazard ratios for mood may no longer be significant because the estimates of mood were taken at the beginning of the study, which can be as far back as approximately 18 years ago, and therefore no longer significantly relate to the outcome variables. This would not be surprising as mood states fluctuate as part of the human condition and it is likely that participants who were suffering from mood symptoms are no longer significantly affected by this condition. This finding may also be influenced by a secondary positive effect of improved medication in treating the disease. It is likely that as opposed to a less optimistic outlook for individuals at the beginning of the study diagnosed as HIV+, these same individuals are now somewhat less affected by depression in general. It is also possible that as opposed to situational and transitory mood states, more entrenched trait-related mood disorders may have a stronger association with clinical outcomes. If this is true then individuals with a potential trait-related depressive disorder may have in essence self-selected their way out of the follow-up analyses. Many of these participants could have already reached clinical endpoints such as death during the original observation period. A recent study by Cook et al. (2004)

supports our explanation of the findings indicating that chronic versus intermittent depression was significantly related to mortality in a sample of 2059 HIV+ women over a period of 7.5 years after controlling for important variables such as antiretroviral therapy, medication adherence, substance use, and demographic factors.

Intelligence and reserve theory

While the chronicity or trait-related classification of depression had some influence on each outcome in the original study, its influence dropped in the replication study, which captured the primary period of HAART. This was not the case for IQ, which remained a stable predictor in both studies for time to AIDS, dementia, and death. The hazards for reaching each outcome in the replication study varied from 1.29 for AIDS, to 1.48 for dementia and 1.33 for death. With respect to dementia, an incremental decrease in Shipley IQ resulted in a 48% increase in the likelihood of dementia.

Individual differences in intelligence, as reflected in the Shipley, have consistently shown remarkable stability from childhood throughout the adult lifespan (Arbuckle, Gold, Andres, Schwartzman, & Chaikelson, 1992; Arbuckle, Maag, Pushkar, & Chaikelson, 1998; Gold, Andres, Etezadi, Arbuckle, Schwartzman, & Chaikelson, 1998; Plassman, Welsh, Helm, Brandt, Page, & Brietner, 1995). It has been shown that measures of general intelligence, unlike component abilities, are more resistant to the effects of mild to moderate brain injury (Levin, Grafman, & Eisenberg, 1987). Individual differences in general intelligence have shown strong heritability in most of the long-term follow-up studies, including the recent Swedish study of octogenarian identical twins (see Gottesmann, 1997; Plomin, 1999; Bouchard, 1998; McClearn et al., 1997 for reviews). The heritability indices for component processes (e.g., memory, crystallized abilities), while important, are less robust than for general measures of intelligence, which are presumed to be associated with "g" (Thompson et al., 2001; Posthuma, De Gens, Baare, HulshoffPol, Kahn, & Boomsma, 2002). There is more on this below.

The biological origins of intelligence are also strongly linked to structural measures of brain size and volume and have consistently shown modest associations ($r^2 = .40$ to $.50$) after correcting for restricted ranges of measures (see Wickett, Vernon, & Lee, 2000; Rushton & Ankney, 1996; and Tan, Tan, Polat, Ceylan, Suma, & Okur, 1999 for reviews). More compelling evidence has recently shown that individual differences in the size of these structures (total brain size, total gray and white matter volume and frontal volume) are even more strongly heritable ($H^2 = 0.80$ to 0.90) with minimal environmental influences (Thompson et al., 2001; Posthuma et al., 2002). The robust heritability indices for individual differences in brain structure and intelligence raise the question of whether some of the genes influencing specific brain structures may partly overlap with genes influencing intelligence. Thompson et al. (2001) found that cognitive function (primarily general intelligence or "g") that linked with brain structure occurred in those structures under stronger genetic control.

Posthuma et al. (2002) investigated the correlation between brain volume and cognition in twin samples to identify genetic and environmental components in a large group of monozygotic and dizygotic pairs. They found strong heritability indices between whole brain gray and white matter and measures of working memory and "g" that Thompson et al. (2002) found were linked to frontal gray matter. The negligible influences of environmental exposure on individual differences in these brain regions was surprising, particularly in light of the heritability of white matter volume where neural connectivity has been hypothesized to be under strong environmental influence (Posthuma et al., 2002). However, one must note that there were other critical brain structures (e.g., medial temporal, hippocampal) that showed low heritability and are the very structures that play a critical role in declarative memory. Interestingly, studies have also recently shown a low heritability for individual differences in declarative memory (McClearn et al., 1997) raising the question of whether these structures' functions are also under more environmental control, as with crystallized ability.

It seems to be that measures of general intelligence or g may have stronger genetic structural linkages to the construct of both brain reserve and cognitive reserve, the latter of which may indirectly mediate the primary temporal paths to cognitive aging, dementia and death (Hardy, Satz, D'Elia, & Uchijama, 2006). In a series of four recent brain activation studies on network expression after cognitive challenge, intelligence has been shown to be a strong indicator of network expression (Stern, 2002; Stern, Zarahn, Hilton, Flynn, DeLaPaz, & Rakitin, 2003; Scarmeas & Stern, 2004). Stern (2002) has recently conceptualized brain reserve as a passive construct, in contrast to cognitive reserve as a more active construct. This may be somewhat misleading because of the strong linkages between the two constructs, each of which captures an active and dynamic synergy between biological and environmental forces (Satz, 1993). We hypothesize that general intelligence, unlike component processes, represents a more valid marker of both brain and cognitive reserve, the latter of which may better capture the biological and environmental synergy in the brain reserve construct.

Clearly HIV/AIDS provides an ideal venue for studying the mediating effects of brain reserve capacity. HIV replicates within the central nervous system, and brain-related symptoms such as dementia are caused by HIV or opportunistic infections. In the present study we were able to access large longitudinal resources (MACS) permitting an assessment of brain-related functioning across a span of time that is unique to HIV.

Acknowledgments

Data in this manuscript were collected by the Multicenter AIDS Cohort Study (MACS) with centers (Principal Investigators) located at The Johns

Hopkins Bloomberg School of Public Health (Joseph Margolick); Howard Brown Health Center and Northwestern University Medical School (John Phair); University of California, Los Angeles (Roger Detels); University of Pittsburgh (Charles Rinaldo); and Data Analysis Center (Lisa Jacobson). The MACS is funded by the National Institute of Allergy and Infectious Diseases, with additional supplemental funding from the National Cancer Institute; and the National Heart, Lung, and Blood Institute: UO1-AI-35042, 5-M01-RR-00052 (GCRC), UO1-AI-35043, UO1-AI-37984, UO1-AI-35039, UO1-AI-35040, UO1-AI-37613, and UO1-AI-35041.

References

Arbuckle, T. Y., Gold, D. P., Andres, D., Schwartzman, A., & Chaikelson, J. (1992). The role of psychosocial context, age, and intelligence in memory performance of older men. *Psychology & Aging*, *7*(1), 25–36.

Arbuckle, T. Y., Maag, U., Pushkar, D., & Chaikelson, J. S. (1998). Individual differences in trajectory of intellectual development over 45 years of adulthood. *Psychology and Aging*, *13* (4), 663–675.

Arendt, G., Hefter, H., Nelles, H. W., Hilperath, R., & Strohmeyer, G. (1993). Age-dependent decline in cognitive information processing of HIV-positive individuals detected by event-related potential recordings. *Journal of Neurology Sciences*, *115*, 223–229.

Basso, M. R., & Bornstein, R. A. (2000). Effects of immunosuppression and disease severity upon neuropsychological function in HIV infection. *Journal of Clinical and Experimental Neuropsychology*, *22*, 104–114.

Bouchard, T. J., Jr. (1998). Genetic and environmental influences on adult intelligence and special mental abilities. *Human Biology*, *70*, 257–279.

Burack, J. H., Barrett, D. C., Stall, R. D., Chesney, M. A., Ekstrand, M. L., & Coates, T. J. (1993). Depressive symptoms and CD4 lymphocyte decline among HIV-infected men. *Journal of the American Medical Association*, *270*, 2568–2573.

Cook, J. A., Grey, D., Burke, J., Cohen, M. H., Gurtman, A. C., Richardson, J. L., et al. (2004). Depressive symptoms and AIDS-related mortality among a multisite cohort of HIV-positive women. *American Journal of Public Health*, *94* (7), 1133–1140.

Detels, R., Munoz, A., McFarlane, G., Kingsley, L. A., Margolick, J. B., Giorgi, J., et al. (1998). Effectiveness of potent antiretroviral therapy on time to AIDS and death in men with known HIV infection duration. *Journal of the American Medical Association*, *280* (17), 1497–1503.

Enger, C., Graham, N., Peng, Y., Chmiel, J. S., Kingsley, L. Q., Detels, R., et al. (1996). Survival from early, intermediate, and late stages of HIV infection. *Journal of the American Medical Association*, *275*, 1329–1334.

Farinpour, R., Miller, E. N., Satz, P., Selnes, O. A., Cohen, B. A., Becker, J. T., et al. (2003). Psychosocial risk factors of HIV morbidity and mortality: Findings from the multicenter AIDS cohort study (MACS). *Journal of Clinical and Experimental Neuropsychology*, *25*(5), 654–670.

Gold, D. P., Andres, D., Etezadi, J., Arbuckle, T., Schwartzman, A., & Chaikelson, J. (1998). Structural equation model of intellectual change and continuity and predictors of intelligence in older men: Erratum. *Psychology and Aging, 13* (3), 434.

Gottesman, I. I. (1997). Twins: En route to QTLS for cognition. *Science, 276,* 1522–1523.

Hardy, D. J., Satz, P., D'Elia, L. F., & Uchijama, C. L. (2006). Age related group and individual differences in aircraft pilot cognition. *International Journal of Aviation Psychology* (in press).

Levin, H. S., Grafman, J., & Eisenberg, H. (Eds.) (1987). *Neurobehavioral recovery from head injury.* New York: Oxford University Press.

Lyketsos, C. G., Hoover, D. R., Guccione, M., Senterfitt, W., Dew, M. A., Wesch, J., et al., for the Multicenter AIDS Cohort Study (1993). Depressive symptoms as predictors of medical outcomes in HIV infection. *Journal of the American Medical Association, 270,* 2563–2567.

McArthur, J. C., Hoover, D. R., Bacellar, H., Miller, E. N., Cohen, B. A., Becker, J. T., et al., for the Multicenter AIDS Cohort Study (1993). Dementia in AIDS patients: Incidence and risk factors. *Neurology, 43,* 2245–2252.

McClearn, G. E., Johansson, B., Berg, S., Pederson, N. L., Ahern, F., Petrill, S. A. & Plomin, R. (1997). Substantial genetic influence on cognitive abilities in twins 80 or more years old. *Science, 6* (276), 1560–1563.

Plassman, B. L., Welsh, K. A., Helm, M., Brandt, J., Page, W. F., & Brietner, J. C. (1995). Intelligence and education as predictors of cognitive state in late life: A 50-year follow-up. *Neurology, 45* (8), 1446–1450.

Plomin, R. (1999). Genetics and general cognitive ability. *Nature, 402*(Suppl 6761), C25–C29.

Posthuma, D., De Geus, E. J., Baare, W. F., HulshoffPol, H. E., Kahn, R. S., & Boomsma, D. I. (2002). The association between brain volume and intelligence is of genetic origin. *Nature Neuroscience, 5* (2), 83–84.

Radloff, L. S. (1977). The CES-D scale: A self-report depression scale for research in the general population. *Applied Psychological Measurement, 1,* 385–401.

Rushton, J. P., & Ankney, C. D. (1996). Brain size and cognitive ability: Correlations with age, sex, social class, and race. *Psychonomic Bulletin & Review, 3* (1), 21–36.

Satz, P. (1993). Brain reserve capacity on symptom onset after brain injury: A formulation and review of evidence of threshold theory. *Neuropsychology, 7* (3), 273–295.

Satz, P., Morgenstern, H., Miller, E. N., Selnes, O. A., McArthur, J. C., Cohen, B. A., et al. (1993). Low education as a possible risk factor for cognitive abnormalities in HIV-1: Findings from the Multicenter AIDS Cohort Study. *Journal of the Acquired Immune Deficiency Syndrome, 6,* 503–511.

Scarmeas, N., & Stern, Y. (2004). Cognitive reserve: Implications for diagnosis and prevention of Alzheimer's disease. *Current Neurology and Neuroscience Reports, 4* (5), 374–380.

Shipley, W. C. (1946). *Institute of living scale.* Los Angeles: Western Psychological Services.

Stern, Y. (2002). What is cognitive reserve? Theory and research application of the reserve concept. *Journal of the International Neuropsychological Society, 8* (3), 448–460.

Stern, R. A., Silva, S. G., Chaisson, N., & Evans, D. L. (1996). Influence of cognitive reserve on neuropsychological functioning in asymptomatic human immuno-deficiency virus-1 infection. *Archives of Neurology, 53,* 148–153.

Stern, Y., Zarahn, E., Hilton, H. J., Flynn, J., DeLaPaz, R., & Rakitin, B. (2003). Exploring the neural basis of cognitive reserve. *Journal of Clinical and Experimental Neuropsychology, 25* (5), 691–701.

Tan, Ü., Tan, M., Polat, P., Ceylan, Y., Suma, S., & Okur, A. (1999). Magnetic resonance imaging brain size/IQ relations in Turkish university students. *Intelligence, 27* (1), 83–92.

Thompson, P. M., Cannon, T. D., Narr, K. L., van Erp, T., Poutenan, V., Huttenen, M., et al. (2001). Genetic influences on brain structure. *Nature Neuroscience, 4* (12), 1253–1258.

Van Gorp, W. G., Miller, E. N., Marcotte, T. D., Dixon, W., Paz, D., Selnes, O., et al. (1994). The relationship between age and cognitive impairment in HIV-1 infection: Findings from the Multicenter AIDS Cohort Study and a clinical cohort. *Neurology, 44*, 929–935.

Wickett, J. C., Vernon, P. A., & Lee, D. H. (2000). Relationships between factors of intelligence and brain volume. *Personality & Individual Differences, 29* (6), 1095–1122.

13 Literacy and cognitive decline among ethnically diverse elders

Jennifer J. Manly, Nicole Schupf, Ming-Xin Tang, Christopher C. Weiss, and Yaakov Stern

This chapter presents research concerned with relations between literacy level and cognitive function among ethnically diverse elders. We show evidence that literacy has a profound effect on neuropsychological measures across verbal and nonverbal domains, and that this effect is independent of other demographic and experiential factors such as age, years of education, sex, ethnicity, and language use. Differences in organization of visuospatial information, lack of previous exposure to stimuli, and difficulties with interpretation of the logical functions of language are possible factors that affect test performance of elders with low levels of literacy. Furthermore, it appears that reading level is a sensitive predictor of baseline cognitive test performance, and also that low literacy skills are associated with more rapid memory decline and higher risk of development of dementia.

Education, dementia, and cognitive decline among elders

Low education level has been established as a significant risk factor for Alzheimer's disease (AD) and other dementias (Kawas & Katzman, 1999). A higher prevalence of Alzheimer's disease and dementia among elders with low levels of education has been found in Brazil (Caramelli et al., 1997), China (Hill et al., 1993; Zhang et al., 1990), Finland (Sulkava et al., 1985), France (Dartigues et al., 1991), Italy (Bonaiuto et al., 1990; Prencipe, Casini, Ferretti, Lattanzio, Fiorelli, & Culasso, 1996), Israel (Korczyn, Kahana, & Galper, 1991; Bowirrat, Treves, Friedland, & Korczyn, 2001), the Netherlands (Ott et al., 1995), Sweden (Fratiglioni et al., 1991; Gatz, Svedberg, Pederson, Mortimer, Berg, & Johansson, 2001) among twins, and the United States (Gurland et al., 1995; Callahan, Hall, Hui, Musick, Unverzagt, & Hendrie, 1996; Mortel, Meyer, Herod, & Thornby, 1995). Higher incidence of dementia has been demonstrated in several studies (Stern et al., 1994; Letenneur, Commenges, Dartigues, & Barberger-Gateau, 1994; Evans et al., 1993; White et al., 1994). Cognitive decline appears to be faster (Stern, Albert, Tang, & Tsai, 1999; Unverzagt, Hui, Farlow, Hall, & Hendrie, 1998; Teri, McCurry, Edland, Kukull, & Larson, 1995) and associated with increased risk of mortality (Stern, Tang, Denaro, & Mayeux, 1995) among highly educated minorities with Alzheimer's disease, which suggests that the level of brain pathology is greater by the time well educated individuals show the signs of dementia.

The studies cited above demonstrated a link between education and dementia or Alzheimer's disease. But there is also evidence for a role of education in age-related cognitive decline. Several studies of normal aging have found more rapid cognitive and functional decline in individuals with lower educational attainment (Albert et al., 1995; Chodosh, Reuben, Albert, & Seeman, 2002; Butler, Ashford, & Snowdon, 1996; Farmer, Kittner, Rae, Bartko, & Regier, 1995; Christensen et al., 1997; Snowdon, Ostwald, & Kane, 1989). These studies suggest that the same education-related factors that delay the onset of dementia also allow individuals to cope more effectively with changes encountered in normal aging.

Cognitive reserve has been suggested as the mechanism for the link between low education and higher risk of dementia observed in these studies (Stern, 2002; Mortimer, 1988; Katzman, 1993; Satz et al., 1993). Reserve, or the brain's ability to tolerate the effects of dementia pathology, may result from native ability or from the effects of lifetime experience. Years of education may serve as a proxy for reserve whether it results from ability or experience. In passive models of reserve (Stern, 2002), education would be a proxy for the brain's capacity (synaptic density or complexity) to tolerate either gradual or sudden insult. In active models, years of education would be an indicator of the brain's ability to compensate for pathology through more efficient use of existing cognitive networks or recruitment of alternate networks.

However, there are cases in which the relationship between education and risk for cognitive impairment or dementia is weakened or absent. Two large international studies of incident dementia found that illiteracy or low levels of education did not increase the risk of Alzheimer's disease among elders in India (Chandra et al., 2001) and West Africa (Hendrie, 2001; Hall et al., 1998). In fact, these studies had the lowest prevalence and incidence rates of dementia observed to date, despite the fact that a large proportion of the populations lacked formal schooling or literacy training. This paradox serves to illuminate the difficulty in comparing cultural groups with disparate backgrounds. Reserve is measured by proxy variables (such as years of education, occupational level, or IQ measures), but there are a number of ways in which cultural, racial, and economic factors may affect the predictive power of these proxies.

Ethnicity and native ability

Studies showing that early intellectual or linguistic ability predicts who will develop dementia clinically in later life (Whalley, Starr, Athawes, Hunter, Pattie, & Deary, 2000) or neuropathologically (Snowdon, Kemper, Mortimer, Greiner, Wekstein, & Markesbery, 1996) provide strong support for the theory that years of education are a proxy for brain or cognitive characteristics that are already present at birth. That is, the same cognitive strengths or robust brain structures that allow for academic or occupational success, are also are less susceptible to sudden or gradual insult.

However, years of education may not be an accurate representation of native ability among minority or immigrant elders whose educational opportunities were limited due to institutionalized racism and poverty. Minorities with strong intellectual abilities may not achieve high level academic or occupational success because their opportunities are limited by societal forces, such as racism, segregation, or poverty, beyond their native intellect or drive to succeed. Although such individuals may be powerful or influential in their community, their abilities may not be reflected in years of schooling or traditional indicators of occupational status. Thus the relationship between years of education and native ability would be weakened among ethnic minorities, leading to underestimates of the relationship between education and cognitive decline.

In prior research on cognitive reserve, evidence for the relatively weak association between years of education and dementia risk among African Americans is provided by a study conducted in Indianapolis (Hall, Gao, Unverzagt, & Hendrie, 2000). Childhood residence (rural versus urban) and educational level were evaluated in a random sample of 223 African American elders, 180 of whom were neurologically normal and 43 who had AD. Childhood rural residence, combined with fewer than 7 years of school, was associated with an increased risk of AD. The authors hypothesized that low education by itself is not a major risk factor within African Americans, but is a marker for other deleterious socioeconomic or environmental influences in childhood. The major limitation of this study is its cross-sectional design, since African American elders with low education who were raised in rural settings might have performed badly on the cognitive tests used to diagnose dementia simply as a function of their cultural and educational background.

Native ability has also been operationalized using tests such as IQ measures or vocabulary tests. There is ample evidence that scores on traditional cognitive tests underestimate the functional abilities of African Americans (see review, Manly & Jacobs, 2001) and other ethnic minorities (Ardila, 1995; Wong, Strickland, Fletcher-Janzen, Ardila, & Reynolds, 2000) at least in part due to subjects' lack of familiarity with items, or level of comfort and confidence during the testing session. Therefore, indices of reserve (whether assessed either in childhood or as an adult) may also underestimate the strength of the relationship between native ability and protection from cognitive decline among ethnic minorities.

Ethnicity and educational experience

Rather than a reflection of innate ability, years of education could be an indicator of lifetime experiences that change the brain during childhood or adult life and thus create a reserve against disease pathology. However, use of years of education to represent a direct effect of experience on the brain or cognition is problematic when employed among ethnic minorities. This is due to the increased discordance between years of education and quality of education among ethnic minorities. Although it is common for investigators to use covariance, matching procedures, or education-corrected norms in order to "equate" ethnic groups on years of education before interpreting neuropsychological test performance, these techniques ignore ethnic discrepancies in quality of education.

Along with several other authors (Kaufman, Cooper, & McGee, 1997; Whitfield & Baker-Thomas, 1999; Loewenstein, Arguelles, Arguelles, & Linn-Fuentes, 1994), we argue that due to the disparities in quality of education, matching on quantity of formal education does not necessarily mean that the quality of education received by each racial group is comparable. The source of this discordance between years of education and achievement has been investigated through studies of school characteristics, such as pupil expenditures, teacher quality, pupil/teacher ratios, presence of special facilities such as science laboratories, length of school year/days attended, and peer characteristics such as the educational background and aspirations of other children in the school. Figure 13.1 provides an example by displaying

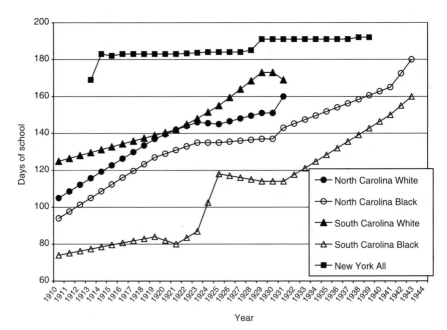

Figure 13.1   Length of school year in North Carolina, South Carolina, and New York from 1910 to 1943. Source: United States Department of Health, Education, and Welfare Office of Education. Biennial Survey of Education in the United States (DHHS Publication No. 1919). Washington, DC, US Government Printing Office.

length of school year in elementary schools in selected states for African American and White schools during the years in which many elders attended school. These school variables have been shown to account for much of the difference in achievement and other outcomes (e.g., wage earnings), between African Americans and Whites (Hanushek, 1989; Hedges, Laine, & Greenwald, 1994; O'Neill, 1990). The unequal distribution of funds to segregated African American schools in the South in the first half of the twentieth century, and the subsequent lower quality of education, was related to lower earnings among African Americans in a number of studies (Margo, 1985, 1990; Smith & Welch, 1977; Smith, 1984; Welch, 1966, 1973; Card & Krueger, 2003).

Our group sought to determine if discrepancies in quality of education could explain differences in cognitive test scores between African American and White elders matched on years of education (Manly, Jacobs, Touradji, Small, & Stern, 2002). A comprehensive neuropsychological battery was administered to a sample of nondemented African American and non-Hispanic White participants in an epidemiological study of normal aging and dementia in the northern Manhattan community. The Reading Recognition subtest from the Wide Range Achievement Test—Version 3 (WRAT-3) was used as an estimate of quality of education. African American elders obtained significantly lower scores than Whites on measures of word list learning and memory, figure memory, abstract reasoning, fluency, and visuospatial skill even though the groups were matched on years of education. However, after adjusting the scores for WRAT-3 reading score, the overall effect of race was greatly reduced and racial differences on all tests (except category fluency and a drawing measure) became nonsignificant. Reading score also attenuated the effect of race after accounting for an estimate of test-wiseness. Test-wiseness is defined as the ability to use the format and characteristics of a test to achieve a high score (Scruggs & Lifson, 1985), and the use of deduction and item cues to answer questions (Borrello & Thompson, 1985). This finding suggests that years of education is an inadequate measure of the educational experience among multicultural elders, and that adjusting for quality of education may improve the specificity of certain neuropsychological measures across racial groups.

The literacy advantage

We propose that the use of literacy as an estimate of the quality of education will serve as a more meaningful proxy for reserve among ethnic minorities. The utility of literacy in studies of cognitive ability among normal elders was recently demonstrated by our group in research that sought to determine if discrepancies in quality of education could explain differences in neuropsychological test scores between African American and White elders matched on years of education. A comprehensive cognitive battery was administered to a sample of nondemented African American and non-Hispanic White participants in an epidemiologic study of normal aging and dementia in the northern Manhattan community. The Reading Recognition subtest from the Wide Range Achievement Test—Version 3 (WRAT-3) was used as an estimate of quality of education. African American elders obtained significantly lower scores than Whites on measures of word list learning and memory, figure memory, abstract reasoning, fluency, and visuospatial skill even though the groups were matched on years of education. However, after adjusting the scores for WRAT-3 reading score, the overall effect of race was greatly reduced and racial differences on all tests (except category fluency and a drawing measure) became nonsignificant. This study suggests that literacy could be a more sensitive proxy for reserve than years of education because it more accurately reflects the quality of the educational experience provided to ethnic minority elders. In addition, literacy could be a more accurate reflection of native ability because it does not assume that all individuals get the same amount of learning from a certain grade level; the fact that some excel more than others or seek learning outside school will be reflected in measurements of literacy.

Literacy and age-related memory decline

Ardila and his colleagues (Ardila, Ostrosky-Solis, Rosselli, & Gomez, 2000) conducted a cross-sectional study of 865 Spanish-speaking Mexican adults between the ages of 16 and 85. They found that verbal memory performance declined more sharply with age among illiterates than among people with 10 or more years of education. Measures of other cognitive domains (such as visuospatial skill, attention, and verbal fluency) showed other patterns of change with age by education level. The authors did not indicate how illiteracy was determined (it appears to be equivalent with having no formal schooling), and thus the effects of literacy and years of education are indistinguishable. Further, the cross-sectional design leaves open the possibility that the interactions between age and education are cohort effects.

We designed a study to explore the relationship of literacy level to change in memory ability over time among an ethnically diverse sample of English-speaking nondemented elders (Manly, Touradji, Tang, & Stern, 2003). Specifically, we wanted to determine if literacy was a stronger predictor of memory decline (and thus a more sensitive indicator of reserve) than years of education or racial/ethnic classification, although each of these variables was expected to influence baseline scores. We focused our analyses on immediate and delayed recall measures from a verbal word list learning task, since these measures are sensitive to age-related memory decline and the earliest signs of Alzheimer's disease. Because our focus was on age-related memory change, participants were selected into the study only if their overall cognition and functioning in daily activities were normal, and they were nondemented, at all four time points. We measured literacy level using the

Wide Range Achievement Test—Version 3 (WRAT-3) (Wilkinson, 1993) Reading Recognition subtest. On this test, participants were asked to name letters and pronounce words out of context, which were listed in order of decreasing familiarity and increasing phonological complexity. The high literacy group ($n = 69$) was 61% White, 39% African American, and 0% Hispanic, while the low literacy group ($n = 67$) was 24% White, 67% African American and 9% Hispanic. The literacy groups did not differ from each other on age or gender composition. Mean follow-up duration was about 5 years and did not differ within the two literacy groups. Using generalized estimating equations analysis, we found that elders with both high and low levels of literacy declined in immediate (Figure 13.2) and delayed (Figure 13.3) memory over time; however, the decline was more rapid among low literacy elders. This suggests that high literacy skills do not provide complete preservation of memory skills but rather a slowing of age-related decline. There were no interactions between time and either years of education or ethnicity, suggesting that in this diverse population of normal elders, literacy

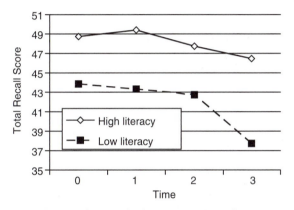

Figure 13.2   Change in Selective Reminding Test total recall score over time.

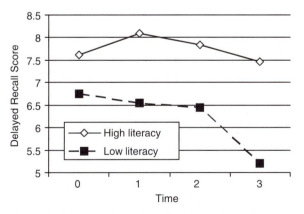

Figure 13.3   Change in Selective Reminding Test delayed recall score over time.

was the most sensitive predictor of memory decline. Unlike many prior studies that examined the relationship of education to dementia or normal aging, we did not find that low education (less than 12 years) was a risk factor for cognitive decline.

Literacy and incident dementia

Our next study was designed to determine if literacy was a significant predictor of incident dementia, and to determine the relative risk associated with low literacy in relation to ethnicity and years of education. For this study, we selected participants who were not demented at baseline (based on a physician's independent evaluation). Follow-up evaluations occurred every 18 months with repeat medical, neurologic, psychiatric, and neuropsychological examinations. Participants were followed for an average of about 4 years. At follow-up, at a consensus conference, information from the assessments was reviewed. The diagnosis of AD was based on the National Institute of Neurological and Cognitive Disorders and Stroke/Alzheimer's Disease and Related Disorders Association criteria (McKhann, Drachman, Folstein, Katzman, Price, & Stadlan, 1984). Analysis of the final sample, 1192 participants, revealed that there were significantly more incident cases of dementia over the follow-up period among those in the low literacy groups. Table 13.1 shows that the relative risk (RR) associated with non-white ethnicity to incident dementia was 2.3 (95% CI: 1.5, 3.7) after adjustment for sex and age at baseline. The RR relating non-white ethnicity and dementia remained unchanged even after adding years of education into the model, which was also a significant predictor of incident dementia. However, after literacy level was entered into the model, the risk associated with non-white ethnicity was attenuated and became nonsignificant, while the risk associated

Table 13.1 Adjusted Cox model showing relative risk for incident dementia among 1192 participants

Variables in the model	Model 1		Model 2		Model 3	
	Relative risk (95% CI)	p value	Relative risk (95% CI)	p value	Relative risk (95% CI)	p value
Sex	1.0 (0.7–1.7)	.770	1.0 (0.6–1.5)	.835	1.0 (0.6–1.1)	.941
Age	1.2 (1.1–1.8)	.000	1.2 (1.1–1.2)	.000	1.2 (1.1–1.2)	.000
White vs. non-white	2.3 (1.5–3.7)	.000	2.0 (1.3–3.3)	.003	1.4 (0.9–2.3)	.177
Years of education			2.5 (1.4–4.5)	.002	2.0 (1.1–3.7)	.017
Reading level					3.0 (1.5–6.0)	.002

Table 13.2 Hazard ratios and 95% confidence intervals relating years of education and reading level to incident dementia. The models are adjusted for age, gender, and ethnicity, and are based on a sample of 1192 participants

Years of education— reading level profile	At risk	Cases	Relative risk (95% confidence intervals)	p value
High education High reading level	304	5	1	–
Low education High reading level	185	6	1.3 (0.4–4.2)	.698
High education Low reading level	187	9	2.0 (0.6–6.1)	.232
Low education Low reading level	516	72	4.7 (1.8–12.2)	.001

with fewer than 12 years of education remained essentially unchanged. Finally, the risk of incident dementia associated with membership in the four education (low vs. high) by literacy (low vs. high) groups was examined after adjusting for sex, age, and ethnicity. Table 13.2 demonstrates that as compared to the high education–high literacy group, although the risk increased gradually in the low education–high literacy and then the high education–low literacy groups, only the risk associated with the low education–low literacy group was significantly different. This demonstrated that both years of education and literacy were strong predictors of incident dementia; however, literacy significantly attenuated the effect of ethnicity while accounting for years of education did not. Although there was some evidence that the increase in risk associated with literacy was a stronger predictor of dementia risk than years of education, the effect of years of school remained significant after literacy was added, and only the low education–low literacy group was at significantly higher risk for dementia as compared to the high education–high literacy group.

Conclusion

Literacy level is a crucial predictor of cognitive test performance among ethnically diverse elders. We found that that ethnic minorities were more likely to be among the group in which years of education was high but literacy level was low. Based on the results of this work, we propose that regardless of race/ethnicity, literacy measures educational experience more accurately than years of education, and thus is a superior assessment of the knowledge, strategy, and skills needed to perform well on traditional neuropsychological tasks. Test scores adjusted for literacy level can be used to predict performance more accurately than if only years of education and racial classification are used.

Not only does literacy influence the specificity of neuropsychological measures, but it is also a powerful predictor of cognitive decline and incident dementia. It is likely that among ethnic minorities, literacy is a more accurate reflection of native ability than years of education. While educational experience certainly contributes to literacy skills, individuals may have opportunities to enhance their literacy throughout their lifetime that are not reflected by years of education. Gifted individuals will be more likely to develop literacy skills regardless of their opportunity to attend formal schooling. Our findings extend previous studies that showed literacy captures an aspect of educational experience that is not accounted for by years of education alone, and that it can add to the prediction of how ethnically and linguistically diverse individuals should perform on cognitive tests (Weiss, Reed, Kligman, & Abyad, 1995; Manly et al., 1999; Manly et al., 2002; Reis & Castro-Caldas, 1997). The meaning of years of education is not commensurate between ethnic and racial groups (Kaufman & Cooper, 1995), making literacy a more sensitive indicator of the educational experience of minority elders. When comparing ethnic groups, differences in the availability of educational opportunity are likely to predominate. Racism, poverty, and other societal forces may have prevented some individuals with high native ability from gaining literacy skills, so literacy scores are a better proxy for quality of education in between-group comparisons. Within the same ethnic or racial group, disparities in educational opportunity may not be as strong, making literacy more likely to reflect ability to achieve academic success. In this case, literacy may be more appropriately used as a proxy for an individual's innate intellectual ability. Research on cognitive reserve could benefit from such an indicator to help deconstruct the various components of educational experience that might contribute to resistance against pathology.

Research interest in the effects of literacy on cognition began when Vygotsky (1962, 1978) suggested that the development and organization of basic psychological processes such as abstraction, inference, and memory depended on the type of symbols (e.g., writing systems) used by the individual in their environment. Luria (1976) found that illiterate, unschooled individuals solved cognitive problems in a context-bound manner and were more influenced by the perceptual and functional attributes of a stimulus than were schooled literates, who were more responsive to abstract concepts and logical relationships among stimuli. As a result of their studies of the Vai people in Liberia, Scribner and Cole (1981) concluded that although literacy is not necessary for the development of logic, abstraction, memory, and communication skills, the nature of writing systems and the way in which they are used affect the organization and expression of these cognitive abilities. More recently, researchers have begun to hypothesize that learning to read and write may fundamentally change the functional architecture of the brain (Petersson, Reis, & Ingvar, 2001), allowing it to actively compensate for age-related changes. Literacy changes the way we process and represent information, primarily phonological (Scribner & Cole, 1981; Lecours et al., 1987; Matute, Leal, Zaraboso, Robles, & Cedillo, 1997; Rosselli, Ardila, &

Rosas, 1990; Petersson et al., 2001) but also nonverbal stimuli (Ardila, Rosselli, & Rosas, 1989; Manly et al., 1999). The process of acquiring and using literacy skills may also increase the synaptic density of the brain, like other factors that contribute to an "enriched environment" (Diamond, 1988).

Research on literacy and cognitive reserve requires longitudinal design. Analysis of change over time and incident dementia avoids detection bias, because variables such as years of education, literacy, and cultural background that affect baseline measurement are likely to have a similar effect on subsequent measurements. However, the assumption that these biases will not affect change in score over time is problematic if well educated, highly literate, and culturally mainstream individuals are able to benefit from practice more than less educated, low literate ethnic minorities.

Although the utility of single-word reading measures such as the WRAT-3 in premorbid IQ estimation is controversial (Storandt, Stone, & LaBarge E., 1995; O'Carroll, 1995; Johnstone, Callahan, Kapila, & Bouman, 1996; Johnstone & Wilhelm, 1996; Dura, Myers, & Freathy, 1989), one longitudinal study of incident dementia (Schmand, Geerlings, Jonker, & Lindeboom, 1998) concluded that reading level remains a valid estimate of premorbid ability in mild and questionable dementia. Ideally, childhood measures of literacy would be used to predict development of cognitive decline later in life, thus avoiding confounding from effects of preclinical dementia on reading skill. This technique was elegantly demonstrated in studies showing that low scores on measures of intelligence in childhood (Whalley et al., 2000) and low linguistic ability in the early twenties (Snowdon et al., 1996) were associated with low cognitive test scores and dementia in old age.

Future study should detail the relationship of literacy to functional change or memory complaints over time; if high literacy reflects reserve, it should also be associated with relative preservation of activities of daily living. This approach would avoid the problems of shared variance that arise when one verbal test (literacy) is used to predict another (verbal memory). In addition, there is an enormous amount of work to be done with immigrant groups, in which issues of language and acculturation complicate cognitive assessment and evaluation of literacy level.

Literacy level is a strong correlate of quality of schooling. Literacy involves not only the ability to read and write script, but also the knowledge of how and in what context to apply literacy skills for specific purposes. All reading and writing tasks involve skills such as encoding language into graphic symbols, visual and motor abilities to form and decode characters, words, or sentences, and retrieving word representations from memory (Scribner & Cole, 1981). However, the growing acceptance of the importance of lifelong learning has influenced current measures to move away from assessment of a set of "isolated" cognitive skills such as decoding or reading recognition. Instead, literacy is viewed as an advancing set of skills, knowledge, and information processing strategies that individuals apply within specific contexts that are influenced by culture (Kirsch, 2001; Heath, 1983).

For this reason, we look forward to studying all aspects of literacy, not just reading level, as predictors of cognitive change and indicators of cognitive reserve.

Acknowledgments

This research was supported by federal grants AG16206 (J. Manly), AG07232 (R. Mayeux), and the Alzheimer's Association.

References

Albert, M. S., Jones, K., Savage, C. R., Berkman, L., Seeman, T., Blazer, D., et al. (1995). Predictors of cognitive change in older persons: MacArthur studies of successful aging. *Psychology and Aging, 10,* 578–589.

Ardila, A. (1995). Directions of research in cross-cultural neuropsychology. *Journal of Clinical and Experimental Neuropsychology, 17,* 143–150.

Ardila, A., Ostrosky-Solis, F., Rosselli, M., & Gomez, C. (2000). Age-related cognitive decline during normal aging: The complex effect of education. *Archives of Clinical Neuropsychology, 15,* 495–513.

Ardila, A., Rosselli, M., & Rosas, P. (1989). Neuropsychological assessment in illiterates: Visuospatial and memory abilities. *Brain and Cognition, 11,* 147–166.

Bonaiuto, S., Rocca, W. A., Lippi, A., Luciani, P., Turtu, F., Cavarzeran, F., et al. (1990). Impact of education and occupation on prevalence of Alzheimer's disease (AD) and multi-infarct dementia (MID) in Appignano, Macerata Province, Italy. *Neurology, 40*(Suppl. 1), 346.

Borrello, G. M., & Thompson, B. (1985). Correlates of selected test-wiseness skills. *Journal of Experimental Education, 53,* 124–128.

Bowirrat, A., Treves, T., Friedland, R. P., & Korczyn, A. D. (2001). Prevalence of Alzheimer's type dementia in an elderly Arab popultion. *European Journal of Epidemiology, 8,* 119–123.

Butler, S. M., Ashford, J. W., & Snowdon, D. A. (1996). Age, education, and changes in the Mini-Mental State Exam scores of older women: Findings from the Nun Study. *Journal of the American Geriatrics Society, 44,* 675–681.

Callahan, C. M., Hall, K. S., Hui, S. L., Musick, B. S., Unverzagt, F. W., & Hendrie, H. C. (1996). Relationship of age, education, and occupation with dementia among a community-based sample of African Americans. *Archives of Neurology, 53,* 134–140.

Caramelli, P., Poissant, A., Gauthier, S., Bellavance, A., Gauvreau, D., Lecours, A. R., et al. (1997). Educational level and neuropsychological heterogeneity in dementia of the Alzheimer type. *Alzheimer Disease and Associated Disorders, 11,* 9–15.

Card, D., & Krueger, B. (2003). School resources and student outcomes: An overview of the literature and new evidence from North and South Carolina. *The Journal of Economic Perspectives, 10,* 31–50.

Chandra, V., Pandav, R., Dodge, H. H., Johnston, J. M., Belle, S. H., DeKosky, S. T., et al. (2001). Incidence of Alzheimer's disease in a rural community in India: The Indo-US study. *Neurology, 57,* 985–989.

Chodosh, J., Reuben, D. B., Albert, M. S., & Seeman, T. E. (2002). Predicting cognitive impairment in high-functioning community-dwelling older persons:

MacArthur Studies of Successful Aging. *Journal of the American Geriatrics Society, 50,* 1051–1060.

Christensen, H., Korten, A. E., Jorm, A. F., Henderson, A. S., Jacomb, P. A., Rodgers, B., et al. (1997). Education and decline in cognitive performance: Compensatory but not protective. *International Journal of Geriatric Psychiatry, 12,* 323–330.

Dartigues, J. F., Gagnon, M., Michel, P., Letenneur, L., Commenges, D., Barberger-Gateau, P., et al. (1991). Le programme de recherche paquid sur l'epidemiologie de la demence methodes et resultats initiaux. *Revue Neurologique (Paris), 147,* 225–230.

Diamond, M. C. (1988). *Enriching heredity: The Impact of the environment on the anatomy of the brain.* New York: The Free Press.

Dura, J. R., Myers, E. G., & Freathy, D. T. (1989). Stability of the Wide Range Achievement Test in an adolescent psychiatric inpatient setting. *Educational & Psychological Measurement, 49,* 253–256.

Evans, D. A., Beckett, L. A., Albert, M. S., Hebert, L. E., Scherr, P. A., Funkenstein, H. H., et al. (1993). Level of education and change in cognitive function in a community population of older persons. *Annals of Epidemiology, 3,* 71–77.

Farmer, M. E., Kittner, S. J., Rae, D. S., Bartko, J. J., & Regier, D. A. (1995). Education and change in cognitive function: The epidemiologic catchment area study. *Annals of Epidemiology, 5,* 1–7.

Fratiglioni, L., Grut, M., Forsell, Y., Viitanen, M., Grafstrom, M., Holmen, K., et al. (1991). Prevalence of Alzheimer's disease and other dementias in an elderly urban population: Relationship with age, sex and education. *Neurology, 41,* 1886–1892.

Gatz, M., Svedberg, P., Pederson, N. L., Mortimer, J. A., Berg, S., & Johansson, B. (2001). Education and the risk of Alzheimer's disease: Findings from the study of dementia in Swedish twins. *Journals of Gerontology, 56B,* 292–300.

Gurland, B. J., Wilder, D., Cross, P., Lantigua, R., Teresi, J. A., Barret, V., et al. (1995). Relative rates of dementia by multiple case definitions, over two prevalence periods, in three cultural groups. *American Journal of Geriatric Psychiatry, 3,* 6–20.

Hall, K. S., Gao, S., Unverzagt, F. W., & Hendrie, H. C. (2000). Low education and childhood rural residence: Risk for Alzheimer's disease in African Americans. *Neurology, 54,* 95–99.

Hall, K. S., Gureje, O., Gao, S., Ogunniyi, A., Hui, S. L., Baiyewu, O., et al. (1998). Risk factors and Alzheimer's disease: A comparative study of two communities. *Australian and New Zealand Journal of Psychiatry, 32,* 698–706.

Hanushek, E. (1989). The impact of differential expenditures on school performance. *Educational Researcher, 18,* 45–51.

Heath, S. B. (1983). *Ways with words.* Cambridge: Cambridge University Press.

Hedges, L. V., Laine, R. D., & Greenwald, R. (1994). Does money matter? A meta-analysis of studies of the effects of differential school inputs on student outcomes. *Educational Researcher, 23,* 5–14.

Hendrie, H. C. (2001). Exploration of environmental and genetic risk factors for Alzheimer's Disease: The value of cross cultural studies. *Current Directions in Psychological Science, 10,* 98–101.

Hill, L. R., Klauber, M. R., Salmon, D. P., Yu, E. S. H., Liu, W. T., Zhang, M., et al. (1993). Functional status, education, and the diagnosis of dementia in the Shanghai survey. *Neurology, 43,* 138–145.

Johnstone, B., Callahan, C. D., Kapila, C. J., & Bouman, D. E. (1996). The comparability of the WRAT-R Reading Test and NAART as estimates of premorbid intelligence in neurologically impaired patients. *Archives of Clinical Neuro-psychology*, *11*, 513–519.

Johnstone, B., & Wilhelm, K. L. (1996). The longitudinal stability of the WRAT-R reading subtest: Is it an appropriate estimate of premorbid intelligence? *Journal of the International Neuropsychological Society*, *2*, 282–285.

Katzman, R. (1993). Education and the prevalence of dementia and Alzheimer's disease. *Neurology*, *43*, 13–20.

Kaufman, J. S., & Cooper, R. S. (1995). Epidemiologic research on minority health: In search of the hypothesis. *Public Health Reports*, *110*, 662–666.

Kaufman, J. S., Cooper, R. S., & McGee, D. L. (1997). Socioeconomic status and health in blacks and whites: The problem of residual confounding and the resilience of race. *Epidemiology*, *8*, 621–628.

Kawas, C. H., & Katzman, R. (1999). Epidemiology of dementia and Alzheimer's disease. In R. D. Terry, R. Katzman, S. S. Sisodia, & K. L. Bick (Eds.), *Alzheimer's disease* (pp. 95–116). Philadelphia: Lippincott Williams & Wilkins.

Kirsch, I. S. (2001). *The International Adult Literacy Survey (IALS): Understanding what was measured*. Unpublished manuscript.

Kirsch, I. S., Jungeblut, A., Jenkins, L., & Kolstad, A. (1993). *Adult literacy in America: The National Adult Literacy Survey. National Center for Education Statistics, US Department of Education*. Washington, DC: US Government Printing Office.

Korczyn, A. D., Kahana, E., & Galper, Y. (1991). Epidemiology of dementia in Ashkelon, Israel. *Neuroepidemiology*, *10*, 100.

Lecours, A. R., Mehler, J., Parente, M. A., Caldeira, A., Cary, L., Castro, M. J., et al. (1987). Illiteracy and brain damage. 1. Aphasia testing in culturally contrasted populations (control subjects). *Neuropsychologia*, *25*, 231–245.

Letenneur, L., Commenges, D., Dartigues, J. F., & Barberger-Gateau, P. (1994). Incidence of dementia and Alzheimer's disease in elderly community residents of south-western France. *International Journal of Epidemiology*, *23*, 1256–1261.

Loewenstein, D. A., Arguelles, T., Arguelles, S., & Linn-Fuentes, P. (1994). Potential cultural bias in the neuropsychological assessment of the older adult. *Journal of Clinical and Experimental Neuropsychology*, *16*, 623–629.

Luria, A. R. (1976). *Cognitive development, its cultural and social foundations*. Cambridge, MA: Harvard University Press.

Manly, J. J., & Jacobs, D. M. (2001). Future directions in neuropsychological assess-ment with African Americans. In F. R. Ferraro (Ed.), *Minority and cross-cultural aspects of neuropsychological assessment* (pp. 79–96). Lisse, Netherlands: Swets and Zeitlinger.

Manly, J. J., Jacobs, D. M., Sano, M., Bell, K., Merchant, C. A., Small, S. A., et al. (1999). Effect of literacy on neuropsychological test performance in nondemented, education-matched elders. *Journal of the International Neuropsychological Society*, *5*, 191–202.

Manly, J. J., Jacobs, D. M., Touradji, P., Small, S. A., & Stern, Y. (2002). Reading level attenuates differences in neuropsychological test performance between African American and White elders. *Journal of the International Neuropsychological Society*, *8*, 341–348.

Manly, J. J., Touradji, P., Tang, M.-X., & Stern, Y. (2003). Literacy and memory decline among ethnically diverse elders. *Journal of Clinical and Experimental Neuropsychology*, *5*, 680–690.

Margo, R. A. (1985). *Disenfranchisement, school finance, and the economics of segregated schools in the United States south, 1890–1910*. New York: Garland Publishing.

Margo, R. A. (1990). *Race and schooling in the South, 1880–1950: An economic history*. Chicago: University of Chicago Press.

Matute, E., Leal, F., Zaraboso, A., Robles, A., & Cedillo, C. (1997). Influence of literacy level on stick constructions in non-brain-damaged subjects. [Abstract]. *Journal of the International Neuropsychological Society, 3*, 32.

McKhann, G., Drachman, D., Folstein, M., Katzman, R., Price, D., & Stadlan, E. (1984). Clinical diagnosis of Alzheimer's disease: Report of the NINCDS-ADRDA Work Group under the auspices of the Department of Health and Human Services Task Force on Alzheimer's disease. *Neurology, 34*, 939–944.

Mortel, K. F., Meyer, J. S., Herod, B., & Thornby, J. (1995). Education and occupation as risk factors for dementia of the Alzheimer and ischemic vascular types. *Dementia, 6*, 55–62.

Mortimer, J. A. (1988). Do psychosocial risk factors contribute to Alzheimer's disease. In A. S. Henderson & J. H. Henderson (Eds.), *Etiology of dementia of Alzheimer's type* (pp. 39–52). Chichester: John Wiley and Sons.

O'Carroll, R. (1995). The assessment of premorbid ability: A critical review. *Neurocase, 1*, 83–89.

O'Neill, J. (1990). The role of human capital in earning differences between Black and White men. *Journal of Economic Perspectives, 4*, 25–45.

Ott, A., Breteler, M. M., van Harskamp, F., Claus, J. J., van der Cammen, T. J., Grobbee, D. E., et al. (1995). Prevalence of Alzheimer's disease and vascular dementia: Association with education. The Rotterdam study [see comments]. *British Medical Journal, 310*, 970–973.

Petersson, K. M., Reis, A., & Ingvar, M. (2001). Cognitive processing in literate and illiterate subjects: A review of some recent behavioral and functional neuroimaging data. *Scandinavian Journal of Psychology, 42*, 251–267.

Prencipe, M., Casini, A. R., Ferretti, C., Lattanzio, M. T., Fiorelli, M., & Culasso, F. (1996). Prevalence of dementia in an elderly rural population: Effects of age, sex, and education. *Journal of Neurology, Neurosurgery & Psychiatry, 60*, 628–633.

Reis, A., & Castro-Caldas, A. (1997). Illiteracy: A cause for biased cognitive development. *Journal of the International Neuropsychological Society, 3*, 444–450.

Rosselli, M., Ardila, A., & Rosas, P. (1990). Neuropsychological assessment in illiterates. II. Language and praxic abilities. *Brain and Cognition, 12*, 281–296.

Satz, P., Morgenstern, H., Miller, E. N., Selnes, O. A., McArthur, J. C., Cohen, B. A., et al. (1993). Low education as a possible risk factor for cognitive abormalities in HIV-1: Findings from the Multicenter AIDS Cohort Study (MACS). *Journal of Acquired Immune Deficiency Syndromes, 6*, 503–511.

Schmand, B., Geerlings, M. I., Jonker, C., & Lindeboom, J. (1998). Reading ability as an estimator of premorbid intelligence: Does it remain stable in emergent dementia? *Journal of Clinical and Experimental Neuropsychology, 20*, 42–51.

Scribner, S., & Cole, M. (1981). *The psychology of literacy*. Cambridge; MA: Harvard University Press.

Scruggs, T. E., & Lifson, S. A. (1985). Current conceptions of test-wiseness: Myths and realities. *School Psychology Review, 14*, 339–350.

Smith, J. P. (1984). Race and human capital. *American Economic Review, 4*, 685–698.

Smith, J. P., & Welch, F. (1977). Black–White male wage ratios: 1960–1970. *American Economic Review, 67*, 323–328.

Snowdon, D. A., Kemper, S. J., Mortimer, J. A., Greiner, L. H., Wekstein, D. R., & Markesbery, W. R. (1996). Linguistic ability in early life and cognitive function and Alzheimer's disease in late life. Findings from the Nun Study. *Journal of the American Medical Association, 275*, 528–532.

Snowdon, D. A., Ostwald, S. K., & Kane, R. L. (1989). Education, survival and independence in elderly Catholic sisters, 1936–1988. *American Journal of Epidemiology, 130*, 999–1012.

Stern, Y. (2002). What is cognitive reserve? Theory and research application of the reserve concept. *Journal of the International Neuropsychological Society, 8*, 448–460.

Stern, Y., Albert, S., Tang, M.-X., & Tsai, W.-Y. (1999). Rate of memory decline in AD is related to education and occupation: Cognitive reserve? *Neurology, 53*, 1942–1947.

Stern, Y., Gurland, B., Tatemichi, T. K., Tang, M. X., Wilder, D., & Mayeux, R. (1994). Influence of education and occupation on the incidence of Alzheimer's disease. *Journal of the American Medical Association, 271*, 1004–1010.

Stern, Y., Tang, M. X., Denaro, J., & Mayeux, R. (1995). Increased risk of mortality in Alzheimer's disease patients with more advanced educational and occupational attainment. *Annals of Neurology, 37*, 590–595.

Storandt, M., Stone, K., & LaBarge E. (1995). Deficits in reading performance in very mild dementia of Alzheimer type. *Neuropsychology, 9*, 174–176.

Sulkava, R., Wikstrom, J., Aromaa, A., Raitasalo, R., Lahtinen, V., Lahtela, K., et al. (1985). Prevalence of severe dementia in Finland. *Neurology, 35*, 1025–1029.

Teri, L., McCurry, S. M., Edland, S. D., Kukull, W. A., & Larson, E. B. (1995). Cognitive decline in Alzheimer's disease: A longitudinal investigation of risk factors for accelerated decline. *Journals of Gerontology: Biological Sciences & Medical Sciences, 50A*, M49–M55.

Unverzagt, F. W., Hui, S. L., Farlow, M. R., Hall, K. S., & Hendrie, H. C. (1998). Cognitive decline and education in mild dementia. *Neurology, 50*, 181–185.

Vygotsky, L. S. (1962). *Thought and language*. Cambridge, MA: MIT Press.

Vygotsky, L. S. (1978). *Mind in society: The development of higher psychological processes*. Cambridge, MA: Harvard University Press.

Weiss, B. D., Reed, R., Kligman, E. W., & Abyad, A. (1995). Literacy and performance on the Mini-Mental State Examination. *Journal of the American Geriatric Society, 43*, 807–810.

Welch, F. (1966). Measurement of the quality of education. *American Economic Review, 56*, 379–392.

Welch, F. (1973). Black–White differences in returns to schooling. *American Economic Review, 63*, 893–907.

Whalley, L. J., Starr, J. M., Athawes, R., Hunter, D., Pattie, A., & Deary, I. J. (2000). Childhood mental ability and dementia. *Neurology, 55*, 1455–1459.

White, L., Katzman, R., Losonczy, K., Salive, M., Wallace, R., Berkman, L., et al. (1994). Association of education with incidence of cognitive impairment in three established populations for epidemiological studies of the elderly. *Journal of Clinical Epidemiology, 47*, 363–374.

Whitfield, K. E., & Baker-Thomas, T. (1999). Individual differences in aging minorities. *International Journal of Aging and Human Development, 48*, 73–79.

Wilkinson, G. S. (1993). *Wide Range Achievement Test 3—Administration Manual.* Wilmington, DE: Jastak Associates, Inc.

Wong, T. M., Strickland, T. L., Fletcher-Janzen, E., Ardila, A., & Reynolds, C. R. (2000). Theoretical and practical issues in the neuropsychological assessment and treatment of culturally dissimilar patients. In E. Fletcher-Janzen, T. L. Strickland, & C. R. Reynolds (Eds.), *Handbook of cross-cultural neuropsychology* (pp. 3–18). New York: Kluwer Academic Publishers.

Zhang, M., Katzman, R., Salmon, D., Jin, H., Cai, G., Wang, Z., et al. (1990). The prevalence of dementia and Alzheimer's disease in Shanghai, China: Impact of age, gender and education. *Annals of Neurology, 27*, 428–437.

14 Brain reserve and risk of dementia: Findings from the Nun Study

James A. Mortimer, David A. Snowdon, and William R. Markesbery

Characteristics established in early life, including educational attainment and brain size, have been implicated as risk factors for dementia and intellectual decline in late life. In particular, low educational attainment has been shown to be a risk factor for prevalent dementia (Bowirrat, Friedland, Farrer, Baldwin, & Korczyn, 2002; Callahan, Hall, Hui, Musick, Unverzagt, & Hendrie, 1996; Canadian Study of Health and Aging, 1994; Chibnall & Eastwood, 1998; Dartigues et al., 1991; De Ronchi, Fratiglioni, Rucci, Paternico, Graziani, & Dalmonte, 1998; Haan, Mungas, Gonzalez, Ortiz, Acharya, & Jagust, 2003; Hall et al., 1998; Kokmen, Beard, O'Brien, & Kurland, 1993; Ott et al., 1995; Precipe M., Casini, Ferretti, Lattanzio, Fiorelli, & Culasso, 1996; Ravaglia et al., 2002; Schmand et al., 1997; Zhang et al., 1990) and incident dementia (Di Carlo et al., 2002; Evans et al., 1997; Fratiglioni et al., 1997; Karp, Kareholt, Qiu, Bellander, Winblad, & Fratiglioni, 2004; Launer et al., 1999; Letenneur, Gilleron, Commenges, Helmer, Orgogozo, & Dartigues, 1999; Lindsay et al., 2002; Ott, van Rossum, van Harskamp, van de Mheen, Hofman, & Breteler, 1999; Stern, Gurland, Tatemichi, Tang, Wilder, & Mayeux, 1994; Wilson et al., 2002; Zhang, Katzman, Yu, Liu, Xiao, & Yan, 1998), although a few studies have failed to confirm this association (Beard, Kokmen, Offord, & Kurland, 1992; Cobb, Wolf, Au, White, & D'Agostino, 1995; Graves et al., 1996a).

Smaller brain size attained in childhood (Dobbing & Sands, 1973), estimated radiographically (Mori et al., 1997; Schofield, Mosesson, Stern, & Mayeux, 1995; Wolf, Julin, Gertz, Winblad, & Wahlund, 2004) or from head circumference (Graves, Mortimer, Larson, Wenzlow, Bowen, & McCormick, 1996b; Reynolds, Johnson, Dodge, DeKosky, & Ganguli, 1999; Schofield, Logroscino, Andrews, Albert, & Stern, 1997), has been associated with increased prevalence (Schofield et al., 1997; Wolf et al., 2004), incidence (Borenstein-Graves et al., 2001), earlier onset of symptoms (Schofield et al., 1995) and increased severity of cognitive deficit (Graves et al., 1996b; Mori et al., 1997; Schofield et al., 1997) in Alzheimer's disease, as well as with lower scores on cognitive screening tests in a community sample of non-demented older adults (Reynolds et al., 1999). However, two negative studies have been published, in which total intracranial volume, a measure of maximum attained brain size, was found not to be associated with presence of Alzheimer's disease (Edland et al., 2002; Jenkins, Fox, Rossor, Harvey, & Rossor, 2000).

Higher educational attainment and larger brain size generally have been viewed as protective factors that increase brain reserve and therefore delay the appearance of dementia symptoms in individuals with brain pathology. It is likely that brain reserve is a multifactorial concept, related to the number of neurons, the density of their interconnections, and the number and sophistication of cognitive strategies for solving problems (Mortimer, 1997). In this regard, larger brain size and higher educational attainment may be expected to act synergistically, with those possessing the combination of a large brain and an extensive education deriving the greatest benefit. We tested this hypothesis by examining the reduction in risk of prevalent dementia resulting from having a larger brain, a higher education, or both.

The sample consisted of a subset of participants from the Nun Study, a longitudinal study of aging and dementia, who are evaluated annually for cognitive function and followed to autopsy. Data from those who were autopsied were used to assess associations of head circumference and educational attainment with neuropathological outcomes, for comparison with the associations with clinical dementia.

Methods

Participants in the Nun Study are members of the School Sisters of Notre Dame congregation and live in communities in the Midwestern, Eastern, and Southern United States. The Nun Study is described in more detail elsewhere (Snowdon, 1997; Snowdon, Greiner, Mortimer, Riley, Greiner, & Markesbery, 1996; Snowdon, Kemper, Mortimer, Greiner, Wekstein, & Markesbery, 1997). In 1991 and 1992, 678 sisters aged 75 to 102, who agreed to annual evaluation and brain donation after death, were enrolled. Participants included both individuals who were initially demented and those free of dementia. Cognitive and physical function were assessed annually, and all participants agreed to brain donation at death. All participants or their legal guardians gave informed consent to their participation in this study.

Cognitive function was evaluated annually with the CERAD (Consortium to Establish a Registry for Alzheimer's Disease) neuropsychological battery (Morris et al., 1989). This battery assesses memory, concentration, language, visuospatial ability and orientation to time and place. Performance-based testing was used to evaluate basic and instrumental activities of daily living (Kuriansky & Gurland, 1976; Potvin et al., 1972).

Participants were considered to be demented when all of the following conditions were met (Snowdon et al., 1997): (1) impairment in memory (defined by a score of < 4 on the Delayed Word Recall Test), (2) impairment in one or more other areas of cognition (defined by scores of < 11 on Verbal Fluency, < 13 on Boston Naming or < 8 on Constructional Praxis), (3) impairment in basic or instrumental activities of daily living (defined by inability to use a telephone, handle money, or dress oneself), and (4) evidence of a decline in ability from a previous level attributable to cognitive impairment. Cut-off scores selected to define cognitive impairment on tests were based on scores less than the fifth percentile for normal controls in CERAD (Welsh et al., 1994).

Gross and microscopic evaluations of the brains of participants who died during the study were performed by a neuropathologist who was blinded to their cognitive test scores and functional assessments. The intact brain and 1.5 cm thick coronal sections were examined for the presence of cerebral cortical atrophy, vascular lesions, and other alterations. For histopathological diagnosis, multiple sections of neocortex, hippocampus, entorhinal cortex, amygdala, basal ganglia, brainstem, and cerebellum were stained with hematoxylin and eosin as well as with the modified Bielschowsky stain. Senile plaques and neurofibrillary tangles were counted in the five most severely involved microscopic fields of the middle frontal gyrus (Brodmann area 9), inferior parietal lobule (areas 39/40), and middle temporal gyrus (area 21). Bielschowsky stained sections were used to count senile plaques (both diffuse and neuritic) per $10 \times (2.35 \text{ mm}^2)$ microscopic field and the number of neurofibrillary tangles per $20 \times (0.586 \text{ mm}^2)$ microscopic field.

To meet the study's neuropathological criteria for Alzheimer's disease, participants were required to have: (1) abundant senile plaques in the frontal, temporal, or parietal lobe, i.e., 16 or more senile plaques per mm^2 (consistent with Khachaturian criteria; Khachaturian, 1985), (2) neuritic plaques in at least one lobe, and (3) neurofibrillary tangles in at least one lobe.

Information on educational attainment was obtained from the convent archives. Sisters who completed less than 16 years of education were coded as having low educational attainment; those with 16 or more years of education were coded as having high educational attainment.

Head circumference was measured by placing a measuring tape over the eyebrows and passing it around the head to fit snugly over the most posterior protuberance of the occiput (Cameron, 1978). Circumference was recorded in inches and converted to centimeters. This measure was added between 4 and 5 years after the initiation of the study and therefore was only available for a sample ($N = 294$) of the original cohort ($N = 678$).

Hierarchical multiple logistic regression was used to estimate the association between dementia and the following variables entered on the first step: educational attainment, head circumference, age, and the presence of one or more apolipoprotein E $\varepsilon 4$ alleles. On a subsequent step, an interaction term for educational attainment and head circumference was added. Multiple logistic regression was used to estimate satisfaction of neuropathological criteria for Alzheimer's disease relative to head circumference and educational attainment, adjusting for the effects of age at the most recent evaluation and the presence of one or more apolipoprotein E $\varepsilon 4$ alleles. Interaction between head circumference and educational attainment also was assessed using the method described by Ottman (1990). In this method, risk to individuals with both exposures is compared to those with only one or the other exposure and to those with neither exposure (reference category).

Findings

All 294 participants were Caucasian females. For this group, data were available on educational attainment, age, and dementia status at the most recent annual evaluation. Three participants were missing data on apolipoprotein E genotype, resulting in a sample size of 291 for analyses that included this variable. Comparison of the characteristics of the sample with the original longitudinal cohort ($N = 678$) showed little difference in mean age at the most recent evaluation (89.34 years for the sample vs. 89.66 years for the cohort), years of education (15.79 for the sample vs. 15.87 for the cohort), percentage demented at the most recent evaluation (37.76 for the sample vs. 37.17 for the cohort), or percentage carrying one or more apolipoprotein E ε4 alleles (22.00 for the sample vs. 22.83 for the cohort).

Figures 14.1 and 14.2 show the distributions of educational attainment and head circumference in the sample of 294 participants. Because most of the participants were teachers, their mean education (15.87 years) was high for American women of similar age.

Figure 14.3 shows the percentage of participants who were demented by head circumference tertile and education. Sisters whose head circumferences were in the highest tertile and those with high educational attainment had the lowest probability of being demented. Education appeared to play an important role in determining dementia risk among sisters with head

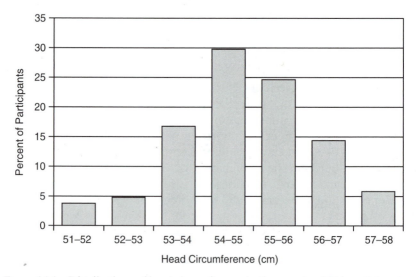

Figure 14.1   Distributions of head circumference in the sample of 294 participants.

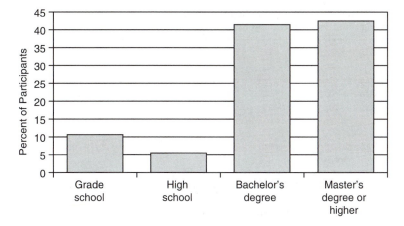

Figure 14.2 Distribution of educational attainment in the sample of 294 participants.

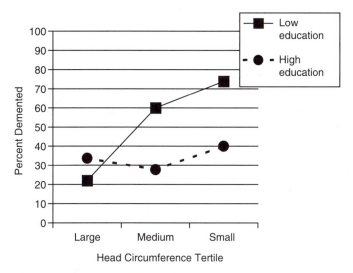

Figure 14.3 Percentage of individuals who were demented in six groups defined by educational attainment (high = bachelor's degree or higher, low = less than a bachelor's degree) and head circumference tertile.

circumference in the lower two tertiles. Among those with head circumference in the low or middle tertile, the likelihood of dementia was significantly higher for individuals with fewer than 16 years of education compared to those with 16 years or more ($\chi^2 = 15.5$, $p < .0001$). By contrast, among those with head circumferences in the highest tertile, there was no difference between individuals with low versus high education in the frequency of dementia ($\chi^2 = 0.49$, $p = .48$).

Table 14.1 Results of hierarchical logistic regression analysis predicting dementia from educational attainment and head circumference, and their interaction ($N = 291$)

Step	Variable(s) entered	χ^2	Odds ratio (95% CI)	Likelihood ratio χ^2
1	Attained education (years)	14.9***	0.84 (0.77–0.92)	
	Head circumference (cm)	2.6	0.86 (0.72–1.03)	
	Age at most recent evaluation (years)	17.7****	1.13 (1.07–1.19)	
	Presence of one or more apolipoprotein E ε4 alleles (1 = yes, 0 = no)	6.9**	2.38 (1.24–4.54)	
				47.3****
2	Attained education (years) × head circumference (cm)	6.5*		
				55.0****

* $p < .05$; ** $p < .01$; *** $p < .001$; **** $p < .0001$

Table 14.1 shows the results of a hierarchical logistic regression analysis predicting dementia in which years of education, head circumference, age at the most recent cognitive evaluation, and presence of one or more apolipoprotein E ε4 alleles were entered on the first step. Significant associations were present between dementia and education, age and the presence of apolipoprotein E ε4. The addition of an interaction term for years of education and head circumference significantly increased the model χ^2 (residual χ^2 test, $p = .011$).

Table 14.2 shows unadjusted and multivariate-adjusted odds ratios for dementia in groups with different combinations of head circumference and educational attainment. Individuals with head circumferences in the lower two tertiles who had less than 16 years of education were four times as likely to present with dementia as those with head circumferences in the highest tertile who completed 16 or more years of education (reference group). However, there was no elevation of risk among those with a large

Table 14.2 Odds ratios and prevalence of dementia in groups defined by educational attainment and head circumference ($N = 294$)

< 16 years of education	Head circumference in lowest two tertiles	Unadjusted odds ratio of dementia (95% CI)	Adjusted odds ratio of dementia (95% CI)*	Prevalence of dementia (cases/100)	# at risk
Yes	Yes	4.3 (1.9–9.6)	4.1 (1.7–9.9)	68.4	38
Yes	No	0.6 (0.1–2.9)	0.7 (0.1–3.9)	22.2	9
No	Yes	1.0 (0.5–1.7)	1.0 (0.6–1.8)	33.5	158
No	No	1.0 (reference)	1.0 (reference)	33.7	89

* Adjusted for age at most recent evaluation and presence of one or more apolipoprotein E ε4 alleles.

head circumference who had completed less than 16 years of education, or those with a small head circumference who had completed 16 or more years of education, when these groups were compared with those with both high education and large head circumference.

Autopsy data were available for 60 of the 294 participants. The mean interval between the final cognitive evaluation and death was 0.9 years. Thirty-four of these individuals fulfilled study neuropathological criteria for Alzheimer's disease; 26 did not. Educational attainment was unrelated to the fulfillment of neuropathological criteria in individuals with head circumference in the lower two tertiles ($\chi^2 = 0.11$, $p = .74$) as well as in those with head circumference in the highest tertile ($\chi^2 = 0.32$, $p = .57$). In a multiple logistic regression model controlling for age at the most recent evaluation and the presence of one or more apolipoprotein E ε4 alleles, neither educational attainment nor head circumference was associated with satisfaction of neuropathological criteria for Alzheimer's disease (Table 14.3). In addition, there was no significant interaction between these variables (not shown), although the power to detect such an interaction was low.

Comment

Educational attainment was significantly associated with dementia, controlling for age at the most recent evaluation and the presence of one or more apolipoprotein E ε4 alleles. Individuals with either a head circumference in the highest tertile or with more than 16 years of education were protected from being demented relative to those with both small head circumference and lower educational attainment. The findings are consistent with previous studies demonstrating significant associations between dementia and low education (Callahan et al., 1996; Canadian Study of Health and Aging, 1994; Chibnall & Eastwood, 1998; Dartigues et al., 1991; De Ronchi et al., 1998; Di Carlo et al., 2002; Evans et al., 1997; Fratiglioni, Viitanen, von Strauss, Tontodonati, Herlitz, & Winblad, 1997; Haan et al., 2003; Hall et al., 1998; Karp et al., 2004; Kokmen et al., 1993; Launer et al., 1999; Letenneur et al., 1999; Lindsay et al., 2002; Ott et al., 1995, 1999; Precipe et al., 1996;

Table 14.3 Results of multiple logistic regression analysis showing odds ratios of satisfaction of neuropathological criteria for Alzheimer's disease related to educational attainment and head circumference ($N = 60$)

Variable	Odds ratio	95% Confidence Interval	p
< 16 years of education (1 = yes, 0 = no)	2.05	0.51–8.19	.31
Head circumference (cm)	1.20	0.79–1.81	.40
Age at most recent evaluation (years)	0.96	0.86–1.07	.43
Presence of one or more apolipoprotein E ε4 alleles (1 = yes, 0 = no)	19.55	2.26–169.1	.007

Schmand et al., 1997; Stern et al., 1994; Wilson et al., 2002; Zhang et al., 1990, 1998). In contrast to the associations of head circumference and educational attainment with dementia, neither of these factors was associated with fulfillment of neuropathological criteria for Alzheimer's disease, which was the underlying cause of dementia in 78 percent of the autopsied sisters with this syndrome.

Those with both smaller head circumference and low educational attainment were four times as likely to be demented as those with other combinations of head circumference and education. The lack of an additional benefit from having a larger brain and higher education in comparison with having only one of these characteristics is surprising. The extra brain reserve provided by either a larger brain or higher education may be sufficient to substantially reduce the probability of dementia.

The presence of an association of the combination of low education and smaller head circumference with increased risk of dementia, and the lack of associations of these variables with fulfillment of neuropathological criteria for Alzheimer's disease, suggest that education and head size may be acting to *modify* the appearance of dementia in individuals with an underlying dementing illness. We have proposed that there are two sets of risk factors for Alzheimer's disease: those related to the development of the underlying pathology and those related to clinical expression of a dementing illness (Mortimer, 1995). The finding in our study that the satisfaction of neuropathological criteria for Alzheimer's disease was unrelated to educational attainment is consistent with Bennett et al. (2003), who reported that education was not related to a global Alzheimer pathology score or to scaled scores of neuritic plaques, diffuse plaques, or neurofibrillary tangles. These investigators concluded that education modifies the effect of Alzheimer's disease pathology on cognition.

Katzman et al. (1988) were the first to show that clinical expression of Alzheimer's disease was related to brain size; persons with larger brains were more likely to remain non-demented despite having similar numbers of Alzheimer lesions to those who were demented. Other studies (Crystal et al., 1988; Morris et al., 1996) have identified substantial percentages (43–67%) of individuals who remained non-demented during life, but fulfilled neuropathological criteria for Alzheimer's disease at autopsy. In the present study, 16 of the 34 participants (47%) who satisfied Alzheimer's disease neuropathological criteria remained non-demented through the last evaluation. Only 27 participants who died with dementia received a neuropathological diagnosis. Of these, 18 fulfilled neuropathological criteria for Alzheimer's disease at autopsy. In the larger cohort, 101 of 129 sisters who were demented during life (78%) fulfilled neuropathological criteria for Alzheimer's disease at autopsy. Whereas the percentage of sisters who were autopsied is too small to examine the role of head circumference in modifying the clinical expression of neuropathologically defined Alzheimer's disease per se, the fact that most sisters who were demented suffered from this illness suggests that head circumference is very likely to modify the expression of Alzheimer's disease.

Two published studies (Edland et al., 2002; Jenkins et al., 2000) did not find a significant association between intracranial volume, a measure of maximum attained brain size, and the presence of Alzheimer's disease. Jenkins et al. (2000) compared total intracranial volume in 85 Alzheimer patients and 52 volunteer controls. Educational attainment in these groups was not specified, so it is impossible to assess the role played by this variable in modifying the association between intracranial volume and Alzheimer's disease. Edland et al. (2002) compared total intracranial volume in 166 Alzheimer patients and 184 controls. Analyses were not stratified by educational attainment; therefore it was not possible to judge whether there was an interaction effect between brain size and educational attainment such as that found in the present study. These authors suggested that their sample was relatively advantaged, which may have reduced the number of individuals with smaller brain sizes related to poor nutrition during development.

The mechanism by which education modifies the expression of dementia is unknown. At least three explanations can be given: (1) low educational attainment may be related to exposures that increase the risk of dementia during life; (2) higher education level may lead to greater neuronal connectivity early in life that persisted through the life course, or (3) higher education level may be related to lifelong mental stimulation and neuronal growth (Mortimer & Graves, 1993). Given the uniform lifestyles of the Catholic sisters, it is unlikely that differential exposures explain the association between education and dementia that was found. Low and high educated sisters had similar social activities and support, did not smoke or drink excessive amounts of alcohol, had similar income throughout adult life, lived in the same houses and ate food prepared in the same kitchens, and had equal access to preventative and medical care services. It is more likely that an association of education with continued stimulation and growth may have led to increased neuronal connectivity, providing a buffer against neuronal decay and cell loss that occurs in Alzheimer's disease.

References

Beard, C. M., Kokmen, E., Offord, K. P., & Kurland, L. T. (1992). Lack of association between Alzheimer's disease and education, occupation, marital status, or living arrangement. *Neurology, 42*, 2063–2068.

Bennett, D. A., Wilson, R. S., Schneider, J. A., Evans, D. A., Mendes de Leon, C. F., Arnold, S. E., et al. (2003). Education modifies the relation of AD pathology to level of cognitive function in older persons. *Neurology, 60*, 1909–1915.

Borenstein-Graves, A., Mortimer, J. A., Bowen, J. D., McCormick, W. C., McCurry, S. M., Schellenberg, G. D., et al. (2001). Head circumference and incident Alzheimer's disease: Modification by apolipoprotein E. *Neurology, 57*, 1453–60.

Bowirrat, A., Friedland, R. P., Farrer, L., Baldwin, C., & Korczyn, A. (2002). Genetic and environmental risk factors for Alzheimer's disease in Israeli Arabs. *Journal of Molecular Neuroscience, 19*, 239–245.

Callahan, C. M., Hall, K. S., Hui, S. L., Musick, B. S., Unverzagt, F. W., & Hendrie, H. C. (1996). Relationship of age, education, and occupation with dementia among a community-based sample of African-Americans. *Archives of Neurology, 53*, 134–140.

Cameron, N. (1978). *The methods of auxological anthropometry.* In F. Falkner & J. M. Tanner (Eds.), *Human growth, Vol. 2: Postnatal growth.* New York: Plenum Press.

Canadian Study of Health and Aging (1994). The Canadian Study of Health and Aging: Risk factors for Alzheimer's disease in Canada. *Neurology, 44*, 2073–2080.

Chibnall, J. T., & Eastwood, R. (1998). Postsecondary education and dementia risk in older Jesuit priests. *International Psychogeriatrics, 10*, 359–368.

Cobb, J. L., Wolf, P. A., Au, R., White, R., & D'Agostino, R. B. (1995). The effect of education on the incidence of dementia and Alzheimer's disease in the Framingham Study. *Neurology, 45*, 1707–1712.

Crystal, H., Dickson, D., Fuld, P., Masur, D., Scott, R., Mehler, M., et al. (1988). Clinico-pathologic studies in dementia: Nondemented subjects with pathologically confirmed Alzheimer's disease. *Neurology, 38*, 1682–1687.

Dartigues, J. F., Gagnon, M., Michel, P. L. L., Commenges, D., Barberger-Gateau, P., Auriacombe, S., et al. (1991). The Paquid research program on the epidemiology of dementia. Methods and initial results. *Revue Neurologique, 147*, 225–230.

De Ronchi, D., Fratiglioni, L., Rucci, P., Paternico, A., Graziani, S., & Dalmonte, E. (1998). The effect of education of dementia occurrence in an Italian population with middle to high socioeconomic status. *Neurology, 50*, 1231–1238.

Di Carlo, A., Baldereschi, M., Amaducci, L., Lepore, V., Bracco, L., Maggi, S., et al. (2002). Incidence of dementia, Alzheimer's disease, and vascular dementia in Italy. The ILSA Study. *Journal of the American Geriatrics Society, 50*, 41–48.

Dobbing, K., & Sands, J. (1973). Quantitative growth and development of the human brain. *Archives of Diseases in Childhood, 49*, 757–767.

Edland, S. D., Xu, Y., Plevak, M., O'Brien, P., Tangalos, E.G., Petersen, R.C., et al. (2002). Total intracranial volume: Normative values and lack of association with Alzheimer's disease. *Neurology, 59*, 272–274.

Evans, D. A., Hebert, L. E., Beckett, L. A., Scherr, P. A., Albert, M. S., Chown, M. J., et al. (1997). Education and other measures of socioeconomic status and risk of incident Alzheimer disease in a defined population of older persons. *Archives of Neurology, 54*, 1399–1405.

Fratiglioni, L., Viitanen, M., von Strauss, E., Tontodonati, V., Herlitz, A., & Winblad, B. (1997). Very old women at highest risk of dementia and Alzheimer's disease: Incidence data from the Kungshomen Project, Stockholm. *Neurology, 48*, 132–138.

Graves, A. B., Larson, E. B., Edland, S. D., Bowen, J. D., McCormick, W. C., McCurry, S. M., et al. (1996a). Prevalence of dementia and its subtypes in the Japanese American population of King County, Washington state. The Kame Project. *American Journal of Epidemiology, 144*, 760–771.

Graves, A. B., Mortimer, J. A., Larson, E. B., Wenzlow, A., Bowen, J. D., & McCormick, W. C. (1996b). Head circumference as a measure of cognitive reserve: Association with severity of impairment in Alzheimer's disease. *British Journal of Psychiatry, 169*, 86–92.

Haan, M. N., Mungas, D. M., Gonzalez, H. M., Ortiz, T. A., Acharya, A., & Jagust, W. J. (2003). Prevalence of dementia in older Latinos: The influence of type 2 diabetes mellitus, stroke and genetic factors. *Journal of the American Geriatrics Society*, *51*, 169–177.

Hall, K., Gureje, O., Gao, S., Ogunniyi, A., Hui, S.L., Baiyewu, O., et al. (1998). Risk factors and Alzheimer's disease: A comparative study of two communities. *Australian & New Zealand Journal of Psychiatry*, *32*, 698–706.

Jenkins, R., Fox, N. C., Rossor, A. M., Harvey, R. J. & Rossor, M. N. (2000). Intracranial volume and Alzheimer's disease: Evidence against the cerebral reserve hypothesis. *Archives of Neurology*, *57*, 220–224.

Karp, A., Kareholt, I., Qiu, C., Bellander, T., Winblad, B., & Fratiglioni, L. (2004). Relation of education and occupation-based socioeconomic status to incident Alzheimer's disease. *American Journal of Epidemiology*, *159*, 175–183.

Katzman, R., Terry. R., DeTeresa, R., Brown, T., Davies, P., Fuld, P., et al. (1988). Clinical, pathological, and neurochemical changes in dementia: A subgroup with preserved mental status and numerous neocortical plaques. *Annals of Neurology*, *23*, 138–144.

Khachaturian, Z. S. (1985). Diagnosis of Alzheimer's disease. *Archives of Neurology*, *42*, 1097–1105.

Kokmen, E., Beard, C. M., O'Brien, P. C., & Kurland, L. T. (1993). Educational attainment and Alzheimer's disease: Reassessment of the Rochester, Minnesota data (1975–1984). *Neurology*, *43*, A317.

Kuriansky, J., & Gurland, B. (1976). The performance test of activities of daily living. *International Journal of Aging and Human Development*, *7*, 343–352.

Launer, L. J., Andersen, K., Dewey, M. E., Letenneur, L., Ott, A., Amaducci, L. A., et al. (1999). Rates and risk factors for dementia and Alzheimer's disease: Results from EURODEM pooled analyses. *Neurology*, *52*, 78–84.

Letenneur, L., Gilleron, V., Commenges, D., Helmer, C., Orgogozo, J. M., & Dartigues, J. F. (1999). Are sex and educational level independent predictors of dementia and Alzheimer's disease? Incidence data from the PAQUID project. *Journal of Neurology, Neurosurgery & Psychiatry*, *66*, 177–183.

Lindsay, J., Laurin, D., Verreault, R., Hebert, R., Helliwell, B., Hill, G. B., et al. (2002). Risk factors for Alzheimer's disease: A prospective analysis from the Canadian Study of Health and Aging. *American Journal of Epidemiology*, *156*, 445–453.

Mori, E., Hirono, N., Yamashita, H., Imamura, T., Ikejiri, Y., Ikeda, M., et al. (1997). Premorbid brain size as a determinant of reserve capacity against intellectual decline in Alzheimer's disease. *American Journal of Psychiatry*, *154*, 18–24.

Morris, J. C., Heyman, A., Mohs, R. C., Hughes, J. P., van Belle, G., et al. (1989). The Consortium to Establish a Registry for Alzheimer's Disease (CERAD). Part I. Clinical and neuropsychological assessment of Alzheimer's disease. *Neurology*, *39*, 1159–1165.

Morris, J. C., Storandt, M., McKeel, D. W., Jr., Rubin, E. H., Price, J. L., Grant, E. A., et al. (1996). Cerebral amyloid deposition and diffuse plaques in "normal" aging: Evidence for presymptomatic and very mild Alzheimer's disease. *Neurology*, *46*, 707–719.

Mortimer, J. A. (1995). The continuum hypothesis of Alzheimer's disease and normal aging: The role of brain reserve. *Alzheimer's Research*, *1*, 67–70.

Mortimer, J. A. (1997). Brain reserve and the clinical expression of Alzheimer's disease. *Geriatrics*, *52*, S50–S53.

Mortimer, J. A., & Graves, A. B. (1993). Education and other socioeconomic determinants of dementia and Alzheimer's disease. *Neurology, 43*, S39–S44.

Ott, A., Breteler, M. M., van Harskamp F., Claus, J. J., van der Cammen, T. J., Grobbee, D. E., et al. (1995). Prevalence of Alzheimer's disease and vascular dementia: Association with education. The Rotterdam study. *British Medical Journal, 310* (6985), 970–3.

Ott, A., van Rossum, C. T. M., van Harskamp, F., van de Mheen, H., Hofman, A., & Breteler, M. M. (1999). Education and the incidence of dementia in a large population-based study: The Rotterdam Study. *Neurology, 52*, 663–666.

Ottman, R. (1990). An epidemiologic approach to gene–environment interaction. *Genetic Epidemiology, 7*, 177–185.

Potvin, A. R., Tourtellotte, W. W., Dailey, J. S., Alberts, J. W., Walker, J. E., Pew, R. W., et al. (1972). Simulated activities of daily living examination. *Archives of Physical Medicine & Rehabilitation, 53*, 476–489.

Precipe, M., Casini, A. R., Ferretti, C., Lattanzio, M. T., & Fiorelli, M., & Culasso, F. (1996). Prevalence of dementia in an elderly rural population: Effects of age, sex, and education. *Journal of Neurology, Neurosurgery, and Psychiatry, 60*, 628–633.

Ravaglia, G., Forti, P., Maioli, F., Sacchetti, L., Mariani, E., Nativio, V., et al. (2002). Education, occupation, and prevalence of dementia: Findings from the Conselice study. *Dementia & Geriatric Cognitive Disorders, 14*, 90–100.

Reynolds, M. D., Johnson, J. M., Dodge, H. H., DeKosky, S. T., & Ganguli, M. (1999). Small head size is related to low Mini-Mental State Examination scores in a community sample of nondemented older adults. *Neurology, 53*, 228–229.

Schmand, B., Smit, J., Lindeboom, J., Smits, C., Hooijer, C., Jonker, C., et al. (1997). Low education is a genuine risk factor for accelerated memory decline and dementia. *Journal of Clinical Epidemiology, 50*, 1025–1033.

Schofield, P. W., Logroscino, G., Andrews, H. F., Albert, S., & Stern, Y. (1997). An association between head circumference and Alzheimer's disease in a population-based study of aging and dementia. *Neurology, 49*, 30–37.

Schofield, P. W., Mosesson, R. E., Stern, Y., & Mayeux, R. (1995). The age at onset of Alzheimer's disease and an intracranial area measurement. A relationship. *Archives of Neurology, 52*, 95–98.

Snowdon, D. A. (1997). Aging and Alzheimer's disease: Lessons from the Nun Study. *Gerontologist, 37*, 150–156.

Snowdon, D. A., Greiner, L. H., Mortimer, J. A., Riley, K. P., Greiner, P. A., & Markesbery, W. R. (1997). Brain infarction and the clinical expression of Alzheimer disease. The Nun Study. *Journal of the Americal Medical Association, 277*, 813–817.

Snowdon, D. A., Kemper, S. J., Mortimer, J. A., Greiner, L. H., Wekstein, D. R., & Markesbery, W. R. (1996). Linguistic ability in early life and cognitive function and Alzheimer's disease in late life: Findings from the Nun Study. *Journal of the American Medical Association, 275*, 528–532.

Stern, Y., Gurland, B., Tatemichi, T. K., Tang, M. X., Wilder, D., & Mayeux, R. (1994). Influence of education and occupation on the incidence of Alzheimer's disease. *Journal of the American Medical Association, 271*, 1004–1010.

Welsh, K. A., Butters, N., Mohs, R. C., Beekly, D., Edland, S., Fillenbaum, G., et al. (1994). The Consortium to Establish a Registry for Alzheimer's Disease (CERAD). Part V. A normative study of the neuropsychological battery. *Neurology, 44*, 609–614.

Wilson, R. S., Bennett, D. A., Bienias, J. L., Aggarwal, N. T., Mendes de Leon, C. F., Morris, M. C., et al. (2002). Cognitive activity and incident AD in a population-based sample of older persons. *Neurology, 59,* 1910–1914.

Wolf, H., Julin, P., Gertz, H. J., Winblad, B., & Wahlund, L.O. (2004). Intracranial volume in mild cognitive impairment, Alzheimer's disease and vascular dementia: Evidence for brain reserve? *International Journal of Geriatric Psychiatry, 19,* 995–1007.

Zhang, M. Y., Katzman, R., Salmon, D., Jin, H., Cai, G. J., Wang, Z. Y., et al. (1990). The prevalence of dementia and Alzheimer's disease in Shanghai, China: Impact of age, gender, and education. *Annals of Neurology, 27,* 428–437.

Zhang, M., Katzman, R., Yu, E., Liu, W., Xiao, S. F., & Yan, H. (1998). A preliminary analysis of incidence of dementia in Shanghai, China. *Psychiatry and Clinical Neuroscience, 52,* S291–S294.

15 Imaging cognitive reserve

Yaakov Stern

The concept of cognitive reserve (CR) posits that individual differences in the way tasks are processed might provide differential reserve against brain pathology, or age-related changes. For example, brain networks that are more efficient or flexible may be less susceptible to disruption. Many of the chapters in this volume review the evidence for the existence of cognitive reserve. This chapter reviews research that is designed to ask a related question: What are the neural processes that underlie cognitive reserve? If the basis of cognitive reserve is a differential use of cognitive strategies and their underlying brain networks, then imaging should be able to provide some insight into the neural implementation of cognitive reserve.

Using functional imaging to study cognitive reserve makes demands on this technique that may not be relevant to other cognitive neuroimaging studies. The first part of this chapter is devoted to a review of conceptual and design issues that are particularly relevant for functional imaging studies of cognitive reserve. The second part reviews some imaging studies from my group that illustrate many of these issues.

Theoretical and design issues

Goal of neuroimaging studies of reserve

Many neuroimaging studies are aimed at functional localization. The question they ask is: What area or set of brain areas mediate a specific cognitive function, such as verb generation or object recognition? In contrast, the question faced in studying cognitive reserve is a different one. We seek to isolate brain networks whose differential expression may allow one person to cope with brain pathology more readily than another. Since the nature and underlying cognitive operations of such a network are not clear, the task at hand might be described as studying the relationship between task-related brain activation and proxies for cognitive reserve, as opposed to performance of the task itself.

If cognitive reserve really is subserved by a set of cognitive networks that is more resilient or more adaptive in the face of brain damage, then it is unlikely that the brain networks subserving cognitive reserve are equivalent to those required to perform any one particular task. Rather, it is more likely that a "cognitive reserve network" would be elicited by many tasks. It is only by subserving some general function that supercedes those tapped by specific tasks that cognitive reserve might allow someone to cope with pathology and maintain effective functioning for a longer period of time. Thus, when using neuroimaging to investigate the neural instantiation of cognitive reserve, the research question being asked differs markedly from that in the more typical cognitive activation study.

Studying individual differences

Another important point is that cognitive neuroimaging studies of the neural basis of cognitive reserve aim to explore individual variability in task-related activation. The typical neuroimaging study seeks the aspects of activation that are common to all of the subjects in the study. In a two-group study design comparing young and old subjects, for example, the inter-individual variability within each age group is typically treated as error. When dealing with questions about cognitive reserve, however, we are precisely interested in the variability within the groups, since it is this variability that might provide reserve for one person and not another. Several design approaches have been taken to address within-group variability. One approach has been to subdivide the elders into those who do and do not perform effectively and to compare both of these groups to younger individuals (e.g., Cabeza, Anderson, Locantore, & McIntosh, 2002). While not operating at the level of individual variability, this approach does attempt to address the fact that there is within-group variability and that it is precisely this variability that we wish to elucidate. Another approach is to utilize analytic techniques that preserve the data of each individual subject. For example, imaging data can be analyzed with regression techniques that evaluate, individual by individual, the relationship between some aspect of activation and some proxy for cognitive reserve. This approach is reviewed in the description of some of our studies below. A third approach, also discussed below, is to first use standard voxel-wise or covariance approaches to identify brain areas or "brain networks" that are associated with task performance. Follow-up analyses can then evaluate the relationship between each subject's expression of this network and measured proxies of cognitive reserve, as well as the implication of differential network expression for task performance.

One set of concepts that might be useful in helping to design studies of the neural basis of cognitive reserve is that of efficiency and capacity. Figure 15.1 illustrates some hypothetical data that may help to clarify these concepts. On the x axis is increasing task demand. This refers to a hypothetical within-subject manipulation where the difficulty of the task is increased in a parametric manner. The y axis represents task-related activation either at

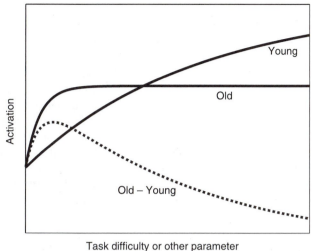

Figure 15.1 Hypothetical relationship between task demand and task-related activation.

one particular brain location or throughout some brain network. The figure demonstrates hypothesized curves relating task demand to task-related activation in young and old individuals. Note two features of these curves. First, the rate of rise in the curve might be an index of the efficiency of the system. Thus in this hypothetical example the rate of rise is much slower in the young subjects than in the older subjects. This might indicate that the brain network is more efficient in the younger subjects. Simplistically, at any particular level of difficulty, the task can be mediated by less activation in the young people than in the old. A second feature of these curves is that they reach an asymptote, potentially indicative of the capacity of the system. In these hypothetical curves, the brain network has a greater capacity in the younger subjects than in the older subjects, suggesting that it might continue to respond effectively in the face of increased task demand. Intuitively, these concepts of efficiency and capacity of brain networks might be important components underlying cognitive reserve such that networks with greater efficiency and capacity might be more able to withstand disruption and still operate effectively. One might predict that individuals with higher reserve would show greater efficiency and/or greater capacity. It is worth noting that differential efficiency and capacity can occur within young or older people, as opposed to just between them, and evidence of greater efficiency in young adults with higher reserve is demonstrated in one of the studies reviewed below.

Figure 15.1 is also useful for illustrating another important design issue. At any fixed point, a task might be more difficult or demanding for one group than another. For example, if a young and an old group are given a 7-word memory test, this task might be trivial for the young subjects, but demanding for the older subjects. This divergence in relative difficulty for the two groups might lead to differences in task-related activation in any particular brain area or network. Note in the illustration that at relatively low task demand, greater activation might be seen in old people than in young people. Conversely, at higher task demand, greater activation might be seen in the young subjects than in the old. This has two important implications. First, differential activation in and of itself is very difficult to interpret. Using the same task at different levels of difficulty, one might find greater or less activation in the young subjects. In order to derive meaning from differential activation across groups, the investigator must have good control over the relative difficulty of the task in the two groups. One may do this by carefully matching task performance across the two groups. For example, several investigators have taken great pains to ensure that, as a group, old and young subjects' behavioral performance on their activation task was matched. An alternate approach, which was implemented in the studies described below, is to titrate task difficulty in each individual subject in order to ensure that each subject is performing the task at a comparable level.

More recently, my group has moved to a more comprehensive approach to the issue of task difficulty. Specifically, we are attempting to understand the nature of task-related activation over a range of task difficulty, and the way in which this differs between young and old subjects. Then, when linked to task performance, one might begin to understand the relationship between task activation and task difficulty. This should yield a better picture of the differences between young and old people, and might in turn provide a greater insight into cognitive reserve.

There is also a related issue underlying this discussion that is important to make explicit. When comparing two groups, such as old and young individuals, it is very important to understand whether the two groups are activating the same brain network, albeit with differing efficiency and/or capacity, or whether one of the groups is using a completely different network than the other. Even a carefully designed study of young and old people that parametrically varies task difficulty within subjects might yield data that would be inconclusive in this regard. Thus, in the illustration, we have situations where the same task, at different levels of task demand, may yield greater and lesser activation in the two groups. This could be because the underlying neural network differs in the two groups or that the network is actually the same but is operating at different efficiency and capacity. Because the same network can vary in its degree of expression, voxel-based analyses of imaging data as traditionally applied are not sufficient to make this discrimination. The existence of voxel-wise differences in this case does not imply distinct spatial patterns. Potential analytic solutions to this problem are illustrated in the studies described below.

Neural reserve and neural compensation

The discussion to this point provides some of the background for my assertion that it is important to divide the neural basis of cognitive reserve into two separate classes. Essentially, I wish to differentiate between situations where the patient uses the same brain networks as unimpaired individuals, as opposed to situations when alternate, potentially compensatory, networks are used. Cognitive reserve may be a function of differential efficiency or capacity of pre-existing networks that allows someone to continue functioning in the face of brain damage. In this case, the brain-damaged individual would be using the same brain networks as an unimpaired individual, albeit with potentially less efficiency and/or capacity. On the other hand, cognitive reserve may also operate by the recruitment of alternate strategies or alternate brain networks that are invoked to compensate for the disruption of the more typically used strategies or networks. Thus someone with greater cognitive reserve might be more able to adapt and invoke more useful new, alternate networks.

When the same brain network is recruited by both groups, I would argue that this should not be called compensation. I therefore have suggested the term "neural reserve" for this situation. In contrast, I have suggested the term "neural compensation" only for situations in which it can be demonstrated that the older group is using some alternate network that is not used by the younger group (Stern et al., 2005).

The term "neural reserve" is meant to encompass the idea that cognitive reserve is a representation of individual differences in task processing that probably developed throughout the life span. For example, in some studies described below, we can show that young, healthy subjects show differential recruitment of a brain network during task performance as a function of IQ, a proxy for cognitive reserve.

"Neural compensation" is reserved for a situation where it can be demonstrated that the more impaired group is using a different network than the unimpaired group. This different network can take several forms. One possibility is that the impaired group is using a completely different set of brain areas (or network) than the unimpaired group. Another possibility is that the impaired group continues to use the same brain areas, but that the network itself is reorganized. Note that this term does not imply that the alternate mode of processing is beneficial. An example of this latter possibility is presented below. Thus it need not be demonstrated that the use of this compensatory network allows an individual to perform better at the task or that it returns the impaired individual to normal performance. While this is an important question to be asked in regard to a compensatory network, I do not feel that demonstrating a relationship between differential expression of a compensatory network and superior performance is required. That is because it is possible that a compensatory network could serve to maintain performance when the network that usually mediates performance is damaged. In this case, network expression might not be associated with superior performance, but simply with the maintenance of the ability to perform.

Of course, a compensatory network can be associated with superior performance. In the "compensatory reallocation" model, those who make use of a compensatory network perform better than those who do not. An example of this is the hemispheric asymmetry reduction in older adults or HAROLD hypothesis (Cabeza, 2002). In sum, this hypothesis posits that better functioning older adults will evidence additional compensatory activation in homologous areas contralateral to those typically activated by younger adults. In contrast, poorer functioning elders will not evidence this compensatory activation.

Much of the literature does not differentiate between neural reserve and neural compensation. More generally, the differentiation between differential expression of the same network and the expression of new, compensatory networks has not received sufficient consideration. Many papers comparing two groups, for example an old and a young group, focus on differential task-related activation across groups. If the older group has reduced activation in some area, the investigators might relate their poorer performance to that reduction. Alternately, if the older group has increased activation in some area, investigators might hypothesize that this area is compensatory, i.e., that the older group must be recruiting this area in order to compensate for age-related deficits. As should be clear from the discussion above, this simplistic approach has obvious drawbacks.

Review of studies

Supporting the concept of CR, studies of Alzheimer's disease (AD) patients have used resting cerebral blood flow (CBF) as a surrogate for AD pathology (DeCarli et al., 1992; Friedland, Brun, & Bundinger, 1985; McGeer, McGeer, Harrop, Akiyama, & Kamo, 1990). In patients matched for clinical severity, these studies have found negative correlations between resting CBF and education, IQ, occupation and leisure (Stern, Alexander, Prohovnik, & Mayeux, 1992; Stern et al., 1995; Alexander, Furey, Grady, Pietrini, Mentis, & Schapiro, 1997; Scarmeas et al., 2003a). The negative correlations are consistent with the prediction that at any given level of clinical disease severity, a subject with a higher level of CR should have greater AD pathology (i.e., lower CBF).

The studies of resting CBF provide support for the concept of CR, and suggest that two individuals with the same amount of brain pathology may appear completely different clinically. However the resting CBF studies cannot elucidate the neurophysiologic substrate of CR. The logic behind the functional imaging studies that my group has undertaken is simply that if we can identify differential task-related activation as a function of proxies for CR, this might give us a clue as to how CR is implemented.

Based on the discussion above regarding neural reserve and neural compensation, we can predict that there should be differences in task-related neural processing in individuals of any given age as a function of CR. These activation differences across subjects should be present not only in individuals affected by brain pathology, but even in healthy young individuals. This differential activation would be associated with neural reserve. Once we identify brain networks associated with CR in healthy young individuals, we can then test whether these networks are also expressed in individuals who may suffer from insult to the brain associated with aging. For this purpose, the present review compares and contrasts activation in old and young individuals.

This chapter reviews four papers detailing the results of two related studies that used the same paradigm in an attempt to identify the neurophysiologic substrate underlying cognitive reserve. For each study, the data were analyzed in two different ways, first with voxel-based techniques and then with co-variance approaches. The first set of analyses focuses on neural reserve in young, healthy individuals. Testing for a relationship between a cognitive reserve index such as IQ and differential activation in young subjects has the advantage that one need not be concerned about the confound of between-subject variability in age-related brain pathology. The second set of analyses compares activation in old and young subjects, allowing us to search for the use of compensatory networks in the older subjects.

Both studies used a continuous nonverbal recognition task. The basic task consisted of the serial presentation of one or more single un-nameable shapes, followed by a series of the same number of recognition probes. For each probe, the subject used a button press to indicate whether or not they had just seen the item. There were two task conditions. In the low demand condition, each study item was followed by a recognition probe. In the titrated demand condition, subjects studied a longer list of items, and then responded to an equally long set of recognition probes. Prior to scanning, the study list size of the titrated demand condition was adjusted for each subject, such that recognition accuracy was 75%. This procedure was intended to match task difficulty (as operationalized by level of performance) across subjects. In reference to the previous discussion of Figure 15.1, the titration procedure is designed to ensure that all subjects are working at the same level of task demand or difficulty. This, in turn, allows us to interpret activation differences without the concern that they are simply related to differential difficulty of the task across subjects or groups.

Our intention was to explore how individual differences in cognitive reserve are related to changes in neural activity as the subjects move from the low to the titrated demand task. Our prediction was that certain aspects of task-related activation would be related to cognitive reserve. This simplifies to a prediction that there will be a correlation between measures of cognitive reserve and the change in activation from low to titrated demand.

Neuroimaging studies in young adults

The first study (Stern, Zarahn, Hilton, Delapaz, Flynn, & Rakitin, 2003) used 19 healthy young adults between the ages of 18 and 30. We used the raw score of the National Adult Reading test (NART) (Nelson, 1982; Grober & Sliwinski, 1991) as a proxy measure for cognitive reserve. This test is a good estimate of verbal IQ, and reading measures have been used effectively as measures of reserve in the past. The data analytic approach in this study was to look voxel by voxel to find brain areas in which the change in event-related fMRI response amplitude from low to titrated demand conditions (T-L) correlated with an individual subject's NART scores. During the study phase of the task (i.e., when subjects were viewing the shapes to remember them later), positive correlations between T-L and NART were seen in left middle frontal gyrus and negative correlations were seen at right superior frontal gyrus, middle frontal gyrus, precentral gyrus, medial frontal gyrus, and insular. We also found brain areas that showed correlations between T-L and NART scores during the recognition phase of the task.

Thus the primary finding of this study was that, both during study and during subsequent retrieval, brain areas were noted where there was a systematic relationship between CR and brain activation. These correlations support the hypotheses that neural processing differs as a function of CR. This differential processing may help to explain individual differences in capacity or efficiency, and may underlie reserve against age-related or other pathologic changes.

In subsequent analyses (Habeck, Hilton, Zarahn, Flynn, Moeller, & Stern, 2003), we analyzed the data from 17 of the subjects from this study using a covariance approach: ordinal trend canonical variates analysis (OrT CVA) (Habeck, Krakauer, Ghez, Sackeim, Eidelberg, Stern et al., 2005). This analysis identifies a covariance pattern (or "brain network") whose expression increases from the low to the titrated demand condition for as many subjects as possible. Once a brain network whose subject expression systematically increased in expression from low to titrated demand was identified, we examined the relationship between individual subjects' change in network expression across the two conditions and their NART scores.

The ordinal trend analysis was first performed on imaging data from the study phase of the task. There we identified a covariance pattern whose change in expression from the low to the titrated demand condition increased for 15 of the 17 subjects. This brain network reflects activity in all areas of the brain, however some areas are more involved in this network than others. Further, the identification of a covariance pattern implies that change in activation in one area is related to change in another area. This relationship can be positive or negative. Thus, as the brain network expression increases, some brain areas show increased activation and some show decreased activation. Areas that were associated with increases in activation from the low to the titrated condition for the majority of subjects were found in cerebellar locations. Areas associated with decreased activity from low to titrated demand conditions were attained in precuneus, anterior singular gyrus, bilateral thalamus, right insular, right middle temporal gyrus and bilateral inferior frontal gyrus. The key finding for our purposes was that the larger the increase in activation from low to titrated demand condition in a subject, the lower their NART IQ. That is, subjects with lower CR showed the greatest changes in expression of this brain network across the two difficulty conditions. These findings were independent of any differences in the study list size across subjects.

Once a brain network is identified in one task condition, one can apply it prospectively to data from another task condition and investigate the association of network expression with other experimental variables. In this case, we examined whether the network identified during study also changed its expression across the low to titrated demand condition during the recognition phase of the task. Indeed, we found that network expression increased from low to titrated demand during recognition in the same manner as it did during encoding. Further, across subjects, the change in expression from low to titrated demand condition in the test phase again correlated significantly with NART IQ.

Thus this analysis identified a brain network that showed increased expression as the load associated with the task increased. That is, as we moved from a low demand task to a titrated demand task, increased expression of this network was noted. Further, this change in activation across tasks was associated with CR: individuals with lower CR showed greater levels of change in network expression. These results complement those of the first set of analyses. We have now found a brain network that appears to be differentially expressed as a function of CR. We consider this network a good example of the concept of neural reserve.

Neuroimaging studies in young and old adults

The second study (Scarmeas et al., 2003b) used the same nonverbal activation task. In this study we used PET as the imaging modality, and both old and young subjects were included. Seventeen young adults and 19 healthy elderly adults participated. The cognitive reserve variable that we used in this study was a factor score that summarized years of education and scores on two IQ indices: the NART and WAIS-R vocabulary score. As in the other study, subjects were scanned while performing the low and titrated demand tasks.

This study used a similar analytic approach to that described above. We began by searching for voxels in which there was a correlation between the CR measure and the change in activation from the low to the titrated condition. As in our initial study, areas where such a correlation is found would be likely candidates for mediating CR. Indeed, we found such areas in both the young and the old subjects. The more crucial analysis for a theoretical point of view was to search for areas in which the relationship between task-related activation and cognitive reserve differed in young and old subjects. For example, Figure 15.2 illustrates a voxel in the cingulate gyrus where the relationship between task-related activation and CR was positive in the young subjects, and negative in the old. If we assume that people with more CR are doing a task in a more optimal manner, then the positive relationship in the young would suggest that it is more adaptive to show increased activation at this brain location as a task gets more difficult. However, the older subjects with more reserve are doing exactly the opposite. This finding suggests that there has been some reorganization of the networks underlying task performance in the old subjects versus the young subjects. This reorganization has resulted in the optimal activation of this brain area in old subjects with high reserve being in the opposite direction than that in young subjects with high reserve. We speculate that the older subjects are using a brain area differently than the younger subjects in order to compensate for the effects of aging. We hypothesize that the source of this change in brain utilization is the age-related neural changes in the older group. Thus this study points to a set of brain areas where there may be reorganization of brain responses as a response to aging. This change in network utilization would be a candidate for what we have termed neural compensation.

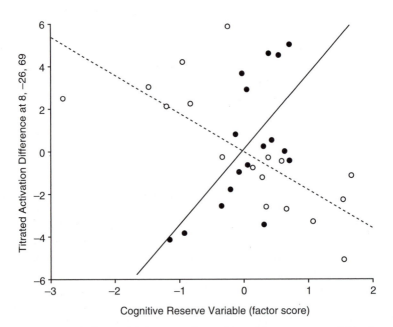

Figure 15.2   Voxel-wise multiple regression of cognitive reserve variable (*x* axis) against the change in activation from the low to the titrated demand condition (*y* axis) for the age groups in voxel $x = 8$, $y = 26$, $z = 69$ (cingulate gyrus; Brodmann's area 31). Young in black circles—solid regression line, old in white circles—dashed regression line.

In a separate analysis of these data (Stern et al., 2005), we used covariance analysis to identify a set of functionally connected regions that changed in expression across the two task conditions and was differentially expressed by the young and elderly subjects. The regions most active in this brain network consisted of right hippocampus, posterior insula, thalamus, and right and left operculum; and concomitant deactivation in right lingual gyrus, inferior parietal lobe, association cortex, left posterior cingulate, and right and left calcarine cortex. The mean expression of this topography was more positive for the older group.

Since young subjects operate without the burden of any age-related physiologic changes, we began by evaluating expression of this network in the young group. The mean expression of this network in the young subjects was lower than that in the old subjects, but the correlation between network expression and reserve was positive. Thus in the transition from low to titrated demand condition the higher their level of CR, the more young subjects increased their activation in regions with positive loadings, with concomitantly decreased activation in regions with negative loadings. The differential utilization of this topography by young subjects as a function of CR is consistent with our prediction of the behavior of a neural reserve network.

In the elders, the correlation between the CR index and their expression of the age-related topography was negative. That is, the higher their level of CR, the more old subjects increased their activation in regions with negative loadings and decreased their activation in regions with positive loadings in the transition from the low to the titrated demand condition. Thus, as in the young subjects, individual differences in elder subjects' network expression in response to increased task demand correlated with a measure of CR. However, the direction of this relationship was the opposite of that seen in the young subjects.

Since the young subjects have no age-related neural changes, we can speculate that the different relationship between CR and topographic expression in the two groups is due to some age-related physiological change in the older subjects. As a response to these changes, perhaps as a function of longer-term brain adaptation, the older subjects make use of an altered network, causing the activation of the regions captured in the covariance pattern to switch sign. This results in higher CR being associated with increased utilization of some brain areas with more positive network expression in one group, and more negative expression in the other. The age-related changes in network expression are thus most consistent with our definition of neural compensation.

One point that is stressed in all of these studies is the careful control of task difficulty. Without control of difficulty, we cannot be sure that between-subject differences in activation are not simply a function of differences in the difficulty of the task for each subject. In the described studies, we used a titration procedure for this purpose. Another approach that we have implemented in ongoing studies is to parametrically vary task difficulty within each subject. This allows us to understand the neural response to changing task difficulty, how this response varies as a function of CR, and whether this response is affected by age or disease.

In summary, the studies reviewed represent the first steps in identifying the neural implementation of CR, and the concepts of neural reserve and compensation. We have begun with a nonverbal memory task, but have been generalizing our application of these concepts to other tasks as well. If cognitive reserve, as we conceive of it, allows people to cope with brain pathology and maintain effective functioning, then its implementation should not be specific to any particular task.

Acknowledgments

This work was supported by NIH grant RO1 AG26158.

References

Alexander, G. E., Furey, M. L., Grady, C. L., Pietrini, P., Mentis, M. J., & Schapiro, M. B. (1997). Association of premorbid function with cerebral metabolism in Alzheimer's disease: Implications for the reserve hypothesis. *American Journal of Psychiatry*, *154*, 165–172.

Cabeza, R. (2002). Hemispheric asymmetry reduction in older adults: The HAROLD model. *Psychology & Aging*, *17*, 85–100.

Cabeza, R., Anderson, N. D., Locantore, J. K., & McIntosh, A. R. (2002). Aging gracefully: Compensatory brain activity in high-performing older adults. *Neuroimage*, *17*, 1394–1402.

DeCarli, C., Atack, J. R., Ball, M. J., Kay, J. A., Grady, C. L., Fewster, P., et al. (1992). Post-mortem regional neurofibrillary tangle densities but not senile plaque densities are related to regional cerebral metabolic rates for glucose during life in Alzheimer's disease patients. *Neurodegeneration*, *1*, 113–121.

Friedland, R. P., Brun, A., & Bundinger, T. F. (1985). Pathological and positron emission tomographic correlations in Alzheimer's disease. *Lancet*, *1*, 1–228.

Grober, E., & Sliwinski, M. (1991). Development and validation of a model for estimating premorbid verbal intelligence in the elderly. *Journal of Clinical and Experimental Neuropsychology*, *13*, 933–949.

Habeck, C., Hilton, H. J., Zarahn, E., Flynn, J., Moeller, J. R., & Stern, Y. (2003). Relation of cognitive reserve and task performance to expression of regional covariance networks in an event-related fMRI study of non-verbal memory. *Neuroimage*, *20*, 1723–1733.

Habeck, C., Krakauer, J. W., Ghez, C., Sackeim, H. A., Eidelberg, D., Stern, Y., et al. (2005). A new approach to spatial covariance modeling of functional brain imaging data: Ordinal trend analysis. *Neural Computation*, *17*, 1602–1645.

McGeer, E. G., McGeer, P. L., Harrop, R., Akiyama, H., & Kamo, H. (1990). Correlations of regional postmortem enzyme activities with premortem local glucose metabolic rates in Alzheimer's disease. *Journal of Neuroscience Research*, *27*, 612–619.

Nelson, H. E. (1982). *The National Adult Reading Test (NART): Test manual*. Windsor, UK: NFER-Nelson.

Scarmeas, N., Zarahn, E., Anderson, K. E., Habeck, C. G., Hilton, H. J., Flynn, J., et al. (2003a). Association of leisure activities with cerebral blood flow in Alzheimer's disease: Implications for the cognitive reserve hypothesis. *Archives of Neurology, 60,* 359–365.

Scarmeas, N., Zarahn, E., Anderson, K. E., Hilton, H. J., Flynn, J., Van Heertum, R. L., et al. (2003b). Cognitive reserve modulates functional brain responses during memory tasks: A PET study in healthy young and elderly subjects. *Neuroimage, 19,* 1215–1227.

Stern, Y., Alexander, G. E., Prohovnik, I., & Mayeux, R. (1992). Inverse relationship between education and parietotemporal perfusion deficit in Alzheimer's disease. *Annals of Neurology, 32,* 371–375.

Stern, Y., Alexander, G. E., Prohovnik, I., Stricks, L., Link, B., Lennon, M. C., et al. (1995). Relationship between lifetime occupation and parietal flow: Implications for a reserve against Alzheimer's disease pathology. *Neurology, 45,* 55–60.

Stern, Y., Habeck, C., Moeller, J. R., Scarmeas, N., Anderson, K. E., Hilton, H. J., et al. (2005). Brain networks associated with cognitive reserve in healthy young and old adults. *Cerebral Cortex, 15,* 394–402.

Stern, Y., Zarahn, E., Hilton, H. J., Delapaz, R., Flynn, J., & Rakitin, B. (2003). Exploring the neural basis of cognitive reserve. *Journal of Clinical and Experimental Neuropsychology, 5,* 691–701.

16 Cognitive reserve in healthy aging and Alzheimer disease: Evidence for compensatory reorganization of brain networks

Cheryl L. Grady

Age differences in cognitive function have been studied for many years, and of all the cognitive domains, memory has probably been studied the most. This rich literature has shown that older adults have particular difficulty with episodic memory, defined as the conscious recollection of events that have occurred in a person's experience (Tulving, 1983). In the laboratory, these age differences in episodic memory are seen in a reduced ability to learn and retrieve lists of stimuli (for a review see Craik & Bosman, 1992). Reductions in recall of real-life, autobiographical memories also have been reported (Levine, Svoboda, Hay, Winocur, & Moscovitch, 2002; Marchal et al., 1992). Age-related difficulties in episodic memory may be related to deficits in encoding new material (Craik & Byrd, 1982), as well as to reductions in the adequacy of retrieval (Burke & Light, 1981). Substantial age-related declines also are seen on working memory tasks (for reviews see Balota, Dolan, & Duchek, 2000; Zacks, Hasher, & Li, 2000), but semantic memory, or the accumulation of knowledge about the world, is maintained in older adults (Craik & Jennings, 1992).

Dysfunction in episodic memory also is a hallmark of Alzheimer disease (AD), and is one of the earliest and most devastating symptoms (Grady et al., 1988; Jacobs, Sano, Dooneief, Marder, Bell, & Stern, 1995; Price, Gurvit, Weintraub, Geula, Leimkuhler, & Mesulam, 1993; Zec, 1993). This early impairment of episodic memory in AD is consistent with the damage to medial temporal structures, including the hippocampus and entorhinal cortex, that is thought to occur early in the disease (Braak, Braak, & Bohl, 1993; Kemper, 1994). Unlike healthy aging, semantic memory also is impaired early in AD, although to a lesser extent than episodic memory (Chan, Butters, & Salmon, 1997; Ober & Shenaut, 1999). This deficit generally consists of lost access to specific information about object attributes (Binetti, Magni, Cappa, Padovani, Bianchetti, & Tabucchi, 1995; Giffard et al., 2001; Hodges, Salmon, & Butters, 1992).

In recent years, functional neuroimaging has been used to study how these differences in memory between young and old adults, and between healthy older adults and patients with AD, are expressed in terms of brain activity. When brain activity in young and older adults is compared on a task, there are at least three possible outcomes in any given brain area: (1) young and old groups could have equivalent brain activity, (2) older adults could show less activity, or (3) old adults could show greater activity. Reduced activity in the elderly can reasonably be assumed to reflect a reduced level of functioning, particularly when accompanied by poorer performance on the task. Equivalent activity is generally considered evidence for spared function in the elderly. The major challenge facing researchers in this field is how to interpret increased recruitment of additional or different brain activity in the elderly or in patients with dementia.

The complexity of this issue is illustrated by patterns of age differences found in prefrontal cortex. First, there is evidence that older adults who perform better on memory tasks recruit prefrontal cortex to a greater degree than those perfoming less well (Cabeza, Anderson, Locantore, & McIntosh, 2002; Grady, Bernstein, Siegenthaler, & Beig, 2002; Grady, McIntosh, & Craik, 2003), suggesting that this increased frontal activity can compensate for reduced activity elsewhere in the brain. As a consequence of this compensation, task performance is maintained or improved. On the other hand, prefrontal cortex increases its activity when tasks emphasize executive functions (e.g., D'Esposito, Detre, Alsop, Shin, Atlas, & Grossman, 1995; D'Esposito, Postle, Ballard, & Lease, 1999) or become more difficult (e.g., Braver, Cohen, Nystrom, Jonides, Smith, & Noll, 1997; Grady et al., 1996). It is possible then that increased prefrontal activity in the elderly under some conditions may reflect greater need or use of executive functions at lower levels of task demand than would be necessary for activation of this area in young adults. In this case the increased activity in prefrontal cortex might not be related at all to performance on the particular task, but would reflect a type of non-selective recruitment in older adults (Logan, Sanders, Snyder, Morris, & Buckner, 2002). It is also possible that greater recruitment of prefrontal cortex could represent a failure of some cognitive process in older adults, or engagement of less effective strategies for carrying out the task, that would be associated with worse performance. A potential example of this kind of result is the report that prefrontal activity is associated with slower reaction times in the elderly (Grady, 2002). In short, there are a number of ways in which different recruitment of specific brain areas could be interpreted in older adults or AD patients, and the mechanism may vary with the particular task demands under study.

The best way to resolve this issue may be to systematically relate behavioral performance with brain activity. This is the approach I have taken in much of my own research, and in this chapter I evaluate whether these experiments have supported the idea of compensatory activity in older adults or patients with AD. The focus in this review is on memory experiments, but results from experiments on other types of cognitive processing are also covered. In addition, this work has made extensive use of multivariate analyses of measurements of covariance among brain areas and between brain activity and performance indices. Multivariate approaches, such as principal component analysis or partial least squares (Friston, Frith, Liddle, & Frackowiak, 1993; McIntosh, 1999; Moeller & Strother, 1991), are used to identify brain areas that show the same pattern of functional changes during the experimental tasks. Groups of regions thus identified can be thought of as the networks that underlie cognitive processing. Functional connectivity is another type of network-based approach and involves assessing how activity in a given region covaries with activity in other areas of the brain during a task (Friston et al., 1993; Horwitz, 1994; McIntosh, 1999). This type of correlation can be done on a pairwise region basis or across the whole brain, and it requires no assumptions about how the influence of one region on another is actually brought about. Effective connectivity, on the other hand, is a related type of analysis that models the way brain areas influence one another, and tests whether the model fits the data at hand (Aertsen, Bonhoeffer, & Kruger, 1987; Friston, 1994; McIntosh & Gonzalez-Lima, 1994). In a practical sense, the two ways of assessing connectivity can be thought of as measuring correlations among a group of brain regions (functional connectivity) and decomposing this correlation matrix to determine the direction of influences, i.e., from one region to another, as well as the magnitude of these influences (effective connectivity). Thus connectivity approaches emphasize the functional interactions among brain areas and the ways in which these interactions mediate cognitive processing, rather than the activity in any individual brain region. One way of thinking about this approach that has come from the use of network analysis is that of a *neural context* (McIntosh, 2000). At any instance, the interactions of a given brain region may shift from one afferent/efferent source to another, resulting in a change in cognition or behavior. Across several different tasks, a brain area may show the same activity pattern but serve different functions because of the relation of that activity with other brain regions. The important factor is not that a particular event occurred at a particular site, but rather under what *neural context* did that event occur—in other words, what was the rest of the brain doing? The work described below attempts to answer this question, and to see what impact the answer has on behavioral outcome.

Evidence for compensation in healthy aging

My colleagues and I have searched for evidence of compensatory brain activity in older adults during both the encoding and the retrieval phases of episodic memory. In one such experiment, we examined the functional connectivity of the hippocampus during encoding in young and old adults, and the way in which this connectivity was related to recognition performance (Grady, McIntosh, & Craik, 2003). In this experiment young and older adults viewed pictures of common objects, and words corresponding to common objects, while undergoing positron emission tomography (PET) scans to measure brain activity. The stimuli were judged based on a semantic task (animacy) or a perceptual task (size or letter case). Later, after the scans were over, recognition memory for the words and pictures was tested. Both groups showed increased activity in medial temporal regions during picture encoding (Grady, McIntosh, Rajah, Beig, & Craik, 1999). In subsequent analyses we focused on the semantic encoding tasks, as recognition of items encoded using this task was equivalent in the young and old adults. This allowed us to examine connectivity differences due to age unconfounded by any differences that might be associated with performance level. Activity in the right hippocampus during encoding was associated with better subsequent memory despite the fact that activity in this area was not increased overall during word encoding. The functional connectivity of the hippocampus and activity in the rest of the brain was assessed, and the relation of the identifed network to recognition was determined to see if activity in the network *as a whole* mediated memory performance. During encoding of both words and pictures in young adults, hippocampal activity was correlated with activity in ventral prefrontal and extrastriate regions, and increased activity in all these regions was associated with better recognition (Figure 16.1). In contrast, older adults showed correlations between hippocampal activity and dorsolateral prefrontal and parietal regions, and positive correlations between activity in these regions and better memory performance. The results of this study provide evidence that aging is associated with alterations in hippocampal function, including how it is functionally connected with prefrontal cortex. The most important result was that these alterations have an impact on memory performance. The ventral/dorsal distinction seen with age suggests a shift in the cognitive resources utilized from more perceptually based processes (mediated by extrastriate cortex) to those involved in executive and organizational functions (mediated by dorsolateral prefrontal cortex (PFC)). This result also can be seen as evidence for compensation, i.e., older adults showed an encoding network that differed from that seen in young adults, and those individuals best able to recruit this network showed better memory.

We found similar evidence for recruitment of age-specific networks for face memory (Grady et al., 2002). In this experiment young and old adults encoded unfamilar faces and subsequently had their memory tested for these faces. Using the same multivariate approach (partial least squares, or PLS) that we had used for the functional connectivity analysis described above, we determined the network of regions that was associated with better performance on these face memory tasks. In young adults, better face memory was associated with more activity in medial temporal regions and ventral frontal cortex. In contrast, better memory in older adults was correlated with more activity in dorsolateral prefrontal and parietal regions. This result is strikingly similar to that found for words and objects, both of which suggest compensatory recruitment of dorsolateral prefrontal and parietal cortices in older adults during episodic memory tasks.

A more recent study used the same multivariate approach to examine the brain networks involved in performing recognition of words and objects (Grady, McIntosh, & Craik, 2005). This experiment used the same stimuli as

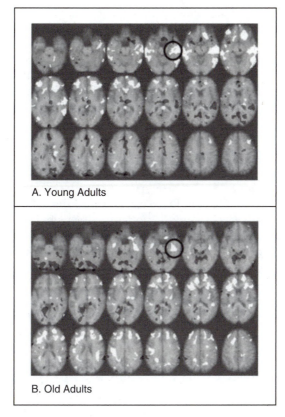

A. Young Adults

B. Old Adults

Figure 16.1   Brain areas where activity during object encoding was significantly correlated with activity in right hippocampus and with subsequent recognition performance in young adults (A) and old adults (B) are shown on
standard magnetic resonance images ranging from −28 mm to +48 mm
relative to the AC–PC line (the left side of the brain is seen on the left
side of the images). The right hippocampal region used for this connectivity analysis is indicated by the black circles. Regions shown in white
had positive correlations with activity in the hippocampus and recognition accuracy, whereas those in black had negative correlations with
both indices. Data are from Grady, McIntosh, and Craik (2003).

in the previous study, but the participants were scanned during recognition
rather than at encoding. Both young and old adults showed increased activity
during recognition, compared to a control task, in bilateral PFC. Young
adults showed greater activation of left hippocampus and lateral temporal
cortex during recognition, whereas older adults showed greater activity in
the right dorsolateral PFC. Age differences also were seen in correlations
between brain activity and memory performance. Better recognition performance in young adults was associated with activity in the right parahippocampal gyrus, anterior cingulate and inferior parietal cortex. In older
adults better recognition performance was correlated with increasing activity

in a number of prefrontal regions, temporal cortex, and occipital areas. These positive correlations included the right PFC region where older adults had greater activation. In addition, activity in this right PFC region was negatively correlated with medial temporal activity in both groups. There are several important aspects to these results. First, activity in the medial temporal lobe (MTL) was negatively correlated with activity in PFC during recognition in both young and older adults; unlike encoding, where MTL and PFC activity were positively correlated. This indicates that the functional connectivity of these two regions is task-dependent, as well as age-dependent. Second, MTL activity during recognition was associated with better memory only in young adults, again unlike encoding. This result suggests that MTL function in older adults during memory tasks can be disrupted, as previous studies have reported (Cabeza, Daselaar, Dolcos, Prince, Budde, & Nyberg, 2004; Grady et al., 1995; Mitchell, Johnson, Raye, & D'Esposito, 2000). Finally, the finding of a relation between dorsolateral PFC activity and performance only in older adults is consistent with that found during word and picture encoding and during face memory, adding further support for a compensatory role for this region. Further, the negative relation between MTL activity and PFC activity suggests that older individuals who recruit PFC to a greater degree may do so as a response to less effective processing by the MTL.

Several groups have used a different approach to assessing brain activity in the context of task performance but have found similar results. Morcom, Good, Frackowiak, and Rugg (2003) used event-related functional MRI (fMRI) to measure brain activity in young and old adults while they made animacy decisions about words. Activity was then examined for those words that later were successfully recognized. Activity during the animacy task in left inferior prefrontal cortex and the left hippocampus was greater for subsequently recognized words in both age groups. However, older adults also showed the same association between more activity and subsequent recognition in right prefrontal cortex. Gutchess et al. (2005) used a similar approach to study scene encoding in young and older adults. Compared to activity for forgotten items, activity during encoding of scenes that were subsequently remembered was greater in inferior frontal and lateral occipital regions for both younger and older adults. Older adults showed less activation than young adults in the parahippocampus bilaterally and more activation than young adults in frontal cortex. Moreover, correlations between inferior frontal and parahippocampal activity were significantly negative only for old adults. This result is similar to our finding, mentioned above, of negative correlation between MTL and PFC in older adults during recognition. These two studies are consistent with our work in showing that the MTL is consistently involved in memory function in young adults, but is often reduced in older adults. In addition all of these experiments indicate that the frontal regions assume a larger role in supporting successful recognition memory with increasing age.

Age differences in working memory (WM) and the relation between these differences and performance also have been studied using a number of different tasks. In one such experiment, young and old adults were imaged while they performed a delayed visual discrimination task, in which they determined which of two successively presented sine-wave gratings had the highest spatial frequency (Della-Maggiore, Sekuler, Grady, Bennett, Sekuler, & McIntosh, 2000; McIntosh et al., 1999). Behavioral performance was equal for the two groups, and activity in the hippocampus was positively correlated with performance across groups. However, an analysis of the cortical regions that were functionally connected to the hippocampus showed that a different hippocampal network supported performance in the elderly. The young adults engaged a network that included anterior prefrontal cortex, fusiform gyrus, and posterior cingulate gyrus. In contrast, the network recruited by the old included dorsolateral prefrontal cortex, middle cingulate gyrus, and caudate nucleus. Recruitment of a distinct corticolimbic network for visual WM in the elderly suggests that aging results in the modification of large-scale network operations, which in turn have an impact on WM, as well as on episodic memory. In addition the recruitment by older adults of dorsolateral PFC on this WM task, as well as on episodic tasks, suggests that this may be a general response across multiple cognitive domains.

In another experiment young and old adults performed a delayed match-to-sample task for faces, in which the delay between the sample and choice faces was varied from 1 to 21 seconds (Grady, McIntosh, Bookstein, Horwitz, Rapoport, & Haxby, 1998). Reaction time was slower and accuracy lower in the old group, but not markedly so. Many brain regions showed similar activity during these tasks in both young and old adults, including left anterior prefrontal cortex, which had increased activity with delay, and ventral extrastriate cortex, which showed decreased activity with delay. However, old adults had less modulation of activity across delay in right ventro-lateral prefrontal cortex, and greater activation in left dorsolateral prefrontal cortex compared to young adults. Activity in frontal regions was differentially related to performance in that it was associated with decreasing response times in the young group and increasing response times in the older individuals. Thus, despite the finding that performance on these memory tasks and associated activity in a number of brain areas are relatively preserved in old adults, differences elsewhere in the brain suggest that different strategies or cognitive processes are used by the elderly to maintain memory representations over short periods of time.

Before going on to the next section on dementia, it is important to consider how reliable or how generalizable age differences are across experiments. I have already presented evidence that a number of studies have shown similar age differences in how brain activity is related to memory performance, with notable consistencies in PFC. The issue of generality also has been addressed directly in two studies. In one of these, a meta-analysis of brain activity in young and old adults was carried out using data across three face processing experiments: episodic memory, working memory, and degraded face perception (Grady, 2002). Each experiment contained an easy face matching condition and a more difficult processing condition. Young adults showed greater activity in bilateral prefrontal cortex during the memory tasks, compared to face matching, but no difference in prefrontal activity between degraded and nondegraded perception. Older adults, on the other hand, had greater prefrontal activity in both memory and degraded perceptual tasks compared to matching. This suggests that increased prefrontal activity is task-specific in young adults, but, in old adults, is a more general response to increased cognitive effort or need for resources.

Using another approach Cabeza et al. (2004) scanned younger and older adults while they performed three different tasks: working memory, visual attention and episodic retrieval. In all three tasks, older adults showed less occipital and hippocampal activity and more prefrontal and parietal activity compared to younger adults. The age reductions across the three tasks were interesting in light of suggestions that there is a "common cause" of cognitive aging (Salthouse, Atkinson, & Berish, 2003; Salthouse & Ferrer-Caja, 2003), and indicate that both sensory processing and memory encoding could be involved in such a common cause. The prefrontal increase was interpreted as further evidence for functional compensation in the elderly participants. Taken together with the meta-analysis, these results indicate that some of the age differences in brain activity that have been reported, particularly alterations of prefrontal and MTL activity, generalize across task conditions and appear to play an important role in multiple cognitive domains.

Evidence for compensation in Alzheimer disease

There are fewer studies examining the relation between brain activity and behavior in patients with AD, and some of this work is covered in other chapters in this volume. Some early experiments found that individuals with AD had increased activity in prefrontal regions compared with healthy age-matched controls during cognitive tasks (Backman, Andersson, Nyberg, Winblad, Nordberg, & Almkvist, 1999; Becker, Mintun, Aleva, Wiseman, Nichols, & DeKosky, 1996; Grady et al., 1993; Woodard, Grafton, Votaw, Green, Dobraski, & Hoffman, 1998). This was typically interpreted as compensatory reallocation of cognitive resources, but direct evidence for a facilitating effect on performance was scarce. To address this issue we measured neural activity during semantic and episodic memory tasks in mildly demented AD patients and healthy elderly controls (Grady, McIntosh, Beig, Keightley, Burian, & Black, 2003). Activity was increased in a similar set of regions in both groups, and in both tasks, including left prefrontal and occipital cortex. However, when the functional connectivity of the left prefrontal region was assessed, different patterns of connectivity were found in the two groups. Controls recruited a left hemisphere network of regions, including temporal and occipital cortex, in both the semantic and episodic tasks. Patients engaged a unique network that included temporal and occipital cortex, but involved both hemispheres. Of particular interest was that the patients also recruited bilateral dorsolateral prefrontal regions into this network. Critically, activity in this entire network of regions in the patient group was correlated with better performance on both the semantic and episodic tasks. This provides direct evidence that AD patients, like healthy elderly, can use additional neural resources in prefrontal cortex, presumably those mediating executive functions, to compensate for losses of cognitive function.

We have also found altered networks in AD patients during working memory tasks. We used the same delayed match-to-sample face task mentioned above (Grady et al., 1998), with delays from 1 to 16 seconds between the sample and choice faces. There was no change in recognition accuracy with increasing delay in controls, whereas patients showed impaired recognition over all delays that worsened as delay increased. Both groups showed increased activity in right prefrontal cortex with increasing memory delay, but the functional connectivity of right PFC differed between the groups. Controls showed connectivity between right prefrontal cortex and left prefrontal regions, as well as with visual regions and the right hippocampus. In the patients, activity in right prefrontal cortex was correlated mainly with other prefrontal regions. These results support the idea of a functional disconnection between prefrontal cortex and hippocampus, and suggest that memory breakdown in early AD is related to a reduction in the integrated activity within a distributed network that includes these two areas. However increased activity in right prefrontal regions was associated with better memory performance in both groups, and activity in left prefrontal cortex was also associated with better memory in the patients. This result is similar to that seen in the previously mentioned experiment, and in fact there were common areas of PFC where increased activity was associated with better performance in AD patients for semantic memory, episodic memory, and working memory (Figure 16.2). This suggests that AD patients can recruit some of the same regions to support performance as healthy elders do (e.g., right PFC) but recruitment of PFC in AD patients is more widespread. This similarity may indicate that frontal recruitment may be a general compensatory mechanism in response to functional loss due to a variety of causes.

In addition to the frontal changes, and of more relevance to the idea of compensation, activity in the left amygdala was increased with memory delay in this face task in the AD patients. This activity also was correlated with better recognition performance in this group. This pattern of activity was not seen in the healthy elderly group. In addition the functional connectivity of the amygdala differed between groups. Areas where activity was correlated with the left amygdala in AD patients included the bilateral posterior parahippocampal gyri, a number of left prefrontal regions, anterior and posterior cingulate, thalamus, and insula. The control group had a relatively restricted set of regions where activity correlated with the left

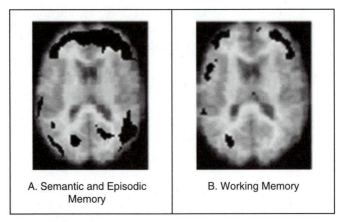

A. Semantic and Episodic
Memory

B. Working Memory

Figure 16.2   Brain areas where activity is associated with better task performance in
mildly demented AD patients during semantic and episodic memory
tasks (A) and a face working memory task (B). In both cases better task
performance was associated with more activity in the areas shown in
black, most notably bilateral prefrontal regions. Data are from Grady et
al. (2003) and Grady, Furey, Pietrini, Horwitz, and Rapoport (2001).

amygdala, mainly temporal and occipital areas. This result is interesting,
given the role of the amygdala in assessing emotional expressions in faces
(Morris et al., 1996), even when this emotional content is not the focus of
attention (Critchley et al., 2000; Keightley, Winocur, Graham, Mayberg,
Hevenor, & Grady, 2003), as was the case in this working memory task. This
result suggests that the patients may have processed the emotional content of
the faces even though not instructed to do so, and to a greater degree than did
the controls. Further, the positive association between amygdala activity and
memory performance in the patients suggests a possible compensatory role
for this region in face memory, in addition to that suggested for frontal
cortex.

Results consistent with the idea that AD patients recruit different networks involving the frontal lobes also has been found in a non-memory task.
We used a face matching task similar to that discussed above (Grady, 2002) in
a group of mildly demented AD patients and healthy controls (Grady et al.,
1993). Activation patterns in the AD group were similar to controls in areas
known to be responsible for object and face processing, i.e., the ventral visual
processing stream (Haxby, Horwitz, Ungerleider, Maisog, Pietrini, & Grady,
1994; Kanwisher, McDermott, & Chun, 1997; Ungerleider & Mishkin, 1982),
but they showed greater relative activation in dorsal prefrontal cortices compared to controls. More importantly, the AD patients showed a pattern of
interactions in the ventral stream network that was decidedly different from
controls (Horwitz et al., 1995). AD patients had a functional disconnection
of occipitotemporal and frontal regions, similar to the disconnection between
MTL and frontal regions seen during WM (see above). However, increased

functional connectivity was observed in the patients among prefrontal regions, as we also observed during memory tasks.

Unresolved issues

It is clear from the evidence to date that both healthy aging and early stage AD are associated with alterations of the brain networks that underlie cognition. Further, these alterations are frequently, although not invariably, associated with better task performance, and hence provide evidence in favor of the compensation hypothesis. This evidence has fueled considerable interest in the neuroscience of cognitive aging, and in the process has uncovered more questions about how such compensation might work and how it might arise. In the remaining section of this chapter I discuss these questions and how we might go about answering them.

One question is whether changes in brain activity with age indicate that young and old adults use different cognitive processes to carry out the same task, even if they presumably follow the same set of instructions, or whether over time different brain areas come to be used for the same cognitive process. That is, does a given cognitive process become represented differently in the brain as we age? Another way of expressing this question is to ask if these differences that we see in brain activity with age are changes in how cognition is carried out or changes in strategy use by older adults. In some sense the answer to this question may not be a critical one, as cognitive strategies and the brain activity that mediates them are very closely intertwined. Researchers in the field of functional neuroimaging routinely make inferences from cognitive strategy to brain area and vice versa, and it is not clear if the two can be separated. A more reasonable question to ask may be which comes first, the change in brain function necessitating a change in strategy or a change in strategy that is reflected in brain activity. Unfortunately it may be very difficult to distinguish between these two alternatives except by longitudinal studies.

On the other hand, one way to think about this question is to ask whether rehabilitation or cognitive training can influence brain activity as well as behavior. That is, if older adults are taught different strategies to use for memory, does this lead to more recruitment of prefrontal cortex as well as improvement in memory tasks? If the answer is "yes," then this suggests that it is at least possible that some of the compensatory changes noted in older brains have occurred because individuals have adopted different strategies. In addition, the question of whether compensation can be taught is interesting in its own right. Studies to address this issue are currently underway so we may have some answers to these questions in the near future.

Another important question about alterations in cognitive networks with age is when in the life span these changes occur. It is likely that the differences in brain activity seen in older adults have developed gradually over time, but it is not known at what age these changes would begin. It is conceivable that our brains are continually changing over the life span, with new experiences and as new information is acquired, and that the effects of advanced age are just part of this evolution. Longitudinal studies would address this problem, but given the difficulty of doing these, studying a middle aged group along with a young and an old sample would begin to address this issue.

There also are issues specific to connectivity studies that have yet to be resolved. For example, results to date indicate that older adults engage different brain networks even when their performance on the task in question is equivalent to that seen in young adults. This raises the question of whether old and young groups will *always* be different in terms of their cognitive networks, or whether there are some task conditions in which these would be the same. It is possible, and perhaps likely, that for simple perceptual or sensorimotor tasks, such as pressing a button to a specified stimulus, the recruited network would not differ with age, but this has not been tested. Clearly, there must be constraints on the degree to which networks can be altered, as well as aspects that remain invariant with age, but these limits have not been determined. In addition, most tasks involve more than one cognitive process, as well as motor components, so that multiple networks are probably active simultaneously. Little is known about how these processes and networks interact with one another in young adults, much less in older adults.

Another interesting question is the extent to which the network alterations seen in older adults are due to changes in the function of the brain regions themselves or to changes in the white matter tracts that connect the regions. Communication between cortical regions could be reduced or altered because the neurons in the regions themselves have altered function or because the fibers that connect them are damaged or less efficient. Changes with age in white matter, and the impact of these on cognition, have been documented (e.g. DeCarli et al., 1995; Garde, Mortensen, Krabbe, Rostrup, & Larsson, 2000; Gunning-Dixon & Raz, 2000; Pfefferbaum, Sullivan, Hedehus, Lim, Adalsteinsson, & Moseley, 2000) but how these changes affect functional connectivity of gray matter regions during cognitive tasks is unknown. Recent evidence (see review by Buckner, 2004) indicates that age differences in white matter are more prominent in frontal than posterior brain areas. Others have also reported that frontal regions have more atrophic changes in older adults than other brain areas (Raz, 2000). These structural changes are consistent with age changes in frontal activity that suggest non-selectivity, but not with evidence that frontal cortex is most often recruited for compensatory purposes. Clearly we have much to learn about the complex interplay between brain structure and function, and how this interaction is affected by age.

The influence of other factors on cognitive networks and age-related changes in these networks is another area where much is unknown. One such factor is education, which has been shown to have a protective effect against decline in cognitive function in healthy older adults and in patients with dementia. For example, more years of education have been associated with a slower age-related decline in memory (Colsher & Wallace, 1991; Evans et al.,

1993), mental status (Lyketsos, Chen, & Anthony, 1999; Starr, Deary, Inch, Cross, & MacLennan, 1997), and verbal ability (Arbuckle, Maag, Pushkar, & Chaikelson, 1998; Christensen et al., 1997). We found that in young adults education was negatively correlated with frontal activity, whereas in older adults education was positively correlated with frontal activity (Springer, McIntosh, Winocur, & Grady, 2005). Medial temporal activity was associated with more education in young adults, but less education in older adults. This finding is consistent with the evidence of greater frontal recruitment by older adults and suggests that frontal cortex is engaged particularly by those older adults who are highly educated. Thus it may be that compensatory brain activity in older adults is most likely to be seen in those with higher education. Other variables, such as personality traits or mood, have yet to be examined, but also could be influencing brain network activity in older adults.

Finally, the observant reader will have noticed that the discussion of age differences in this review has focused on areas of the brain that are "activated" during task performance, i.e., have increased activity over some baseline condition. However, recent research has indicated the importance of "deactivations," or those areas where activity actually goes down during performance of a task. These areas, called the "default mode" network (Raichle, MacLeod, Snyder, Powers, Gusnard, & Shulman, 2001), are thought to accompany the monitoring and evaluating of one's environment and internal milieu, and are suppressed when participants are engaged in a specific task. A reduction in the suppression of default mode activity has been noted in healthy older adults, compared to young adults (Lustig et al., 2003), and in patients with AD (Greicius, Srivastava, Reiss, & Menon, 2004; Lustig et al., 2003). A reduction in the ability to suspend non-task related, or "default mode" activity might reflect an alteration in the balance between default mode and task-related activity that could adversely affect multiple cognitive domains. Still to be determined is how an altered balance between default mode and task-specific activity influences the changes in cognitive networks observed in older adults.

Conclusion

Functional neuroimaging has provided some intriguing insights into the field of cognitive aging, but has provided us with some new challenges as well. The use of network approaches to image analysis has, in particular, provided information about how brain areas work together to mediate memory function and how these networks change with age or with degenerative brain disease. Perhaps the most important use of this approach is to examine how changes in the functional organization of these networks impacts on the ability of individuals to carry out cognitive functions, such as remembering new information. Evidence to date would suggest that increased recruitment of dorsolateral prefrontal cortex and functional interactions between dorsolateral prefrontal and medial temporal regions are associated with better memory performance in older adults. These alterations in the memory networks may thus be compensatory, at least for some types of tasks. Clearly the goals of future research will be to understand the task conditions that promote this compensation, the role of the various brain areas in aiding memory function, and how these compensatory mechanisms can be elicited to enhance rehabilitation efforts.

References

Aertsen, A., Bonhoeffer, T., & Kruger, J. (1987). Coherent activity in neuronal populations: analysis and interpretation. In E. R. Caianiello (Ed.), *Physics of cognitive processes* (pp. 1–34). Singapore: World Scientific Publishing.

Arbuckle, T. Y., Maag, U., Pushkar, D., & Chaikelson, J. S. (1998). Individual differences in trajectory of intellectual development over 45 years of adulthood. *Psychology and Aging*, *13*, 663–675.

Backman, L., Andersson, J. L. R., Nyberg, L., Winblad, B., Nordberg, A., & Almkvist, O. (1999). Brain regions associated with episodic retrieval in normal aging and Alzheimer's disease. *Neurology*, *52*, 1861–1870.

Balota, D. A., Dolan, P. O., & Duchek, J. M. (2000). Memory changes in healthy older adults. In E. Tulving & F. I. M. Craik (Eds.), *The Oxford handbook of memory* (pp. 395–409). New York: Oxford University Press.

Becker, J. T., Mintun, M. A., Aleva, K., Wiseman, M. B., Nichols, T., & DeKosky, S. T. (1996). Compensatory reallocation of brain resources supporting verbal episodic memory in Alzheimer's disease. *Neurology*, *46*, 692–700.

Binetti, G., Magni, E., Cappa, S. F., Padovani, A., Bianchetti, A., & Trabucchi, M. (1995). Semantic memory in Alzheimer's disease: An analysis of category fluency. *Journal of Clinical & Experimental Neuropsychology*, *17*, 82–89.

Braak, H., Braak, E., & Bohl, J. (1993). Staging of Alzheimer-related cortical destruction. *European Neurology*, *33*, 403–408.

Braver, T. S., Cohen, J. D., Nystrom, L. E., Jonides, J., Smith, E. E., & Noll, D. C. (1997). A parametric study of prefrontal cortex involvement in human working memory. *NeuroImage*, *5*, 49–62.

Buckner, R. L. (2004). Memory and executive function in aging and AD: Multiple factors that cause decline and reserve factors that compensate. *Neuron*, *44*, 195–208.

Burke, D. M., & Light, L. L. (1981). Memory and aging: The role of retrieval processes. *Psychological Bulletin*, *90*, 513–546.

Cabeza, R., Anderson, N. D., Locantore, J. K., & McIntosh, A. R. (2002). Aging gracefully: Compensatory brain activity in high-performing older adults. *NeuroImage*, *17*, 1394–1402.

Cabeza, R., Daselaar, S. M., Dolcos, F., Prince, S. E., Budde, M., & Nyberg, L. (2004). Task-independent and task-specific age effects on brain activity during working memory, visual attention and episodic retrieval. *Cerebral Cortex*, *14*, 364–375.

Chan, A. S., Butters, N., & Salmon, D. P. (1997). The deterioration of semantic networks in patients with Alzheimer's disease: A cross-sectional study. *Neuropsychologia*, *35*, 241–248.

Christensen, H., Korten, A. E., Jorm, A. F., Henderson, A. S., Jacomb, P. A., Rodgers, B., et al. (1997). Education and decline in cognitive performance: Compensatory but not protective. *International Journal of Geriatric Psychiatry, 12*, 323–330.

Colsher, P. L., & Wallace, R. B. (1991). Longitudinal application of cognitive function measures in a defined population of community-dwelling elders. *Annals of Epidemiology, 1*, 215–230.

Craik, F. I. M., & Bosman, E. A. (1992). Age-related changes in memory and learning. In H. Bouma & J. Graafmans (Eds.), *Gerontechnology: Proceedings of the first international conference on technology and aging* (pp. 79–92). Eindhoven: IOS Press.

Craik, F. I. M., & Byrd, M. (1982). Aging and cognitive deficits: The role of attentional resources. In F. I. M. Craik & S. Trehub (Eds.), *Aging and cognitive processes* (pp. 191–211). New York: Plenum Press.

Craik, F. I. M., & Jennings, J. M. (1992). Human memory. In F. I. M. Craik & T. A. Salthouse (Eds.), *The handbook of aging and cognition* (pp. 51–110). Hillsdale, NJ: Lawrence Erlbaum Associates, Inc.

Critchley, H., Daly, E., Phillips, M., Brammer, M., Bullmore, E., Williams, S., et al. (2000). Explicit and implicit neural mechanisms for processing of social information from facial expressions: A functional magnetic resonance imaging study. *Human Brain Mapping, 9*, 93–105.

DeCarli, C., Murphy, D. G., Tranh, M., Grady, C. L., Haxby, J. V., Gillette, J. A., et al. (1995). The effect of white matter hyperintensity volume on brain structure, cognitive performance, and cerebral metabolism of glucose in 51 healthy adults. *Neurology, 45*, 2077–2084.

Della-Maggiore, V., Sekuler, A. B., Grady, C. L., Bennett, P. J., Sekuler, R., & McIntosh, A. R. (2000). Corticolimbic interactions associated with performance on a short-term memory task are modified by age. *Journal of Neuroscience, 20*, 8410–8416.

D'Esposito, M., Detre, J. A., Alsop, D. C., Shin, R. K., Atlas, S., & Grossman, M. (1995). The neural basis of the central executive system of working memory. *Nature, 378*, 279–281.

D'Esposito, M., Postle, B. R., Ballard, D., & Lease, J. (1999). Maintenance versus manipulation of information held in working memory: An event-related fMRI study. *Brain and Cognition, 41*, 66–86.

Evans, D. A., Beckett, L. A., Albert, M. S., Hebert, L. E., Scherr, P. A., Funkenstein, H. H., et al. (1993). Level of education and change in cognitive function in a community population of older persons. *Annals of Epidemiology, 3*, 71–77.

Friston, K. J. (1994). Functional and effective connectivity: A synthesis. *Human Brain Mapping, 2*, 56–78.

Friston, K. J., Frith, C. D., Liddle, P. F., & Frackowiak, R. S. J. (1993). Functional connectivity: The principal-component analysis of large (PET) data sets. *Journal of Cerebral Blood Flow and Metabolism, 13*, 5–14.

Garde, E., Mortensen, E. L., Krabbe, K., Rostrup, E., & Larsson, H. B. (2000). Relation between age-related decline in intelligence and cerebral white-matter hyperintensities in healthy octogenarians: A longitudinal study. *Lancet, 356*, 628–634.

Giffard, B., Desgranges, B., Nore-Mary, F., Lalevee, C., de la Sayette, V., Pasquier, F., et al. (2001). The nature of semantic memory deficits in Alzheimer's disease: New insights from hyperpriming effects. *Brain, 124*, 1522–1532.

Grady, C. L. (2002). Age-related differences in face processing: A meta-analysis of three functional neuroimaging experiments. *Canadian Journal of Experimental Psychology, 56*, 208–220.

Grady, C. L., Bernstein, L., Siegenthaler, A., & Beig, S. (2002). The effects of encoding task on age-related differences in the functional neuroanatomy of face memory. *Psychology and Aging, 17*, 7–23.

Grady, C. L., Furey, M. L., Pietrini, P., Horwitz, B., & Rapoport, S. I. (2001). Altered brain functional connectivity and impaired short term memory in Alzheimer's disease. *Brain, 124*, 739–756.

Grady, C. L., Haxby, J. V., Horwitz, B., Gillette, J., Salerno, J. A., Gonzalez-Aviles, A., et al. (1993). Activation of cerebral blood flow during a face perception task in patients with dementia of the Alzheimer type. *Neurobiology of Aging, 14*, 35–44.

Grady, C. L., Haxby, J. V., Horwitz, B., Sundaram, M., Berg, G., Schapiro, M. B., et al. (1988). Longitudinal study of the early neuropsychological and cerebral metabolic changes in dementia of the Alzheimer type. *Journal of Clinical and Experimental Neuropsychology, 10*, 576–596.

Grady, C. L., Horwitz, B., Pietrini, P., Mentis, M. J., Ungerleider, L. G., Rapoport, S. I., et al. (1996). The effect of task difficulty on cerebral blood flow during perceptual matching of faces. *Human Brain Mapping, 4*, 227–239.

Grady, C. L., McIntosh, A. R., Beig, S., Keightley, M. L., Burian, H., & Black, S. E. (2003). Evidence from functional neuroimaging of a compensatory prefrontal network in Alzheimer disease. *Journal of Neuroscience, 23*, 986–993.

Grady, C. L., McIntosh, A. R., Bookstein, F., Horwitz, B., Rapoport, S. I., & Haxby, J. V. (1998). Age-related changes in regional cerebral blood flow during working memory for faces. *NeuroImage, 8*, 409–425.

Grady, C. L., McIntosh, A. R., & Craik, F. I. (2003). Age-related differences in the functional connectivity of the hippocampus during memory encoding. *Hippocampus, 13*, 572–586.

Grady, C. L., McIntosh, A. R., & Craik, F. (2005). Task-related activity in prefrontal cortex and its relation to recognition memory performance in young and old adults. *Neuropsychologia, 43*, 1466–1481.

Grady, C. L., McIntosh, A. R., Horwitz, B., Maisog, J. M., Ungerleider, L. G., Mentis, M. J., et al. (1995). Age-related reductions in human recognition memory due to impaired encoding. *Science, 269*, 218–221.

Grady, C. L., McIntosh, A. R., Rajah, M. N., Beig, S., & Craik, F. I. M. (1999). The effects of age on the neural correlates of episodic encoding. *Cerebral Cortex, 9*, 805–814.

Greicius, M. D., Srivastava, G., Reiss, A. L., & Menon, V. (2004). Default-mode network activity distinguishes Alzheimer's disease from healthy aging: Evidence from functional MRI. *Proceedings of the National Academy of Science USA, 101*, 4637–4642.

Gunning-Dixon, F. M., & Raz, N. (2000). The cognitive correlates of white matter abnormalities in normal aging: A quantitative review. *Neuropsychology, 14*, 224–232.

Gutchess, A. H., Welsh, R. C., Hedden, T., Bangert, A., Minear, M., Liu, L. L., et al. (2005). Aging and the neural correlates of successful picture encoding: Frontal activations compensate for decreased medial temporal activity. *Journal of Cognitive Neuroscience, 17*, 84–96.

Haxby, J. V., Horwitz, B., Ungerleider, L. G., Maisog, J. M., Pietrini, P., & Grady, C. L. (1994). The functional organization of human extrastriate cortex: A PET-rCBF study of selective attention to faces and locations. *Journal of Neuroscience, 14,* 6336–6353.

Hodges, J. R., Salmon, D. P., & Butters, N. (1992). Semantic memory impairment in Alzheimer's disease: Failure of access or degraded knowledge? *Neuropsychologia, 30,* 301–314.

Horwitz, B. (1994). Data analysis paradigms for metabolic-flow data: Combining neural modeling and functional neuroimaging. *Human Brain Mapping, 2,* 112–122.

Horwitz, B., McIntosh, A. R., Haxby, J. V., Furey, M., Salerno, J., Schapiro, M. B., et al. (1995). Network analysis of PET-mapped visual pathways in Alzheimer type dementia. *NeuroReport, 6,* 2287–2292.

Jacobs, D. M., Sano, M., Dooneief, G., Marder, K., Bell, K. L., & Stern, Y. (1995). Neuropsychological detection and characterization of preclinical Alzheimer's disease. *Neurology, 45,* 957–962.

Kanwisher, N., McDermott, J., & Chun, M. M. (1997). The fusiform face area: A module in human extrastriate cortex specialized for face perception. *Journal of Neuroscience, 17,* 4302–4311.

Keightley, M. L., Winocur, G., Graham, S. J., Mayberg, H. S., Hevenor, S. J., & Grady, C. L. (2003). An fMRI study investigating cognitive modulation of brain regions associated with emotional processing of visual stimuli. *Neuropsychologia, 41,* 585–596.

Kemper, T. L. (1994). Neuroanatomical and neuropathological changes during aging and in dementia. In M. L. Albert & E. J. E. Knoepfel (Eds.), *Clinical neurology of aging* (2nd ed., pp. 3–67). New York: Oxford University Press.

Levine, B., Svoboda, E., Hay, J., Winocur, G., & Moscovitch, M. (2002). Aging and autobiographical memory: Dissociating episodic from semantic retrieval. *Psychology and Aging, 17,* 677–689.

Logan, J. M., Sanders, A. L., Snyder, A. Z., Morris, J. C., & Buckner, R. L. (2002). Under-recruitment and nonselective recruitment: Dissociable neural mechanisms associated with aging. *Neuron, 33,* 827–840.

Lustig, C., Snyder, A. Z., Bhakta, M., O'Brien, K. C., McAvoy, M., Raichle, M. E., et al. (2003). Functional deactivations: Change with age and dementia of the Alzheimer type. *Proceedings of the National Academy of Science USA, 100,* 14504–14509.

Lyketsos, C. G., Chen, L. S., & Anthony, J. C. (1999). Cognitive decline in adulthood: an 11.5-year follow-up of the Baltimore Epidemiologic Catchment Area study. *American Journal of Psychiatry, 156,* 58–65.

Marchal, G., Rioux, P., Petit-Taboue, M. C., Sette, G., Travere, J. M., Le Poec, C., et al. (1992). Regional cerebral oxygen consumption, blood flow, and blood volume in healthy human aging. *Archives of Neurology, 49,* 1013–1020.

McIntosh, A. R. (1999). Mapping cognition to the brain through neural interactions. *Memory, 7,* 523–548.

McIntosh, A. R. (2000). Towards a network theory of cognition. *Neural Networks, 13,* 861–870.

McIntosh, A. R., & Gonzalez-Lima, F. (1994). Structural equation modeling and its application to network analysis in functional brain imaging. *Human Brain Mapping, 2,* 2–22.

McIntosh, A. R., Sekuler, A. B., Penpeci, C., Rajah, M. N., Grady, C. L., Sekuler, R., et al. (1999). Recruitment of unique neural systems to support visual memory in normal aging. *Current Biology*, *9*, 1275–1278.

Mitchell, K. J., Johnson, M. K., Raye, C. L., & D'Esposito, M. (2000). fMRI evidence of age-related hippocampal dysfunction in feature binding in working memory. *Cognitive Brain Research*, *10*, 197–206.

Moeller, J. R., & Strother, S. C. (1991). A regional covariance approach to the analysis of functional patterns in positron emission tomographic data. *Journal of Cerebral Blood Flow and Metabolism*, *11*, A121–A135.

Morcom, A. M., Good, C. D., Frackowiak, R. S., & Rugg, M. D. (2003). Age effects on the neural correlates of successful memory encoding. *Brain*, *126*, 213–229.

Morris, J. S., Frith, C. D., Perrett, D. I., Rowland, D., Young, A. W., Calder, A. J., et al. (1996). A differential neural response in the human amygdala to fearful and happy facial expressions. *Nature*, *383*, 812–815.

Ober, B. A., & Shenaut, G. K. (1999). Well-organized conceptual domains in Alzheimer's disease. *Journal of the International Neuropsychological Society*, *5*, 676–684.

Pfefferbaum, A., Sullivan, E. V., Hedehus, M., Lim, K. O., Adalsteinsson, E., & Moseley, M. (2000). Age-related decline in brain white matter anisotropy measured with spatially corrected echo-planar diffusion tensor imaging. *Magnetic Resonance in Medicine*, *44*, 259–268.

Price, B. H., Gurvit, H., Weintraub, S., Geula, C., Leimkuhler, E., & Mesulam, M. (1993). Neuropsychological patterns and language deficits in 20 consecutive cases of autopsy-confirmed Alzheimer's disease. *Archives of Neurology*, *50*, 931–937.

Raichle, M. E., MacLeod, A. M., Snyder, A. Z., Powers, W. J., Gusnard, D. A., & Shulman, G. L. (2001). A default mode of brain function. *Proceedings of the National Academy of Science USA*, *98*, 676–682.

Raz, N. (2000). Aging of the brain and its impact on cognitive performance: Integration of structural and functional findings. In F. I. M. Craik & T. A. Salthouse (Eds.), *Handbook of aging and cognition—II* (pp. 1–90). Mahwah, NJ: Lawrence Erlbaum Associates, Inc.

Salthouse, T. A., & Ferrer-Caja, E. (2003). What needs to be explained to account for age-related effects on multiple cognitive variables? *Psychology and Aging*, *18*, 91–110.

Salthouse, T. A., Atkinson, T. M., & Berish, D. E. (2003). Executive functioning as a potential mediator of age-related cognitive decline in normal adults. *Journal of Experimental Psychology: General*, *132*, 566–594.

Springer, M. V., McIntosh, A. R., Winocur, G., & Grady, C. L. (2005). The relation between brain activity during memory tasks and years of education in young and old adults. *Neuropsychology*, *19*, 181–192.

Starr, J. M., Deary, I. J., Inch, S., Cross, S., & MacLennan, W. J. (1997). Blood pressure and cognitive decline in healthy old people. *Journal of Human Hypertension*, *11*, 777–781.

Tulving, E. (1983). *Elements of episodic memory*. New York: Oxford University Press.

Ungerleider, L. G., & Mishkin, M. (1982). Two cortical visual systems. In D. J. Ingle, M. A. Goodale, & R. J. W. Mansfield (Eds.), *Analysis of visual behavior* (pp. 549–586). Cambridge, MA: MIT Press.

Woodard, J. L., Grafton, S. T., Votaw, J. R., Green, R. C., Dobraski, M. E., & Hoffman, J. M. (1998). Compensatory recruitment of neural resources during overt rehearsal of word lists in Alzheimer's disease. *Neuropsychology, 12*, 491–504.

Zacks, R. T., Hasher, L., & Li, K. Z. H. (2000). Human memory. In F. I. M. Craik & T. A. Salthouse (Eds.), *The handbook of aging and cognition* (2nd ed., pp. 200–230). Mahwah, NJ: Lawrence Erlbaum Associates, Inc.

Zec, R. F. (1993). Neuropsychological functioning in Alzheimer's disease. In R. W. Parks, R. F. Zec, & R. S. Wilson (Eds.), *Neuropsychology of Alzheimer's disease and other dementias* (pp. 3–80). New York: Oxford University Press.

17 A neurocognitive overview of aging phenomena based on the event-related brain potential (ERP)

David Friedman

The last decade of cognitive aging research has demonstrated convincingly that not all aspects of cognition show losses with similar trajectories as individuals age. For example, within the domain of memory function, performance on episodic tasks that require the reinstatement of the surrounding spatio- (where) and temporal- (when) context (i.e., source) of a previous event, shows large age-related decline (Spencer & Raz, 1995). By contrast, retrieving the content does not. Working memory (WM), the process by which information is coded into a short-term buffer, actively maintained and subsequently retrieved, also shows age-related decrement (Jonides, Marshuetz, Smith, Reuter-Lorenz, Koeppe, & Hartley, 2000). On the other hand, simple, old/new recognition memory does not show as dramatic a decrement and, in some studies, shows no age-related deficit at all (Craik & McDowd, 1987).

It is also widely known that a good deal of performance variability exists within the normally aging population. Hence the general trends suggested by the preceding paragraph do not apply to all elderly individuals. For example, it has been noted in the behavioral (Li, Lindenberger, Freund, & Baltes, 2001) and physiological (Cabeza, Daselaar, Dolcos, Prince, Budde, & Nyberg, 2004) literatures that some older individuals "compensate" for the deleterious effects of aging. Some have argued, based primarily on the results of recent hemodynamic imaging studies (Cabeza, 2002; Grady, 2000), that this neurocognitive compensation takes the form of the activation of neural networks different from those recruited by the young. This "compensation" hypothesis suggests that similar performance to that of the young is enabled by recruiting different brain regions not activated by the young. Strong evidence for the compensation view would seem to require that elderly individuals who show the pattern in question also demonstrate better performance than those elderly subjects who do not.

Potential contributors to individual differences in performance and perhaps the recruitment of different brain networks are educational level and socioeconomic status (SES), which are often linked in their modulating effects on cognitive task performance. For example, low educational levels have been shown to be a risk factor for the development of dementia, whereas high levels of education have been associated with better cognitive test performance in the non-demented elderly (e.g., Stern, Albert, Tang, & Tsai, 1999). These kinds of observations have led to the "cognitive reserve" hypothesis, i.e., that education (or its surrogates, such as SES) may provide a buffer or reserve capacity for the deleterious effects of aging on brain function (see Stern, 2002 for a review). This hypothesis predicts that, in the normally aging adult, greater levels of education should be associated with greater changes in brain structure and function. Support for this hypothesis has been reported by Coffey, Saxton, Ratcliff, Bryan, and Lucke (1999), who showed that higher levels of educational attainment were associated with greater degrees of cerebral atrophy in the non-demented elderly. Because of limitations inherent in all cross-sectional designs, this finding requires replication. Nevertheless, it is an intriguing result that might help explain some of the age-related differences in electrical activity observed at the scalp, as well as age-related changes observed in fMRI investigations of cognitive aging.

A continually expanding literature implicates age-related change in frontal lobe processing in the etiology of cognitive aging phenomena, including performance decrements on episodic memory, working memory, and novelty detection tasks (for a review, see West, 1996). This "frontal lobe deficit hypothesis" receives support from a wide variety of research domains, including structural and functional neuroimaging, performance on standard neuropsychological tests presumed to tap the integrity of the frontal cortex, and performance decrements on experimental tasks on which patients with circumscribed frontal lobe lesions perform poorly (see Friedman, 2000 for a review).

The frontal lobes might be implicated in age-related compensation. Episodic memory, working memory and paradigms that necessitate switching tasks or responses, require strategic or executive processes (which are initiated in prefrontal cortex), as all require the management of information that is retrieved from more posterior cortical areas. For example, neuropsychological as well as functional neuroimaging data have provided compelling evidence that the prefrontal cortex is a critical element in the retrieval of source information during episodic memory tasks (Cabeza et al., 1997), the maintenance and selection of information on line during working memory tasks (Rowe, Toni, Josephs, Frackowiak, & Passingham, 2000), and in assessments of executive function such as task switching (Braver, Reynolds, & Donaldson, 2003). Performance on all of these tasks shows age-related decline. Another functional neuroimaging technique, the event-related brain potential (ERP), has also been used in the assessment of episodic (Wilding, 2001) and working memory (McEvoy, Pellouchoud, Smith, & Gevins, 2001), as well as during task (Friedman, Nessler, Johnson, & Bersick, 2004; Karayanadis, Coltheart, Michie, & Murphy, 2003) and response (Fabiani & Friedman, unpublished observations) switching. Although it is difficult to infer the intracranial source of ERP activity simply from inspection of the potentials recorded on the scalp, this technique has also yielded evidence consistent with prefrontal cortical contributions to episodic source retrieval (Friedman & Johnson, 2000; Wilding & Rugg, 1996), working memory (Nielsen-Bohlman & Knight, 1995), and task switching (Friedman et al., 2004). Here too, the limited evidence suggests age-related decrement in the ERP correlates of source retrieval (Trott, Friedman, Ritter, Fabiani, & Snodgrass, 1999), working memory (Gaeta, Friedman, & Hurlie, un- published manuscript; McEvoy et al., 2001), and task switching (Friedman et al., 2004).

An important goal of cognitive aging research, as assessed by ERP methods (and other neurophysiological techniques), will be to understand which variables underlie the relations between ERP parameters and cognitive function. Based on the frontal lobe deficit hypothesis, a potential contri- buting factor could be the extent of performance decrement on tests that putatively assess the integrity of prefrontal cortex. In fact, Glisky and her colleagues (Glisky, Rubin, & Davidson, 2001) have demonstrated that lowered performance on "frontal lobe" tests can explain a large percentage of the variance in individual differences of older adults on performance in source memory paradigms. This technique has not been employed to the same extent with physiological measures.

In the current chapter, a selective review of age-related studies from this laboratory is undertaken. As a whole, the results of these investigations suggest that there are differences in ERP patterns of elderly participants that may help explain age-related performance differences. To anticipate my conclusions, some of these patterns may be "compensatory," while others may be "inefficient," but it is too early at the current state of knowledge, at least with ERP measures, to conclude that this is the only way of explaining the neurophysiological patterns that underlie the changes in cognition that are seen with increasing age.

Studies of episodic memory

I turn first to a consideration of recency/recognition memory tasks where it appears that some individuals in the older population may compensate for the adverse effects of aging on neurocognition by activating frontal cortex more than their poorer performing counterparts. Fabiani, Friedman, Cheng, Wee, and Trott (1999) designed an ERP study to follow up a previous behavioral recency/recognition investigation (Fabiani & Friedman, 1997). In this adaptation of the recency/recognition paradigm, a large number of pictures were first presented singly in continuous sequence. These are labeled "information only" trials. Subjects were instructed to memorize the stimuli for subsequent testing within the succeeding sequence of trials. The informa- tion only phase was followed by intermixed information only and test trials, with the latter comprising pairs of stimuli. For all test trials, subjects were instructed that they were to press the button corresponding to the side of the object that had been presented most recently. On *recency only trials*, the pair

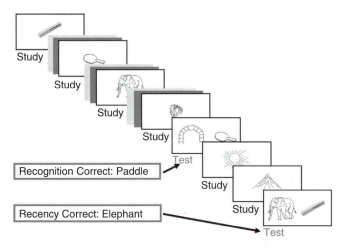

Figure 17.1   Schematic diagram of the construction of the recency recognition paradigm. The task began with information only trials (single objects). Following information only trials, test trials (paired objects) and information only trials were intermixed. Subjects always responded to test trials on the basis of which object was most recently presented. On *recognition only* trials, one old and one new object was presented; on *recency only* trials, both objects were old.

consisted of two previously presented old items (Figure 17.1). On *recognition only trials*, there was one old and one new item. Importantly, subjects need not be aware of whether the trial is testing recency or recognition memory, as the procedure is identical in the two cases and the trials are intermixed. Thus any performance difference observed between recency and recognition cannot be attributed to differences in task requirements.

Due to our interest in individual differences in the aging population, the elderly participants were categorized according to SES, and the ERP data were assessed separately for low and high SES groups. The high SES group had also experienced a greater number of years of education. If the compensation hypothesis has merit, then we would expect that ERP waveform morphology would differ between the high and low SES groups and would be associated with higher performance levels in the high SES group.

The Old–High and Old–Low groups did not differ reliably on recognition performance. However the Old–High group (mean = 60%) outperformed the Old–Low group (mean = 50% or chance performance) during recency trials. Moreover, while the young adults (mean = 63%) produced better performance than the Old–Low subjects, the Old–High and young adults did not differ reliably in recency accuracy.

Figure 17.2 depicts the grand averaged ERPs associated with correctly recognized recency trials in the young adult group and in the low and high SES groups. Note that the waveforms in the Old–High ·group show considerably larger negativity than those of either the young or the Old–Low

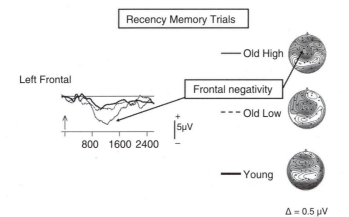

Figure 17.2 Grand mean ERPs elicited by correctly identified recency trials in three groups of participants. The *Old–High* group ($N = 8$) comprises subjects with high educational levels; the *Old–Low* group ($N = 7$) comprises subjects with low levels of educational attainment. The young group comprises 16 young adult subjects. The data are depicted at a left prefrontal electrode site where the differences among groups were greatest. Note the large negativity in the waveforms of the Old–High group. The surface voltage scalp distributions (SP data computed as the averaged voltage between 985 and 1220 ms) are depicted to the right of the waveforms. The Δ refers to the separation (in μV) between isopotential lines. Small filled squares represent the recording sites. The shaded areas reflect negative activity; the unshaded areas, positive activity.

groups. This negativity does not appear to reflect qualitatively different cognitive activity in the two groups of older adults, as the topographic maps look highly similar, with the maps of the young and both older age groups showing centrally oriented negative foci. This suggests that similar underlying neural networks were recruited. However, for the Old–High subjects, but not the young or the Old–Low group, this negative activity was much larger during recency trials than recognition trials (the latter are not depicted). These recency vs. recognition ERP comparisons appear to mirror directly the performance data, i.e., no differences between Old–High and Old–Low groups during recognition trials, but a reliable difference between these groups during recency trials. In combination with the finding that the Old–High group did not differ from the young adult group in accuracy of recency judgments, these data suggest the possibility that the larger, frontally oriented negativity reflects compensatory neural activity in the Old–High SES group.

Future ERP work in the domain of the cognitive aging of memory should involve the search for individual differences. Changes in ERP parameters such as component amplitude and scalp distribution among groups of elders characterized as either high or low performers on the basis of memory performance, neuropsychological test performance, and/or other demographic variables (e.g., education) should enable the investigator to determine if the observed differences are "compensatory" or "inefficient" (see Cabeza, 2002).

Studies of executive function

Based on hemodynamic activation in the brain, age-related changes in working memory (Rypma & D'Esposito, 2000; Jonides et al., 2000) and task-switching (Smith, Geva, Jonides, Miller, Reuter-Lorenz, & Koeppe, 2001) also appear to be due, at least in part, to age-related changes in frontal lobe function. Hence the next series of studies I describe sought to determine if ERP and behavioral measures of working memory, task- and response-switching would also suggest a frontal lobe locus of age-related differences in executive function.

Working memory

Gaeta et al. (unpublished manuscript) presented single digits sequentially in strings with lengths of either 4, 5, 7, 9, or 11 digits. During the updating task (UT), subjects were instructed to remember, in order of presentation, the last four digits for a subsequent match/non-match probe test. During the delayed matching to sample task (DMS), participants were asked to remember the first four digits for the subsequent match/non-match probe test. For both, a test stimulus comprised four digits in the same or different order from the four relevant digits in the previous study string. A match occurred if the probe stimulus was identical in sequence to the four previously studied digits. The design is schematically illustrated in Figure 17.3.

DMS performance did not differ between the age groups, whereas the older subjects showed longer response times and a somewhat lower percentage of hits and a greater percentage of false alarms in the UT task. Figure 17.4 depicts the ERPs elicited by the 1st, 3rd, and 4th digits during the study phase for the DMS task and the 1st, 4th, and 5th digits for the UT task in young and old age groups. Under DMS conditions, a positive component of maximum amplitude (peak latency approx. 500–600 ms) was always elicited by the fourth stimulus in a study string. This stimulus was the last one that needed to be encoded for the subsequent match/non-match task and, there-fore, delivered all the task-relevant information (Sutton, Braren, Zubin, & John, 1965). There were no age differences in ERP parameters during the DMS task, and for both age groups there was a marked increase in positive activity (i.e., P300 or P3b) from the 3rd to the 4th digit. Under UT con-ditions, the positive component of greatest amplitude was always elicited by the 5th digit in the study string, as shown in the right two columns of wave-forms in Figure 17.4. The 5th digit was the first to indicate that the contents of WM needed to be updated. Unlike the data resulting from the DMS task, in the UT task there are notable age differences associated with the 5th digit

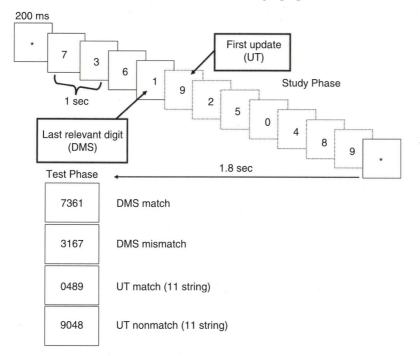

200 ms

7 3 6

1 sec

Last relevant digit (DMS)

First update (UT)

Study Phase

1 9 2 5 0 4 8 9 *

1.8 sec

Test Phase

7361	DMS match
3167	DMS mismatch
0489	UT match (11 string)
9048	UT nonmatch (11 string)

Figure 17.3 Schematic diagram of the working memory paradigm for both the delayed matching to sample (DMS) and updating (UT) tasks.

in the string; whereas the ERP data of the young show a large increment in positive activity, those of the older adults do not. Coupled with the reliable age difference in UT performance, the data suggest that, when confronted with the requirement to remove or suppress a digit currently residing in working memory and simultaneously add the current digit to a fluid WM representation, older adults do not do as well as their young adult counterparts.

To determine the difference due to the necessity to update WM, difference waveforms (not shown) were computed by subtracting the ERPs elicited by the 4th digit from the ERPs elicited by the 5th digit. Current source density (CSD) maps of scalp activity (not depicted) showed that, for the old group only, there was an area of prefrontal scalp positive activity. This age-related difference in topography was reliable. The prefrontal activity in the data of the elderly might reflect the recruitment of "executive processes" required to manage the greater informational demands of the UT task. The frontal focus observed for the elderly, but not the young, may be indicative of compensation for a decline in the efficacy of the updating process, as the elderly performed at a slightly lower level than the young. This latter interpretation is consistent with hemodynamic imaging studies that have provided evidence of age-related differences in frontal lobe activity during working memory tasks (Grady et al., 1994; Jonides et al., 2000).

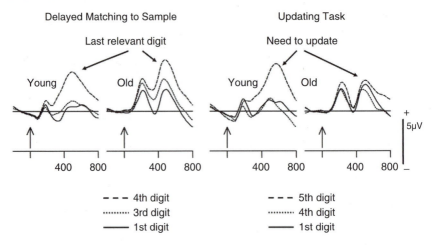

Figure 17.4   Grand mean ERPs averaged across subjects within each age group elicited by the 1st, 3rd, and 4th digits in the delayed matching to sample (DMS) task, and by the 1st, 4th, and 5th digits during the updating task (UT). The data were recorded at the midline central scalp site (Cz). During the DMS task, the 4th digit provided all the information the subject needed to perform the task; during the UT, the 5th digit signaled the need to update the contents of working memory. Arrows mark stimulus onset. The ERP data have been collapsed across all study strings. Modified from Gaeta et al. (unpublished manuscript).

Task- and response-switching

Rapidly and flexibly adjusting behavior to environmental demands is the hallmark of cognitive control. Task- and response-switching paradigms assess this by requiring participants to change rapidly from one task set to a completely different task regime. This involves the coordination of multiple cognitive operations (Monsell, 2003). For example, processes involved on the trial indicating that a switch is required include inhibiting the previous task or response set and concurrently reconfiguring stimulus–response requirements by retrieving the current task or response set. This "new" set must then be maintained on line in working memory until the next switch is indicated.

Consistent with processes involved in cognitive control relying on prefrontal cortex, hemodynamic investigations of task-switching generally suggest that, although a network of brain regions is recruited, areas of the prefrontal cortex play critical roles in mediating performance (Braver et al., 2003). Cognitive aging investigations support the hypothesis that old adults are impaired, relative to young adults, when the kinds of executive processes recruited by task- and response-switching must be engaged (Meiran, Gotler, & Perlman, 2001; Salthouse, Fristoe, McGuthry, & Hambrick, 1998). Further, these difficulties might be due to age-related alterations in prefrontal cortical control mechanisms, in keeping with the "frontal lobe deficit" hypothesis of cognitive aging (West, 1996).

In the studies I describe, we sought to characterize age-related differences in the ERP correlates of task- and response-switching. There are, to our knowledge, no previous age-related ERP studies of task- or response-switching, although the results of a few ERP investigations of young adults have been published (Rushworth, Passingham, & Nobre, 2002).

Response-switching

Because of our finding that the elderly continue to show activation over prefrontal scalp to novel environmental sounds that are repeatedly presented (Fabiani & Friedman, 1995), we (Fabiani & Friedman, unpublished observations) created a design in which these same stimuli served as cues to signal that a response switch was necessary. Fourteen young and 14 elderly adults participated. Environmental sound stimuli served as cues. Sounds whose sources reflected "living" concepts were chosen, and only those sounds high in name agreement (i.e., the majority of subjects produced the appropriate name when hearing the sound) were employed (Fabiani, Kazmerski, Cycowicz, & Friedman, 1996). During two blocks of trials, subjects were required to detect the rare occurrence of deviant, target tones (12% probability of occurrence), and the frequent occurrence of standard stimuli (76% of trials) via choice reaction time. Participants began with a specific response/hand configuration (e.g., left hand assigned to target, right to standard) and were required to switch to the opposite response/hand mapping whenever they heard an infrequent environmental sound (12% of trials). These latter cues did not require a response.

Although the brain's response to the environmental sound cues is of interest, I focus here on the ERPs elicited by standard stimuli occurring one trial before and one trial after the cue to shift response/hand mapping. These are also important because the trial immediately after the cue should show an effect (relative to the standard preceding the cue) of the necessity to reconfigure response hand assignments.

As might have been expected, older adults failed to switch response hands appropriately on 31% of trials (SD = 19), whereas the young adults failed on only 7% of switch trials (SD = 7). In both young and old adults, reaction time was reliably prolonged on the standard trial following the switch cue relative to the standard trial preceding the cue, as depicted in Figure 17.5. However the switch costs for the young (mean = 52 ms) and old (mean = 64 ms) did not differ.

The ERPs elicited by the standards preceding and following the cue are depicted in Figure 17.6A along with their surface potential scalp distributions (17.6B). For the young, relative to the standard preceding the cue, the standard following the cue shows enhanced positive activity which is characterized by a parietal scalp focus. By contrast, for the old adults, the

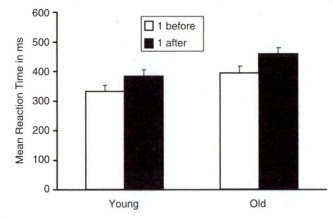

Figure 17.5   Grand mean reaction times for the young and old adults associated with the standards preceding (1 before) and following (1 after) the environmental sound switch cue. Error bars represent the standard error of the mean.

standard following the cue is characterized by negative-going activity with a frontally oriented scalp topography. A graphical depiction of the differences between the young and old adults is presented in Figure 17.6C.

The response time (RT) prolongation is undoubtedly due to the additional processing necessary to switch hands appropriately. For example, the previous response hand assignments would have to be inhibited and the new ones retrieved, stored and maintained in working memory (until the next cue signaling a response hand switch). This interpretation is supported by the fact that the RTs associated with the second standard following the switch cue were highly similar to the RTs to the standards immediately preceding the cue. This was the case for both young and old adults.

Despite the between-age-group similarity in RT responding, the ERPs following the cue were characterized by positivity in the data of the young and negativity in those of the elderly. This suggests a fundamental difference in the way in which the two groups handled the change in response/hand mapping. The positive activity in the ERPs of the young is most likely an instance of the P300 or P3b. This activity has been hypothesized to reflect categorization of task relevant events (Friedman, Cycowicz, & Gaeta, 2001), as well as the updating of information in working memory (Barcelo, Perianez, & Knight, 2002). Updating is a somewhat ambiguous term, and it is likely that there are several processes that could be subsumed under this construct. For example, updating would be likely to include the processes of temporary storage and maintenance of information in working memory. Although no consensus exists as to the functional role of the P3b, the positive activity in the data of the young might reflect the storage and/or maintenance of the new response/hand assignments in working memory. One speculative possibility is that, for the elderly, this process takes longer, consistent with

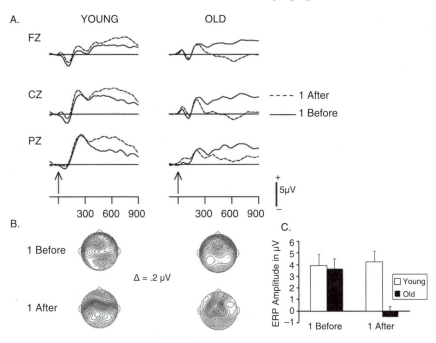

Figure 17.6   (A) Grand mean ERPs averaged across subjects within the young (left-hand panel) and old (right-hand panel) age groups. The data were recorded at midline central scalp sites. The ERPs are depicted for the standards preceding (1 before) and following (1 after) the environmental sound cue. (B) The surface potential scalp topographies associated with each of these events are presented below the corresponding young and old waveforms. The Δ refers to the separation (in μV) between isopotential lines. The shaded areas reflect negative activity, the unshaded areas, positive activity. Small dots represent the electrode locations. (C) Grand mean averaged voltages, measured between 600 and 700 ms post-stimulus, associated with the ERP waveforms illustrated in (A). Error bars represent the standard error of the mean.

the cognitive slowing hypothesis of cognitive aging (Salthouse, 1996). The frontally oriented scalp distribution of the negative activity may be consistent with the necessity of the older adults to recruit prefrontal control processes at a time when the young no longer need to. This notion receives some support from the finding that, in the data of the elderly, the second standard trial following the switch (not depicted) was associated with a large-amplitude positivity demonstrating a similar scalp distribution to that shown in the young adult data on the first trial following the switch.

I turn now to a description of a task-switching paradigm we have been using which, like the response-switching paradigm described above, is thought to be a quintessential executive function highly dependent on pre-frontal cortex and its interconnections.

Task-switching

Using fMRI, DiGirolamo et al. (2001) reported that medial and dorsolateral frontal cortices, theorized to subserve executive processes, showed large areas of activation in both young and old adults during trials in which subjects had to switch between task sets. However, the young activated these regions only when switching between tasks was required. By contrast, the old recruited them during switch as well as no-switch trials, the latter trials presumably not involving heavy executive demands. In the paradigm I describe, ERP and behavioral data were compared for switch trials and no-switch trials. The P3 component elicited during switch trials has been related to some of the executive processes, such as task-set reconfiguration, described above (Rushworth et al., 2002). To the extent that DiGirolamo et al.'s (2001) results generalize to the ERP data, it was expected that large-amplitude, frontally oriented P3 components would occur on switch compared to no-switch trials in young adults, but that similar amplitude P3 components with similar topographies would be associated with both types of trials in older adults.

A schematic of the experimental design is depicted in Figure 17.7. There were 15 young adults and 10 older adults who participated. The task was adapted from Salthouse et al. (1998). Single digits were presented sequentially and speeded and accurate choice button press responses were made according to the instructions appropriate to one of two tasks. In the *more than/less than task*, the subject responded based on whether the digit was more or less than 5. In the *odd/even task*, the subject responded based on whether the digit was odd or even. The requirement to switch was signaled by a black square around the current digit (Figure 17.7). During no-switch trials, subjects performed the same task without switches.

Preliminary reaction time and ERP data are depicted, respectively, in Figure 17.8A and 17.8B (Friedman et al., 2004), in which the data have been collapsed across tasks. There are two major findings that are of interest. First,

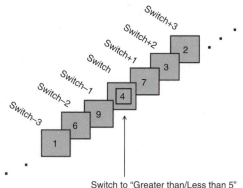

Figure 17.7 Schematic diagram of the task-switching paradigm.

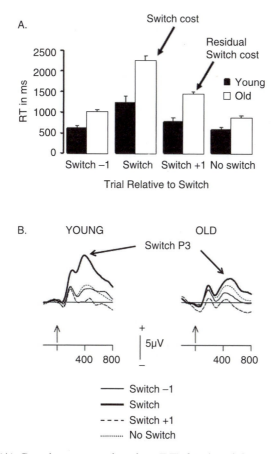

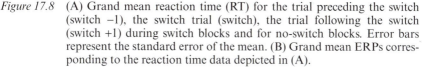

Figure 17.8 (A) Grand mean reaction time (RT) for the trial preceding the switch (switch −1), the switch trial (switch), the trial following the switch (switch +1) during switch blocks and for no-switch blocks. Error bars represent the standard error of the mean. (B) Grand mean ERPs corresponding to the reaction time data depicted in (A).

the old adults show greater RT switch and residual switch costs than the young adults. The switch cost is calculated as the difference in RT between the switch trial and the trial preceding the switch. For the young, this cost is 618 ms; for the old, it is 1232 ms. The switch cost is undoubtedly due to several processes engendered by the switch cue: the need to inhibit the previous task set, retrieve the current task set, and maintain it online until the next switch is indicated. The residual switch cost—presumably due to the subject's continued need to reconfigure the new task set—is calculated by subtracting the RT on the pre-switch trial from that on the immediate post-switch trial; these costs for the young are 155 ms, while for the old they are nearly two and a half times as great at 411 ms.

The second finding of note is that, relative to all other trial types, switch trials for the young were associated with a large-amplitude P3 component (approx. 400–450 ms). In the context of Johnson's (1986) model of P3 amplitude, the large P3s on the switch trial would reflect processing of the additional task information related to the initial performance of the new task set and inhibition of the previous task set. This positivity most likely reflects the output of a widespread cortical network responsible for coordinating these several processes, consistent with the fronto-central and temporo-parietal scalp foci evident in the topographic data (not depicted). The scalp-recorded topographic foci are roughly consistent with hemodynamic assessments of task-switching behavior mentioned earlier, as well as with ERP data (Rushworth et al., 2002).

By contrast with the data of the young, for the old there is a much smaller amplitude increase on switch trials relative to all other trial types. This is consistent with the older group's poorer RT performance on switch trials compared to the young. Moreover, by contrast with the young, the old showed frontally oriented scalp activity for all trial types, whereas the young only showed an anterior scalp topography for the switch trial (not depicted). The presence of similar amplitude P3 components with frontal scalp distributions for all trial types in the data of the elderly but only for the switch trial in the data of the young is reminiscent of the hemodynamic data of DiGirolamo et al. (2001). Consistent with those data, the current results suggest that the older adults may have had to continually recruit prefrontal executive processes even when no such cognitive control demands were inherent in the task condition. Perhaps this neural recruitment is important in counteracting the declines in cognitive function associated with normal aging.

One possibility for the oft-reported age-related decline in episodic memory performance might be age-related changes in those cognitive control mechanisms that enable the recruitment of appropriate strategies during encoding and/or retrieval. In a preliminary attempt to explore this possibility, the amplitude of the P3 component on switch and no-switch trials was correlated across young and old subjects with the sensitivity measure, Pr (Snodgrass & Corwin, 1988), obtained from a simple old/new recognition memory task (Nessler, Friedman, Bersick, & Johnson, 2004). These two trial types were chosen because the switch trial presumably engenders a great deal of executive processing, whereas this should not be the case for the no-switch trial. The correlation between the switch trial P3 measured at FCz and Pr was 0.37 (p <.04), whereas for the no-switch trial, this value was 0.13 (non-significant). Although a modest correlation based on preliminary data, the relation between the measure of episodic memory sensitivity and switch trial P3 amplitude does suggest that at least some of the variance in episodic memory function may be explained by measures of executive function.

Compensating for the deleterious effects of aging

Generally, it is not at all clear how to conclude that a brain activity pattern is "compensatory" or "inefficient." This is due, in part, to the small number of cognitive aging studies that have considered these factors, as well as to the small number of investigations that have been specifically designed with these questions in mind. For example, one difficulty in making this kind of interpretation is the finding that some brain activity is neither compensatory nor inefficient. Rather, the age-related changes that are observed might simply be due to "aging" per se and have no bearing on cognitive function (McIntosh et al., 1999).

Stern (2003) argues that the term "compensation" "be reserved for a specific response to brain dysfunction or damage" (p. 590). In this sense, compensation refers to maintained or improved performance via the recruitment of brain regions or networks not activated when the brain is healthy. As mentioned, in the recency/recognition study by Fabiani et al. (1999), high SES participants showed *greater* activity over prefrontal scalp than did the low SES subjects, and produced better recency performance accuracies than the low SES participants. This provides some basis for an interpretation in terms of "compensation." That is, because the high-performing older volunteers showed recency performance equivalent to that of the young adults, the greater frontal scalp activity observed in the data of these older subjects might indicate additional prefrontal recruitment that aids in maintaining performance levels.

An investigation by Logan, Sanders, Snyder, Morris, and Buckner (2002) suggests that a distinction between invariant aging patterns (i.e., those putatively unalterable by cognitive and/or pharmacologic interventions) and functional compensatory changes (those that might be alterable) may coexist in elderly samples. Similarly, a recent investigation by Cabeza et al. (2004) speaks to these issues and comes to somewhat similar conclusions. These two studies make the point that the issues of "compensation" and "inefficiency" are fairly complex, and will require further investigation before firm conclusions can be reached. The Cabeza et al. and Logan et al. designs and results suggest that, by including several levels of experimental manipulation as well as more groups of older adults stratified by age, and/or performance and demographic characteristics, hypotheses concerning "compensation" and "inefficiency" could be more easily formulated, with the results not as subject to post hoc interpretation as appears to be the case currently.

One potential solution may be to screen the elderly sample a priori on the basis of critical performance and demographic measures, such as long-term memory function, frontal lobe function, and/or educational levels and socioeconomic status. The choice would depend on the hypotheses under study. For example, if the "frontal lobe deficit" hypothesis was under investigation, one might choose frontal lobe assessments for characterizing the sample. The elderly sample would then be categorized on the basis of high and low performance on one or more of these indices. In these circumstances, a scenario might be that good performers recruit a compensatory neural network and do not differ behaviorally from the young on the experimental task in question; by contrast, poor performers might recruit a similar network to the young, but use it "inefficiently," resulting in a poorer performance than the young and the high performing old.

Conclusions

This review is based on selected sets of ERP data from this laboratory. None-theless, it is clear that we are at a very early stage of understanding the basis of age-related compensatory neural changes based on ERP data. To my knowledge, aside from the ERP studies described in the current chapter, there are no other published ERP investigations that have examined the issue of compensation specifically. Hence, it is important to be cautious in attempting to draw conclusions at this point. The ERP provides fine-grained temporal precision currently unavailable with fMRI methods. Note that, in all of the ERP investigations described in the current chapter, the critical neural events reflecting either age-related or condition-related differences occurred within the first 250–800 ms post-stimulus. This same degree of temporal resolution is unavailable with current fMRI techniques. On the other hand, fMRI allows excellent spatial resolution, whereas intracranial sources of scalp-recorded activity are more difficult to infer. Hence, an approach in which both techniques are combined will most likely lead to breakthroughs in knowledge. This kind of approach has been successful in other domains (see Rugg, 1998 and Luck, 1999 for discussions) but, to date, has not been applied to the study of cognitive aging. The future looks bright, and further research will undoubtedly yield a better understanding of the mechanisms underlying the preservation and dissolution of neurocognitive functions as humans age.

Acknowledgments

The author thanks Mr. Charles L. Brown, III for computer programming, and Mr. Michael Bersick, Mr. Jeff Cheng, Ms. Letecia Latif, Mr. Jason Frangos, Ms. Bridget Pierpont, and Ms. Efrat Schori for technical assistance. The author thanks Drs. Monica Fabiani, Helen Gaeta, Doreen Nessler, and Ray Johnson, Jr. for their invaluable contributions to the research reported here. Preparation of this chapter was supported in part by grants AG05213 and AG09988 from the NIA, and by the New York State Department of Mental Hygiene.

This manuscript is a revised and updated version of a previously published paper (Friedman, 2003).

References

Barcelo, F., Perianez, J. A., & Knight, R. T. (2002). Think differently: A brain orienting response to task novelty. *Neuroreport, 13*(15), 1887–1892.

Braver, T. S., Reynolds, J. R., & Donaldson, D. I. (2003). Neural mechanisms of transient and sustained cognitive control during task switching. *Neuron, 39*(4), 713–726.

Cabeza, R. (2002). Hemispheric asymmetry reduction in older adults: The HAROLD model. *Psychology and Aging, 17*(1), 85–100.

Cabeza, R., Daselaar, S. M., Dolcos, F., Prince, S. E., Budde, M., & Nyberg, L. (2004). Task-independent and task-specific age effects on brain activity during working memory, visual attention and episodic retrieval. *Cerebral Cortex, 14*(4), 364–375.

Cabeza, R., Mangels, J., Nyberg, L., Habib, R., Houle, S., McIntosh, A. R., et al. (1997). Brain regions differentially involved in remembering what and when: A PET study. *Neuron, 19*(4), 863–870.

Coffey, C. E., Saxton, J. A., Ratcliff, G., Bryan, R. N., & Lucke, J. F. (1999). Relation of education to brain size in normal aging: Implications for the reserve hypothesis. *Neurology, 53*(1), 189–196.

Craik, F. I. M., & McDowd, J. M. (1987). Age differences in recall and recognition. *Journal of Experimental Psychology: Learning, Memory, and Cognition, 13*, 474–479.

DiGirolamo, G. J., Kramer, A. F., Barad, V., Cepeda, N. J., Weissman, D. H., Milham, M. P., et al. (2001). General and task-specific frontal lobe recruitment in older adults during executive processes: An fMRI investigation of task-switching. *Neuroreport, 12*(9), 2065–2071.

Fabiani, M., & Friedman, D. (1995). Changes in brain activity patterns in aging: The novelty oddball. *Psychophysiology, 32*(6), 579–594.

Fabiani, M., & Friedman, D. (1997). Dissociations between memory for temporal order and recognition memory in aging. *Neuropsychologia, 35*(2), 129–141.

Fabiani, M., Friedman, D., Cheng, J., Wee, E., & Trott, C. T. (1999). Use it or lose it: Effects of aging and education on brain activity in the performance of recency and recognition memory tasks [Abstract]. *Journal of Cognitive Neuroscience, 11*, (Supplement), 73.

Fabiani, M., Kazmerski, V. A., Cycowicz, Y. M., & Friedman, D. (1996). Naming norms for brief environmental sounds: Effects of age and dementia. *Psychophysiology, 33*(4), 462–475.

Friedman, D. (2000). Event-related brain potential investigations of memory and aging. *Biological Psychology, 54*(1–3), 175–206.

Friedman, D. (2003). Cognition and aging: A highly selective overview of event-related potential (ERP) data. *Journal of Clinical and Experimental Neuropsychology, 25*, 702–720.

Friedman, D., & Johnson, R. (2000). Event-related potential (ERP) studies of memory encoding and retrieval: A selective review. *Microscopy Research and Technique, 51*(1), 6–28.

Friedman, D., Cycowicz, Y. M., & Gaeta, H. (2001). The novelty P3: An event-related brain potential (ERP) sign of the brain's evaluation of novelty. *Neuroscience and Biobehavioral Reviews, 25*(4), 355–373.

Friedman, D., Nessler, D., Johnson, R. Jr., & Bersick, M. (2004). Age-related changes in task switching: An ERP analysis. *Journal of Cognitive Neuroscience, 40*(Supplement), 28.

Gaeta, H., Friedman, D., & Hurlie, J. (unpublished manuscript). *Age-related differences in the neural correlates of working memory.*

Glisky, E. L., Rubin, S. R., & Davidson, P. S. R. (2001). Source memory in older adults: An encoding or retrieval problem? *Journal of Experimental Psychology: Learning, Memory, and Cognition, 27*, 1131–1146.

Grady, C. L. (2000). Functional brain imaging and age-related changes in cognition. *Biological Psychology, 54*(1–3), 259–281.

Grady, C. L., Maisog, J. M., Horwitz, B., Ungerleider, L. G., Mentis, M. J., Salerno, J. A., et al. (1994). Age-related changes in cortical blood flow activation during visual processing of faces and location. *Journal of Neuroscience, 14*(3 Pt 2), 1450–1462.

Johnson, R., Jr. (1986). A triarchic model of P300 amplitude. *Psychophysiology, 23*, 367–384.

Jonides, J., Marshuetz, C., Smith, E. E., Reuter-Lorenz, P. A., Koeppe, R. A., & Hartley, A. (2000). Age differences in behavior and PET activation reveal differences in interference resolution in verbal working memory. *Journal of Cognitive Neuroscience, 12*(1), 188–196.

Karayanadis, F., Coltheart, M., Michie, P. T., & Murphy, K. (2003). Electrophysiological correlates of anticipatory and poststimulus components of task switching. *Psychophysiology, 40*, 329–348.

Li, K. Z., Lindenberger, U., Freund, A. M., & Baltes, P. B. (2001). Walking while memorizing: Age-related differences in compensatory behavior. *Psychological Science, 12*(3), 230–237.

Logan, J. M., Sanders, A. L., Snyder, A. Z., Morris, J. C., & Buckner, R. L. (2002). Under-recruitment and non-selective recruitment: Dissociable neural mechanisms associated with aging. *Neuron, 33*, 827–840.

Luck, S. J. (1999). Direct and indirect integration of event-related potentials, functional magnetic resonance images, and single-unit recordings. *Human Brain Mapping, 8*, 115–120.

McEvoy, L. K., Pellouchoud, E., Smith, M. E., & Gevins, A. (2001). Neurophysiological signals of working memory in normal aging. *Cognitive Brain Research, 11*(3), 363–376.

McIntosh, A. R., Sekuler, A. B., Penpeci, C., Rajah, M. N., Grady, C. L., Sekuler, R., et al. (1999). Recruitment of unique neural systems to support visual memory in normal aging. *Current Biology, 9*(21), 1275–1278.

Meiran, N., Gotler, A., & Perlman, A. (2001). Old age is associated with a pattern of relatively intact and relatively impaired task-set switching abilities. *Journals of Gerontology: Psychological Sciences, 56*(2), 88–102.

Monsell, S. (2003). Task switching. *Trends in Cognitive Sciences, 7*(3), 134–140.

Nessler, D., Friedman, D., Bersick, M., & Johnson, R., Jr. (2004). Two presentations are better than one: Elderly benefit behaviorally but age-related ERP differences remain [Abstract]. *Psychophysiology, 41* (Suppl.) 579.

Nielsen-Bohlman, L., & Knight, R. T. (1995). Prefrontal alterations during memory processing in aging. *Cerebral Cortex, 5*(6), 541–549.

Rowe, J. B., Toni, I., Josephs, O., Frackowiak, R. S., & Passingham, R. E. (2000). The prefrontal cortex: Response selection or maintenance within working memory? *Science, 288*(5471), 1656–1660.

Rugg, M. D. (1998). Convergent approaches to electrophysiological and hemo-dynamic investigations of memory. *Human Brain Mapping, 6,* 394–398.

Rushworth, M. F., Passingham, R. E., & Nobre, A. C. (2002). Components of switch-ing intentional set. *Journal of Cognitive Neuroscience, 14*(8), 1139–1150.

Rypma, B., & D'Esposito, M. (2000). Isolating the neural mechanisms of age-related changes in human working memory. *Nature Neuroscience, 3*(5), 509–515.

Salthouse, T. A. (1996). The processing-speed theory of adult age differences in cognition. *Psychological Review, 103*(3), 403–428.

Salthouse, T. A., Fristoe, N., McGuthry, K. E., & Hambrick, D. Z. (1998). Relation of task switching to speed, age, and fluid intelligence. *Psychology and Aging, 13*(3), 445–461.

Smith, E. E., Geva, A., Jonides, J., Miller, A., Reuter-Lorenz, P., & Koeppe, R. A. (2001). The neural basis of task-switching in working memory: Effects of perform-ance and aging. *Proceedings of the National Academy of Sciences, 98*(4), 2095–2100.

Snodgrass, J. G., & Corwin, J. (1988). Pragmatics of measuring recognition memory: Applications to dementia and amnesia. *Journal of Experimental Psychology: General, 117*(1), 34–50.

Spencer, W. D., & Raz, N. (1995). Differential effects of aging on memory for content and context: A meta-analysis. *Psychology and Aging, 10,* 527–539.

Stern, Y. (2002). What is cognitive reserve? Theory and research application of the reserve concept. *Journal of the International Neuropsychological Society, 8*(3), 448–460.

Stern, Y. (2003). The concept of cognitive reserve: A catalyst for research. *Journal of Clinical and Experimental Neuropsychology, 25*(5), 589–593.

Stern, Y., Albert, S., Tang, M. X., & Tsai, W. Y. (1999). Rate of memory decline in AD is related to education and occupation: Cognitive reserve? *Neurology, 53*(9), 1942–1947.

Sutton, S., Braren, M., Zubin, J., & John, E. R. (1965). Evoked-potential correlates of stimulus uncertainty. *Science, 150,* 1187–1188.

Trott, C. T., Friedman, D., Ritter, W., Fabiani, M., & Snodgrass, J. G. (1999). Episodic priming and memory for temporal source: Event-related potentials reveal age-related differences in prefrontal functioning. *Psychology and Aging, 14*(3), 390–413.

West, R. L. (1996). An application of prefrontal cortex theory to cognitive aging. *Psychological Bulletin, 120,* 272–292.

Wilding, E. L. (2001). Event-related functional imaging and episodic memory. *Neuro-science and Biobehavioral Reviews, 25,* 545–554.

Wilding, E. L., & Rugg, M. D. (1996). An event-related potential study of recognition memory with and without retrieval of source. *Brain, 119,* 889–905.

18 Adult neurogenesis and regeneration in the brain

Yevgenia Kozorovitskiy and Elizabeth Gould

Multiple regenerative mechanisms are initiated after brain damage occurs. Some of these, such as metabolic compensation, reactive synaptogenesis and collateral sprouting, involve neurons that survived the damage. However, in cases of severe damage or degeneration, these mechanisms are not sufficient, and the addition of new neurons may be a prerequisite for functional recovery. It is now generally accepted that new neurons are added to the adult mammalian brain. This raises the possibility that naturally occurring neurogenesis may be useful for repairing the damaged adult brain. Indeed, several studies have shown that damage to the adult brain can stimulate neurogenesis. Yet the production of new neurons is only one of multiple steps necessary to restore damaged neural circuits to their original state or the functional equivalent. Studies carried out on intact animals have identified conditions that affect the production and survival of new neurons in adult brains. This chapter considers the evidence for compensatory neurogenesis in the adult mammalian brain, with a view toward applying information from the undamaged brain to studies of regeneration.

Mechanisms of brain repair

> once the development was ended, the founts of growth and regeneration of the axons and dendrites dried up irrevocably. In adult centres the nerve paths are something fixed, ended, immutable. Everything may die, nothing may be regenerated. It is for the science of the future to change, if possible, this harsh decree.
>
> (Ramon y Cajal, *Degeneration and Regeneration of the Nervous System*, 1928, p. 750)

Over a century ago, Santiago Ramon y Cajal observed that in contrast to the high regenerative capacity of the peripheral nervous system, the adult mammalian brain is limited in its ability to regenerate. In humans, failure to recover completely after substantial brain injury or disease supports this view. And yet, scientific advances over the past few decades have begun to respond to Cajal's challenge.

Although rarely complete in severe cases, some spontaneous recovery of function usually occurs after brain damage. Until recently, regeneration was thought to involve primarily surviving neural circuitry. Well-studied examples of such processes include metabolic compensation, reactive synaptogenesis, and axon collateral sprouting. For example, Parkinson's disease is characterized by the death of dopaminergic neurons in the substantia nigra. In the rat model of this neurodegenerative disease, surviving substantia nigra neurons appear to increase their turnover of dopamine. In pre-symptomatic animals with neuronal damage in this brain region, a change in the proportion of intracellular dopamine to its metabolite compensates for the damaged cells until more than 70% of dopaminergic neurons in the affected areas are depleted (Zigmond, Abercrombie, Berger, Grace, & Stricker, 1990).

Metabolic compensation can parallel morphological changes in the brain. New synapses can be established on surviving neurons that may compensate for the destroyed cells. This process, reactive synaptogenesis, was first described in the septal nucleus of the adult rat (Raisman, 1969) and has been studied extensively in the dentate gyrus, where it occurs in parallel with axon collateral sprouting following destruction of entorhinal cortex projections to the hippocampus (Lynch, Matthews, Mosko, Parks, & Cotman, 1972; Peterson, 1987). Although collateral sprouting—the growth of new axon branches from terminal ends of healthy or injured neurons into denervated areas—is often observed in the injured central nervous system, axonal regeneration may be limited by factors associated with glial scarring, which forms a mechanical, and possibly chemical, barrier (Schwab, 1990). Collateral sprouting, reactive synaptogenesis and metabolic compensation are all relatively local events that may not provide enough new substrate for full recovery of function. New neuron formation may be necessary for successful recovery, especially in cases of extensive damage.

The longstanding general belief that the adult brain is incapable of producing new neurons was in agreement with the clinical observations of limited recovery after brain damage. However, studies carried out over the past few decades suggest not only that neurons are produced in the adult brain, but also that the rate of their generation can be enhanced by damage. We review evidence for compensatory neurogenesis following brain damage and then examine how neurogenesis is regulated in the intact normal brain, with a view towards applying this knowledge to questions of brain regeneration.

Compensatory neuron production in the adult brain

Beginning about 40 years ago and extending to the present day, numerous studies have provided evidence that neurons are formed in the intact adult mammalian brain (Fuchs & Gould, 2000). Adult neurogenesis has been reported in the dentate gyrus (Altman & Das, 1965; Kaplan & Hinds, 1977; Eriksson et al., 1998), the olfactory bulb (Kaplan & Hinds, 1977; Altman,

1969; Luskin, 1993; Doetsch & Alvarez-Buylla, 1996), the amygdala (Bernier, Bedard, Vinet, Levesque, & Parent, 2002), several regions of the basal ganglia (Zhao et al., 2003; Chmielnicki, Benraiss, Economides, & Goldman, 2004; Baker, Baker, & Hagg, 2005; Dayer, Cleaver, Abouantoun, & Cameron, 2005), and in the neocortex (Altman, 1969; Bernier et al., 2002; Dayer et al., 2005; Kaplan, 1981; Gould, Vail, Wagers, & Gross, 2001), although findings in these latter areas remain controversial (Rakic, 1985; Kornack & Rakic, 2001; Koketsu, Mikami, Miyamoto, & Hisatsune, 2003). The existence of naturally occurring neurogenesis from an endogenous pool of stem or progenitor cells suggests that the adult brain may be capable of replenishing cell populations following damage; a process that could be a starting point for recovery of function.

Recent studies have suggested that, at least in some brain regions, loss of neurons is associated with compensatory neurogenesis (Figure 18.1). These reports describe neuron production in response to injury that can be divided into three groups: (1) damage to an area that normally exhibits adult neurogenesis results in a local increase in the rate of neuron production—*local compensatory neurogenesis*; (2) damage to an area that does not normally exhibit substantial adult neurogenesis results in an increase in the rate of neuron production in another, intact, area that normally displays adult neurogenesis—*distal compensatory neurogenesis*; and (3) damage to a neuronal population in an area that does not normally exhibit high levels of adult neurogenesis results in the *induction of compensatory neurogenesis*.

Local compensatory neurogenesis

With regard to the first example of local compensation, multiple studies suggest that brain regions known to undergo extensive neurogenesis in adulthood, such as the mammalian olfactory bulb and the dentate gyrus, as well as the avian song system, respond to cell death with enhanced production of new neurons. In mammals, aspiration of the olfactory bulb accelerates the pace of cell renewal from the subventricular zone (Schwob, 2002). Likewise, lesion-induced granule neuron death in the dentate gyrus, whether caused by excitotoxic or mechanical means, increases the number of newly born neurons on the same side of the brain (Gould and Tanapat, 1997) (see Figure 18.1A). In these circumstances, the rate of cell proliferation correlates positively with the extent of damage, and the majority of new cells survive for at least 3 weeks, long after they start expressing biochemical markers of granule cells. However, these new cells do not appear to restore the granule cell layer to its previous, undamaged, structural state. Despite the increase in production of new granule cells, areas of damage and gliosis remain. Additional evidence in support of increased neurogenesis in the subventricular zone and the dentate gyrus following different types of neuronal loss includes data from studies of ischemia (Jin et al., 2001; Liu, Solway, Messing, & Sharp, 1998; Sharp, Liu, & Bernabeu, 2002), as well as seizures induced by

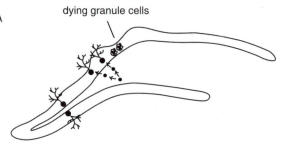

A

dying granule cells

Granule cell replacement in the adult dentate gyrus

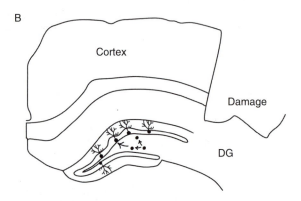

B

Cortex

Damage

DG

Enhanced granule cell genesis after cortical damage

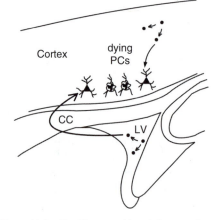

C

Cortex

dying
PCs

CC

LV

Pyramidal cell replacement in adult neocortex

Figure 18.1 Three types of compensatory neurogenesis in the adult mammalian brain. (A) Local compensatory neurogenesis. Lesion-induced granule neuron death in the dentate gyrus increases the number of new granule neurons on the ipsilateral side of the brain (Gould & Tanapat, 1997). (B) Distal compensatory neurogenesis. Cortical injury bilaterally increases the number of new granule neurons in the dentate gyrus (Kernie, Erwin, & Parada, 2001). (C) Induction of compensatory neurogenesis. Highly targeted apoptosis of cerebral cortex, which normally do not exhibit substantial levels of neurogenesis in the adult, leads to the production of replacement pyramidal neurons (Magavi & Macklis, 2002).

pilocarpine (Parent, Yu, Leibowitz, Geschwind, Sloviter, & Lowenstein, 1997; Parent, Valentin, & Lowenstein, 2002a) and kainic acid treatment (Gray & Sundstrom, 1998).

Similar findings have been reported in the avian song system where more controlled photolytic destruction of neurons has been induced. In this system, targeted death of high vocal center neurons in adult male canaries results in an increase in the recruitment of homotypic new neurons to this area (Scharff, Kirn, Grossman, Macklis, & Nottebohm, 2000). Moreover, this increase in neuron recruitment is associated with some degree of functional recovery; all experimental subjects that exhibited song deterioration showed subsequent improvement over the following 3 months.

Distal compensatory neurogenesis

Neurogenesis in regions that normally undergo continual neuron replacement can also be stimulated by destruction of distant regions in the brain (see Figure 18.1B). For example, cortical injury in mice has been shown to enhance the production of new granule cells in the dentate gyrus (Kernie et al., 2001). The authors report a significant increase in cell proliferation in the dentate gyrus, both contralateral and ipsilateral to the site of damage. In addition, aspiration lesions of parts of the adult rat cortex also enhance cell proliferation in the subventricular zone (Szele & Chesselet, 1996). Collectively, these data suggest that communication signals between dying neurons or nearby cells and precursors travel across relatively long distances. The mobilization of neuronal precursors or stem cells in distal areas could signify the recruitment of alternate circuitry, aimed at recovery of function. Meanwhile, it remains to be determined whether distal enhancement of proliferation is truly reparative in that it leads to functional improvement.

Induction of compensatory neurogenesis

Recently, damage-induced neurogenesis in neuronal populations that do not normally undergo neuronal replacement, such as cortical and hippocampal pyramidal cells as well as striatal neurons, has been described (see Figure 18.1C). While the majority of new neurons in adulthood are confined to the mammalian olfactory bulb and the dentate gyrus, a low but steady level of neuron production may persist in the intact rodent and primate neocortex (Bernier et al., 2002; Dayer et al., 2005; Gould et al., 2001). Damage can enhance the production of new neurons in the cerebral cortex as well, although it is unclear whether the same neuronal populations are involved in the neuronal turnover in the intact and the damaged cortex. Region and cell type specific neurogenesis has been induced by highly targeted apoptosis of neurons in the cerebral cortex of mice (Magavi, Leavitt, & Macklis, 2000; Magavi & Macklis, 2002). First, the authors selectively depleted small groups of pyramidal cells with cortico-thalamic projections.

This targeted depletion stimulated the production of new pyramidal neurons. Here, compensation occurred through mobilization of resident precursors as well as through a new population of cells originating near the subventricular zone in response to damage.

In the damaged hippocampus, as in the damaged cortex, pyramidal cells can be produced in adulthood (Nakatomi et al., 2002). Transient ischemia results in the production of new cells with the morphological, ultrastructural and biochemical features of pyramidal neurons in the CA1 region. Regeneration of this cell population is associated with behavioral and electrophysiological indices of functional recovery. Similar findings have been reported in the striatum of animals after ischemic damage to this region. In this area, which normally undergoes scarce adult neurogenesis, a substantial number of new neurons were observed after blood flow occlusion and subsequent cell death (Arvidsson, Collin, Kirik, Kokaia, & Lindvall, 2002). Others, however, have found that new striatal neurons generated after ischemia have migrated from the subventricular zone (Parent, Vexler, Gong, Derugin, & Ferriero, 2002b). The activation of local, previously suppressed, progenitors and the engagement of distal progenitors from neurogenic zones could both contribute to rebuilding the damaged brain. The activation of local progenitors may occur on a faster scale relative to the engagement of the more numerous progenitors from the established highly neurogenic zones.

The data on inducing cell proliferation in areas that do not normally undergo substantial neurogenesis in adulthood suggest that, in the future, therapies involving endogenous precursor cells may be useful for the treatment of brain damage after trauma or neurodegenerative diseases. At the same time they raise important questions about the obstacles preventing spontaneous functional recovery in neurodegenerative diseases. While it is possible that clinical conditions associated with neuronal death are accompanied by enhanced neurogenesis, this potential reparative step may be functionally ineffective because other disruptive degenerative profiles remain. For example, the degenerative process in conditions like Alzheimer's disease results in multiple abnormalities, such as neurofibrillary tangles, senile plaques, and associated microglia. These abnormalities may contribute to the inability of the brain to self-repair following neurodegeneration. Thus, even though neurogenesis can be induced or enhanced by neurodegeneration, the proper integration of the replacement neurons is not assured. The brains of Alzheimer's patients and transgenic animal models show increased expression of immature neuronal markers in the hippocampus, which points to increased rates of neurogenesis (Jin et al., 2004). However, β-amyloid has been shown to impair proliferation and differentiation of neuronal precursors in vitro, through mechanisms related to oxidative stress and calcium homeostasis (Haughey, Nath, Chan, Borchard, Rao, & Mattson, 2002). The same study also showed that, in a transgenic mouse overexpressing human β-amyloid precursor protein (APP), the amyloid plaques are associated with a 55% reduction in BrdU labeling compared to controls. So, even though Alzheimer's disease may be associated with enhanced neurogenesis, compensation via enhanced neurogenesis may not be successful due to amyloid accumulation. Reactive neurogenesis in adulthood has also been reported following neuronal death in brain regions that are compromised in other neurodegenerative diseases, such as Parkinson's and Huntington's (Zhao et al., 2003; Tattersfield, Croon, Liu, Kells, Faul, & Connor, 2004). The progressive nature of these diseases may override any positive effects of compensatory neurogenesis.

Many events in the damaged brain could block the new cells from establishing the appropriate connections. One typical response to damage that may prevent new neurons from integrating properly is the excessive proliferation of glia. The glial scar that rapidly forms at an injury site serves to confine inflammatory and necrotic-apoptotic responses and seals the potentially damaged blood–brain barrier. The glial scar may become a biochemical and physical block to functional regeneration (Schwab, 1990; but see Liberto, Albrecht, Herx, Yong, & Levison, 2004, for a contrasting view). Studies describe two types of cells that shield the damaged region: oligodendrocytes and astrocytes. The former produce growth inhibitory proteoglycans such as NG2, neurocan and phosphocan (Chen, Ughrin, & Levine, 2002). Oligodendrocyte conglomerates also form a wall through which axons or migrating neurons cannot penetrate. Proliferating astrocytes, which represent a large proportion of the glial scar, normally support the energy requirements of neuronal cells and aid survival by releasing cytokines and trophic factors (Collazos-Castro & Nieto-Sampedro, 2001). Recently, stem cells with the characteristics of dentate gyrus astrocytes were shown to be the actual precursors of adult-born granule cells in the region (Seri, Garcia-Verdugo, McEwen, & Alvarez-Buylla, 2001). After traumatic brain injury, however, the local proliferating cells preferentially produce glia, which make up the glial scar (Kernie et al., 2001). Still, the evidence that astrocytes and neural stem cells either are the same or derive from the same precursor population presents the possibility that neuron production could be selectively induced in nearby endogenous stem cells at the scene of the damage.

The consequences of hippocampal seizures illustrate that new neurons do not always form normal and functional connections. Pilocarpine-induced seizures result in increased cell death paralleled by an enhancement in the numbers of new granule cells in the dentate gyrus. These new cells migrate to an aberrant location on the border of the dentate gyrus and the CA3 region and may contribute to further development of seizures (Scharfman, Goodman, & Sollas, 2000). This raises the important consideration of whether adult-generated neurons in the damaged brain are capable of replacing developmentally generated neurons in function. Studies suggest that adult-generated cells, possibly including those born in response to damage, produce action potentials (Nakatomi et al., 2002; van Praag, Schinder, Christie, Toni, Palmer, & Gage, 2002). Recent evidence points to several morphological and electrophysiological differences between adult and developmentally born neurons.

New neurons may differ both structurally and functionally from those produced during development. On entering CA3, their axons diverge less than the axons of developmentally generated granule cells (Hastings, Seth, Tanapat, Rydel, & Gould, 2002). Adult-generated neurons are characterized by low capacitance and high input resistance (Ambrogini et al., 2004), an insensitivity to GABAergic inhibition, and a lower threshold for LTP induction (Wang, Scott, & Wojtowicz, 2000; Schmidt-Hieber, Jonas, & Bischofberger, 2004). These characteristics of adult-born neurons resemble the qualities of immature neurons during development, suggesting that, in adult animals, new neurons may have enhanced activity levels relative to surrounding developmentally generated cells. The qualities of adult-generated cells reveal a strong potential to contribute to recovery from brain damage (see Figure 18.2).

One longstanding view is that to restore damaged neural circuitry to its original state is a prerequisite to functional recovery (see Figure 18.2A and 18.2B). If this were the case, adult-generated cells would need all the characteristics of the cells they are replacing in order to be functionally successful. Since morphological and electro-physiological characteristics of new adult neurons appear to differ from developmentally generated neurons, one path for therapeutic intervention is to manipulate the proliferating population to express the qualities of cells lost to damage or disease.

Another approach to the question of recovery from brain damage is not based on the assumption that compensation for lost neurons needs to be isomorphic. After all, the therapeutic goal is functional, rather than

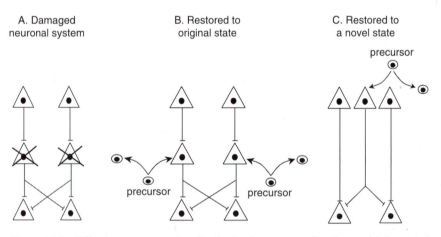

Figure 18.2   Effective compensation for brain damage can involve multiple neural states. (A) A feed-forward neural system damaged at a specific level. (B) New neurons from proliferating precursors restore the system to its original state. (C) New neurons from proliferating precursors restore the system to a novel state that could be functionally similar to (B).

structural, recovery. It is possible that compensation through alternate circuitry may prove equally efficient, compared to restructuring the old circuits. For example, when one level in a feed-forward neuronal system is destroyed (see Figure 18.2A), one way of rebuilding the system is to increase the number of neurons in the areas preceding the damaged site (see Figure 18.2C). The possibility of functional compensation without preserving identical structure is consistent with the data on the biophysical characteristics of adult-born neurons. Recent findings on the role of the new neurons in learning strengthen the possibility that adult neurogenesis could prove useful in compensating for brain damage or neurodegeneration.

Adult-generated neurons in the dentate gyrus play a role in certain types of hippocampal-dependent learning. For example, decreases in neurogenesis induced by the anti-mitotic DNA methylating agent methylazoxymethanol acetate (MAM) or irradiation temporarily disrupt performance on some hippocampal-dependent tasks, including trace eye-blink and trace fear conditioning, as well as memory in the spatial version of the water maze task (Shors, Miesegaes, Beylin, Zhao, Rydel, & Gould, 2001; Shors, Townsend, Zhao, Kozorovitskiy, & Gould, 2002; Snyder, Hong, McDonald, & Wojtowicz, 2005). The connection between new neurons and learning is bi-directional: adult neurogenesis is important for some forms of learning and memory, while learning, in turn, increases the number of newly generated neurons. Learning several types of hippocampal-dependent tasks is associated with a long-term increase in neurogenesis, lasting long after the time the hippocampus is required for recall of the memory (Gould, Beylin, Tanapat, Reeves, & Shors, 1999; Leuner, Mendolia-Loffredo, Kozorovitskiy, Samburg, Gould, & Shors, 2004). Studies elucidating the function of the adult-generated neurons confirm that new cells could be useful under conditions of damage. In fact, a recent study showed that reducing adult neurogenesis exacerbates behavioral deficits after ischemia (Raber et al., 2004). This suggests that adult-generated neurons may play a role in learning in both the intact and the damaged brain.

Many studies have attempted to identify factors and conditions that regulate the number of new neurons in the intact adult brain. It is possible that this information may aid in testing the possible strategies for inducing effective regeneration in the damaged brain.

Regulation of adult neurogenesis in the intact brain

The regulation of adult neurogenesis in the intact brain has been studied most extensively in the mammalian hippocampus. Although our understanding of the mechanisms underlying the regulation of adult neurogenesis remains incomplete, an array of modulators that comprise neural, hormonal and experiential factors has been identified (see Table 18.1). These include factors synthesized by the brain, factors produced in the periphery, and environmental influences.

Table 18.1 Regulation of adult neurogenesis in the intact brain

Neural	Hormonal	Experiential
Glutamate (NMDA)[1, 2] ↓	Glucocorticoids[8, 9] ↓	Stress[12] ↓
Nitric oxide[3, 4] ↓	Estrogens[10, 11] ↑	Complex environments[13–15] ↑
Serotonin[5, 6] ↑		Learning[16] ↑
Growth factors (e.g.,		Dominance[17, 18] ↑
IGF-1)[7] ↑		Physical activity[19] ↑

Notes: This table documents some of the better-studied regulators of adult neurogenesis in the intact brain, comprising neural, hormonal and experiential factors. A better knowledge of these factors and other cues that remain to be identified will increase the likelihood that adult neurogenesis can be used to enhance functional recovery from brain damage. The reference list (numbers 1–24, see References section) includes selected examples of studies on each topic. Arrows indicate direction of the effect on adult neurogenesis.

Different factors that regulate adult neurogenesis do not necessarily act independently of one another. For example, serotonin may be involved in the effect of nitric oxide on neurogenesis (Park, Kang, Kwon, Chung, Ahn, & Huh, 2001; Gibbs, 2003). Evidence suggests a possible involvement of brain-derived neurotrophic factor (BDNF) in the modulation of adult neurogenesis by both serotonin and nitric oxide (Cheng, Wang, Cai, Rao, & Mattson 2003; Mattson, Maudsley, & Martin, 2004). BDNF has trophic effects on serotonergic neurons in the brain, and manipulating serotonin activity bidirectionally alters gene expression of BDNF (Zetterstrom, Pei, Madhav, Coppell, Lewis, & Grahame-Smith, 1999).

Certainly, neural, hormonal and experiential influences on adult neurogenesis are interconnected. For instance, stress and the main stress hormones, glucocorticoids, decrease adult neurogenesis through activation of the NMDA glutamate receptor (Cameron, McEwen, & Gould, 1995; Cameron, Tanapat, & Gould, 1998; McEwen, 1996); moreover, blocking the stress-induced rise in glucocorticoids counteracts the inhibitory effect of stress on cell proliferation (Tanapat, Hastings, Rydel, Galea, & Gould 2001). In the hippocampus, in addition to decreased rates of adult neurogenesis, the negative consequences of chronic stress include long-term potentiation (LTP) inhibition, excitotoxicity, reduced dendritic branching, and deficits in episodic and spatial memory (Luine, Villegas, Martinez, & McEwen, 1994; McEwen, 2000). Any such changes are capable of exerting a negative influence on recovery from brain damage.

Stress is not the only experiential factor that influences numerous brain parameters. Living in complex environments alters multiple brain measures, in addition to enhancing adult neurogenesis. Following the lead of Rosenzweig and his laboratory in the 1960s, many studies have shown that living in enriched laboratory environments enhances the levels of the enzyme acetylcholinesterase, complexity of dendritic branching, dendritic spine density, cell body size, glial numbers, and cortical thickness, among other measures

(Rosenzweig, Bennett, & Krech, 1964; Diamond et al., 1966; Mollgaard, Diamond, Bennett, Rosenzweig, & Lindner, 1971; West & Greenough, 1972; Greenough & Volkmar, 1973; Globus, Rosenzweig, Bennett, & Diamond, 1973; Diamond, Johnson, Ingham, Rosenzweig, & Bennett, 1975; Rosenzweig & Bennett, 1996). Although the addition of new neurons arguably holds the most hope for compensation in cases of very extensive brain damage, clearly, many of these neural changes could potentially aid in recovery.

The findings on the effects of environment on adult neurogenesis raise the important issue of whether control animals in experiments aimed at understanding the intact and the damaged brain are, in fact, deprived of the minimal experiential stimulation required for the production and maintenance of an optimal number of new neurons. Control conditions for laboratory rats are usually single-sex groups of very few animals, housed in small cages with unlimited access to food and water. The imposed restrictions of socialization and space, together with the absence of natural competition for nourishment and reproduction, suggest that these animals may represent a highly deprived population, with potentially altered brain morphology and function. Laboratory control conditions may be even more problematic for nonhuman primates living in captivity, because these animals typically show complex social and cognitive capabilities. Data gathered in environmental enrichment paradigms may provide information about the brain in more natural settings. Still, the relevance of these studies to human brain function is difficult to interpret, since even a deprived human environment is highly complex in comparison to the surroundings of a typical laboratory control animal.

A caveat to keep in mind when applying the information on adult neurogenesis gathered in the intact brain to studies of regeneration is that the regulatory processes for the intact and the damaged brain may differ. For example, nitric oxide is known as a negative neural regulator of adult neurogenesis. This diffusable transcellular signaling molecule decreases cell proliferation in the intact brain and may mediate the switch from proliferation to differentiation (Gibbs, 2003; Packer et al., 2003; Moreno-Lopez, Romero-Grimaldi, Noval, Murillo-Carreters, Matarredona, & Estrada, 2004). Consistently, one study found that knockouts of neuronal nitric oxide synthase (the enzyme that synthesizes nitric oxide) had enhanced levels of both basal and ischemia-induced neurogenesis. However, other groups show that nitric oxide is necessary for ischemia-induced neurogenesis in some cases, and has additional protective effects in promoting angiogenesis and as an antioxidant (Zhang et al., 2001; Zhu, Liu, Sun, & Lu, 2003; Keynes & Garthwaite, 2004). Glutamate is another regulatory factor that may differ in its effects on adult neurogenesis in intact and damaged brains. Although the actions of this neurotransmitter at NMDA receptors inhibit proliferation of precursor cells in the normal dentate gyrus (Cameron et al., 1998), blocking NMDA receptors prevents the ischemia-induced rise in adult

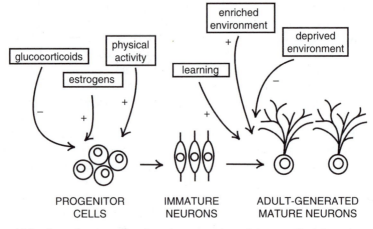

Figure 18.3   Some hormonal and environmental modulators of adult neurogenesis. Estrogens and glucocorticoids affect proliferation of neuronal precursors, while environmental factors, such as learning, physical activity, and the level of environmental complexity, tend to influence survival time of adult-born neurons.

neurogenesis (Arvidsson et al., 2002). Thus glutamate may play additional protective roles in the damaged brain. The multifaceted effects of nitric oxide, glutamate and other modulatory factors on damage-induced neurogenesis require further study.

In summary, over the past decade many factors that modulate neuronal proliferation and survival in the adult mammalian brain have been identified, and a systematic picture of neurogenesis regulation is beginning to emerge (Figure 18.3). A thorough grasp of the factors that regulate adult neurogenesis in the intact brain may be necessary, although not sufficient, for efforts to enhance the brain's natural capacity to self-repair.

Strategies for augmenting compensatory neurogenesis

Studies of neurogenesis in the intact brain have guided the experiments aimed at understanding the damaged brain. Results of recent investigations suggest that living in a more complex environment is conducive to brain restoration or maintenance under conditions of damage. For example, living in an enriched environment slows functional deterioration in a rat model of Huntington disease (Hockly et al., 2002), increases synaptic density in cortical regions of control and postischemic rats (Johansson & Belichenko, 2002), and improves performance on tasks that involve damaged brain areas (Galani, Jarrard, Will, & Kelche, 1997). In light of the evidence that living in enriched environments enhances adult neurogenesis in the intact brain, in addition to upregulating many other structural parameters, it seems reasonable to suppose that environmental complexity could enhance damage-induced neurogenesis in the adult brain and contribute to functional recovery. The current evidence regarding this possibility is scant and inconclusive. On one hand, living in complex environments has been shown to enhance adult neurogenesis after seizures; this effect is accompanied by improved performance in the water maze (Faverjon et al., 2002), and protection from future seizures (Auvergne et al., 2002). On the other hand, some studies show no effect of environmental enrichment on ischemia-induced adult neurogenesis (Komitova, Perfilieva, Mattsson, Eriksson, & Johansson, 2002), or even an exacerbation of ischemic cell death (Farrell, Evans, & Corbett, 2001). Intriguingly, the last study found that living in a complex environment led to improvement in maze task performance of ischemic animals. It appears that living conditions can impact the damaged brain and aid in functional recovery in multiple ways, only some of which involve adult neurogenesis.

Stress, yet another experiential regulator of adult neurogenesis in the intact brain, has been shown to exacerbate damage due to excitotoxicity (Stein-Behrens, Mattson, Chang, Yeh, & Sapolsky, 1994). Despite this finding, no studies have examined whether stressful situations impair compensatory neurogenesis. If stressful experience regulates damage-induced adult neurogenesis, then previous accounts of this phenomenon may have underestimated the magnitude of damage-induced neurogenesis. Experimental animals may be housed under potentially stressful conditions, such as in a novel post-surgical environment, post-surgical pain, or social isolation. Numerous studies have suggested that neural and hormonal factors can alter the structural and functional outcomes of brain damage. For example, endogenous glutamate released after traumatic brain injury, or stress, exacerbates cell death (Moghaddam, Bolinao, Stein-Behrens, & Sapolsky, 1994; Palmer, Marion, Botscheller, Swedlow, Styren, & DeKosky, 1993). Since glutamate is known to inhibit proliferation of the precursor cells (Cameron et al., 1998), it is possible that this neurotransmitter could contribute to poor functional outcome after injury by enhancing cell death and suppressing new cell production (but see Arvidsson et al., 2002).

Some progress has been made in exploring the possibility that peptide signaling molecules alter damage-induced neurogenesis. For example, fibroblast growth factor (FGF) has been shown to be important for neurogenesis in the intact *subventricular zone* and in the dentate gyrus after ischemia or traumatic brain injury (Yoshimura et al., 2001; Yoshimura et al., 2003; Zheng, Nowakowski, & Vaccarino, 2004). Overexpression of vascular endothelial growth factor (VEGF) leads to enhancement in adult neurogenesis that parallels improved learning in a spatial maze (Cao et al., 2004). Infusion of EGF together with albumin greatly enhances post-ischemic neuronal replacement in the striatum (Teramoto, Qiu, Plumier, & Moskowitz 2003). Moreover, intraventricular infusions of both EGF and FGF enhance the production of CA1 hippocampal pyramidal cells after damage, while also ameliorating behavioral deficits (Nakatomi et al., 2002). That is, compensatory neurogenesis, enhanced by growth factor administration, correlates with improved performance on the Morris water maze task, a test that requires an intact CA1 pyramidal cell field.

Advances in the study of adult neurogenesis over the past decade have changed the way the adult brain is viewed. Not only are new cells produced under normal conditions, but their generation can also be enhanced by damage. Yet, in many instances, damage-induced neurogenesis fails either to restore brain circuitry to its original state or to lead to complete functional recovery. Knowledge about conditions that regulate adult neurogenesis in the absence of damage may be applicable to questions of regeneration. However, to optimize the proportion of adult-born compensatory neurons that successfully undergo differentiation, integration into appropriate circuitry, and long-term survival, more of the cues controlling these processes need to be identified and thoroughly characterized.

References

Altman, J. (1969). Autoradiographic and histological studies of postnatal neurogenesis. IV. Cell proliferation and migration in the anterior forebrain, with special reference to persisting neurogenesis in the olfactory bulb. *Journal of Comparative Neurology, 137*, 433–457.

Altman, J., & Das, G. D. (1965). Autoradiographic and histological evidence of postnatal hippocampal neurogenesis in rats. *Journal of Comparative Neurology, 124*, 319–335.

Ambrogini, P., Lattanzi, D., Ciuffoli, S., Agostini, D., Bertini, L., Stocchi, V., et al. (2004). Morpho-functional characterization of neuronal cells at different stages of maturation in granule cell layer of adult rat dentate gyrus. *Brain Research, 1017*, 21–31.

Arvidsson, A., Collin, T., Kirik, D., Kokaia, Z., & Lindvall, O. (2002). Neuronal replacement from endogenous precursors in the adult brain after stroke. *Nature Medicine, 8*, 963–970.

Auvergne, R., Lere, C., El Bahh, B., Arthaud, S., Lespinet, V., Rougier, A., et al. (2002) Delayed kindling epileptogenesis and increased neurogenesis in adult rats housed in an enriched environment. *Brain Research, 954*, 277–285.

Baker, S. A., Baker, K. A., & Hagg, T. (2005). D3 dopamine receptors do not regulate neurogenesis in the subventricular zone of adult mice. *Neurobiological Disorders, 18*, 523–527.

Bernier, P. J., Bedard, A., Vinet, J., Levesque, M., & Parent, A. (2002). Newly generated neurons in the amygdala and adjoining cortex of adult primates. *Proceedings of the National Academy of Science USA, 99*, 11464–11469.

Cahal, Santiago Ramon y (1991). *Cajal's degeneration and regeneration of the nervous system* (J. DeFelipe & E. C. Jones, Eds., R. M. May, Trans.). New York: Oxford University Press. (original work published 1928)

Cameron, H. A., McEwen, B. S., & Gould, E. (1995). Regulation of adult neurogenesis by excitatory input and NMDA receptor activation in the dentate gyrus. *Journal of Neuroscience, 15*, 4687–4692.

Cameron, H. A., Tanapat, P. & Gould, E. (1998). Adrenal steroids and N-methyl-D-aspartate receptor activation regulate neurogenesis in the dentate gyrus of adult rats through a common pathway. *Neuroscience, 82*, 349–354.

Cao, L., Jiao, X., Zuzga, D. S., Liu, Y., Fong, D. M., Young, D., et al. (2004). VEGF links hippocampal activity with neurogenesis, learning and memory. *Nature Genetics, 36*, 827–835.

Chen, Z. J., Ughrin, Y., & Levine, J. M. (2002). Inhibition of axon growth by oligodendrocyte precursor cells. *Molecular and Cellular Neuroscience, 20*, 125–139.

Cheng, A., Wang, S., Cai, J., Rao, M. S., & Mattson, M. P. (2003). Nitric oxide acts in a positive feedback loop with BDNF to regulate neural progenitor cell proliferation and differentiation in the mammalian brain. *Developmental Biology, 258*, 319–333.

Chmielnicki, E., Benraiss, A., Economides, A. N., & Goldman, S. A. (2004). Adenovirally expressed noggin and brain-derived neurotrophic factor cooperate to induce new medium spiny neurons from resident progenitor cells in the adult striatal ventricular zone. *Journal of Neuroscience, 24*, 2133–2142.

Collazos-Castro, J. E., & Nieto-Sampedro, M. (2001). Developmental and reactive growth of dentate gyrus afferents: Cellular and molecular interactions. *Restorative Neurology and Neuroscience, 19*, 169–187.

Dayer, A. G., Cleaver, K. M., Abouantoun, T., & Cameron, H. A. (2005). New GABAergic interneurons in the adult neocortex and striatum are generated from different precursors. *Journal of Cell Biology, 168*, 415–427.

Diamond, M. C., Johnson, R. E., Ingham, C., Rosenzweig, M. R., & Bennett, E. L. (1975). Effects of differential experience on neuronal nuclear and perikarya dimensions in the rat cerebral cortex. *Behavioral Biology, 15*, 107–111.

Diamond, M. C., Law, F., Rhodes, H., Lindner, B., Rosenzweig, M. R., Krech, D., et al. (1966). Increases in cortical depth and glia numbers in rats subjected to enriched environment. *Journal of Comparative Neurology, 128*, 117–126.

Doetsch, F., & Alvarez-Buylla, A. (1996). Network of tangential pathways for neuronal migration in adult mammalian brain. *Proceedings of the National Academy of Science USA, 93*, 14895–14900.

Eriksson, P. S., Perfilieva, E., Bjork-Eriksson, T., Alborn, A. M., Nordborg, C., Peterson, D. A., et al. (1998). Neurogenesis in the adult human hippocampus. *Nature Medicine, 4*, 1313–1317.

Farrell, R., Evans, S., & Corbett, D. (2001). Environmental enrichment enhances recovery of function but exacerbates ischemic cell death. *Neuroscience, 107*, 585–592.

Faverjon, S., Silveira, D. C., Fu, D. D., Cha, B. H., Akman, C., Hu, Y., et al. (2002). Beneficial effects of enriched environment following status epilepticus in immature rats. *Neurology, 59*, 1356–1364.

Fuchs, E., & Gould, E. (2000). Mini-review: In vivo neurogenesis in the adult brain: Regulation and functional implications. *European Journal of Neuroscience, 12*, 2211–2214.

Galani, R., Jarrard, L. E., Will, B. E., & Kelche, C. (1997). Effects of postoperative housing conditions on functional recovery in rats with lesions of the hippocampus, subiculum, or entorhinal cortex. *Neurobiology of Learning and Memory, 67*, 43–56.

Gibbs, S. M. (2003). Regulation of neuronal proliferation and differentiation by nitric oxide. *Molecular Neurobiology, 27*, 107–120.

Globus, A., Rosenzweig, M. R., Bennett, E. L., & Diamond, M. C. (1973). Effects of differential experience on dendritic spine counts in rat cerebral cortex. *Journal of Comparative Physiology and Psychology, 82*, 175–181.

Gould, E., & Tanapat, P. (1997). Lesion-induced proliferation of neuronal progenitors in the dentate gyrus of the adult rat. *Neuroscience, 80*, 427–436.

Gould, E., Beylin, A., Tanapat, P., Reeves, A., & Shors, T. J. (1999). Learning enhances adult neurogenesis in the hippocampal formation. *Nature Neuroscience, 2*, 260–265.

Gould, E., Vail, N., Wagers, M., & Gross, C. G. (2001). Adult-generated hippocampal and neocortical neurons in macaques have a transient existence. *Proceedings of the National Academy of Science USA, 98*, 10910–10917.

Gray, W. P., & Sundstrom, L. E. (1998). Kainic acid increases the proliferation of granule cell progenitors in the dentate gyrus of the adult rat. *Brain Research, 790*, 52–59.

Greenough, W. T., & Volkmar, F. R. (1973). Pattern of dendritic branching in occipital cortex of rats reared in complex environments. *Experimental Neurology, 40*, 491–504.

Hastings, N. B., Seth, M. I., Tanapat, P., Rydel, T. A., & Gould, E. (2002). Granule neurons generated during development extend divergent axon collaterals to hippocampal area CA3. *Journal of Comparative Neurology, 452*, 324–333.

Haughey, N. J., Nath, A., Chan, S. L., Borchard, A. C., Rao, M. S., & Mattson, M. P. (2002). Disruption of neurogenesis by amyloid beta-peptide, and perturbed neural progenitor cell homeostasis, in models of Alzheimer's disease. *Journal of Neurochemistry, 83*, 1509–1524.

Hockly, E., Cordery, P. M., Woodman, B., Mahal, A., van Dellen, A., Blakemore, C., et al. (2002). Environmental enrichment slows disease progression in R6/2 Huntington's disease mice. *Annals of Neurology, 51*, 235–242.

Jin, K., Minami, M., Lan, J. Q., Mao, X. O., Batteur, S., Simon, R. P., et al. (2001). Neurogenesis in dentate subgranular zone and rostral subventricular zone after focal cerebral ischemia in the rat. *Proceedings of the National Academy of Science USA, 98*, 4710–4715.

Jin, K., Peel, A. L., Mao, X. O., Xie, L., Cottrell, B. A., Henshall, D. C., et al. (2004). Increased hippocampal neurogenesis in Alzheimer's disease. *Proceedings of the National Academy of Science USA, 101*, 343–347.

Johansson, B. B., & Belichenko, P. V. (2002). Neuronal plasticity and dendritic spines: Effect of environmental enrichment on intact and postischemic rat brain. *Journal of Cerebral Blood Flow and Metabolism, 22*, 89–96.

Kaplan, M. S. (1981). Neurogenesis in the 3-month-old rat visual cortex. *Journal of Comparative Neurology, 195*, 323–338.

Kaplan, M. S., & Hinds, J. W. (1977). Neurogenesis in the adult rat: Electron microscopic analysis of light radioautographs. *Science, 197*, 1092–1094.

Kernie, S. G., Erwin, T. M., & Parada, L. F. (2001). Brain remodeling due to neuronal and astrocytic proliferation after controlled cortical injury in mice. *Journal of Neuroscience Research, 66*, 317–326.

Keynes, R. G., & Garthwaite, J. (2004). Nitric oxide and its role in ischaemic brain injury. *Current Molecular Medicine, 4*, 179–191.

Koketsu, D., Mikami, A., Miyamoto, Y., & Hisatsune, T. (2003). Nonrenewal of neurons in the cerebral neocortex of adult macaque monkeys. *Journal of Neuroscience, 23*, 937–942.

Komitova, M., Perfilieva, E., Mattsson, B., Eriksson, P. S., & Johansson, B. B. (2002). Effects of cortical ischemia and postischemic environmental enrichment on hippocampal cell genesis and differentiation in the adult rat. *Journal of Cerebral Blood Flow and Metabolism, 22*, 852–860.

Kornack, D. R., & Rakic, P. (2001). Cell proliferation without neurogenesis in adult primate neocortex. *Science, 294*, 2127–2130.

Leuner, B., Mendolia-Loffredo, S., Kozorovitskiy, Y., Samburg, D., Gould, E., & Shors, T. J. (2004). Learning enhances the survival of new neurons beyond the time when the hippocampus is required for memory. *Journal of Neuroscience, 24*, 7477–7481.

Liberto, C. M., Albrecht, P. J., Herx, L. M., Yong, V. W., & Levison, S. W. (2004). Pro-regenerative properties of cytokine-activated astrocytes. *Journal of Neurochemistry, 89*, 1092–1100.

Liu, J., Solway, K., Messing, R. O., & Sharp, F. R. (1998). Increased neurogenesis in the dentate gyrus after transient global ischemia in gerbils. *Journal of Neuroscience, 18*, 7768–7778.

Luine, V., Villegas, M., Martinez, C., & McEwen, B. S. (1994). Repeated stress causes reversible impairments of spatial memory performance. *Brain Research, 639*, 167–170.

Luskin, M. B. (1993). Restricted proliferation and migration of postnatally generated neurons derived from the forebrain subventricular zone. *Neuron, 11*, 173–189.

Lynch, G., Matthews, D. A., Mosko, S., Parks, T., & Cotman, C. (1972). Induced acetylcholinesterase-rich layer in rat dentate gyrus following entorhinal lesions. *Brain Research, 42*, 311–318.

Magavi, S. S., & Macklis, J. D. (2002). Induction of neuronal type-specific neurogenesis in the cerebral cortex of adult mice: Manipulation of neural precursors in situ. *Brain Research. Developmental Brain Research, 134*, 57–76.

Magavi, S. S., Leavitt, B. R., & Macklis, J. D. (2000). Induction of neurogenesis in the neocortex of adult mice. *Nature, 405*, 951–955.

Mattson, M. P., Maudsley, S., & Martin, B. (2004). BDNF and 5-HT: A dynamic duo in age-related neuronal plasticity and neurodegenerative disorders. *Trends in Neuroscience, 27*, 589–594.

McEwen, B. S. (1996). Gonadal and adrenal steroids regulate neurochemical and structural plasticity of the hippocampus via cellular mechanisms involving NMDA receptors. *Cellular and Molecular Neurobiology, 16*, 103–116.

McEwen, B. S. (2000). Effects of adverse experiences for brain structure and function. *Biological Psychiatry, 48*, 721–731.

Moghaddam, B., Bolinao, M. L., Stein-Behrens, B., & Sapolsky, R. (1994). Glucocorticoids mediate the stress-induced extracellular accumulation of glutamate. *Brain Research, 655*, 251–254.

Mollgaard, K., Diamond, M. C., Bennett, E. L., Rosenzweig, M. R., & Lindner, B. (1971). Quantitative synaptic changes with differential experience in rat brain. *International Journal of Neuroscience, 2*, 113–127.

Moreno-Lopez, B., Romero-Grimaldi, C., Noval, J. A., Murillo-Carretero, M., Matarredona, E. R., & Estrada, C. (2004). Nitric oxide is a physiological inhibitor of neurogenesis in the adult mouse subventricular zone and olfactory bulb. *Journal of Neuroscience, 24*, 85–95.

Nakatomi, H., Kuriu, T., Okabe, S., Yamamoto, S., Hatano, O., Kawahara, N., et al.

(2002). Regeneration of hippocampal pyramidal neurons after ischemic brain injury by recruitment of endogenous neural progenitors. *Cell, 110*, 429–441.

Packer, M. A., Stasiv, Y., Benraiss, A., Chmielnicki, E., Grinberg, A., Westphal, H., et al. (2003). Nitric oxide negatively regulates mammalian adult neurogenesis. *Proceedings of the National Academy of Science USA, 100*, 9566–9571.

Palmer, A. M., Marion, D. W., Botscheller, M. L., Swedlow, P. E., Styren, S. D., & DeKosky, S. T. (1993). Traumatic brain injury-induced excitotoxicity assessed in a controlled cortical impact model. *Journal of Neurochemistry, 61*, 2015–2024.

Parent, J. M., Valentin, V. V., & Lowenstein, D. H. (2002a). Prolonged seizures increase proliferating neuroblasts in the adult rat subventricular zone-olfactory bulb pathway. *Journal of Neuroscience, 22*, 3174–3188.

Parent, J. M., Vexler, Z. S., Gong, C., Derugin, N., & Ferriero, D. M. (2002b). Rat forebrain neurogenesis and striatal neuron replacement after focal stroke. *Annals of Neurology, 52*, 802–813.

Parent, J. M., Yu, T. W., Leibowitz, R. T., Geschwind, D. H., Sloviter, R. S., & Lowenstein, D. H. (1997). Dentate granule cell neurogenesis is increased by seizures and contributes to aberrant network reorganization in the adult rat hippocampus. *Journal of Neuroscience, 17*, 3727–3738.

Park, C., Kang, M., Kwon, Y. K., Chung, J. H., Ahn, H., & Huh, Y. (2001). Inhibition of neuronal nitric oxide synthase enhances cell proliferation in the dentate gyrus of the adrenalectomized rat. *Neuroscience Letters, 309*, 9–12.

Peterson, G. M. (1987). The response of the associational afferents to the dentate gyrus to simultaneous or sequential elimination of the commissural and entorhinal afferents. *Brain Research Bulletins, 19*, 245–259.

Raber, J., Fan, Y., Matsumori, Y., Liu, Z., Weinstein, P. R., Fike, J. R. et al. (2004). Irradiation attenuates neurogenesis and exacerbates ischemia-induced deficits. *Annals of Neurology, 55*, 381–389.

Raisman, G. (1969). Neuronal plasticity in the septal nuclei of the adult rat. *Brain Research, 14*, 25–48.

Rakic, P. (1985). Limits of neurogenesis in primates. *Science, 227*, 1054–1056.

Rosenzweig, M. R., & Bennett, E. L. (1996). Psychobiology of plasticity: Effects of training and experience on brain and behavior. *Behavioral Brain Research, 78*, 57–65.

Rosenzweig, M. R., Bennett, E. L., & Krech, D. (1964). Cerebral effects of environmental complexity and training among adult rats. *Journal of Comparative Physiology and Psychology, 57*, 438–439.

Scharff, C., Kirn, J. R., Grossman, M., Macklis, J. D., & Nottebohm, F. (2000). Targeted neuronal death affects neuronal replacement and vocal behavior in adult songbirds. *Neuron, 25*, 481–492.

Scharfman, H. E., Goodman, J. H., & Sollas, A. L. (2000). Granule-like neurons at the hilar/CA3 border after status epilepticus and their synchrony with area CA3 pyramidal cells: Functional implications of seizure-induced neurogenesis. *Journal of Neuroscience, 20*, 6144–6158.

Schmidt-Hieber, C., Jonas, P., & Bischofberger, J. (2004). Enhanced synaptic plasticity in newly generated granule cells of the adult hippocampus. *Nature, 429*, 184–187.

Schwab, M. E. (1990). Myelin-associated inhibitors of neurite growth and regeneration in the CNS. *Trends in Neuroscience, 13*, 452–456.

Schwob, J. E. (2002). Neural regeneration and the peripheral olfactory system. *The Anatomical Record, 269*, 33–49.

Seri, B., Garcia-Verdugo, J. M., McEwen, B. S., & Alvarez-Buylla, A. (2001). Astro-cytes give rise to new neurons in the adult mammalian hippocampus. *Journal of Neuroscience, 21*, 7153–7160.

Sharp, F. R., Liu, J., & Bernabeu, R. (2002). Neurogenesis following brain ischemia. *Brain Research. Developmental Brain Research, 134*, 23–30.

Shors, T. J., Miesegaes, G., Beylin, A., Zhao, M., Rydel, T., & Gould, E. (2001). Neurogenesis in the adult is involved in the formation of trace memories. *Nature, 410*, 372–376.

Shors, T. J., Townsend, D. A., Zhao, M., Kozorovitskiy, Y., & Gould, E. (2002). Neurogenesis may relate to some but not all types of hippocampal-dependent learning. *Hippocampus, 12*, 578–584.

Snyder, J. S., Hong, N. S., McDonald, R. J., & Wojtowicz, J. M. (2005). A role for adult neurogenesis in spatial long-term memory. *Neuroscience, 130*, 843–852.

Stein-Behrens, B., Mattson, M. P., Chang, I., Yeh, M., & Sapolsky, R. (1994). Stress exacerbates neuron loss and cytoskeletal pathology in the hippocampus. *Journal of Neuroscience, 14*, 5373–5380.

Szele, F. G., & Chesselet, M. F. (1996). Cortical lesions induce an increase in cell number and PSA-NCAM expression in the subventricular zone of adult rats. *Journal of Comparative Neurology, 368*, 439–454.

Tanapat, P., Hastings, N. B., Rydel, T. A., Galea, L. A., & Gould, E. (2001). Exposure to fox odor inhibits cell proliferation in the hippocampus of adult rats via an adrenal hormone-dependent mechanism. *Journal of Comparative Neurology, 437*, 496–504.

Tattersfield, A. S., Croon, R. J., Liu, Y. W., Kells, A. P., Faull, R. L., & Connor, B. (2004). Neurogenesis in the striatum of the quinolinic acid lesion model of Huntington's disease. *Neuroscience, 127*, 319–332.

Teramoto, T., Qiu, J., Plumier, J. C., & Moskowitz, M. A. (2003). EGF amplifies the replacement of parvalbumin-expressing striatal interneurons after ischemia. *Journal of Clinical Investigations, 111*, 1125–1132.

van Praag, H., Schinder, A. F., Christie, B. R., Toni, N., Palmer, T. D., & Gage, F. H. (2002). Functional neurogenesis in the adult hippocampus. *Nature, 415*, 1030–1034.

Wang, S., Scott, B. W., & Wojtowicz, J. M. (2000). Heterogenous properties of dentate granule neurons in the adult rat. *Journal of Neurobiology, 42*, 248–257.

West, R. W., & Greenough, W. T. (1972). Effect of environmental complexity on cortical synapses of rats: Preliminary results. *Behavioral Biology 7*, 279–284.

Yoshimura, S., Takagi, Y., Harada, J., Teramoto, T., Thomas, S. S., Waeber, C., et al. (2001). FGF-2 regulation of neurogenesis in adult hippocampus after brain injury. *Proceedings of the National Academy of Science USA, 98*, 5874–5879.

Yoshimura, S., Teramoto, T., Whalen, M. J., Irizarry, M. C., Takagi, Y., Qiu, J., et al. (2003). FGF-2 regulates neurogenesis and degeneration in the dentate gyrus after traumatic brain injury in mice. *Journal of Clinical Investigations, 112*, 1202–1210.

Zetterstrom, T. S., Pei, Q., Madhav, T. R., Coppell, A. L., Lewis, L., & Grahame-Smith, D. G. (1999). Manipulations of brain 5-HT levels affect gene expression for BDNF in rat brain. *Neuropharmacology, 38*, 1063–1073.

Zhang, R., Zhang, L., Zhang, Z., Wang, Y., Lu, M., Lapointe, M., et al. (2001). A nitric oxide donor induces neurogenesis and reduces functional deficits after stroke in rats. *Annals of Neurology, 50*, 602–611.

Zhao, M., Momma, S., Delfani, K., Carlen, M., Cassidy, R. M., Johansson, C. B., et al. (2003). Evidence for neurogenesis in the adult mammalian substantia nigra. *Proceedings of the National Academy of Science USA, 100*, 7925–7930.

Zheng, W., Nowakowski, R. S., & Vaccarino, F. M. (2004). Fibroblast growth factor 2 is required for maintaining the neural stem cell pool in the mouse brain subventricular zone. *Developmental Neuroscience, 26*, 181–196.

Zhu, D. Y., Liu, S. H., Sun, H. S., & Lu, Y. M. (2003). Expression of inducible nitric oxide synthase after focal cerebral ischemia stimulates neurogenesis in the adult rodent dentate gyrus. *Journal of Neuroscience, 23*, 223–229.

Zigmond, M. J., Abercrombie, E. D., Berger, T. W., Grace, A. A., & Stricker, E. M. (1990). Compensations after lesions of central dopaminergic neurons: Some clinical and basic implications. *Trends in Neuroscience, 13*, 290–296.

References for Table 18.1

1. Cameron, H. A., McEwen, B. S., & Gould, E. (1995). Regulation of adult neurogenesis by excitatory input and NMDA receptor activation in the dentate gyrus. *Journal of Neuroscience, 15*, 4687–4692.

2. Nacher, J., Rosell, D. R., Alonso-Llosa, G., & McEwen, B. S. (2001). NMDA receptor antagonist treatment induces a long-lasting increase in the number of proliferating cells, PSA-NCAM-immunoreactive granule neurons and radial glia in the adult rat dentate gyrus. *European Journal of Neuroscience, 13*, 512–520.

3. Packer, M. A., Stasiv, Y., Benraiss, A., Chmielnicki, E., Grinberg, A., Westphal, H. et al. (2003). Nitric oxide negatively regulates mammalian adult neuro-genesis. *Proceedings of the National Academy of Science USA, 100*, 9566–9571.

4. Moreno-Lopez, B., Romero-Grimaldi, C., Noval, J. A., Murillo-Carretero, M., Matarredona, E. R., Estrada, C. (2004). Nitric oxide is a physiological inhibitor of neurogenesis in the adult mouse subventricular zone and olfactory bulb. *Journal of Neuroscience, 24*, 85–95.

5. Brezun, J. M., & Daszuta, A. (1999). Depletion in serotonin decreases neuro-genesis in the dentate gyrus and the subventricular zone of adult rats. *Neuroscience, 89*, 999–1002.

6. Malberg, J. E., Eisch, A. J., Nestler, E. J., & Duman, R. S. (2000). Chronic antidepressant treatment increases neurogenesis in adult rat hippocampus. *Journal of Neuroscience, 20*, 9104–9110.

7. Anderson, M. F., Aberg, M. A., Nilsson, M., & Eriksson, P. S. (2002). Insulin-like growth factor-I and neurogenesis in the adult mammalian brain. *Brain Research. Developmental Brain Research, 134*, 115–122.

8. Gould, E., Cameron, H. A., Daniels, D. C., Woolley, C. S., & McEwen, B. S. (1992). Adrenal hormones suppress cell division in the adult rat dentate gyrus. *Journal of Neuroscience, 12*, 3642–3650.

9. Cameron, H. A., & Gould, E. (1994). Adult neurogenesis is regulated by adrenal steroids in the dentate gyrus. *Neuroscience, 61*, 203–209.

10. Tanapat, P., Hastings, N. B., Reeves, A. J., & Gould, E. (1999). Estrogen stimulates a transient increase in the number of new neurons in the dentate gyrus of the adult female rat. *Journal of Neuroscience, 19*, 5792–5801.

11. Tanapat, P., Hastings, N. B., & Gould, E. (2005). Ovarian steroids influence cell proliferation in the dentate gyrus of the adult female rat in a dose- and time-dependent manner. *Journal of Comparative Neurology, 481*, 252–265.

12. Mirescu, C., Peters, J. D., & Gould, E. (2004). Early life experience alters response of adult neurogenesis to stress. *Nature Neuroscience, 7*, 841–846.

13. Barnea, A., & Nottebohm, F. (1994). Seasonal recruitment of hippocampal neurons in adult free-ranging black-capped chickadees. *Proceedings of the National Academy of Science USA, 91*, 11217–11221.

14. Kempermann, G., Kuhn, H. G., & Gage, F. H. (1997). More hippocampal neurons in adult mice living in an enriched environment. *Nature, 386*, 493–495.

15. Nilsson, M., Perfilieva, E., Johansson, U., Orwar, O., & Eriksson, P. S. (1999). Enriched environment increases neurogenesis in the adult rat dentate gyrus and improves spatial memory. *Journal of Neurobiology, 39*, 569–578.

16. Leuner, B., Mendolia-Loffredo, S., Kozorovitskiy, Y., Samburg, D., Gould, E., & Shors, T. J. (2004). Learning enhances the survival of new neurons beyond the time when the hippocampus is required for memory. *Journal of Neuroscience, 24*, 7477–7481.

17. Kozorovitskiy, Y. & Gould, E. (2004). Dominance hierarchy influences adult neurogenesis in the dentate gyrus. *Journal of Neuroscience, 24*, 6755–6759.

18. Pravosudov, V. V., & Omanska, A. (2005). Dominance-related changes in spatial memory are associated with changes in hippocampal cell proliferation rates in mountain chickadees. *Journal of Neurobiology, 62*, 31–41.

19. van Praag, H., Christie, B. R., Sejnowski, T. J., & Gage, F. H. (1999). Running enhances neurogenesis, learning, and long-term potentiation in mice. *Proceedings of the National Academy of Science USA, 96*, 13427–13431.

Author index

Subject index